COMMUNITY UNIT SCHOOL DIST.
NO. 303
ST. CHARLES, ILLINOIS

LINCOLN SCHOOL

# 6

# Concepts in SCIENCE

# Concepts in SCIENCE

6

PAUL F. BRANDWEIN

ELIZABETH K. COOPER

PAUL E. BLACKWOOD

ELIZABETH B. HONE

HARCOURT, BRACE & WORLD, INC.

New York    Chicago    Atlanta    Dallas    Burlingame

## EDITORIAL CONSULTANTS

| | | |
|---|---|---|
| Hubert N. Alyea | Herbert Drapkin | Marguerite Smith |
| Esther L. Bossung | Ruth McDonald | Robert Stollberg |
| Matthew Brennan | Clifford R. Nelson | Violet Strahler |
| Annie Sue Brown | Helio C. Parreira | Richard M. Sutton |
| R. Will Burnett | Hy Ruchlis | Fletcher G. Watson |

## PICTURE CREDITS

**Cover:** Dow Chemical Company. **About This Book:** p. 1, General Motors Futurama. **Unit One:** p. 2, L. Willinger, Marineland, California, Shostal; p. 5, Harbrace; p. 6, left, Karl W. Kenyon from National Audubon Society, right, Winston Pote from Shostal; p. 7, top, General Biological Supply House, Inc., Chicago, bottom, Walter Dawn; p. 8, top, Hermann Eisenbeiss from Photo Researchers, others, Eric Grave from Photo Researchers; p. 13, Harbrace; p. 14, Walter Dawn; pp. 19, 29, 33, Harbrace. **Unit Two:** p. 46, General Electric Company; p. 48, left, Oberlin College, right, Aluminum Company of America; pp. 49, 50, 51, Harbrace; p. 54, top to bottom, Brown Brothers, Bettman Archive, Secretary of Agriculture in the National Archives, Wide World Photos, Inc.; p. 55, top to bottom, U.S. Army Air Forces in the National Archives, Brown Brothers, The National Foundation, Brown Brothers; pp. 58, 59, Harbrace; p. 68, Chicago Natural History Museum; p. 69, both, American Museum of Natural History; pp. 70, 72, Harbrace; p. 79, Thomas B. Hollyman from Photo Researchers; pp. 81, 82, Harbrace; p. 86, International Silk Association; p. 87, bottom, E. I. du Pont de Nemours & Company, others, American Viscose Corp.; p. 93, top, Jerry Cooke, bottom, Fisher Scientific Company; p. 94, left, Institute of Food and Agricultural Sciences, University of Florida, right, Grant Heilman; p. 95, Harbrace. **Unit Three:** p. 98, Chas. Pfizer & Co., Inc.; p. 100, left, Harbrace, right, Walter Dawn; p. 101, Harbrace; p. 102, bottom, Harbrace, others, Walter Dawn; pp. 105, 106, Harbrace; pp. 108, 111, Walter Dawn; p. 112, Harbrace; pp. 113, 114, Walter Dawn; p. 115, Harbrace; p. 120, top, Karsh, Ottawa, bottom, copyright © by Philippe Halsman; p. 124, top, Dr. Guiseppe Penso, bottom left, courtesy of the Virus Laboratory, University of California, Berkeley, bottom right, The National Foundation; p. 125, The National Foundation; p. 128, top, The National Foundation, bottom, Chas. Pfizer & Co., Inc.; p. 134, Harbrace; p. 137, top, Wallace and Tiernan Inc., center, United States Department of Agriculture, bottom, H. J. Heinz Co.; p. 141, General Biological Supply House, Inc., Chicago. **Unit Four:** p. 152, Josef Scaylea from Shostal; pp. 155, 157, 162, 167, 169, Harbrace; p. 172, National Park Service, U.S. Department of the Interior; pp. 173, 177, 178, 181, 185, Harbrace. **Unit Five:** p. 194, Jack Novak from Shostal; pp. 199, 201, 205, 207, 213, Harbrace; p. 215, top, Bibliotheque Nationale, bottom, U.S. Signal Corps in the National Archives; p. 216, Harbrace. **Unit Six:** p. 230, Curt W. Kaldor from Photo Researchers; p. 233, Harbrace; p. 235, Ewing Galloway; pp. 237, 239, 241, 243, Harbrace; p. 244, both, Bureau of Reclamation; p. 245, Harbrace; p. 247, Cotton Ginning Research Laboratory, U.S. Department of Agriculture; p. 249, Harbrace; p. 261, American Telephone and Telegraph Company; pp. 265, 269, Harbrace; p. 277, Westinghouse Electric Corporation. **Unit Seven:** p. 284, Union Carbide Corporation; p. 293, Harbrace; p. 298, courtesy of the University of California Lawrence Radiation Laboratory, Berkeley; p. 306, Harbrace; p. 308, David Lawlor from Shostal; p. 311, Official U.S. Navy Photo; p. 313, Atomic Energy of Canada Limited; p. 315, courtesy of the University of California Lawrence Radiation Laboratory, Berkeley. **Unit Eight:** p. 324, The Upjohn Company; pp. 326, 327, 329, Harbrace; p. 334, Dr. Berwind P. Kaufman, University of Michigan; pp. 336, 338, 339, Harbrace; p. 347, J. L. Stage from Photo Researchers; p. 350, LIFE Magazine © 1953 Time, Inc. All Rights Reserved; p. 351, Richard F. Carter, Chief of Illustration Service, The Rockefeller Institute; p. 357, Santa Gertrudis Breeders International; p. 358, Dr. J. L. Peterson, Department of Plant Biology, Rutgers University; p. 359, Harbrace. **Unit Nine:** p. 364, John Naylor from Shostal; pp. 367, 375, Harbrace; p. 381, top, Lowell Observatory, bottom, Mount Wilson and Palomar Observatories; p. 382, Harbrace; p. 384, Yerkes Observatory, University of Chicago; p. 387, Yerkes Observatory, University of Chicago; p. 388, Mount Wilson and Palomar Observatories; p. 390, copyright 1959, California Institute of Technology and Carnegie Institution of Washington; p. 395, top, Yerkes Observatory, University of Chicago, bottom, Mount Wilson and Palomar Observatories; p. 404, National Aeronautics and Space Administration. **The Art of Investigation:** pp. 408, 410, 411, 412, 413, 414, 419, 420, Harbrace.

## ILLUSTRATORS

All artwork done by Diamond Art Studio and Henri Fluchere. Pp. 251, 252, adapted from National Science Teachers Association; p. 416, Weather Bureau, U.S. Department of Commerce.

PRINTED IN THE UNITED STATES OF AMERICA

# CONTENTS

## About This Book

The elephant is stronger than man; but man invents a derrick and a bulldozer to exert more force than an elephant. Man cannot move a mountain, but he builds machinery that can.

Man cannot fly; but, with his brain and hands, man builds airplanes in which he can fly faster than any bird.

Man cannot live under water; but, with his brain and hands, man builds a nuclear submarine in which he can live under water and travel farther than any fish.

Man cannot swim the ocean; but, with his brain and hands, man builds a ship to take him across.

Man cannot see in the dark; but, with his brain and hands, man has harnessed electricity to light his way at night.

Man can learn; and because he uses his brain and hands, imagination and skill, man can do what no other kind of living thing can do. He thinks and plans and changes the world.

1

# UNIT ONE

# LEARNED AND UNLEARNED BEHAVIOR

You are doing a remarkable thing and thinking nothing of it. What do you think it is that you are doing that is so remarkable? No other kind of living thing can do it.

You are reading a book. In doing so, you are using an organ in your body as no other kind of living thing can. That organ is the brain.

Porpoises and other animals can be trained to perform rather complicated acts, and we consider their performances to be remarkable. They cannot compare with man's achievements.

Look around you; read the newspapers; watch television; listen to the radio; and make a list of man's achievements. The list would include: paper, pens, and pencils; bicycles, automobiles, trains, airplanes, rockets, and spaceships; schools, hospitals, and churches; telegraph, telephone, radio, television, and radar; eyeglasses, microscopes, and telescopes; languages, mathematics, poetry, music, and art. All of these are products of the most remarkable of all organs—the human brain.

So man, with his brain and hands, imagination and skill, thinks and acts and changes his environment to satisfy his needs and desires.

## 1. Perfect—Without Learning

Watch a barn swallow or any other bird build a nest. (Look at the figure marked with the square.) ■ Barn swallows gather mud, plaster it under the eaves of a building or in a barn, and line the nest with feathers. All barn swallows do it, yet they do not have to go to school to learn.

Suppose you could know all your arithmetic, spelling, history, and science, without having to study. Just think how much more you would be able to do.

Yet there are things you can do perfectly from the day you are born. Do you know what they are?

Why not investigate to find out about some of the things you can do

without learning. The investigation on the opposite page is about one of them.

### Perfect Performance—From Birth

No matter how hard you or your partner try not to blink, you will blink anyway without thinking about it.

Blinking is an act which you perform without having to learn how. Blinking is an **inborn,** or **unlearned, act.** Sneezing, coughing, and yawning are three other inborn acts.

Take a deep breath, and hold it as long as you can. If you have a watch, check the time. You will find that you cannot hold your breath for long. You cannot stop your heartbeat at all because you cannot control it. You breathe and your heart beats without your having to think. Breathing and the beating of the heart are inborn (unlearned) acts.

Suppose you had to think about and direct the digestion of your food. You would have time for little else. You may think about what you will eat or about chewing it carefully; but, once the food is swallowed, it is digested in the stomach and in the intestines with no more help from you. Digestion is an inborn act.

Simple inborn, or unlearned, acts, such as coughing, blinking, and yawning are known as **reflex acts.** Reflex acts take place without your having to think, and are part of your **behavior** from the time you are born. You can do them quite well without having to learn.

4

# AN INVESTIGATION into the Things You Can Do from Birth

**Needed:** a partner; a square piece of cellophane; and about six sheets of paper

Crumple the six sheets of paper into six paper balls. ■ Place five where your partner cannot see them, and keep one in your hand.

Then ask your partner to hold the small piece of cellophane in front of his (or her) eyes and to look straight at you. ● Throw the paper ball *gently* against the sheet of cellophane. ▲ Does your partner blink?

Ask your partner to try very hard to keep his eyes open and not to blink, as you throw several more paper balls. Can he do it?

Now exchange and have your partner throw paper balls at you. Try to control your own blinking. Can you?

Did you have to learn how to blink or is blinking an act that can be performed without learning?

**Additional Investigation:** What other acts can be performed without learning? If there is a new baby in your home, observe his behavior. What unlearned acts does the baby perform?

How do you know the baby's acts are unlearned? When do you think learning begins? Record the first act that you think the baby learned to perform.

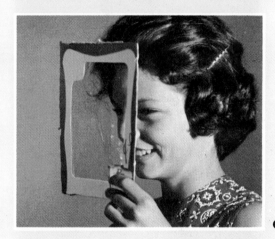

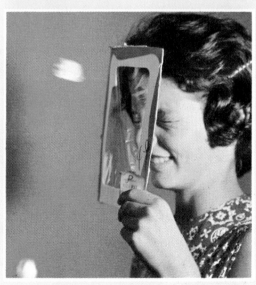

## Inborn Acts in Animals

You may have watched birds build their nests. Does it seem strange to you that all eastern robins build nests that look alike; or that the nests of all mourning doves are the same?■ The nests of all Baltimore orioles are alike and so are those of all broad-tailed humming-birds.● More than that, birds build their nests the very first time they try, without having to learn how. Nest-building is an inborn act in birds, but it is *more* than just a simple reflex act, like blinking.

Some fishes build nests. Their act of nest-building is inborn also. The stickleback, for example, builds a nest of water plants. All sticklebacks build nests and the nests of all stickle-backs look just alike.

Nest-building is inborn; but it is not a simple reflex act such as yawning, coughing, or blinking. When a bird builds a nest, it performs many different acts; so, nest-building is really an unlearned, complicated type of behavior.

Some scientists call complicated, unlearned behavior, such as nest-building, an **instinct.** Perhaps an instinct could be called a series of *complex reflex acts.*

Spinning a web is also a complex reflex act.▲ It is inborn. Have you watched a spider spin a web? The orange garden spider builds a beautiful one. Can you imagine building such a web without having to learn how? Try to make a copy of a spider's web, using string.

**6**

Webs of house spiders are different from those of the garden spider. If you can find the web of a house spider, look at it carefully to see how it is made. The webs are so fine that it is hard to find them until they are covered with dust.

Just as each kind of bird builds its own kind of nest, each kind of spider spins its own kind of web. You may be interested to check this further by finding out how a trap-door spider builds its home.

The important thing to remember is that such acts are inborn. They are fixed behavior patterns.

Some unlearned acts are even more complicated. Have you ever watched a mother cat caring for her kittens?

A group of psychologists (sī·kol′ə-jists), scientists who study behavior, wanted to find out if caring for the young is *really* an unlearned act in certain animals. They took a number of white rats away from their mother as soon as they were born. They kept the baby rats in separate cages, away from all older rats, until they were grown.

When these white rats gave birth to their own young, they cared for them in the same way as any mother rat cares for her young; yet they had never seen it done. ◆ In rats, caring for the young is inborn behavior; but this is not true of all living things.

What is it, really, that is inborn? Perhaps there is an explanation in the way the body works. We will use a simple animal to give us our next clue.

## Inside the Body ("Message" Relays)

We begin by studying the body of a hydra. A hydra is a tiny animal whose nearest relatives are the jellyfish. They live in streams and ponds where they hang from the stems of water plants. They are about a quarter of an inch long—and about as thick as a needle.

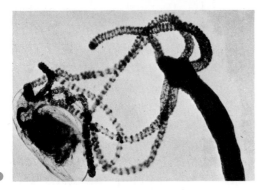

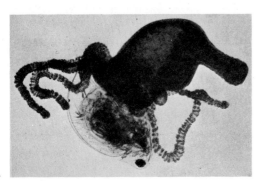

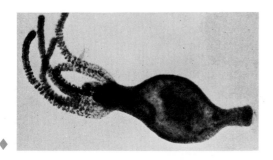

Hydras will grow well in an aquarium, but the aquarium will also need water plants, snails, and even tropical fishes. With a lens you can study the structure and behavior of a hydra. You can watch its **tentacles** (ten′tə-kəls), which seem to be like tiny arms, stretch out in all directions. ■ Hydras feed on small water animals. They can even catch tiny fishes. You may wonder how they do this.

The pictures show a tiny water animal brushing against the tentacles of one of the hydras. The tiny water animal stops suddenly. ● It has been stung by poisonous darts. In the hydra's arms are thousands of tiny poisonous darts, all coiled up, ready to shoot. ▲

When an animal brushes against one of these tentacles, the darts shoot out, and the animal is paralyzed (or anesthetized). Then the tentacles sweep the animal into the hydra's stomach where it is digested. ◆

The poisonous darts shoot out when an animal touches the tiny trigger you see in the picture. ★ ◈ The *touch* of the animal on the trigger of the hydra's tentacles is called a **stimulus** (stim′yə·ləs). A stimulus is anything that results in a **response,** or some kind of activity in a living thing. A stimulus can be one of many things: a touch, a flash of light, something hot or cold or, perhaps, a sound.

Scientists agree that there can be no response without some sort of stimulus. Your eyelids blink *in response* to the stimulus of the thrown paper

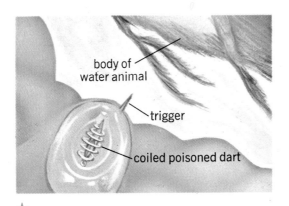

body of
water animal

trigger

coiled poisoned dart

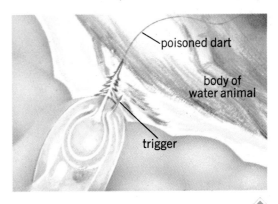

poisoned dart

body of
water animal

trigger

★

ball (page 5). You turn to answer when someone calls your name. The sound of your name is the stimulus which causes a response.

Once an animal brushes against the hydra's tentacles, the muscle cells of the hydra's body respond. They pull the animal into the hydra's stomach. But how does the body "know" that an animal has been caught?

Actually, the hydra does not know what is happening. Its body responds automatically because the "message" is relayed throughout the animal's body by a net of **nerve fibers.** The net of nerve fibers of a hydra extends throughout the animal. A hydra has no real nervous system such as the higher animals have and it has no brain. But even a tiny animal like a hydra has nerve fibers, and nerve fibers carry messages.

We shall call this "message" relay a **nerve impulse.** We are not sure what a nerve impulse is like; but whatever it is, chemical or electrical, that travels along a nerve, it is called a nerve impulse.

Examine the picture of the nerve net of a hydra.◎ Could you make a model of it? The loose weave in cheesecloth is very much like it. Imagine the body of a hydra with a net of nerve fibers arranged like the weave of cheesecloth. Somehow a *stimulus* starts an *impulse* along the *nerve net* so that the hydra *responds.*

Although the hydra is a simple animal, we still do not know exactly what kind of impulse the nerve net carries. Nerves and nerve nets, and the way they carry impulses, are the objects of much investigation.

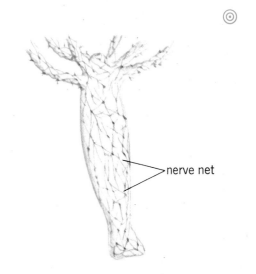

nerve net

**A.** Study the statements below and choose the correct responses. They will help you fix in mind the concepts of this section.

1. An example of an unlearned act is
   a. blinking          b. tying a shoelace

2. An unlearned, or reflex, act is
   a. inborn            b. developed after birth

3. The beating of the heart is a
   a. learned act       b. reflex act

4. Nest-building is
   a. an unlearned act  b. a learned act

5. Nest-building is different from blinking in that it is a
   a. simple reflex act b. complex reflex act

6. In white rats, caring for the young is
   a. a simple reflex act   b. an instinct

7. Nerve impulses in the hydra are carried by a
   a. nerve net         b. stimulus

8. A stimulus brings forth
   a. another stimulus  b. a response

9. A nerve impulse is carried along the nerve. The type of impulse, whether electrical or chemical, is
   a. known             b. unknown

10. The science that is concerned with the way living things behave is called
    a. psychology       b. physics

**B.** Write a paragraph or two on: Stimulus and Response.

1. Peter's father was an excellent tennis player. In time, Peter came to be captain of his school's tennis team.

The neighbors used to say, "Peter is a born tennis player. After all, like father, like son."

Is tennis-playing an inborn act? What is your reasoning?

**2.** Jellyfish are relatives of the hydra. What type of nervous system would you expect them to have?

ON YOUR OWN Do plants have kinds of inborn acts? Try this investigation. Overnight, soak some radish or bean seeds in water. Then line three glass tumblers with blotting paper, as shown in the illustration. ■ Keep some moist cotton at the bottom of each glass. Place at least three seeds between the blotting paper and the glass—about one inch from the rim. When the seedlings have grown above the rim, place one tumbler on its side. Suspend another upside down so that the plants are free to grow. ● Leave the third right side up.

In what direction do the stems of the plants grow? What is your explanation? Can you change their direction of growth?

Scientists call that part of an experiment in which the conditions are unchanged a **control.** In the investigation above, what is the importance of the third tumbler, the one that is standing upright?

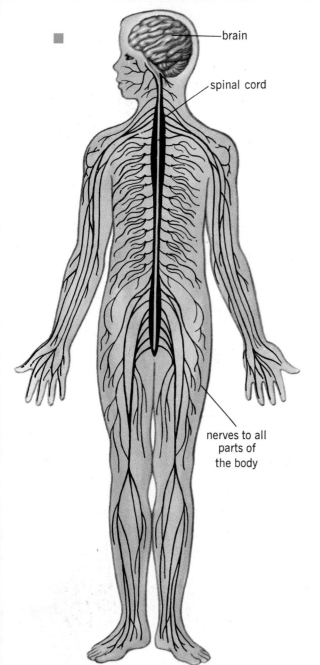

brain

spinal cord

nerves to all
parts of
the body

## 2. From the Hydra
## to Simple Learning

What happens in your body in response to a stimulus? You can observe two of your own reflexes. These reflexes are common to all of us. For a better understanding of them, try the investigation on the opposite page.

Once you have done the investigation, try to explain what happened when the knee was tapped.

### A Study of the Nervous System

Your **nervous system** has **nerves** that connect with the **brain** and the **spinal cord.** (Study the diagram of the nervous system and identify each part.) ■

A nerve is actually made up of many **nerve cells.** Study the diagram of the nerve cell.● Notice the long fiber and the way one cell connects with other nerve cells. All nerve cells are connected; however, they are not scattered loosely over the body. The fibers of the nerve cells are in bundles, and the bundles are called nerves. There is, as you can see, a network of nerves throughout your body. If you stub your toe, the stimulus reaches your brain. You respond perhaps by rubbing the toe with your hand. Your toe, head, and hand are connected by nerves.

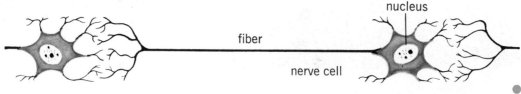

nucleus

fiber

nerve cell

# AN INVESTIGATION into a Common Reflex

**Needed:** a small flashlight; a partner

First, ask your partner to sit on the edge of a table. Be certain that the legs hang loosely and that the feet do not touch the floor.

Now ask him to close his eyes. Then, tap him just below the knee with the edge of your palm, as shown in the picture. 🔥 What happens?

Now it is your turn! Let your partner tap you below the knee. What happens to you? What was the stimulus? What was the response?

Now draw the window blinds or shades, and ask your partner to turn away from the light. Then turn on the

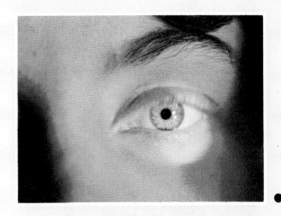

small flashlight, and from the side, flash the light at his eyes. If you use a large flashlight, do not shine the light directly into his eyes. Direct the beam past his head. Observe the pupils of his eyes. What happens? ● ▲

Let your partner observe the same effect on you. What is the stimulus? What is the response?

Here is another important part of this investigation. Ask your partner not to respond to the light. In other words, ask him to control his response.

■

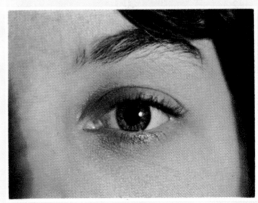

▲

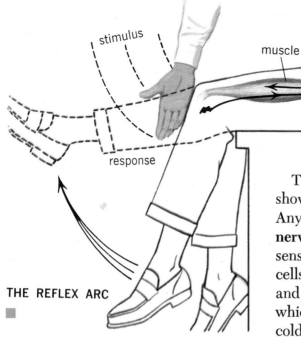

stimulus

muscle

spinal cord

response

## THE REFLEX ARC

Now trace the path of the stimulus (tap on the knee) in the diagram, all the way to the response (kicking out of the leg).■ The brain is not involved in the knee reflex, or **reflex arc.** The spinal cord is the place where the nerves seem to be connected.

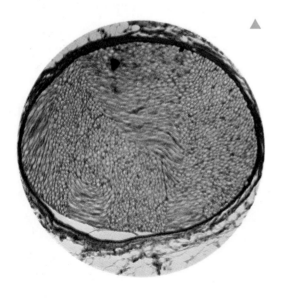

▲

The diagram on the next page shows the reflex arc in greater detail.● Any nerve impulse begins at the **nerve endings.** These nerve endings sense the stimulus. There are nerve cells in your eyes which sense light, and there are nerve cells in your skin which sense a touch, or warmth, or cold. First, then, a stimulus (such as the tap on the knee) is *sensed* or received by a cell known as a **sensory nerve cell.**

Second, the sensory nerve cell in the knee has a long nerve fiber which carries the impulse to the spinal cord. (The microphotograph shows a bundle of nerve fibers.▲ ) In the spinal cord, the impulse is relayed to a **connecting nerve cell** that *receives* the impulse and passes it to another nerve cell known as a **motor nerve cell.** The motor nerve cells end in a muscle or, perhaps, a gland. When the impulse reaches the leg muscle (as in the case of a tap on the knee), the leg kicks out automatically. Such speedy acts, done without thinking, are part of your behavior from birth.

When your salivary glands produce saliva, an impulse has been carried to the glands by a motor nerve. Of course, in the body many nerve cells take part in any responsive act.

Nerve cells of any kind are called **neurons** (noŏr′ons); so a sensory nerve cell is a sensory neuron; a motor nerve cell is a motor neuron. Scientists think there are at least three kinds of neurons which take part in an inborn, or reflex, act. The fiber of a neuron may vary in length; it may be very short or several feet long.

Now, to help you remember, review once again the kinds of neurons that are found in your body. They are:

a. a *sensory neuron.* This nerve cell receives the stimulus, such as the taste of food, and carries a chemical or electrical impulse (or both) to the spinal cord or brain.

b. a *connecting neuron.* This nerve cell connects the sensory neuron with a motor neuron. Connecting neurons are generally found in the spinal cord or brain. A connecting neuron carries the impulse from the sensory neuron to the motor neuron.

c. a *motor neuron.* This nerve cell carries the impulse toward a muscle or gland. That is, motor neurons carry the impulse to the organ which will respond by moving or acting. Recall that your salivary glands respond by forcing saliva into the mouth. Each organ responds in a particular way.

Look again at the diagram of the nerve path of a reflex. Remember that when the spot below the knee is

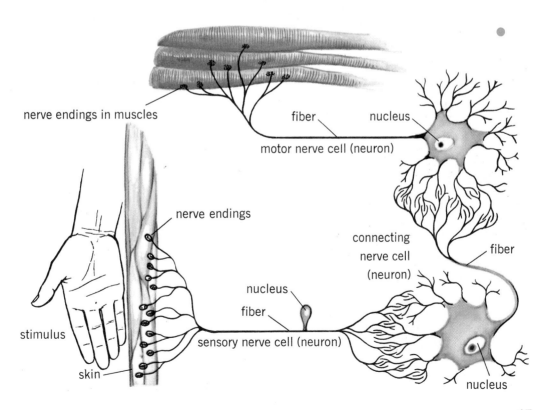

nerve endings in muscles

fiber        nucleus

motor nerve cell (neuron)

nerve endings

connecting
nerve cell
(neuron)        fiber

nucleus

fiber

stimulus

sensory nerve cell (neuron)

skin

nucleus

tapped (a stimulus), the leg kicks out (the response). This act is an inborn, or unlearned, reflex act. For any reflex act, the neurons are already connected and somehow ready to work at birth, but this is by no means the whole story. To learn more about behavior, try to teach a puppy to respond to his name.

### Teaching an Animal

A puppy is born with many reflexes. For instance, it has a scratching reflex.■ If an insect crawls on the puppy, the puppy will scratch. A dog's eyes respond to light. The pupils get smaller in bright light, but widen in the dark. A puppy's heart beats and he breathes, yawns, sneezes, and coughs. All of these are inborn acts; they are reflexes. The neurons which govern these reflex acts are connected at birth and con-

tinue to function as long as the puppy remains alive.

If you have owned a puppy, you may have tried to teach him his name, but it is not likely that he came running to you the first time you called him by name. A response of this sort has to be learned. Responding to the sound of a name is a **learned act,** not a reflex act.

### A Learned Act

Suppose you have a Dalmatian puppy, named "Spot." How would you get him to run to you when you call?

You could start by calling his name each time. Animal trainers, however, would tell you that there is a much easier way. They would suggest that you call him Spot when you give him a dog biscuit. Call him by name when you pat his head or when you call him to play. Why does this work?

Why Spot learns his name more easily this way is explained by psychologists as follows: The food, or a pat on the head, is a **reward** that is given at the same time, or just after, the puppy's name is called. Both the stimulus of the food (the reward) and the stimulus of the sound of the puppy's name reach its brain at almost the same time. Somehow they become related, or, as a psychologist would say, **associated,** in the brain. ●

First the puppy responds to the food or to the pat on the head. That is, he responds at first only to the reward; but the *two* stimuli (the *re-*

*ward* and the *calling of the name*) occur at the same time. Soon the puppy will respond to the name alone. He has learned to respond.

What should you do when the puppy responds to your call of "Spot"? Give him a biscuit the first few times. The next few times, give him a pat on the head. Always reward him when he learns something new until you are sure he has learned. In fact, it is a good idea to give him a pat or reward him some way whenever he pleases you.

## One Explanation of Learning

How would you explain a puppy's response to the sound of his name? Do you agree with the following explanation?

A dog gets hungry. Hunger is inborn. You give the puppy food and he eats. Eating and digesting are inborn responses. The puppy responds to the stimulus of food by running to the food. He is happy, or satisfied, when he feeds. Food is his reward. A reward is useful in training any animal.

Each time you give the puppy his food, you call him "Spot." Each time he comes to the food, you call his name again. When you call his name, the sound "Spot" is a new stimulus. Somehow the *new* stimulus (sound) is associated with the *old* stimulus (food). The response is the same to both. Study the diagram on this page to help fix this idea in mind. The procedure by which Spot "learned" his name is given on the next page.

**17**

a. You would give the puppy something to which he already responds, something he likes. The stimulus of food, for instance, will cause the dog to respond by running to it.

b. You would give him a new stimulus, his name, at the same time you give him the old stimulus, the food.

c. You would repeat this procedure again and again until the dog responds to the new stimulus alone. Then he responds when you call his name, without the stimulus of food. The dog has learned. You have taught him to respond to a new stimulus.

Now that you have an idea how to teach a puppy, can you use a similar idea to teach a fish? Why not try it? Try to train a fish to respond to a flash of light. Do you think it can be done? Plan an investigation into the way a fish can be trained. The first few steps of the investigation are given on the opposite page.

Once you have planned and carried out the investigation, try to explain how you trained the fish to respond to the light of a flashlight.

Scientists have a **theory** to explain this kind of learning and they give their explanation, or theory, a special name. It is called **conditioning** (kən-dish′an·ing). In conditioning, a reward of some kind seems to tie the stimulus and the response together by what is called the **S–R bond** (S, for stimulus and R, for response). ■ In fact, conditioning is sometimes called "S–R bonding." What does the word bonding mean?

Ivan Pavlov, a Russian psychologist, developed the theory of conditioning. Early in the twentieth century, he experimented with dogs in a special way.

Pavlov decided to ring a bell as he gave a dog some food. In other words, the dog was presented with two stimuli at once, food and the sound of a bell. After a few weeks, when the bell was rung, the dog responded to the bell as if he were responding to food. It was as though the dog had acquired a new reflex. Pavlov called the new reflex a *conditioned* reflex.

As you learn more about behavior, you will find that reward or punishment given at the proper time can be very useful in learning.

Pavlov's theory explains how certain reflex acts may be acquired, but it does not explain all about learning. For instance, it does not explain fully the act you may try to learn next.

# AN INVESTIGATION into the Training of a Fish

**Needed:** an aquarium; a flashlight; fish food

Make a plan of the way you would train the fish. You can make use of what you learned about teaching a puppy.

Recall that to train a puppy you should give him a reward when you call him by name. The reward and the sound of his name (the stimuli) are then associated in the brain.

What reward will you give the fish?

What stimulus can be associated with the reward?

What results do you expect?

Can more than one stimulus be used at the same time?

How long will the response continue if you discontinue the reward?

The pictures show a plan that was used by one class to train their pet goldfish to respond to a flash of light. ■ ● ▲ Perhaps you can think of a better way to train a goldfish. For instance, you might use a bell.

**A.** Study the statements below and choose the correct responses. They will help you fix in mind the concepts of this section.

1. The central part of your nervous system is the
   <u>a.</u> brain and spinal cord     b. nerve cell

2. A reflex act, such as the knee reflex, takes place
   a. after thinking     <u>b.</u> without thinking

3. A neuron which ends in a muscle or a gland is a
   a. motor neuron     <u>b.</u> sensory neuron

4. The neuron (connecting neuron) which generally connects motor and sensory neurons may be found
   a. near the muscles     b. in the spinal cord

5. The neurons responsible for a reflex act are
   a. already connected at     b. developed as you
      birth                        learn

6. Answering to a name is a
   a. reflex act     b. learned act

7. To speed up the act of conditioning, it is useful to associate
   a. a reward with the act     b. punishment with
                                   the act

8. S–R bonds help explain
   a. conditioning     b. all learning

**B.** Write a paragraph or two on this topic: Nerve Cells and the Reflex Act.

1. In a camp for boys, one of the older boys was put in charge of a bunkhouse where six other boys lived. He found that it was difficult to get them up in the mornings to do the chores. In order to help them get up on time, he decided to ring a bell.

Once they were awake, he asked the boys to do chores of all kinds—sweeping the bunkhouse, cleaning up, folding their clothes. Soon the boys did not respond to the bell; some went right back to sleep. Others made believe they were asleep.

What do you think was wrong? How would you correct it?

**2.** Psychologists sometimes say that a reward is better than punishment in *establishing (conditioning) a habit.* For example, to train (condition) a dog to keep him from biting the furniture, it is often best to give him a real or a rubber bone. Punishment may keep him from biting the furniture, but it may also condition him to dislike the person punishing him. Do you agree? Give your reasons.

There are a good number of books on training pets. What do they have to say on the value of reward or punishment?

## 3. You Learn a "New" Behavior

Today you may have blinked your eyelids more than 5,000 times. Do you remember each time you blinked?

Today your heart beat thousands of times. Were you aware of your heart beating? You breathed thousands of times. Were you conscious of breathing? You do not think about your heartbeat or your breathing; nor do you think of all the other activities going on inside your body.

Do you remember tying your shoelaces when you put on your shoes this morning? You probably do not remember the details of dressing because you do it without having to think about it.

Whenever you perform an act the same way every time, without thinking, the act is said to be an **automatic**

(ô′tə·mat′ik) **act.** The beating of the heart is an automatic act and so is breathing, blinking, yawning, sneezing, and coughing. All reflexes are automatic; but are all automatic acts reflexes?

Was tying your shoelaces a reflex? Think a moment. Were you able to tie your shoelaces at birth? Of course not. Tying a shoelace is an automatic act, but it is not inborn, or a reflex.

Tying your shoelaces is a simple **habit.** It is something you had to learn. What is the difference then between a reflex and a simple habit?

A reflex is a simple, *unlearned automatic act.* A habit is a *learned automatic act.*

Simple habits are important to you. For one thing, they save you a good deal of time. If you had to think about how to tie your shoelaces each time you put on your shoes, get-

21

**SOME SIMPLE HABITS**

ting dressed would take a long time. ■ Then too, a few simple habits, such as brushing your teeth and washing your hands, help keep you in good health. If you brush your teeth every time you eat, that act will become almost automatic—as will washing your hands before you eat.

Certain kinds of habits, such as brushing your teeth, can be explained by the theory of conditioning. For instance, an S–R bond was formed between the stimulus (finishing your meal) and the response (brushing your teeth). The rewards, better health, a pleasant appearance, and the commendation of your parents may have established the S–R bond.

Like some inborn behavior, habits can become very complicated. For instance, spelling correctly or doing arithmetic are *partly* the result of forming good habits, but complicated ones.

You do not have to think when you spell your name or write the word "science" at the top of a paper you hand in; but no one really knows how a person learns to spell the word "science." No one understands completely how anyone learns to do such complicated things as spelling, or writing, or reading. ● That is, no one really knows as yet how neurons work or how they carry impulses. No one really knows how the brain works or how it "remembers" what it has learned; but the problem is being carefully investigated by many scientists. Some think that the answers lie in the way the stimulus is connected to the response. Psychologists, however, know that many simple things are learned best through practice.

## Forming a Habit

People learn to do all sorts of things as they grow up, and they usually have a reason for learning. One good reason is that learning a habit enables a person to be more efficient. Another reason may be to achieve a reward for learning. The reward may not be something you can see or touch. It may be simply the satisfaction of being able to do something easily. You may not even think of a reward but may learn to do something simply because you want to or have to.

How does one go about learning a simple act? The thing to do is to perform the same act over and over again until it becomes automatic. For instance, you might follow this plan.

First, you have a *goal* to reach. It may be a very simple goal, such as learning to tie your shoelaces.

Second, you *plan* how to reach your goal. For example, you may choose to watch someone else tie a shoelace until you are sure of how it is done.

Third, you *practice* over and over what it is you are learning.

Finally, you can perform the act automatically, without thinking about what you are doing.

Do you dream of being able to do something especially well? Would you like to be a champion swimmer or

diver? an all-star basketball player? Would you like to drive a car? What are your goals? Think about it now, for the earlier you start and the more you learn, the better you will become at whatever you try to do.

Learning to perform automatically enables a person to be more efficient. Some things you learn to do may also be rewarding. For example:

Why would anyone want to learn to ride a bicycle? What is the re-ward? ■ Having fun? Getting exercise? Having better health? Being able to have a newspaper route? Helping your parents by running errands? Getting to school easily? Or is there more than one reason?

Why do you think the boy shown standing alone in the picture would want to learn to ride a bicycle?●

Tying a knot can become a simple habit. Try the investigation on the opposite page to see how long it takes for

# AN INVESTIGATION into the Learning of an Automatic Act

**Needed:** a foot of rope

You can probably tie some kinds of knots, but the kind you will learn to tie here is a special kind.

The pictures show steps in tying a bowline (bō′lin′). ■ It is a very useful knot because it does not slip or become untied.

How fast can you learn to tie the knot? Time yourself. Practice tying the knot until you can do it with your eyes closed. Then compare the time it takes you to learn with the time it takes your classmates. In one class, some of the students learned to tie it faster than others. Some made good tight knots and others made knots that were not so tight. When you can tie a bowline quickly and without wasting time, tying this knot has become a learned automatic act.

**Additional Investigation:** Plan an investigation to find out if age has any effect on the time it takes to learn to tie a new kind of knot. Do older people learn faster than younger ones?

Extend the investigation to include other acts that may become automatic.

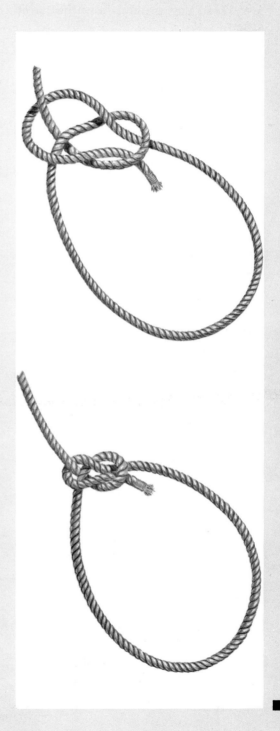

the act to become automatic. You form many simple habits in the same way. Can you explain how the habit was formed?

Brushing your teeth regularly, bathing regularly, and dressing properly are desirable habits. In these instances, the rewards are better health and a pleasing appearance.

Reading, doing arithmetic, spelling, and using the dictionary, all of these are rewarding. Why?

How did you learn to get up at a regular time in the morning? Think back. The reasons may be very complicated, but here is a simple way of looking at this habit and other habits that are like it.

First, you have a goal. Second, you have **insight** into a way of achieving your goal. Third, you practice—until the act becomes a habit.

This manner of learning could be described as the **goal-insight theory.** This theory is based on having a clear goal, insight, and the satisfaction, or reward, of achieving the goal.

## Learning About Learning

Up to this point we have studied reflexes and simple habits. We have investigated habit formation, that is, how an act can become automatic. We have investigated how animals learn by conditioning (page 18).

All learning cannot be explained so simply, however. For instance, under what conditions do people learn best? How do we get an "idea"? a "thought"?

In their attempts to learn about people, scientists often work with animals because they are easier to study than man, especially in the way they learn. Just as rabbits, rats, mice, and guinea pigs have been used in learning how to prevent disease—chimpanzees also have been used to study the learning process. Scientists have learned a great deal from experiments with a chimpanzee by the name of Sultan. They used him in an experiment which tells us something of the way a new idea is developed.

## Sultan Gets an "Idea"

Sultan liked bananas, so they were used as a reward in the learning experiment. A banana was put out of Sultan's reach, but a stick was placed near him (as in the picture). ▮ Almost at once Sultan used the stick to get the banana.● Even when the banana was placed out of reach completely, Sultan would try to use the stick. He had learned how to use a tool (the stick) easily. ▲

Then the psychologists tried something different. Sultan was in his cage as usual, but this time a banana was placed outside the cage—just out of reach of his familiar stick. Another stick was put in the cage. The second stick could be joined to Sultan's first stick, as in the picture. ♦ The problem was: Would Sultan learn to fit the sticks together to reach the banana?★

The scientists doing the experiment reported something like this. First, Sultan tried to reach the banana with

27

one stick, then with the other. He failed. He walked about, screamed, and chattered. Next, he tried to push one stick with the other stick toward the food. He failed, time after time.

Then suddenly, as if in a flash, he fitted the two sticks together and reached the banana. The idea seemed to come in a "flash." The act seemed to take place immediately.

Because of this investigation, scientists who study learning have come to think that many ideas occur in a "flash." Do they really?

### Behind the "Flash"

Do ideas really come out of nowhere? Surely you have had the experience of walking along, or sitting quietly, or reading, or playing—when *suddenly* an "idea" has flashed into your mind.

Recall Sultan's behavior. He had two sticks with which to reach the banana, but they would reach only if they were fitted together. He tried one stick, then the other. He then tried pushing one stick with the other. Finally, with a "flash" of insight he fitted the two sticks together; but remember he had tried other things first *before* he got the "insight."

Somehow he was able to fit his experiences together to form a solution to the problem. The problem: how to reach the banana.

Sultan had needed time to develop insight into solving the problem. During this time he was getting experience by trying different things; and

even though some of his attempts did not work, they gave him an *insight into the solution of the problem.*

Do you learn in the same way when you are trying to solve a problem? Try to find out by doing the investigation on the opposite page.

### A "Flash of Insight"—or Not?

Did you solve the problem? How did you get the insight for a solution to the problem?

Does insight come slowly, bit by bit, or suddenly, after time is spent thinking about it? Perhaps it only seems to come suddenly, without thinking.

If it seems to come suddenly, without thought, your "insight" into the problem has put all the parts together, so the solution comes all at once, as if in a "flash." But a good deal of thought *is* taking place without your knowing about it. The "flash" of insight follows.

Of course, not all problems are solved in a "flash." What information did you need before you could solve the problem? Could you have solved it without knowing

a. that 4 ounces is equal to $\frac{1}{2}$ cup?
b. how big a measuring cup is?
c. that the bottle had just 4 ounces of water in it?

Without information, problems cannot be solved. Without old ideas, new ideas are not so easy to get. In other words, new insights seem to come easier when one has some old ideas to begin with. Insights, or "new ideas," seem to be formed from the

# AN INVESTIGATION into a "Problem" in Learning

**Needed:** a quart jar; a measuring cup; a small bottle (4 oz. or under); a pie plate

Suppose you fill the measuring cup to the top line, and then pour out enough water from the measuring cup (perhaps one half) to fill a bottle which will hold 4 ounces.

Suppose the bottle is filled to the brim, then screw on the cap so that the water will not spill out. It is important to know that there would be half a cup of water in the bottle.

Now set the quart jar on the pie plate and fill it right to the top with water, so it is almost ready to overflow.■

Suppose you were to place the bottle containing the 4 ounces of water into the jar. Be sure to let it drop below the surface of the water.● About how much water would flow out of the jar into the pie plate?

Remove the quart jar from the pie plate, empty the measuring cup, and carefully pour the water from the pie plate into the cup.▲ How full will the cup be?

**29**

association of old ideas and information or perhaps from old ideas with new information.

How does this apply to you in your learning of new things? How does it apply to the scientist who is always learning new things?

## Theories of Learning

We now have two theories which try to explain how we learn. One is the theory of conditioning and the other is the goal-insight theory.

Some psychologists use the theory of conditioning to explain the learning of simple habits—such as responding to a name or tying a shoelace. They use the goal-insight theory to explain the learning of such complex habits as writing, playing the piano, or memorizing a poem.

As you go on in your study of science, you will have reason to wonder if all our behavior can be explained by the theory of conditioning or the goal-insight theory. You may wonder if we really know how learning takes place. You may find that there is much to be learned about learning.

For instance, you may even begin to wonder if you can trust your own senses. Our senses are very important to the learning process. What we know about the environment comes to us through our senses—taste, sight, smell, touch, and hearing. How good are your senses? Why not investigate? You will need several friends to help.

Take turns blindfolding each other with a large handkerchief and see how many things you can identify with your sense of touch. Can you tell the difference between a tomato and an apple, a one-dollar bill and a piece of paper the same size and shape?

Can you identify an apple or a tomato by your sense of smell? Can you distinguish the difference between a piece of onion and a piece of apple if you hold your nose while you are tasting them?

See if you can distinguish sounds and the direction from which they come.

From these investigations you may begin to wonder whether your senses can always be trusted. Can they? How do scientists check the accuracy of their observations?

Scientists use instruments to check the accuracy of their observations. They do not trust their senses alone but use instruments to measure what they observe. They do not trust their sense of touch to say how hot or cold something may be; they use a thermometer. They do not trust their sense of sight to determine the intensity of light; they use a light meter. This is true for every observation; they use accurate instruments to check their observations.

Also, scientists check on each other. They repeat observations and experiments many times to verify what they have observed. One trial is never a sufficient basis for drawing a conclusion. Because they know that their senses may be in error, they check and recheck.

A. Study the statements below and choose the correct responses. They will help you fix in mind the concepts of this section.

1. Coughing is
   a. an inborn automatic act   b. a learned automatic act

2. Writing is
   a. an inborn automatic act   b. a learned automatic act

3. Simple habits are
   a. learned automatic acts   b. inborn automatic acts

4. The theory of learning by *conditioning* cannot explain acts like
   a. writing                   b. tying a shoelace

5. The goal-insight theory is often used to explain the learning of
   a. simple habits             b. complex habits

B. Write a paragraph or two on this topic: How We Learn.

1. Look ahead a bit. Try to answer the following questions about your study habits.
   a. Do you study at home each day?
   b. Do you begin to do your homework at a regular time each day?
   c. Do you study in a quiet place?
   d. Do you have proper tools at hand when you start to study?
   e. Do you plan what you will study first and what you will study later?

After you read the next section, you will be asked these questions again.

2. In asking people to attempt something new, it is usually best to give them a fairly complete explanation of the reasons *why* they should make such an attempt. Then it seems a good idea to discuss also *how* they might start on the new project.

For instance, your brother or sister or a friend may wonder why it is useful to understand fractions in arithmetic. You might explain *why* it is useful and *how* they could go about learning fractions in school.

Show whether your reasons for learning fractions are explained either by

    a. the theory of conditioning;

    b. the goal-insight theory;

    c. or both.

## 4. Making Learning Easy

Set this goal for yourself: To master the habit of studying. Recall that you form many habits of doing things automatically, like tying your shoelaces. You can also form habits, such as study habits, which will help you learn better and more easily. As you advance in school, you will study many different subjects, such as English, mathematics, history, social studies, and science. If you learn to study well, you will gain a better understanding of these subjects.

Learning to study well is a complicated habit. Although it takes a long time to form such a habit, there are some things you can begin to do now.

First, you should know the value of having good study habits. In the next six years or so your business will be that of being a student. Just as the father of a family goes to work each day to earn a living, you go to work each day as a student to learn. What you learn will help determine what you will do all your life. It is important then to become the best student you can—by developing good study habits.

### Developing Good Study Habits

Check yourself. In your notebook, write the answers to the five questions which follow. They are concerned with how you study.

1. Do you study each day?

2. Do you study at a regular time each day?

3. Do you study in a quiet place?

4. Do you have proper tools at hand when you study? (Some of the tools you need are: pen, pencils, erasers, ruler, books, paper, a dictionary, and good lighting.)

5. Do you plan what you will study first and what you will study later?

The answers to these questions are important. If you do not answer "yes" to all five of these questions, find out if you should by doing the investigation on the opposite page. Should you change your study habits?

# AN INVESTIGATION into How Regular Practice Fixes a Simple Habit

**Needed:** at least three friends

Ask two of your friends to write their names with their left hand (or with their right if they are left-handed). Ask them to practice on 2 days out of a 5-day week, for about 40 minutes each day; for example, 40 minutes on Tuesday and 40 minutes on Thursday. ■

Meanwhile, you and another friend in your class should practice writing your names with the hand not normally used; but you should practice once a day for about 15 minutes each day.●

After 5 days, who has had the most practice time? At the end of that time the four of you should meet to see who writes better. Were the results for the students who did not practice regularly different from the results of those who did? How would you explain the resulting differences?

Do you agree that regular practice helps fix a habit?

## Additional Investigations

1. Does regular practice improve your skill in playing a musical instrument? How do you know?

2. Does regular practice improve skill in your favorite sport? Plan an investigation to find out. Make a progress report.

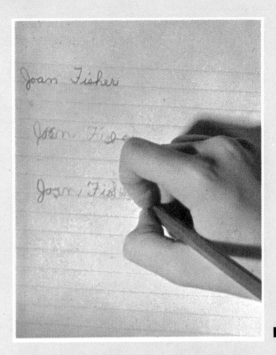

■

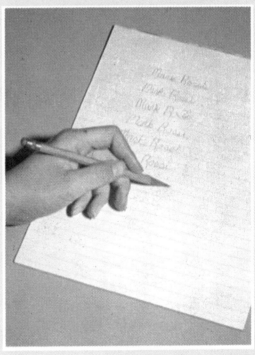

●

Look at the pictures above. ■ ● Why will the boy on the right probably learn faster and better than the boy on the left? Which of the pictures shows the way you study? Do you think there is any connection between the way you study and the kind of marks you get in school?

*Why should you study each day?*

To learn something well you must practice regularly. Regular practice, psychologists have found, helps fix a habit. Thus it is easier to form good study habits by studying an hour every day than by studying several hours one or two days each week.

*Why should you study at a regular time each day?*

When you were very young, you may have been fed whenever you were hungry. Many small babies do not have a regular time to eat, but even if *you* did not, your family did eat at a regular time. Soon you were eating with your family, and eating

at a regular time became a habit. Do you notice now that you get hungry at lunch time—and at dinner time? Your body is ready for lunch or dinner.

In much the same way, if you plan a regular time for study, you will be ready to start work. Being ready, you will pay more attention to your studying. You will therefore learn better and more easily. Each person selects the study time that is best for him. What time is best for you? Is late at night a good time?

Before you choose the time of day to be used as your study period, think of all the things that might interfere with your being able to concentrate. Then choose a time that would have the least interference. For instance:

Could you concentrate on your lessons when your favorite television program is playing?

Could you concentrate when all your friends are at play?

Choose your study time carefully; it makes studying easier.

*Why should you study in a quiet place?*

Try this short investigation to help you decide.

Below are 6 stanzas from "The Day Is Done," a poem by Longfellow. Memorize three stanzas in a quiet place. Time yourself.

THE DAY IS DONE

The day is done, and the darkness
    Falls from the wings of Night,
As a feather is wafted downward
    From an eagle in his flight.

I see the lights of the village
    Gleam through the rain and the
        mist,
And a feeling of sadness comes o'er
        me
    That my soul cannot resist:

A feeling of sadness and longing,
    That is not akin to pain,
And resembles sorrow only
    As the mist resembles the rain.

Come, read to me some poem,
    Some simple and heartfelt lay,
That shall soothe this restless feeling,
    And banish the thoughts of day.

Not from the grand old masters,
    Not from the bards sublime,
Whose distant footsteps echo
    Through the corridors of Time.

For, like strains of martial music,
    Their mighty thoughts suggest
Life's endless toil and endeavor;
    And to-night I long for rest.

Then memorize three more stanzas with the television or the radio on or try to memorize them in a corner of the playground. Time yourself again.

In which place was it easier to memorize: in a quiet place or in a noisy place? How long did it take in either place?

Psychologists have found that it is generally easier for people to study in a quiet place because they can then pay attention more easily to what they are doing.

Do you see why quiet is needed in a library? or in the classroom when you have a reading or a study period?

*Why should you have your study tools at hand?*

Suppose you were trying to solve an arithmetic problem. Suppose, too, that whenever you needed an eraser or a ruler you had to get up to find one. Not only would this waste time but, more important, you would be taking your attention from the arithmetic problem. Once you give attention to a problem, it is best to keep at it until you finish. You reach a solution sooner. This would allow time for all the other things you may want to be doing at home or at school. It is sensible not to waste time.

In addition to having good study habits, it is important that you should have the proper tools. Before you turn the page, jot down a list of all the items that you think are essential as good study tools. Check with the picture on the next page.

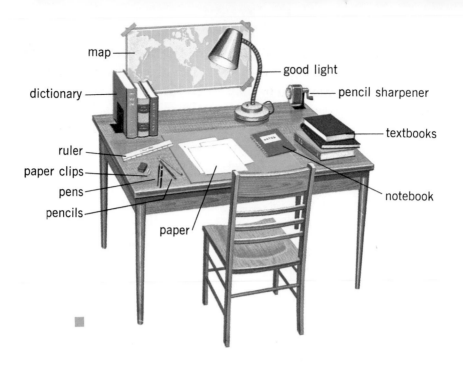

map

dictionary

good light

pencil sharpener

ruler

paper clips

pens

pencils

paper

textbooks

notebook

The picture above shows the tools that you need. ■ You should learn how to use them well. For instance, using a dictionary to help you with words you do not know is one important study habit.

*Why should you plan what you will study first and what you will study later?*

Not everyone finds every subject easy. Some may excel in science and mathematics; others may find English difficult. Suppose you are getting ready to study tomorrow's work. One assignment is in a subject that you find difficult, and another is in one that you find easy.

Would it be best to study the more difficult one first? Psychologists would generally say "yes." It is best to study the more difficult subject first because you would be studying it when you are physically fresh; you are then more alert. When you have finished studying both subjects, it is well to go over the more difficult one again. This will give you another chance to practice the harder subject and to fix it in mind. It seems that the more you practice a difficult subject, the easier it becomes.

There are other useful things you can learn about the practice of studying. Discuss ways of studying with your friends. Some of them may have successful ways of studying, which you may want to use.

The years spent as a student are very important years of your life. Learn to study well, because learning continues as long as you live.

The scientist must be a good student. Scientists are, in fact, students all their lives. They spend their lives in study and investigation.

Scientists have mastered a special way of learning, that is, through investigation. They are careful observers and are always looking for the unusual. The uses of ideas and tools in industry is the subject of the next unit. There you will learn more about the ways of the investigator.

**BEFORE YOU GO ON**

**A.** First, turn your attention once again to the questions on page 32.

Now that you have read this section, have you begun to improve your own study habits?

**1.** What exactly have you done to improve your study habits? Make a list of the changes you have made—or the things you have done.

**2.** How do you plan to study in the future? Make a list of the things you need to do.

**B.** Write a paragraph or two on this topic: "Habit Formation."

**ON YOUR OWN**

Look ahead a bit. Investigate the "Art of Investigation." You will find this section in your book on page 409. Since much of your work in science will be in the form of investigation, it is important for you to develop skill in the ways of a scientist. Find out the meaning of the terms "variable" (vâr′ē·ə·bəl) and "control," in relation to an experiment. Review from previous experiences in science what is meant by a hypothesis and what is meant by a theory.

Plan an investigation with a controlled experiment as part of the investigation. For instance, plan an investigation to determine whether or not plants respond to a stimulus such as light. Do they respond to sound? Do they respond to magnetic force? Do they respond to touch? Do they respond to electric currents?

Take your choice of these suggestions or design an investigation yourself. In this case you are truly on your own. You can let your imagination work for you. Be as original as you possibly can.

## 5. The Main Concept: Changing the Environment Through Learning

Plant a seed in good soil. It can be a bean, or zinnia, or nasturtium seed. Water it. If the seed is planted in a suitable environment, the plant will grow and produce blossoms and more seeds. A bean plant *will not* grow under water, nor on the top of Mount Everest, nor next to a cactus plant on the dry desert. Neither will a zinnia nor a nasturtium plant grow in such places, but some kinds of plants do grow there. Plants are adapted to a *special* environment, a **habitat** (hab′-ə·tat). The habitat for some kinds of plants could be a desert or a mountaintop. For others, the habitat could be the ocean.

The growth of a plant, such as the buttercup shown in the illustration, depends on its surroundings—on a sufficient supply of water, on certain substances found in the soil, and on sunlight. ■

Plants are a part of and make use of their environment. They change their environment by taking certain substances from it, and by adding others to it. However, the environment in which a bean plant has been growing looks the same after the plant has grown as it did before.

A bean plant, like most plants, does not seem to change its environment greatly, and even then, only temporarily. Plants take substances from the air, the water, and the soil, and they use energy from the sun. In turn, they add, as they decay, the materials that were taken. They also add energy; it is stored in the food plants make. Some of the food may be eaten by animals. The animals use the energy and restore some of the materials to their environment. The rest becomes part of the animal.

The same process is true of animals that is true of plants. Animals need food, water, and shelter; they feed on plants or on other animals; they live in and are part of their environment.● Ants build nests and mounds; birds build nests; moles burrow through the ground; but these, like other animals, do not seem to change their environment very much, except as they are part of it, coming and going. Animals, like plants, also return to the environment the materials they have used. There is a continuous exchange of matter and energy between living things and their environment.

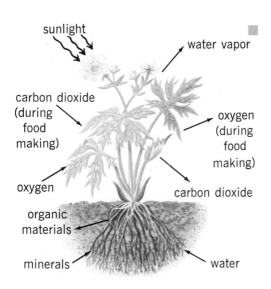

sunlight

water vapor

carbon dioxide (during food making)

oxygen (during food making)

oxygen

carbon dioxide

organic materials

minerals

water

The inborn unlearned behavior helps an animal to live as a part of its special environment, its habitat. Yet some animals, such as the locust, can destroy crops; and large numbers of mice and rats can do great damage. Still, we usually think of animals as being a part of their environment, not changing it very much.

All living things are adapted to their environment. They also are **interdependent** with their environment. The term interdependent means that living things *take* matter and energy from their environment and *return* matter and energy to it. Interdependence is a major concept of science. Wherever you find living things, you will find them interdependent with their environment.

Man also is adapted to and interdependent with his environment. He uses food, water, and oxygen taken from the environment. He returns the matter in other compounds.

However, in one way man is different. His brain enables him to learn about his environment; but a more important fact is that once he has learned, he is able to change his environment.

Man learns, for example, that all matter is made of atoms and molecules, and he changes the way they are put together. The result is that new substances are created. Man invents nylon, stainless steel, and plastics. He even forms new atoms. Of equal importance, his brain makes it possible for him to record what he has learned—in books, on film, or on tapes with a tape recorder. What he learns, man passes on to others.

A newborn infant lives by his reflexes. Soon, through conditioning, the child learns simple habits and his behavior is changed. For instance, he learns to bathe and to dress himself. Simple habits, however, are not enough. Later, he goes to school and learns to read and write; these are more complex habits. He also learns mathematics, science, skills in the gymnasium, and how to play baseball or how to dance. ■

Each boy and girl sets his (or her) own goals and develops insight into ways of reaching them. Boys and girls learn to live in a very complex world, one with many different kinds of people as well as many different kinds of machines.

Adults also spend much of their time learning. They are able to *use* much of what they learn in their daily lives in working with others and in earning a living.

Ancient man learned. He learned to build homes from the wood of trees. He learned to get food from plants and animals.

Much later, man began to build farms and cities. He changed his environment; he changed the face of the earth. Man not only lives in his environment, he learns from it. He develops new ideas and invents new devices and changes his environment.

*Man, like all living things, is interdependent with his environment;* but his ability to acquire new habits through learning makes it possible for him to live in many different environments. In this way, man is unlike any other living thing on earth. Man's creativity gives him a great advantage.

He can live under water but not like fish. He does not have organs which enable him to adapt to a water environment; but he does have an organ which enables him to live in an environment to which he is not adapted.

■ **GROWTH IN LEARNING**

reflexes      conditioned learning      goal-insight learning

That organ is his brain. With his brain he invents a submarine. With his brain he learns new habits which are necessary for him to live successfully in the submarine—under water. With his brain he finds ways to live high in the air, or even in outer space.

Man moves *into* and *out of* many different environments because he is able to learn, to acquire new habits, and to provide for his needs in any environment.

Natural environments change, and animals must adjust to the changes or they cannot survive. Every extinct species became extinct because it could not change or control a new environment. But man can invent new tools, new weapons, and even a whole new environment to suit his fancy. Instead of adjusting to a changing environment, man makes some changes in his environment. This gives man the best chance to survive.

Because man *can* learn, he even changes himself. He learns ways to add years to his life. By changing his diet, he grows taller and healthier.

Man continues to learn. As a scientist, he uses special ways of learning about his environment. The special ways of the scientist are his ways of investigating.● Through these, learning advances at a faster rate than ever before. In fact, the amount of knowledge we are gaining is doubling every 15 years. That is, in 15 years twice as much will be known as is known today. Man hopes that this knowledge will be used for peace.

# Fixing the Main Concepts

Test your understanding of the important concepts of this unit by doing these problems.

1. Suppose you want your cat—or dog—to eat at a certain time. You decide to use a bell to summon your pet. Describe how you would train your pet to respond to the bell.

2. A new puppy howls at night. The girl to whom the puppy belongs goes outside to quiet it every night for the first week.

However, the puppy continues to howl each night. It stops only when the girl goes outside to quiet it. How do you explain what is happening?

What theory of learning are you using in your explanation?

What would *you* do to change the puppy's behavior? Why do you think your method would work?

3. How would you train a fish to come to the side of a glass tank which you tapped?

4. A boy is learning to play basketball. Somehow, his shot at the basket hits the rim most of the time. He gets very discouraged and asks the coach to help him.

The coach of the team knows that the way the boy stands as he throws the ball is causing him to miss the basket. The coach takes him aside and asks him to watch a boy who "shoots baskets" well. In particular, the boy is asked to watch the other boy's feet as he takes his shot.

Use the goal-insight theory of learning to explain what you think the coach is doing.

5. Teachers know that often the difference in learning ability between two boys is not their intelligence level. They know that one boy has better study habits than the other.

From what you know about different students, do you think this is possible?

**6.** Which of the following statements are correct? Give evidence or reasons for your choice.

Good study habits save time.

Good study habits waste time.

Good study habits make learning easier.

Good study habits improve your grades.

Good study habits make no difference.

Study the statements below and choose the correct responses. They will help you fix in mind the concepts of this unit.

1. Of the following, only one is not an inborn automatic act. That one is

a. coughing          c. reading

b. sneezing          d. yawning

2. Of the following, only one is not an inborn automatic act. That one is a

a. spider spinning a web       c. moth flying toward a light

b. robin building a nest       d. baby saying "daddy"

3. Of the following, the neuron which carries the impulse to the muscle is the

a. sensory neuron        c. connecting neuron

b. motor neuron          d. sensory nerve ending

4. The scientist who developed the theory of conditioning is

a. Salk          c. Freud

b. Pavlov        d. Darwin

5. It is thought that a reward fixes the behavior where a new response takes the place of the original response. For instance, a dog that responded only to food now responds to the sound of his name.   This act is explained by the

a. fact that it is an        c. fact that it is
   inborn act                   an instinct

b. theory of                 d. theory of goal-
   conditioning                 insight

**6.** A boy realizes the usefulness of saving money for something he wants to buy. This act is explained in terms of

a. reflexes

b. instincts

c. the theory of conditioning

d. the goal-insight theory

**7.** Man can learn better than any other living thing because of his

a. neurons

b. nerves

c. senses

d. brain

**8.** Practice is essential to the development of

a. an inborn automatic act

b. a reflex

c. a habit

d. an instinct

**9.** The first acts of a baby are

a. habits

b. reflexes

c. learned acts

d. learned automatic acts

**10.** As man grows up he gradually acquires

a. more reflexes

b. more habits

c. fewer reflexes

d. fewer habits

**FOR YOUR READING**

**1.** *Story of People,* by May Edel, published by Little, Brown, Boston, 1953.

This book is a good account of the behaviors of different groups of people. Customs and habits are described.

**2.** *The Friendly Phoebe,* by Berta and Elmer Hader, published by The Macmillan Co., New York, 1953.

This is a story of a newly hatched phoebe and the way it was cared for until it was able to care for itself. In the story is an interesting account of the reflexes and learning ability of a phoebe.

**3.** *The Senses of Animals and Men,* by Lorus J. and Margery Milne, published by Atheneum, 1962.

This book is an introduction to the five basic senses.

The inborn automatic acts of some plants are called *tropisms* (trō′piz·əms).

For instance, stems of plants always seem to grow toward the light. If the action is movement or growth *toward* the stimulus, we say the tropistic response is *positive*. So growth of a plant toward light is a positive tropism. Growth away from a stimulus is called a negative tropism.

### An Investigation into the Behavior of a Plant

Get some oat seed or corn. Plant four seeds in sand in a paper cup. Place each seed about one-half inch below the surface. Keep the sand moist, but to be sure that the sand is not too moist, punch holes in the bottom of the paper cup.

Just as soon as the tips of the plant poke through the surface, place the plants in a shoe box, as shown. ■ Notice the window cut in the box. Then close the cover.

After a few days the plants should look like those in the picture.● Now repeat this with two or three more cups of seeds, except for one difference. When the seeds have grown about one inch, use scissors to snip off the tips of two of the four seedlings in each cup. ▲ Leave two plants with their tips whole. Place the cups in the shoe box once again.

1. What do you observe?
2. Do your observations agree with others in your class?
3. How do you explain your observations?
4. Invent a theory which will help to explain your observations. Recall that a theory is an explanation of observations.

A ■

B ●

C ▲

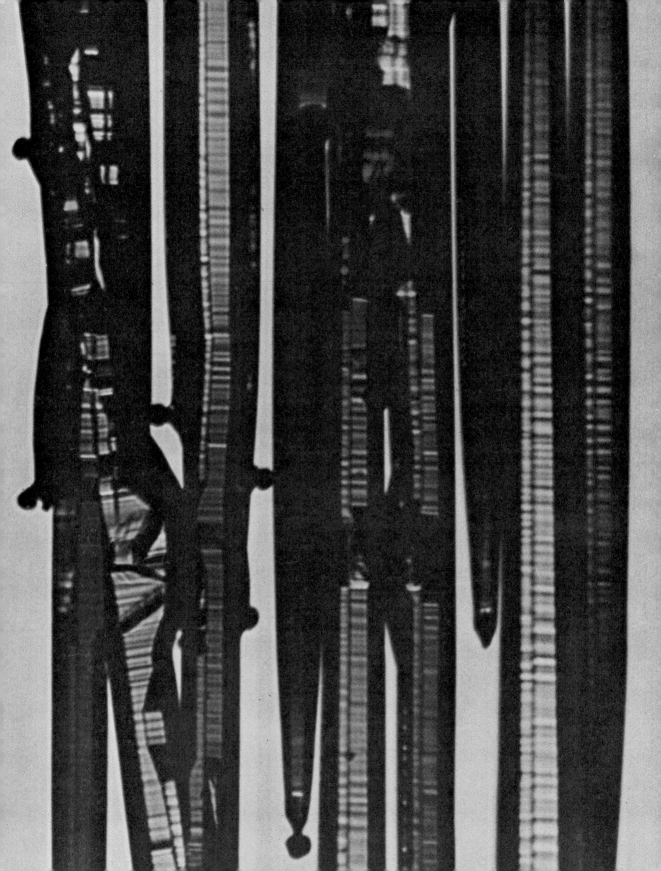

# UNIT TWO

# IDEAS AND TOOLS: FOR NEW PRODUCTS

To walk upon another world for the first time in human history is the greatest adventure ever planned. Yet by the turn of this decade man expects to set foot upon the moon. This adventure will generate a demand for new materials that are stronger, or tougher, or stiffer, or more resistant than existing ones.

Engineers who design structures constantly seek new materials that are stronger and stiffer than existing ones. The microphotograph on the opposite page shows silicon fibers imbedded in aluminum to increase strength but not weight.

Two hundred years ago, there was no penicillin, no nylon, no plastics, no steel bridges, no gasoline, and no aluminum. How did man get along without these things? How did they come about? What new materials will the future demand? Who will discover them, invent them, or design them?

Every significant advance in science is the result of the combined thought of many minds. Through the efforts of the scientists and engineers, each of us is able, through the application of research in astronomy, physics, chemistry, mathematics, medicine, and biology, to develop into a happier, healthier, and more efficient citizen of the universe.

This unit begins a study of the way that man, as scientist and engineer, uses ideas and tools, imagination and skill, to produce new products to meet new demands.

## 1. Charles Hall and His Discovery

About 85 years ago, Charles Martin Hall, a student at Oberlin College, found the objective of his life's work. ■ In his chemistry class the teacher talked about the need for metals, especially aluminum. Aluminum is the most common metal in the earth's crust; but in spite of its abundance it was very expensive at the time that Charles Hall was in college. It was expensive because it was difficult to obtain *pure* aluminum from the earth. The price made its use impractical for buildings and for transportation. An inexpensive method of processing was needed. Scientists realized that quantities of aluminum could be used successfully in building and transportation if only it could be processed easily. All the common metals except aluminum and magnesium had been known and used for hundreds of years. Why, then, wondered Hall, was aluminum so difficult to produce? How and why was Hall able to develop a method for separating aluminum? Why had it not been done 200 years earlier?

After Charles Hall graduated from college, he began to investigate the problem of finding an easier and cheaper way to separate aluminum from its ore. His laboratory was the family woodshed.

One day he was able to give a dozen small pieces of aluminum to his former chemistry teacher. These pieces are sometimes know as "Hall's Jewels." A method similar to the one Hall used is still used today to obtain pure aluminum. It is used to produce very large amounts of the metal at a very low cost.●

## Aluminum Everywhere About You

Aluminum, the most abundant metal in the Earth's crust, is twice as abundant as iron. All igneous rocks contain aluminum, but aluminum usually remains insoluble in the form of clay. So, whenever you take a handful of clay from the ground, you may be picking up a compound containing aluminum. The aluminum is *chemically combined* with several other substances and has been in the earth for millions of years. It was there 2,000 years ago—1,000 years ago. Why then did man not use aluminum earlier? He did not know enough. He did not know as much chemistry and physics as is known today.

Two thousand years ago man did not know aluminum was in the earth. Even 150 years ago aluminum was not used. Man had not learned how to separate the aluminum compound from the crust of the earth, nor how to separate the pure element aluminum from its compound. Before this was possible, the concept of the way **elements** join to form a **compound** had to be understood. This concept is no more than about 150 years old.

At that time, John Dalton, an English school teacher and scientist, had just begun to demonstrate that all matter was made of atoms, and he taught that these atoms combined to form compounds. Charles Martin Hall used this concept in his investigations of a way to separate aluminum from its compound.

It had been known before Hall began *his* work that some kinds of ore, especially the ore called *bauxite* (bôk′sīt), are very rich in a compound called aluminum oxide. ▲ Oxygen is the other element in this compound. The aluminum and oxygen are combined chemically so that it is very hard to separate them. Hall's great discovery was a way of separating aluminum from its partner (oxygen) in aluminum oxide.

The investigation that you find on the next page will give you an idea of how pure aluminum is obtained, although the investigation is done with another metal, copper, which can be separated easily from its most common compound, copper sulfate. In school laboratories, it is not easy to separate aluminum from its compound (the oxide), but the idea is much the same if we try to get the pure metal, copper, from copper sulfate. Try the next investigation.

**49**

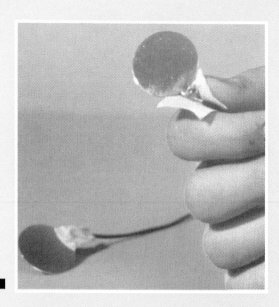

**Needed:** about 3 teaspoonfuls of copper sulfate; two glasses; water; two pieces of insulated wire about 1 foot long; a dry cell; and 1 tablespoon of washing soda

You will also need two small pieces of silver: perhaps two silver coins or old unwanted pieces of jewelry, such as charms from a charm bracelet. Any silver or silver-plated objects will do. *Check with the owner to make sure that the items are no longer wanted.*

Remove the covering from one end of each of the copper wires. Wash the pieces of silver in some hot water and washing soda, to clean their surfaces. It is sometimes necessary to wash the pieces of silver several times to remove any oil or lacquer. When the silver is clean, it will have a dull appearance rather than a bright, shiny one. Tape the end of each piece of wire to a piece of silver, as shown. ■ Remove the covering from about $\frac{1}{2}$-inch of the other end of each wire. Connect these ends to the dry cell, as shown. Use *only one dry cell.* ●

Pour hot water into the glass until it is three-quarters full. Add 1 level teaspoonful of copper sulfate to the hot water, and stir until the compound is dissolved. Then, add 2 more level teaspoonfuls of copper sulfate and stir until they dissolve.

**DANGER:** The compound copper sulfate is poisonous.
**DO NOT GET ANY IN YOUR MOUTH.**
Wash your hands after the investigation.

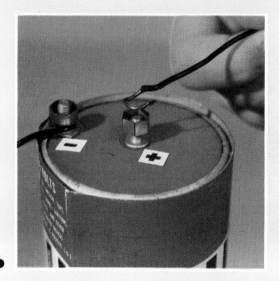

50

# When an Electric Current Is Passed Through Copper Sulfate

Now put the pieces of silver into the solution, but do not let them touch each other. ▲ Leave them until you see that one of the pieces of silver has turned a copper color. ◆

What has happened? First, an electric current goes from the dry cell through the compound copper sulfate.

The coin becomes coated, or plated, with copper. Where could the copper have come from?

If you leave the coin in the **solution** long enough, the blue color seems to disappear. The copper sulfate is gone. What is your explanation?

**Additional Investigation:** To which terminal on the dry cell is the coin that receives the coating of copper connected? What happens if you change the terminal to which each coin is connected?

How would you explain what happens? If you cannot explain it, where would you go to find out?

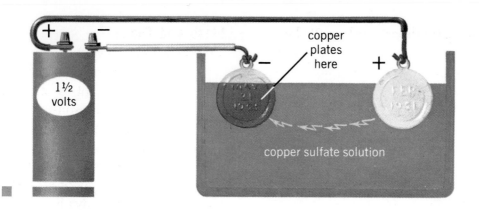

copper plates here

copper sulfate solution

1½ volts

## From Our Copper to Hall's Aluminum

A good explanation of the effect that an electric current has on copper sulfate is this: the copper leaves the solution to plate the silver coin or charm. ■ Electric energy causes the pure copper to separate from its compound, copper sulfate.

Does the same explanation hold true for separating aluminum from aluminum oxide in the ore bauxite? If so, what did Charles Hall need? He needed an electric current. Furthermore, he needed the aluminum oxide in a form that would conduct electricity easily. The aluminum oxide had to be dissolved in a melted substance called *cryolite* (krī′ə·līt); it will not dissolve in water, as copper sulfate does. When Hall passed an electric current through the solution of aluminum oxide and melted cryolite, the pure aluminum came out of the bauxite in the solution.

What an important discovery! Of course, it had been known that an electric current could break up certain substances, but Hall made this idea work for him by inventing a way

of using it. Through his efforts the element aluminum could finally be made useful.

It was the development of the electric generator to replace the battery as a source of electricity that made possible the economical and large-scale production of aluminum. Continued research and development has put aluminum in a very important position. It is second only to iron among metals.

Look at the picture on the opposite page. The aluminum "plates" out and settles on the bottom of the tub as a liquid. ● Then the liquid aluminum is run off at the bottom and cooled to form pure solid aluminum ingots (ing′gəts).

Aluminum may be cast into ingots for rolling into bars, rods, sheets, or foil. It can be drawn into wire, and it can be forged. It can be drawn down to tubes of any desired diameter and wall thickness. It is a good reflector of light and is used in the lighting industry. It is a good conductor of electricity and is used in the electrical industry. It is used to make collapsible toothpaste tubes. Today, ceramic engineers use it to make a variety of things harder and stronger, nose cones on rockets, for instance. There is no foreseeable end to the list of uses for aluminum.

Look about you. You will find many objects made of aluminum: pots, pans, ladders, aluminum foil, and screens. Because it is light in weight, aluminum is used in airplane construction; because of its strength, it is often used to replace steel and copper. Like iron, it does combine with oxygen; it forms aluminum oxide. A thin coating of aluminum oxide, however, protects the pure aluminum beneath it, whereas the coating of rust on a piece of steel does not protect the metal. Sooner or later the steel will rust through.

Under certain conditions, the oxide coating on aluminum will absorb various dye stuffs. Colored aluminum is used extensively for many purposes.

## Ideas and Tools: Relatives in Discovery

A study of the way Hall produced aluminum is important for many reasons. One of the reasons is that it shows the advantage of man's brain. It shows how man can use a discovery to change his environment and, thereby, to improve his way of life. Aluminum compounds always have been in the earth, but bears, or lions, or monkeys are not able to take advantage of them. Man *can* and *does*. He invents not only *new tools* but also *new ideas*, or concepts. It is important that you consider both of these aspects of man's activity as a scientist.

Man is interested in what is going on around him in the universe. He observes, analyzes, and reflects upon what he has observed. He asks endless questions, usually of himself. Some of the best ideas are nothing but questions. In fact, the business of science is one of asking questions. The

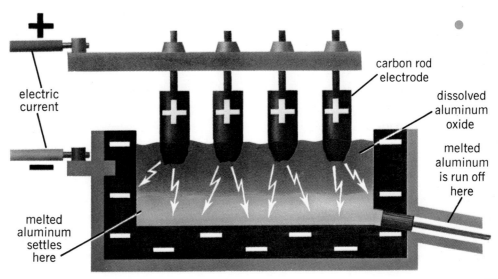

electric current

carbon rod electrode

dissolved aluminum oxide

melted aluminum is run off here

melted aluminum settles here

**Isaac Newton**
(1642–1727)
concepts of motion,
gravitation,
and light

**John Dalton**
(1766–1844)
concept of matter
as particles

**Louis Pasteur**
(1822–1895)
germ theory
of disease

**Albert Einstein**
(1879–1955)
concept of
relativity

kind of science one gets depends on the kind of questions one asks, and some of the answers have become the major *concepts* of science.

As an example, scientists have developed, after many hundreds of years, an explanation of the structure of the material universe—the world of matter. In developing this explanation, they observed and investigated the odd assortment of the billions of things we see around us—rocks, rain, and robins; pencils, paper, and pebbles; sand, salt, and seaweed; trees, toads, and tin; water, wax, and worms; the moon, man, and money.

It is one thing to look at each of these things separately. They seem to have no relationships between them, to be totally different, helter-skelter, scrambled, without order.

It is another thing to discover that all these things *are related* in that they are all made from tiny particles, **atoms** and **molecules.** An understanding of this concept that *all matter is composed of combinations of less than 100 different kinds of tiny particles* brings order out of disorder. The billions of things around us may not be helter-skelter after all; they are indeed related in that they are all composed of atoms and molecules.

Developing concepts, then, about the universe, is one aspect of man's activity as a scientist.

Another aspect of man's activity as a scientist is his interest in using these concepts to invent things that work— tools, machines, or new materials. As we have seen in the case of Charles Martin Hall, this kind of scientist or engineer takes the concepts that have already been developed, and applies them for some special purpose. Charles Hall did this when he separated aluminum from its ore.

Hall used concepts that had been developed by other scientists. For instance, he combined his knowledge of the concept that *matter is made up of particles* with the concept that *energy can be changed from one form to another*. On the basis of his understanding of these two concepts, he split the compound aluminum oxide by means of electric energy. He separated the element from the compound.

You will come across the two aspects of man's activities as a scientist again and again. The one aspect in which he *seeks* to explain what he observes in the universe is usually called pure science. The other aspect, in which he *applies* the concepts of science to invent tools, machines, or materials is called applied science or **technology** (tek·nol′ə·jē).

To use another example, the pure scientist is mainly interested in explaining light; the applied scientist, or engineer, is primarily interested in inventing a light bulb. When the applied scientist works on light bulbs, however, he may actually find out a great deal more about light. In the same way, when the pure scientist investigates light, he may discover a way to make a better light bulb. Ideas and inventions go together.

**Thomas Edison**
(1847–1931)
technology of
electricity

**Guglielmo Marconi**
(1874–1937)
wireless
communications

**Jonas Salk**
(1914–    )
medical research
and development

**Wernher von Braun**
(1912–    )
rocket research
and development

It is very hard to find a person who is a pure scientist only or an applied scientist only. Most scientists are a combination of both. Ideas, or concepts, and tools go hand in hand; but perhaps it is more correct to say that the scientist is interested in concepts, while the engineer is more interested in techniques involved in tools, machines, or materials.

BEFORE YOU GO ON A. Study the statements below and choose the correct responses. They will help you fix in mind the concepts of this section.

1. To get aluminum we must separate it from
   a. cryolite          b. bauxite

2. An electric current can release copper from
   a. copper sulfate          b. aluminum sulfate

3. In order to electroplate a substance, the substance must
   a. conduct electricity          b. not conduct electricity

4. Hall's work in separating aluminum from its ore is an example of
   a. pure science          b. applied science

B. Write a paragraph or two on this topic: Science and Technology.

USING WHAT YOU KNOW Engineers are primarily concerned with advances in technology. (This is not to say that engineers are not interested in pure science.) On the basis of what you now know about technology, who would you say is primarily responsible for work on rockets, scientists interested in pure science or scientists interested in technology?

ON YOUR OWN Which of the following men were more interested in technology than in pure science? The library will help.

Charles Hall          Albert Einstein
Wernher von Braun          Louis Pasteur

northern lights

development
of
organisms

pull of gravity

migration of birds

■ SOME SCIENTIFIC PHENOMENA

## 2. Uses of a Concept

In this part of your book you have been reading about the uses of discovery. You have been focusing attention on how man *uses* the concepts of science to improve his way of living. There is much more to a concept, however, than its use in technology. A concept in science that developed from observation of certain objects and events can often be expanded to explain other objects and events.

Events that the scientist seeks to explain are called phenomena (fi-nom′ə·nə). ■ Examples of such events are weather, the fall of meteors, the revolution of the planets, the pull of gravity, the migration of birds, or the transfer of heat.

Would you be surprised to find that the concept *matter is made of particles* helps us to understand one of the most important phenomena of our environment—**heat?** What is heat? Several investigations may help you to find out. Try those suggested on the following pages.

# AN INVESTIGATION into the Motion of Molecules

**Needed:** two Pyrex beakers; hot and cold water; ink; a medicine dropper; a watch

Fill the two Pyrex beakers almost to the top. One should be filled with very hot water and the other with very cold water. Allow the beakers to stand until the water is quite still.

Put exactly four drops of ink into each with a medicine dropper. ■ Place your watch on a nearby table and note the exact time when the ink was added.

Watch closely! Notice how the ink swirls around and begins to mix with the water.● Notice how the swirls continue to move. Why are they moving even though the water seems to be quite still?

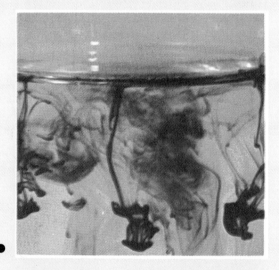

The molecules of ink are mixing with the molecules of water. Are the molecules of ink moving?

Which seems to be moving faster, the swirls of ink in the *hot* or in the *cold* water? Which molecules of water are moving faster, those in the hot water or those in the cold water? ▲

How long does it take the ink to become completely mixed with the hot water?

How long does it take to mix with the cold water? What is your explanation for the difference in time?

Now try the investigation on the opposite page. Analyze the results of each.

# AN INVESTIGATION into the Nature of Heat

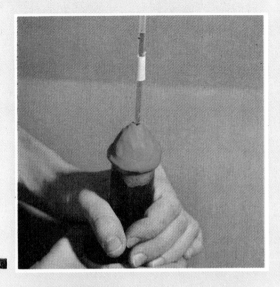 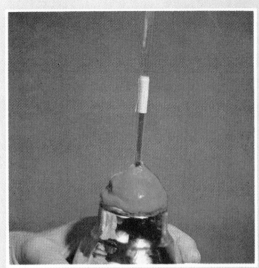

**Needed:** a flask; a small vacuum bottle; modeling clay; a long tube; some water; ink

Set up the flask exactly as shown in the picture. It is important that the flask be filled with water.

Color the water with several drops of ink. Place the modeling clay and tube in the flask. Press down until the water rises part way in the tube.

**a.** Hold your hands around the flask for 5 minutes. What happens? ■

**b.** Repeat the investigation, but use a vacuum bottle (that has been removed from its case) in place of the flask.● Compare the results from both. Get the average from several trials.

A number of students who did this investigation got the results below.

How do you explain their results? How do they compare with yours?

| | Rise of Column of Water (in tube with flask) | Rise of Column of Water (in tube with vacuum bottle) |
|---|---|---|
| **1.** Average of results of investigations by 11 students in a class in New York | $1\frac{1}{2}$ in. | no rise |
| **2.** 22 students in a class in Ohio | $1\frac{7}{16}$ in. | $\frac{1}{16}$ in. |

## The Energy of Moving Molecules

The human body is warm. Some of the *chemical energy* derived from the food we eat is changed to *heat energy*. The rest of this chemical energy is used for movement of the body, for growth, and for other body functions. Some of the heat energy can be transferred from the body to the flask.

How do you know that heat energy is transferred? The evidence is found in the investigation on page 59: the column of liquid rises in the tube from the flask in the same way that a liquid rises in a *thermometer*.

Why does the column of liquid rise? Let us try to apply the concept that *all matter is composed of particles* (in this case the particles are water molecules) to explain why the liquid rises. Reason this way: The liquid is composed of molecules of water. Heat energy is transferred from your body to the water by holding your hands around the flask. ■

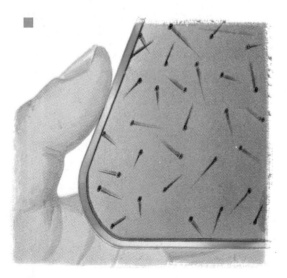

The water expands and occupies more space as it moves up the tube. ● Why? You did not add more molecules of water. Therefore the *same* number of molecules must be occupying *more* space. How can the same number of molecules occupy more space? The motion of molecules is the answer.

The moving ink swirls in the first investigation (page 58) demonstrated that even though the water appeared to be quite still, the particles of water must have been moving in order to mix with the particles of ink. On the basis of this observation we now can add the concept that *molecules of matter are in constant motion* to the concept that matter is composed of molecules.

With this expanded concept we can now explain more fully how the same number of molecules can occupy more space. When the heat from your hands was transferred to the molecules of water in the flask, the molecules began to move faster and faster. (Recall the faster-moving ink swirls in the beaker of hot water on page 58.) As the molecules in the flask moved faster, they pushed farther apart. They bounced faster and harder against the sides of the flask; but the sides of the flask are rigid and do not move, at least not so you can notice. The only way then for the molecules to move farther apart is to move farther up the tube. The **volume** increases while the number of molecules remains the same.

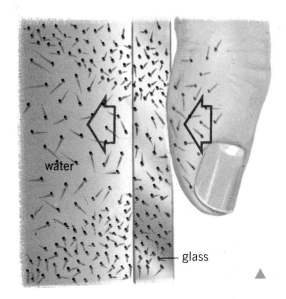

The warmer the liquid becomes, the higher the liquid will rise in the tube. As the liquid cools, the column will fall. You can determine this by putting the flask in a refrigerator for an hour.

If you recall the beakers of hot and cold water on page 58, it was the beaker of hot water that showed the greatest activity (the molecules were moving faster). It is from such observations that scientists have come to explain heat as *the motion of molecules.*

Molecules occupy space. The faster they move, the more space they occupy. This is the reason that a thermometer works. As the temperature rises, the molecules move faster, so that the liquid expands and rises in the tube. What about gases and solids? Do they also expand when the temperature rises?

Anyone who observes what goes on around him realizes that most materials expand as their temperature rises. The expansion of gases is far greater than that of liquids, but gases and liquids expand more than solids.

Designers and builders of many common objects must be aware of expansion and provide for changes in size. Bridges must have joints which allow for the maximum expansion on the hottest day. Cracks are left in sidewalks to keep them from bending under pressure. Do you know of other situations in which expansion could be a problem? Do you know any useful effects of expansion? Remember that expansion occurs when the temperature rises.

The water in the vacuum bottle did not get warmer when you held your hands around it. Why not? Reason this way: Heat is transferred from one place to another by moving molecules. Molecules in the wall of a glass flask will transfer the heat from your hand to the water inside, as shown. ▲

However, a transfer of heat cannot take place easily through the walls of a vacuum bottle. Look at the diagram below. ■ Notice that the vacuum bottle has two layers of glass. Between the layers of the vacuum bottle most of the air has been removed and very few molecules remain. For that reason, heat is not transferred. There is a shortage of moving molecules in a vacuum. The vacuum serves as an **insulator** (in′sə·lā′tər). Insulators slow down the transfer of heat from one place to another. They can be used to keep heat out or to keep heat in. What makes a good insulator?

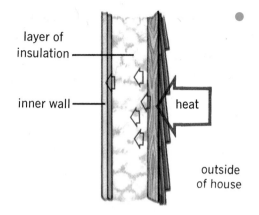

Certain materials can slow down the motion of molecules. They make good insulators also. Insulation, in the walls of a house, traps tiny pockets of air that can help keep heat in (in the winter) or help keep heat out (in the summer). The illustration shows how insulation can be used. ●

### The Nature of Heat

Heat is the energy of moving molecules. The faster they move, the greater the heat. The faster they move, the more space they occupy, if they are not enclosed. Would you say that the molecules of a gas move faster or slower than the molecules of a liquid?

The molecules in ice, water, and water vapor are the same except for their motion. When the molecules in ice or water move fast enough, they can escape and move as individual molecules of water vapor, a gas. Changing from ice to water and then to water vapor is only a matter of transferring heat from one place to another; and heat is the energy of moving molecules.

■ **VACUUM BOTTLE**

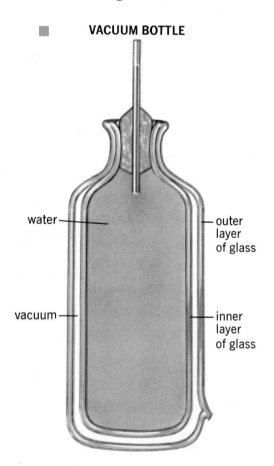

water — — outer layer of glass

vacuum — — inner layer of glass

Moving molecules have **kinetic energy** (ki·net′ik en′ər·jē). Kinetic energy is energy of motion. Fast-moving molecules have more kinetic energy than slow-moving molecules. If heat is the energy of moving molecules, then heat energy is one kind of kinetic energy. This is a very important concept about the nature of heat.

When molecules collide, that is, when molecules bump into one another, some of the kinetic energy of the faster-moving molecules can be transferred to the slower-moving molecules. The amount of energy transferred depends on the mass of the molecules. Why? Kinetic energy depends on both the mass of an object and its velocity. This is an important point to remember about the nature of heat. Now, to the concept that *all matter is made of particles* can be added the concept that *heat is the kinetic energy of molecules* and that energy can be transferred by the collision of particles.

This explanation for the nature of heat is called the **Kinetic Theory of Heat.** ▲ The kinetic theory will be very useful as you study the behavior of molecules. In any event, the kinetic theory enlarges our understanding of the world about us.

The world of matter is a world of particles. Furthermore, these particles of matter have kinetic energy. They are in constant motion. An understanding of the concept of parti-

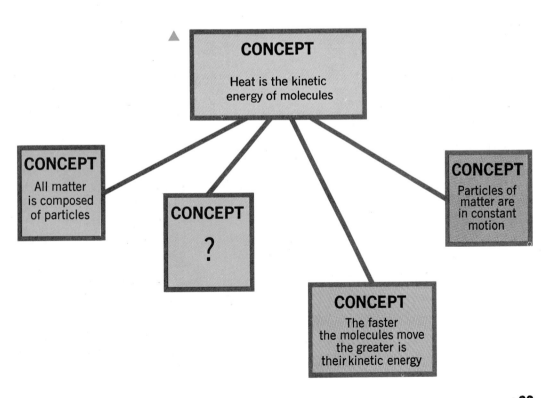

cles in motion results in some very important uses. For instance, by using the concept you can explain the phenomena illustrated below. ■

The scientist *develops* a concept through investigation of the objects and events around him. The engineer *uses* a concept or concepts in a different way from the scientist. The engineer uses concepts to invent many useful tools, materials, and objects. For example, engineers have applied the concept of molecules in motion to the invention of such things as rockets, engines, insulation, valves, and other devices. A few of these devices are shown on the opposite page. ● With these devices he changes the environment and activities of man.

Do you now see how ideas and tools, or science and technology, go hand in hand?

Sometimes, however, the invention comes before the explanation. As the scientist tries to explain the invention, he develops the concept. Once the concept is understood, inventions increase at a much faster rate.

For anyone who is interested in the world around him and is curious about the amazing progress of man's mind, few subjects are more interesting than a history of inventions. You would find how they have changed the patterns of human life down through the ages.

We become aware of this in the next section as we take an imaginary visit to an ancient dump.

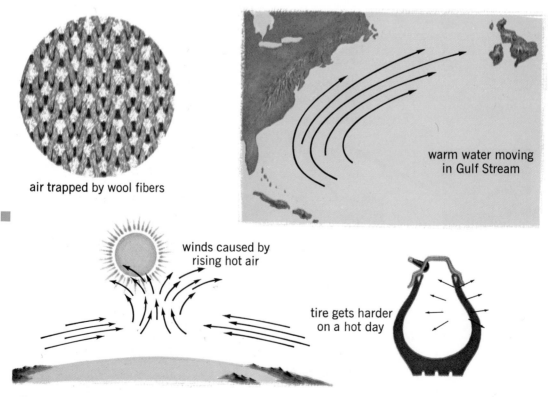

air trapped by wool fibers

warm water moving in Gulf Stream

winds caused by rising hot air

tire gets harder on a hot day

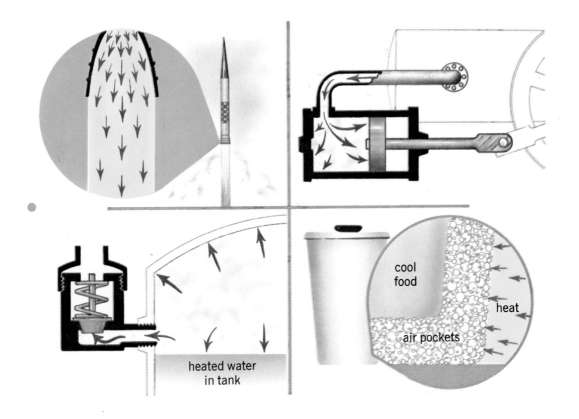

cool food

heat

air pockets

heated water in tank

**A.** Study the statements below and choose the correct responses. They will help you fix in mind the concepts of this section.

1. If there were no light or heat from the sun
   a. all life would cease
   b. the air would remain a liquid

2. *Matter is made up of particles* is a statement of a
   a. scientific event
   b. scientific concept

3. In the body the chemical energy in the food we eat is
   a. completely changed to heat energy
   b. partly changed to heat energy

4. The phenomenon of heat can best be explained this way:
   a. particles of matter are in motion
   b. there is a substance known as heat energy

**65**

**5.** When the motion of particles in a substance is very great, kinetic energy is

    a. high                        b. low

**6.** When the motion of particles in a substance is low, kinetic energy is

    a. high                        b. low

**7.** When the kinetic energy of a substance is increased, its heat is

    a. higher                     b. lower

**8.** The Kinetic Theory of Heat is best used to invent

    a. better insulating          b. ways of getting animals
        materials                  to produce more food

**9.** The development of concepts is primarily (although not always) the work of the

    a. scientist               b. engineer or
                             technologist

**10.** Inventing new materials and machines is primarily (although not always) the work of the

    a. scientist               b. engineer or
                             technologist

**B.** Write a paragraph or two (with examples) on this topic: The Importance of a Concept.

**USING WHAT YOU KNOW**

**1.** Science and technology go hand in hand. Explain how this might be so in the invention of a new kind of tire, one that resists blow-outs more than any present tire.

**2.** Suppose scientists could reduce the temperature of a substance to absolute zero. The temperature of absolute zero means that *no molecules would be in motion*. Describe at least one of the conditions which you would suppose to be true of that substance.

**3.** Cryogenics is a branch of science which deals with very low temperatures. It is a branch in which a great deal of research is being done. Watch for current news items.

You know that accurate measurement is important to the development of any concept in science.

Investigate on your own the way in which the temperature of a substance is measured. The two most common scales used to measure temperature are called the Fahrenheit scale (which is probably familiar to you) and the Celsius scale. ■

What is the freezing temperature of water on the Fahrenheit scale? on the Celsius scale? What is the boiling temperature on each? How many degrees difference is there between boiling and freezing on the two scales?

Can you convert a temperature reading from the Fahrenheit to the Celsius? How would you convert 20° Celsius to the Fahrenheit scale?

Just as we sometimes change feet into meters, there are times when it becomes necessary to change a temperature reading from one scale to the other.

Lacking a scale which gives both readings at once, the following formulas are useful in converting back and forth from Celsius to Fahrenheit:

a. $C = 5/9 \ (F - 32)$
b. $F = (9/5 \times C) + 32$

Explain in your own words the concepts which underlie the development of the thermometer as a tool for the scientist. How many ways do you know that thermometers are useful?

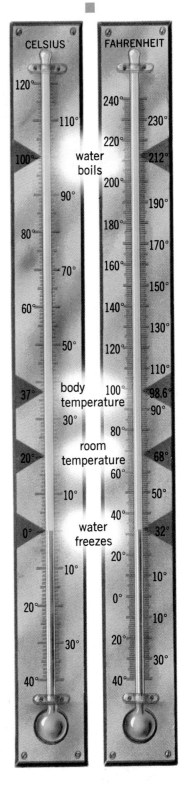

## 3. The Uses of Ideas and Tools: New Metals

Beavers, ants, bees, and swallows are all constructive animals, but their cells, nests, and burrows are the same today as they were years and years ago. They do not change their way of doing things. Man alone among living things can invent and change the natural order. He progresses by means of his inventions.

Sometimes man invents or discovers a way of doing things before he can state the concept which explains it. We go back to ancient man to find an example.

In a way, we are lucky that ancient man had no garbage trucks. When he

finished eating an animal, he threw the bones on the ground or on the floor of his cave, alongside his broken tools. ■ These ancient dumps tell us a great deal about the way ancient man lived.

For instance, as different tribes moved into the caves, they used different tools. Suppose tribe A lived in the caves first and used a kind of axe known as a hand axe. ● Many years later tribe B moved into the caves. Suppose they used axes with a handle or haft and discarded them in the same dump as tribe A. ▲

Scientists of today, digging in the dump, would find the remains of both kinds of axes. The broken tools of the tribe which came first would be found in the dump *below* those of the later tribe. In this way, scientists can tell which tribe came first.

By studying these ancient dumps, called kitchen middens, scientists have been able to piece together a story of how early man used the things he found around him. This story is told in the tools he used.

Study the photograph of some tools of ancient man. ♦ Can you guess which were the tools of the earliest tribes? Check your guesses with the answers given at the bottom of page 71. Which tools were made by the later tribes?

How did early man happen to invent and use tools? This is an important question. No living thing, other than man, has ever been able to do this or is able to do it now. Furthermore, early man learned from the men who came before him, even as you do now.

We have evidence that about a million or so years ago, there lived in Africa a creature that walked upright. Skeletons of these creatures have been found. Near their skeletons have also been found the skeletons of baboons that died because of blows from stones which broke their skulls. Someone had killed them with stones that had been sharpened. Man had found a stone and invented a weapon. He took a stone from nature, changed it, and made it a part of his scheme of things.

## An Advance

For hundreds of centuries man knew nothing about metals, although he did know that with fire metals could be extracted from ores. Any attempt to explain how man discovered metals can only be a calculated guess. In all likelihood, the discovery of metals came about by sheer accident.

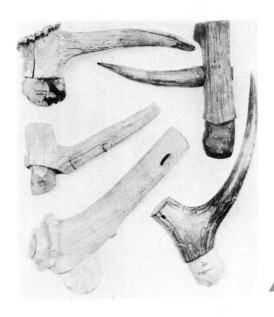

From your study of aluminum remember that man is not always aware of *all* the materials around him. He had to learn from experience *what* the materials are, and *how* they can be used. For example, in the time of early man, coal and oil were present in the crust of the earth, but he did not use them. Copper and gold were there also, undiscovered and unused.

The soil was there, but man had not yet learned to cultivate the soil to grow his crops.

It took thousands of years for man to become a farmer, a *food-producer*. Before he became a food-producer, man had been a *food-gatherer*. That is, he gathered the fruits, berries, and nuts that he found around him. He hunted the animals. In this stage of food-gathering, he did not plant

seeds, nor did he raise his own animals for meat. He was not yet a food-producer.

Before man became a farmer, he had to invent and learn to use the tools he needed to work the earth. It took a long time before he learned to make a plow. The first plow may have been just a stick like the kind still used in some places on the earth. ■

In order for man to become a food-producer—to produce food by planting and harvesting or to produce animals and animal foods (milk, meat, and eggs) by domestication and care, man had to invent tools. He had to invent a technology which would help him produce food. Wooden and stone tools, although useful, were not good enough. They wore out easily; they broke; they were not hard enough.

Soon man was to discover metals. The first metal he discovered, more than 8,000 years ago, was copper. This was a natural discovery, because unlike aluminum, the element copper could be found in many places in its pure form. The copper did not have to be separated from any ore.● Ancient man found deposits of pure copper in many places. Much of it was on top of the ground. He soon learned to shape spearheads and tools out of copper. For many centuries man used weapons and tools made from "native" copper, as it is called. He had no idea that he could get much more copper from ores. He had not yet discovered that metals could be separated from many rocks, or ores.

The discovery of metals happened long before man had any idea what atoms and molecules are. Perhaps the discovery that metals could be separated from ores happened this way.

## An Ancient Fire and a Great Discovery

Imagine a group of men standing around a fire heating and shaping spearheads made of "native" copper, as shown in the picture. This, of course, was a long, long time ago. Scientists believe that somewhere, somehow, in just such a situation as this, man made a great discovery.

The men built their fires with wood, of course (coal and oil had not yet been discovered). To make a hotter fire for softening their spearheads, perhaps they built a wall of stone, with openings for a draft, as in the picture. They would have used the rocks that were available around them. Some of the rocks may have been ores, containing compounds of certain metals.

A wood fire can become very hot. Imagine that some of the rocks used next to the fire contained copper ore. The ore might have been cuprite (kyoo′prīt), which contains the compound copper oxide. In the case of an iron ore, the compound might have been iron oxide. Imagine that in this particular ancient fire the rock contained a copper oxide ore.

Perhaps, then, the discovery of copper was accidental. To see what may have happened, try the investigation on the next page.

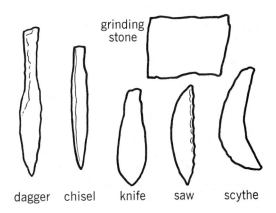

dagger  chisel  knife  saw  scythe

grinding stone

# AN INVESTIGATION into Getting a Metal from Its Compound

**Needed:** some black copper oxide; a hot flame from a Bunsen burner or an alcohol lamp; rubber tubing; a blow pipe; tongs

Take up a bit of the copper oxide in the tongs. Ask your teacher to light the Bunsen burner and to adjust it to get a good blue flame. Then your teacher can hold the piece of copper oxide in the flame with the tongs. ■ Soon the tongs become red hot. ● After a while, they can be opened slightly to allow even more heat to reach the copper oxide, which should stick securely to one side. After several minutes of direct heating, the tongs can be placed on a piece of tile to cool. When the tongs are cool enough, scrape some of the black coating from the copper oxide. Does red, shiny copper appear? ▲

**Additional Investigation:** Repeat the same investigation, only this time use a piece of green copper carbonate (malachite [mal′ə·kīt], another copper ore). Do you again get pure copper? What else is given off?

## The Discovery

Imagine the surprise of the ancient men to find, after the fire had died down, that there were beads of copper on some of the rocks. The rocks were deep down in the fire, where the temperature had been very high. The copper must have come from common ordinary rocks.

In this way a great discovery was made. Apparently, or so ancient man may have reasoned, all one has to do is to build a hot fire near a copper ore, and copper will be found after the fire dies down. The fire must be very hot. Really, a *blast* of fire is needed. Ancient man was no chemist, yet he learned how to obtain copper before he knew about atoms and molecules.

Later on, man learned that this fire-formed metal could be used for purposes other than for the tips of spears. He learned it could be formed into pots and pans. Many thousands of years later (8,000 to 10,000 years later), man learned that copper could be made into wire to carry an electric current. He learned this even before he understood the concept that an electric current is a flow of electrons in a conductor or the reasons why copper is a very good conductor.

Other metals, such as iron, lead, and mercury, may also have been separated from their ores in some of those early fires. Scientists are not completely sure. After all, ancient man did not leave a written record. The alphabet had not yet been invented. We do know, however, that, somehow, early man reasoned that when some kinds of rocks were heated enough, they would yield a metal that was useful in his daily life. He learned by accident and by experience and observation. His observations led him to imitate the natural processes and to invent others.

From what we can guess, early man did not set up an investigation as did Charles Hall or as a modern scientist would do. Early man knew *how* to extract the ore, but an understanding of *why* metal could be obtained from the ore was to come later. Understanding could come only after man had learned enough to build a concept of the structure of matter.

Copper first began to be used about 8,000 years ago, probably in Egypt. No one knows exactly when or how it was discovered, but copper was mined on the island of Cyprus about 5,000 years ago. ■ Cyprus was then known as the Copper Island.

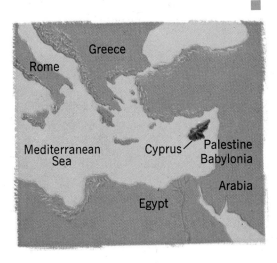

73

meteor fireball

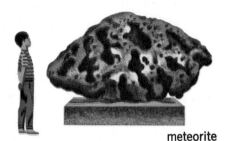

meteorite

On the basis of present evidence, scientists are certain that copper was used long before iron. Perhaps man had selected certain stones for the floor of his hearth because they were brightly colored—blue, green, reddish, or brassy (the colors of copper compounds). In the lower part of the wood fire the temperature was high enough to melt the metal, which was later found in the ashes. It may be well to note here that the invention of the hearth was an important part of this discovery.

About 3,000 (or perhaps 5,000) years ago, iron began to be used. Some scientists believe that the first iron to be used may have come to the earth from outer space as meteors to form meteorites. Meteorites are made primarily of iron together with a few other substances.

## Trial, Error, and Success

Once man began to understand that he could win (separate) a metal from its ore by using heat, he began to heat many different kinds of ores. You might think of it this way. Remember the way you tried tying the bowline knot (Unit One). Perhaps you tried it one way, and then another, and failed. Then another trial, and there was success. *Trial* and *error. Trial* and *error. Trial* and *success!* Much of our learning is achieved in just this way, by trial and error.

Early man may have heated many different ores, and by trial and error, found that heat alone worked on some ores and not on others. In his trials, he found also that a certain temperature was needed for copper ores; a higher temperature for iron ores. Man had to learn by trial and error until he discovered the reason for his failure or success. Once man learned that heat could separate certain compounds, he could use a better method than trial and error. He could base his trials on reason, that is, on a concept of *how* heat could be used to separate metals from their ores.

Let us see how understanding of a concept does away with trial and error and helps man to *plan* his investigations and inventions.

It was ancient man who discovered how to separate certain metals from their ores. Copper is a metal which can be separated most easily. It is extracted from ores containing copper oxide and copper carbonate.

Early man knew nothing about the composition of compounds. We do, so we reason as follows: Somehow, the atoms in copper oxide are not held as tightly as the atoms in some other compounds. A very hot flame can separate the copper from the oxide.

The oxygen leaves the copper and combines with certain of the hot gases in the flame. The oxygen is then carried away in the hot gases.

Iron is a different matter, as you shall see. Nevertheless, ancient man did discover a way of getting iron from its ore (by accident, or so scientists think). Perhaps he tried heat on all kinds of rocks and found that it worked with some and not with others. Thus, from his observations, he began to gather information. Once again, no doubt, a chance observation led to an important discovery, and then to another invention.

Perhaps man realized that green wood cannot reach very high temperatures or that a hot flame was not enough. He may have observed that incompletely burned wood leaves a light porous residue that we call charcoal. Perhaps he found, by accident again, that adding charcoal to his fire made the fire hotter and helped to separate some metals from their ores. Observation is important to invention.

Man's next step, then, was to imitate the natural process and to make charcoal. Charcoal is mainly carbon and is very effective in separating some metals (particularly iron) from their ores. How is this possible?

Suppose the ore is the oxide of a metal, such as iron. It is then possible for the oxygen in the oxide to combine with the carbon. In this way, carbon dioxide (a gas) is formed, and the metal is left behind.

He probably did not learn this the first time. He probably observed *again* and *again* and *again* that he could separate the iron *only* when he had hot glowing carbon (wood coals) in his fire. He learned then to make iron this way: First, get a very hot fire and let it burn until the wood is thoroughly charred, that is, carbonized. Then, add the iron ore. Perhaps he found that blowing air into the fire would help to get a higher temperature. Here again observation was important to progress. Observing the effect that wind has in making a fire burn faster probably led to the idea of an artificial draft.

Oxygen cannot be removed easily from iron oxide by the hot flame alone unless the temperature is extremely high. It can be removed much more easily when the oxygen acts with the carbon to form carbon dioxide ($CO_2$).

$$\text{carbon} \quad + \quad \text{iron oxide} \quad \xrightarrow{\text{high heat}} \quad \text{iron} \quad + \quad \text{carbon dioxide}$$

copper oxide   +   carbon   ⟶   copper   +   carbon dioxide

Ancient man found this out by trial and error; but he did not understand it. Modern man, as a scientist, does understand because he has discovered the differences in the structure and behavior of the atoms and molecules of different substances.

Copper oxide, for example, gives up its oxygen easily, either to carbon or to the hot gases in a flame. Study the figure to find what you would get when the oxygen combines with carbon. ■ The metal is thus freed in its pure state. Other common copper ores contain the sulfides and the carbonates of copper.

When green copper carbonate is heated, carbon dioxide is given off and part of the ore is changed to copper oxide. ● The copper oxide can then be broken down to pure copper by the hot gases in a flame. Carbon dioxide is again given off.

Ancient man did not know that each pure metal (or each pure element) is made of its own particular kind of atom. He did not know that pure iron is an element containing only atoms of iron; but there were

many things that he did know. He discovered metals and the ways of working metals which are still the basis of modern metallurgy. He invented metal furnaces and learned to make charcoal. He combined copper and tin to form bronze, even before he understood the concept of the atom. Understanding the concept was to come later. When man did make this discovery, he was able to put the concept to good use. He was able not only to get iron from its ore but to combine metals in ways that ancient man could not have imagined.

In the process he developed one of the important tools in the technology of making iron and steel. That invention was the blast furnace.

The blast furnace is a vast improvement over rebuilding the fire each time; but remember that it was the prehistoric inventors who extracted the first metals and built the first tools.

Through an understanding of the structure of matter, man was able to build a technology for making iron, one of the most important metals in our civilization.

| copper carbonate | ⟶ | copper oxide | + | carbon dioxide |
| $CuCO_3$ | ⟶ | $CuO$ | + | $CO_2$ |

## Furnaces for Making Iron

Look at the picture of the huge blast furnace, the kind used today for extracting iron. 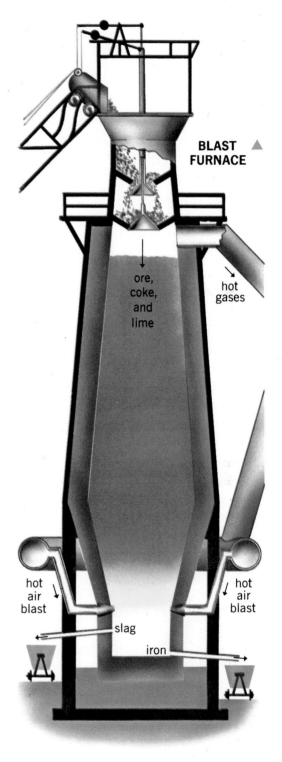 Several different things go into the furnace, but you should now know which two materials *must* go into it. They are iron ore and carbon. The carbon is in the form of coke rather than charcoal. Coke is carbon which is made from coal in a way similar to that in which charcoal is made from wood. The materials which go into making iron are called raw materials. Iron ore, coke, and limestone are the raw materials for extracting iron and making steel.

The coke and the iron ore are heated to a very high temperature in the blast furnace. Hot air is blown in at the bottom to increase the temperature. Carbon from the coke combines with the oxygen in the iron oxide. Carbon dioxide is given off and molten iron is left. This hot molten liquid pours out through another opening at the bottom of the furnace.

If you live in, or travel through, Pennsylvania or Indiana, you may see many huge blast furnaces like the one shown. Iron is reduced in them, and, even more important, modern man has learned to make steel from the refined iron.

Steel is iron that is refined by burning much of the carbon and other impurities out of it and then adding a measured amount of carbon to it. When iron is heated in a blast furnace, much of the carbon remains in the iron. Crude iron is brittle; it breaks

**BLAST FURNACE**

ore, coke, and lime

hot gases

hot air blast

hot air blast

slag

iron

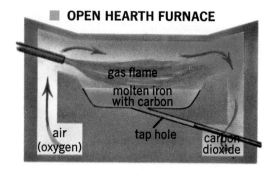

gas flame

molten iron
with carbon

air
(oxygen)

tap hole

carbon
dioxide

## Iron in the Earth

Much of our iron comes from the Great Lakes region. In the hills near Duluth, Minnesota, a city on Lake Superior, is the Mesabi range.

The iron in the Mesabi range is mainly an iron oxide. It may once have been pure iron, but all iron that is exposed to the air soon combines with oxygen to form iron oxide (rust).

In the Mesabi range, the reddish iron ore is scooped out of an open pit. ▲ Then it is shipped to a refining plant to be made into iron and steel.

There is iron ore in every state in the United States, and it can be found in almost every country in the world. The most important iron ore regions are Minnesota, Michigan, Wisconsin, and more recently, Labrador. Almost four out of five tons of iron ore mined in the United States have come from the region around Lake Superior.

easily because it contains leftover carbon. Most of this carbon is burned off in any of several types of furnaces. ■ The most exciting to watch is the Bessemer converter. ●

Fifty years ago, many of the items that people used were made from an iron called cast iron. It was not satisfactory for many purposes. Steel is much better; it is stronger. Today, most of the iron used is in the form of steel. Steel is made stronger by adding other materials and by heat treating; it adds strength but not weight.

## Advancing the Technology of Steel

Chemists and chemical engineers have discovered that metals can be given different properties by adding other substances to them. This special use of substances had to wait until man understood what a substance *is* and what *it is made of*. Once man knew that a pure element was made of only one kind of atom, he could *combine* substances to produce new kinds of compounds. Once he could produce pure substances, he could study their properties. He could then combine substances having different

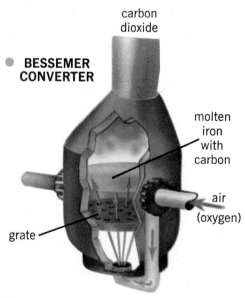

carbon
dioxide

● **BESSEMER CONVERTER**

molten
iron
with
carbon

air
(oxygen)

grate

properties to produce new kinds of metallic substances called **alloys**.

Alloys are combinations of different elements, one of which must be a metal. An alloy has properties different from either of the two elements which were combined. For instance, the chemist adds nickel and chromium to steel to produce a metal called stainless steel that does not rust.

Study the table below. ◆ Do you have any such alloys at home?

Without iron and steel man could not have built tall buildings and bridges. A steel bridge can **corrode** (kə·rōd′) if it is not covered regularly with a protective coat of paint. When it is exposed to air, iron combines with oxygen to form the compound iron oxide, or rust. Thus, steel bridges

### TABLE OF COMMON ALLOYS

| Alloy | Metals contained | Uses |
|---|---|---|
| babbitt | tin, antimony, copper | linings for bearings |
| brass | copper, zinc | cookware, ornaments, fireplace sets |
| bronze | copper, tin | statues, guns, ancient tools |
| coin silver | silver, copper | U.S. coins 10¢ and up |
| dentists' amalgam | copper, mercury | fillings in teeth |
| german silver | copper, zinc, nickel | jewelry |
| nichrome | nickel, chromium | electric wire |
| nickel (coin) | nickel, copper | U.S. 5¢ piece |
| pewter | tin, copper, bismuth, antimony | early American utensils |
| solder | lead, tin | joining metals |
| stainless steel | iron, chromium, nickel | knives, kitchen utensils |
| white gold | gold, nickel, zinc | jewelry, watch cases |

need to be painted regularly to keep them from rusting. To see the effects of rusting, or **corrosion** (kə·rō′zhən), try the investigation on the opposite page.

Perhaps you have some metals in your pocket. Are they pure metals? For instance, is a dime pure silver? Is a penny pure copper? Is a nickel coin pure nickel? Or are they alloys? How could you find out?

Ancient man learned about metals. Perhaps by trial and error, he learned to make bronze, an alloy of copper and tin. He learned about gold, silver, copper, and iron, and the uses of each.

From the beginning, the techniques for working metals developed in three distinct directions. The first was the extraction of the metal from the ore by the use of furnaces. The second was the refinement of a metal by hammering it, and the third, the casting of the pure metals into molds to obtain objects for everyday use or works of art. But something else was important.

If man had confined himself to scratching at the earth's surface, the industry of metals would have ended. He had to dig into the soil and rocks to search for the ore; he had to learn to recognize it. He had to find some way to mine it. In short, in order to be a metal worker, man had to become a miner. He had to learn to light his way, to pump water from the mines, and to bring the ore to the surface.

From chance discoveries man introduced a vast industry; but as he advanced, he invented tools and techniques. His progress became more the result of planning than of chance.

The principle of alloys was discovered by chance and has remained unchanged through the centuries. Some primitive alloys survive today. Today, however, man knows a great deal more about the chemistry of metals, their microscopic structure, and their properties. He produces hundreds of different types of alloys ranging from the bronzes and brasses to the alloys of steel.

The first metals to be used, apart from copper which was often found in its natural state, were gold and, perhaps, silver. Iron came last, because it required higher temperatures and more difficult techniques.

By the middle of the nineteenth century, the groundwork had been laid for Henry Bessemer to design his converter. The production of steel and iron became easy and economical. Metallurgy changed from craftwork to a large-scale industry.

Early man was a discoverer, but he learned mainly by trial and error. Nevertheless, he observed his environment and slowly he learned how to change his environment. Later, much later, he was to become a scientist; and, as a scientist, he would be able to plan investigations.

At the end of this book there is a section titled, **"The Art of Investigation"** (page 409). Why not take a look? You may want to do an investigation on your own soon.

# AN INVESTIGATION into How Fast a Tin Can Rusts

**Needed:** two tin cans; a nail; a damp cloth

Remove the covers from two used cans. Be careful not to cut yourself on rough edges. Wash both cans. On *one* can make five or six long scratches with a nail. ■ Make the scratches deep to remove the tin coating.

Now set the cans aside and cover them loosely with a damp cloth. ● Look at them every day. Keep the cloth damp. Do you see a reddish-brown substance where you scratched the tin? ▲ What is the substance? What is the metal in the can that has been protected by the tin plating?

Why is tin used to protect the iron? **CLUE:** Rusting means the combination of a metal with oxygen. Does tin combine more easily with oxygen than iron?

**Additional Investigation:** In the library look up the term "galvanized." Which metal is used to protect a galvanized pail? What metal underneath is being protected?

## More New Materials

Already the chemical engineer is beginning to replace many metals with other materials. He can do this because he has learned that all matter is made up of *elements* and *compounds,* so he can recombine the elements into newer compounds. Remember that pure gold, silver, and iron are *elements.* Elements contain only one kind of atom. Compounds are made of more than one element. Each compound contains two or more different kinds of atoms that are combined chemically. The pictures show models of two different molecules. ■ ● Which model represents an element? Which model represents a compound?

Man is competing with nature. With his knowledge of chemistry he produces materials which have never before existed on the face of the earth. He is engaged in an industrial activity that affects every part of day-to-day living. He brings to us a whole range of new substances that are manufactured into a variety of articles, from the fountain pen to the telephone.

■

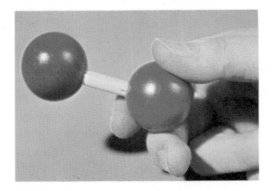

Understanding and applying the concept that matter is made of atoms and molecules has produced this whole new world of synthetic substances.

The chemist has learned how to produce many new compounds in the laboratory. Some of these new compounds have the properties that he wanted from metals. They have *strength; they can be molded* into different shapes; and even more than that, they *do not rust or corrode.*

These new substances that man has developed are not used to build bridges, as yet, but you have already used them for other things. Some of them replace china dishes. Cups, saucers, and plates made from such materials are unbreakable. Furniture has been made from these new substances. Do you know what they are? The new class of substances is called **plastics.** Plastics opened up a new field of technology.

How many different kinds of plastics do you use at home? And for what purposes? dishes? radios? clothing? gadgets? furniture? automobiles? the knobs on your television set?

**A.** Study the statements below and choose the correct responses. They will help you fix in mind the concepts of this section.

**1.** The habits and customs of ancient man can be determined in part from

    a. his writings        b. kitchen middens

**2.** The tools (technology) of ancient man advanced from stone tools to tools made of

    a. copper and iron        b. steel

**3.** Ancient man was first a

    a. food-producer        b. food-gatherer

**4.** Man first discovered how to get metals from ores by

    a. planned        b. trial and error
       investigation

**5.** Before ancient man could get metal from ore, he had to know how to use

    a. fire        b. chemistry

**6.** Ancient man could get metal from ore because he knew

    a. the Kinetic Theory        b. that heat separated
       of Heat                    ores

**7.** An example of the way a substance begins to break down to yield a metal is

$$\text{Copper carbonate} \longrightarrow \text{copper oxide} +$$

    a. oxygen        b. carbon dioxide

**8.** Steel, stainless steel, bronze, and combinations like them are

    a. alloys        b. ores

**9.** A technology can sometimes be developed up to a point. After that, a knowledge of concepts

    a. speeds up the        b. slows down the
       technology                 technology

**B.** Write a paragraph or two on this topic: Blast Furnaces.

1. In your lifetime man began to explore space. He built rockets and spaceships.

The concepts which help us understand gravity and motion of rockets and satellites were developed by Isaac Newton in the seventeenth century. Why did we have to wait so long to send John Glenn and other astronauts into space?

2. We see modern utensils—especially kitchen utensils—being developed of metals like aluminum, stainless steel, or from synthetic materials like plastics.

a. Why is it useful to have kitchen utensils made of these materials?

b. Why is some metal kitchenware coated with enamel?

c. Why were kitchen utensils in the sixteenth and seventeenth centuries made mainly of copper and its alloys?

1. Present a report to your class on the history of plastics. Include something about their chemistry in your report.

2. Make a similar report on silicones (sil′ə·kōnz).

## 4. The Uses of Ideas and Tools: New Fibers

Man makes use of what he finds. When he does not find what he wants, he tries to invent a new material. Ancient man, by trial and error, found a way to make a metal stronger than copper. He made an alloy of copper and tin, an alloy called bronze. He made bronze before he understood the concept that matter is made up of particles and that these could be combined in a variety of ways. Modern man, knowing the concept, invents hundreds of alloys.

Ancient man worked the metals he found and invented *some* alloys. The scientist, with a knowledge of a concept, has a better way to make discoveries than by trial and error alone. Knowledge of a concept helps a scientist or an engineer to plan his investigations and his inventions. A good example is man's invention of plastics and new fibers. The investigations which led to the invention of new fibers were done in a modern laboratory. To a large extent the trials and errors of ancient man were eliminated. The story goes somewhat like this.

## Improving on a Moth

Perhaps you will be surprised to know that man was not satisfied with the product of a moth. This particular moth had served man for many hundreds of years, even before Marco Polo traveled from Italy to China about 650 years ago.

What happens inside the cocoon of a moth? Before we answer, let's go back and take a look at the life history of a moth.

The adult female moth lays eggs which develop and hatch into caterpillars. ■ A caterpillar, or **larva** (lär′-və), as it is called, does not look like an adult moth. The caterpillars, or **larvae,** spend most of their time feeding on green leaves. A larva of this particular moth eats the leaves of the plant, the mulberry plant, on which it hatches. Then, when the larva is full grown, it begins to spin a **cocoon** around itself. The cocoon is useful to the moth, for in it the adult moth develops; but man had other uses for the cocoon of the silk moth.

Have you ever seen a moth larva spin a cocoon? or a spider spin its web? The spider makes a substance inside its body that comes out of the spider as a liquid. In the air the liquid becomes a thin silky thread.

The moth larva makes a thin silky thread too. It spins its web around itself and makes a cocoon. There it rests for a time. In this stage, the moth is a **pupa** (pyo͞o′pə). In the cocoon the pupa changes and it emerges some weeks later as an adult moth.

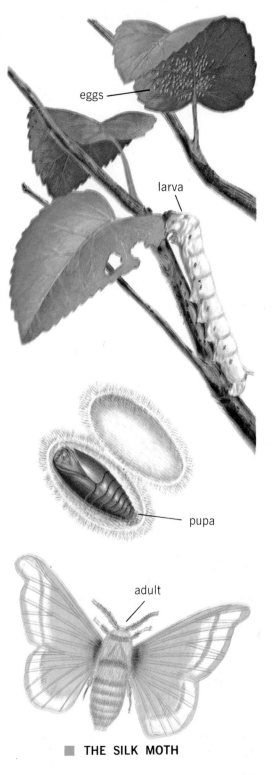

eggs

larva

pupa

adult

■ THE SILK MOTH

85

Thousands of years ago, the Chinese and Japanese learned how to unwind the thread from the cocoon, and how to produce silk thread. The picture shows the cocoons being dried. ■ This kills the pupae which would break the silk filament of their cocoons, if they were allowed to emerge. Of course some of the pupae are allowed to become moths in order to produce more silkworms. After many years the use of silk spread over the world.

Silk is a beautiful and strong material, but it is expensive; silk moths cannot be grown everywhere. It takes a long time for moths to develop from eggs to caterpillars to cocoons to silk threads. Still only the silk moth can produce silk thread. Man was unable to invent something as good as the silk that came from the moth. Trial-and-error methods did not work to produce a good substitute.

## Man Tries to Imitate

The origin of cotton has never been definitely determined; but it has been indicated that cotton cloth was being produced as early as 1500 B.C.

Man learned very early to use the fibers of the cotton plant. He picked the cotton boll and for hundreds of years removed the seeds by hand. This was very expensive labor. Removal of the seeds by hand was so difficult that it required a day for one person to clean a pound of cotton. Eli Whitney went to work and in ten days produced the cotton gin, a machine which separated the fibers from the seeds very easily. He patented the machine in 1794.

Cotton is one of the most valuable of all plants. The uses for its fiber are so varied that it is by far the most important of all textile fibers. Today, however, many synthetic fibers are being used in the textile industry.

Still, in 1794, the concept of the composition of matter was just being developed. The way atoms and molecules combined to form new compounds was not yet fully understood. It wasn't really until the 1850's that the science of chemistry began to develop rapidly.

As chemists learned more about ways of combining molecules, it was natural that they should turn to a study of substances like silk and cotton. They found that they could change cotton into a thread that had *some* of the properties of silk.

One way the chemists found is to dissolve cotton in sodium hydroxide. ● Then, as in the picture, the dissolved cotton is pressed out through tiny holes into a liquid. ▲ It hardens into a fiber which is called **rayon.** ◆

Rayon was first known as "artificial silk" and was considered a substitute for the luxurious fiber. It could be made at less cost.

Spinning a thread by pushing a liquid out through tiny holes is very much what the silkworm did; but rayon has never really had many of the properties of silk. It does not wear as well nor does it take dyes as well as silk.

The chemists, in creating synthetic fibers, decided that the thing to do was to start at the beginning; that is, they decided to start with the atoms which make up a fiber like silk or cotton. For instance, the fiber of the cotton plant is composed of **cellulose** (sel′yə·lōs), a substance containing

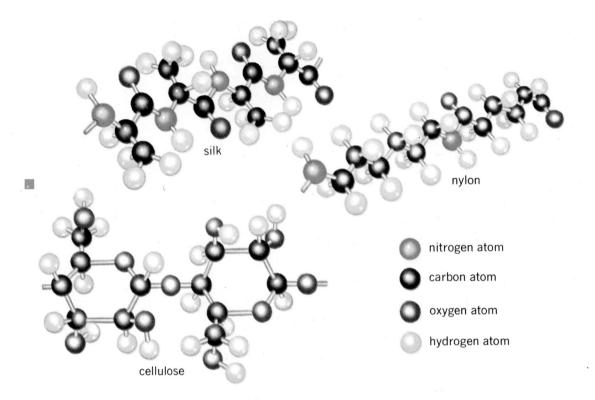

silk

nylon

nitrogen atom

carbon atom

oxygen atom

hydrogen atom

cellulose

carbon, hydrogen, and oxygen. The picture shows a model of a molecule of cellulose. ■ There is, however, at least one more element besides carbon, hydrogen, and oxygen, in a silk fiber. That element is nitrogen, and it is shown in the model of a molecule of silk. ■

After many years of investigation in the laboratory, chemists invented a strong fiber made up of *carbon, hydrogen, oxygen,* and *nitrogen;* but it was not silk. It turned out to be better for many uses. This fiber has many properties like those of silk, but it is much stronger. You have already worn clothes made of this fiber —**nylon.** Look at the picture that shows a model of a nylon molecule. ■

Is it more like the molecule of silk or of cellulose?

The raw materials for the making of nylon are all around us. What is a source of carbon? *Coal.* What is a source of hydrogen? *Water.* What is a source of oxygen and nitrogen? *Air.*

Coal, water, and air are the raw materials from which nylon is made; and the usefulness of nylon seems to be unlimited.●

Man's need for textiles is constant. Ever since he stopped using animal skins for clothing, textiles of one kind or another have been an essential part of civilized living. To what extent the chemist's tube will produce new and better fibers is for the future to determine.

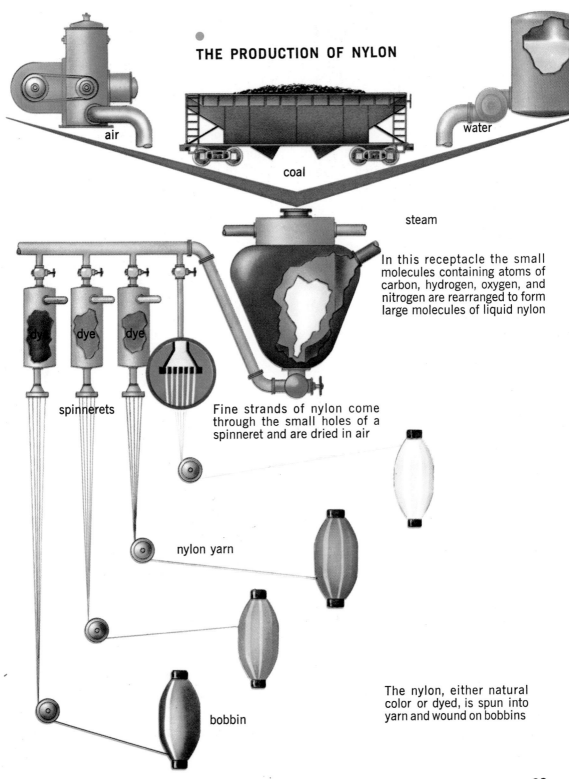

# THE PRODUCTION OF NYLON

air

coal

water

steam

In this receptacle the small molecules containing atoms of carbon, hydrogen, oxygen, and nitrogen are rearranged to form large molecules of liquid nylon

dye    dye    dye

spinnerets

Fine strands of nylon come through the small holes of a spinneret and are dried in air

nylon yarn

bobbin

The nylon, either natural color or dyed, is spun into yarn and wound on bobbins

**89**

Ancient man could not have made rayon and nylon. Ancient man did not know about the building blocks of living things, and he did not know that plants made cellulose from carbon, hydrogen, and oxygen. He did not know that animal fibers were made of these elements plus nitrogen. More than that, ancient man did not even know of the elements on earth. He did not have the ideas, and he did not have the tools.

Again we see how science and technology go hand in hand. This time, however, invention had to wait until scientists had developed the concepts which explain the structure of matter. This was not the way with the discovery of iron. The technology of iron, copper, and gold was well on its way before the science of chemistry was developed. In fact, the invention of the technology of iron gave scientists the facts from which to reason out the structure of matter. On the other hand, the technology (that is, the invention) of new fibers had to wait until scientists understood the structure of matter. Nevertheless, science and technology go hand in hand, although one may advance before the other.

BEFORE YOU GO ON A. Study the statements below and choose the correct responses. They will help you fix in mind the concepts of this section.

**1.** Before man developed the concept *matter is made of atoms and molecules,* he had invented

    a. rayon          b. alloys

**2.** Many times, man used the substances and materials around him. He developed simple ways (a simple technology) of using these materials. In this manner, he developed ways of using

    a. cotton          b. nylon

**3.** In order to get silk, man had to understand the ways of the

    a. moth          b. machine

**4.** Man could not invent new fibers such as nylon until he understood how elements and compounds combine. In other words, man had to wait until the

    a. concepts were          b. machines were
        developed                developed

**5.** To invent new fibers such as nylon and Dacron man had to know more

      a. alchemy                b. technology

**B.** Write a paragraph or two on this topic: A New Technology: Producing New Fibers.

USING WHAT YOU KNOW If chemists and chemical engineers continue to develop a science which enables them to combine elements in different ways and a technology to use this knowledge, we can expect man-made materials to replace those which are made by animals and plants.

Which of these materials can now be replaced by new materials: cotton; silk; wool; linen; wood; horn (from horns of animals); ivory (tusks of elephants); leather (hides of animals)? Add any others you wish.

ON YOUR OWN If you do not know of new materials which could replace any of those listed, you can find some by doing research in the library.

## 5. The Main Concept: Changing the Environment Through Science and Technology

The earth has been here for many millions of years. The riches of the earth's crust have been here as well. It is only in the last 5,000 years that man has really learned to use them; but man has learned to make use of and to change his environment through the partnership of science and technology.

Animals and plants must live in their environment. If the environment changes, the animals and plants must adapt to the changing environment, move on to a new environment, or die and become extinct.

On the other hand, man changes his environment to suit his needs. He can now live under water for months in a nuclear submarine or he can live in a spaceship. He can control his environment by using new ideas to build new tools, or new machines, or new materials.

Early man fed on the earth's plants and animals. He clothed himself in animals' skins. When he discovered fire, he learned to burn wood and to cook his food. Early in his life on this planet man was a food-gatherer. ■

He used stone to make clubs and spears, and soon tipped his spears with stone spearheads. Ten thousand years ago, man learned to tame animals. The dog followed him wherever he traveled. Soon he had other animals, like the horse, in his camp.

He learned to plant seeds in order to grow the plants he liked to eat. He became a farmer. He changed from a food-gatherer to a food-producer. ●

Then, sometime between five and ten thousand years ago, man began to win metals from the earth. He could do this because he had learned to use heat properly. He developed a simple technology by trial and error before he thoroughly understood the concepts underlying his technology. The medieval (mē′dē·ē′vəl) **alchemist** (al′kə·mist) tried to change the elements. He searched for a way of changing lead into gold. He tried many times but failed because he did not understand the structure of matter. ▲

Even though the alchemists failed to change lead into gold, their work developed into the reliable chemical knowledge of today. Their experiments did produce genuine scientific information and discoveries, and the finding of many elements and compounds resulted.

After man developed the concept that matter was made up of atoms and molecules, he learned to combine these particles into new substances. He developed the science of chemistry. Technology became very complex. New substances were produced in great quantities. Man began to make wider use of the earth's raw materials. He planned his investigations. He had become a scientist. For the scientist, the laboratory became his way of life. Instead of depending mostly on trial and error, he began to plan his investigations, to write about his discoveries and ideas, and to exchange them with other scientists and engineers. ◆ He built on the discoveries of other men as well as on his own. And so, science and technology advanced together.

The scientist spends most of his time exploring the universe and trying to find explanations (concepts) of the objects and events he sees. Mainly, the scientist develops new ideas. The engineer develops a way of doing things, a technology based on the concepts of his fellow scientists. The scientist deals with ideas; the engineer develops new tools, machines, or materials. Ideas and tools are partners in progress.

Not satisfied with cotton, man made rayon; not satisfied with silk,

◆

he made nylon. Not satisfied with the oil as it came from the earth, he developed gasoline in his laboratories. Not satisfied entirely with iron, he searched for ways of obtaining aluminum. He found ways of making hundreds of alloys.

▲

Man uses the building blocks (the atoms and molecules) of which his environment is made. He changes them as he makes new discoveries. In this way man has changed his environment. If the discoveries of science and technology are used wisely, they can be used for a better life.

Man, as a chemist, uses his discoveries concerning the building blocks of the earth in a different way from that of other scientists, such as the biologist (bī·ol′ə·jist).

For instance, look at the giant orange shown in the picture. ■ Look at the size of the hog. ● The unusual size of both is the result of discoveries made by the biologist, not the chemist. In other parts of this book you will see how the biologist, in dealing with concepts about organisms, lengthens the life of man. You will see how the **physicist** (fiz′ə·sist), in dealing with concepts of energy, improves the ways in which work can be done.

This book is intended to introduce to you the world which science and technology have made.

In this part of the book you have read about the uses of discovery, the ones made primarily by chemists. The rest of the book will explore the uses of discovery by different kinds of scientists—the physicist, the biologist, the astronomer, and others. In each case, as you examine the uses of discovery, you will see how man (as a scientist) uses his understanding of scientific concepts. This understanding is the base on which science and technology are built.

Tonight, at home, you will be able to control some features of your environment. What will you do to change your environment when it gets dark? when it gets too cold or too warm?

When astronauts and cosmonauts travel in their space capsules and spacesuits, they live in a man-made environment. ▲ As a matter of fact,

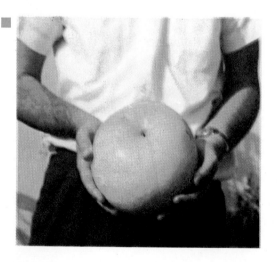

unless man takes his earthly environment with him into space, he hasn't got a chance. For here is a world that has no oxygen, no pressure, no weight. To live and work in orbital flight man must have a miracle package, a life-support system that will provide him with oxygen, water, pressurization, and complete climate control. It also must guard him against temperatures that range from near absolute zero to the reentry heat of thousands of degrees. Such a man-made environment is a product of science and technology.

▲

# Fixing the Main Concepts

**TESTING YOURSELF**     Test your understanding of the important concepts of this unit by doing these problems.

1. You have a five-minute talk to give on the topic "Science and Technology." Organize your talk around these questions: What are the differences between the two? How are they similar? How do they go hand in hand?

2. Nuclear energy plants, nuclear submarines, and other inventions using atomic energy were not built until the 1950's. Why not?

**QUICK TEST**     Study the statements below and choose the correct responses. They will help you fix in mind the concepts of this unit.

1. Science and technology are different in that technology deals mainly with investigations which result in

    a. scientific concepts    b. the invention of devices

**2.** Science and technology are similar in that both are based on

    a. evidence from investigation
    b. ideas arising from argument

**3.** The launching of Telstar, which is a relay station for television, and the building of the X–15 rocket plane were mainly the work of

    a. scientists
    b. engineers

**4.** One of these metals was not used by ancient man. Which one is it?

    a. copper
    b. steel

**5.** Of these, which came first:

    a. the making of iron
    b. the development of the concept that all matter is made of particles

**6.** Of these, which came first:

    a. the making of silk
    b. the making of nylon

**7.** Which of these is more rust-proof:

    a. iron
    b. aluminum

**8.** Better insulators are usually the result of

    a. understanding the concept of kinetic energy
    b. trial and error

**9.** We now accept the concept that all matter is made up of particles. Suppose we find that the matter on the moon is made up of the same kinds of particles as the matter on earth. This would:

    a. not surprise us
    b. surprise us

**10.** In the main, we now accept the concept that the particles of matter are in motion. Because its molecules are in motion, we expect a liquid to evaporate. If it does not,

    a. this should surprise us
    b. it should not surprise us

FOR YOUR
READING These books will help you learn more about the way science and technology go hand in hand.

**1.** *Engineers Did It,* by Duane Bradley, published by Lippincott, Philadelphia, 1958.

This is an interesting account of the world's great engineering feats. There are simple explanations of the scientific concepts underlying them.

**2.** *Aluminum, the Miracle Metal,* by C. B. Colby, published by Coward-McCann, New York, 1960.

Here again is an example of the way science and technology go hand in hand.

ON YOUR OWN Now is a good time to begin to practice the ways of the scientist. Go to the end of the book, on page 409, where you will find a section titled, "The Art of Investigation." There you will find sections titled:

1. Analyzing an Investigation
2. A Word About Words—And a Word About Acts
3. Investigations—On Your Own
4. Selecting Your Own Problem for Investigation

The investigations which are described are ones to which there is no answer in this book, but by designing a proper investigation you can make a discovery yourself. Examine these pages now. Then select a problem to investigate on your own. ■ ●

# UNIT THREE

# IDEAS AND TOOLS: FOR LONGER LIFE

In 1870, rabies was a deadly disease. Joseph Meister had been bitten by a dog with the rabies disease. He would have died—except for Louis Pasteur.

In Pasteur's time it was not known that rabies was caused by a virus; but Louis Pasteur had the idea that germs cause disease and he pursued the idea. Moreover, he had the idea that when weakened disease germs were injected into the body, the body produced substances which destroyed the germs.

Pasteur investigated his ideas. He experimented with rabies and his injections had saved many animals from that dread disease. He had not tried his injections on human beings. Should he or shouldn't he? Faced with the possibility of saving a life, he did inject the weakened rabies virus into Joseph Meister. Joseph Meister lived.

Ever since the time of Pasteur, ideas (such as the germ theory of disease) and tools (such as microscopes and drugs) have been used to conquer disease. This unit is the study of how man uses his brain and his hands, his imagination and his skill, to change his environment and lengthen his life.

# 1. Organisms We Cannot See

The medicine dropper in the picture contains sour milk. ■ It contains many tiny **organisms** (ôr′gən·iz′əmz). In fact, the single drop of milk about to fall from the end of the dropper may contain as many organisms as there are people in the United States.

## A Microscopic View of Tiny Organisms

Organisms too small to be seen by the unaided eye are called **microorganisms** (mī′krō·ôr′gən·iz′əmz). They can be seen only with a microscope. A microscope has several lenses arranged to magnify tiny plants and animals that are invisible to the naked eye. Under a microscope these organisms appear many times larger than they really are. If you look at a drop of sour milk through a microscope, you will see organisms like those shown in the picture. ●

The tiny, rod-shaped organisms are **bacteria.** Bacteria are the smallest living plants. Some kinds of bacteria cause disease but most of them do not. The rod-shaped bacteria shown in the picture are not harmful. They cause milk to sour and therefore are found in sour milk and also in buttermilk. Buttermilk, in fact, is a healthful drink.

Find out more about bacteria and how they grow by doing the investigation on the opposite page.

## Kinds of Bacteria

There are millions of bacteria in one colony. *Some* of them may be harmful, so for reasons of safety, you should examine a colony of bacteria only with the help of your teacher. If your school has a high-powered microscope (400× or more), your teacher may prepare slides with the bacteria from the **cultures** so that you can study them.

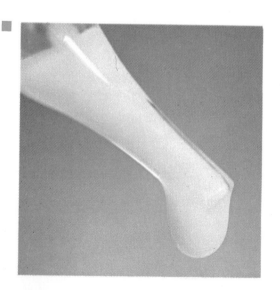

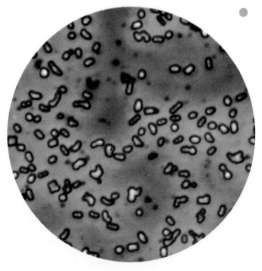

# AN INVESTIGATION into Growing Bacteria

**Needed:** a microscope (400× or more); a medicine dropper; sour milk; two Pyrex dishes; sheets of plastic and rubber bands (or glass lids for the Pyrex dishes); a package of plain gelatin; one bouillon cube

With a medicine dropper, put a drop of sour milk on a clean glass slide. If the drop is very thick, add one drop of water to the slide. Place a cover glass over the drop. Then examine the drop under the microscope. Is what you see similar to that shown in the picture on the opposite page?

A single **bacterium** is invisible to the unaided eye; but when many of them multiply and form **colonies,** you can see the colonies. Grow some colonies of bacteria; but do so *only with the help of your teacher.*

Half-fill two Pyrex dishes with a mixture made as follows:

To a cup of boiling water add the contents from one package of plain gelatin and one bouillon cube. Stir until the ingredients are dissolved. Then add one-half cup cold water and stir. While the mixture is still warm, pour it into the Pyrex dishes. Leave both dishes uncovered for several hours; then put a plastic sheet over each dish and fasten it with a rubber band (or use glass lids). ■ Place one dish in a refrigerator. Leave the other in a warm, dark place.

After several days, do you find blotches, or spots, on the dish left in the warm place? These are the colonies of bacteria. Do they look like those in the picture? ● Were all the bacteria of the same shape?

Look at the dish in the refrigerator. What is the effect of cold on the growth of bacteria?

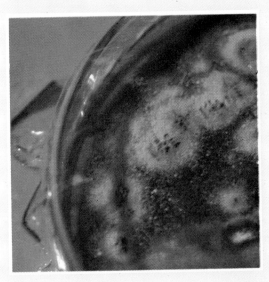

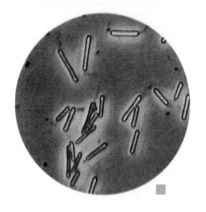 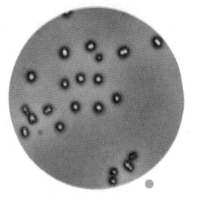 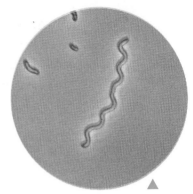

If you were to examine the bacteria under a microscope, you might find three types.

The bacteria shown first are rod-shaped bacteria called **bacilli** (bə-sil′ī). ■ The spherical bacteria are called **cocci** (kok′sī) ●, and a third type, shaped like a corkscrew, is called **spirillum** (spī·ril′əm). ▲ Many corkscrew bacteria in colonies are **spirilla** (spī·ril′lə), plural for spirillum.

These are the three kinds of bacteria that are found all around you. Some of them may be harmful, but most of them are harmless.

Not only do most bacteria not cause disease; some are even useful. Some kinds of bacteria are used in making linen from a plant called flax. Some kinds, called decay bacteria, break down dead animals and plants, and return the matter to the soil. Without such bacteria the world would soon be full of dead things. Imagine a forest full of dead trees, just lying there. In time, no trees could grow, for there would be no **humus** (hyoo′məs) in the soil. Decay bacteria cause dead plants and animals to break down to form humus, an important part of the soil. ◆ Humus restores to the soil the **minerals** that plants need in order to live and grow.

Not all bacteria, however, are beneficial to man. Some are extremely dangerous. They feed on tissues in the body and cause many serious diseases. Scientists and medical doctors are working to rid us of these unwelcome pests, and, thereby, to improve the environment in which we live. The following sections tell of this great battle that goes on between men and disease germs.

**102**

**A.** Study the statements below and choose the correct responses. They will help you fix in mind the concepts of this section.

1. Geraniums and bacteria are alike in that they both
   a. have leaves            b. are plants

2. Geraniums and bacteria are unlike in that bacteria have
   a. no roots               b. roots

3. Look at the drawings of the three microscopic organisms shown below.★ They are all
   a. bacteria               b. bacilli

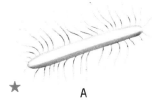 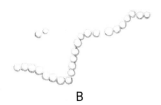 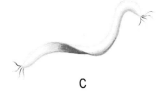

★     A                B              C

4. Bacteria which cause decay are usually
   a. helpful                b. harmful

**B.** Write a paragraph or two on this topic: Some Helpful Bacteria.

1. Why is it important to put certain foods in a refrigerator?

2. Where would most vegetables (for example, lettuce) and fruits (for example, apples or oranges) keep better—in the refrigerator or outside the refrigerator?

3. Of what use are bacteria in a forest?

4. Suppose all bacteria were destroyed. Would this be good for living things?

5. How is it possible to see bacteria without a microscope?

6. Most bacteria are colorless plants containing no chlorophyll. How does this make them different from green plants?

# 2. Unwelcome Organisms

If you have ever had a cold, your body has been attacked by unwelcome organisms. Most colds last only a short time, that is, it usually takes your body only a short time to overcome the organisms that cause a cold. Overcoming attacks by other organisms may take a longer time. What are some of these organisms?

## Nongreen Plants

Bacteria are colorless plants; they have no **chlorophyll**, the green substance found in most plants. Since they have no chlorophyll, bacteria cannot make their own food. They cannot capture the sun's energy as green plants do, so they must get their energy from other living things.

Bacteria are living cells. Like other living cells, they have **cell membranes** on the outside. In addition to a cell membrane, bacteria also have a tough **cell wall** which protects the inside of the cell.

Since a bacterium does have a cell wall, how does food get inside? How do bacteria break down solid food into particles small enough to pass into the bacterial cell?

Bacteria do this in much the same way as do **molds** and other **fungi** (fun′jī). Fungi (the plural of **fungus**, fung′gəs) are nongreen plants. Many fungi grow larger than bacteria, but, like bacteria, these fungi have no chlorophyll. They cannot manufacture their own food and must get their nourishment from other living things. Some common *fungi* are bread mold, mushrooms, and puff balls.

Molds grow in colonies similar to bacteria. They absorb food in much the same way.

To get an idea of how bacteria collected from tne air may cause disease, you can use a substitute, a common mold, in the investigation on the opposite page. The way a fungus plant gets its food will give you a clue as to how bacteria may cause disease.

## The Needs of Fungi

From your investigation, what would you guess are the needs of bacteria, molds, and similar plants? They need a source of *food*, a source of *moisture*, and a *reasonable temperature*. Molds and bacteria grow well at room temperature. Recall your investigation on page 101. Did the bacteria do well in the refrigerator?

What happened to the bread on which the bread mold was growing? Left for a period of time there should be less and less of the bread. As the mold continues to grow, the bread may disappear altogether.

You can explain the change this way. There was an increase in the amount of bread mold. There was a decrease in the amount of bread; the bread had the substances which were needed by the mold for its growth. As the mold grew, the amount of bread decreased. How could the mold absorb the bread?

# AN INVESTIGATION into How Fungus Plants Get Their Food

**Needed:** two dishes (or jars) and covers; some stale bread; a microscope

To grow bread mold, obtain two dishes or jars, with covers. Jars with a screw-top cover will do. Be sure the jars are dry. Break a slice of white bread in half. (Use stale bread, or toast both pieces until they are dry.) Put one piece of bread in each jar. To one piece of

bread add about ten drops of water; add no water to the other. ■ Then screw the cap on each jar.

Put both jars in a dark place at room temperature. Examine each jar every day, and make notes of what you see.●

Examine some bread mold under the microscope. You will see (as shown in the picture) what looks like a bunch of threads. ▲ Each thread has a black ball-like body at one end, which produces **spores.** Each spore can produce a new mold plant.

At the other end of the threads are rootlike structures. Each mold is joined to others by threads that run along the bread.

Do your results agree with those shown? Which one of your jars had the best growth of mold? Why?

# AN INVESTIGATION into the Use of Diastase

**Needed:** bread, as a source of starch; diastase (available at the drugstore); Benedict's solution; a test tube; a source of heat

Plan an investigation to show that diastase acts on starch as saliva does. Your plan must show that diastase breaks down starch. Starch will not dissolve in water. It cannot pass through a cell membrane. Sugar does dissolve in water. It can easily pass through a cell membrane. For this investigation on the action of diastase you will need a way of testing for sugar. ■ ● Your teacher probably has some Benedict's solution on hand. If not, it can be bought at most drugstores. How can Benedict's solution be used to test for sugar? A reference book in the library may help you to find the answer. Bread is mostly starch. How can bread mold change the starch so that it can be absorbed through the cell membrane?

Some plans for investigating the use of diastase are shown on the opposite page. Plan an investigation of your own.

On page 119, you will find Sir Alexander Fleming's design for an investigation. Is your plan similar? Does it include a control?

Bread contains starch, a food substance which does not dissolve in water. A substance must dissolve in water in order to pass through a cell membrane. The bread must be broken down in some way so that it dissolves. Then it can pass through the cell wall and cell membrane.

If you could examine (under the microscope) the bread around the rootlike structures, you would see a clear space as if the bread were being dissolved. Actually, the bread is being **digested.** To *digest* means to break down food so that it can diffuse through cell membranes. How does mold break down the bread?

In most drugstores, you can buy diastase (dī′ə·stās). Diastase is one of a class of substances called **enzymes** (en′zimz). Some enzymes help to break down the starches in food and to change them into sugars. Can diastase change starch into sugar also? You can find out by doing the investigation on the opposite page. ■

■ **POSSIBLE INVESTIGATIONS WITH DIASTASE**

| | | | | |
|---|---|---|---|---|
| **A** | 1. test tube of undissolved starch in water | 2. add diastase | 3. test for sugar | |
| **B** | 1. two test tubes of undissolved starch in water | 2. add diastase to one | 3. test both for starch | 4. test the one with diastase for sugar |
| **C** | 1. two test tubes of undissolved starch in water | 2. add diastase to one | 3. test both for sugar | 4. test a mixture of plain diastase and water for sugar |

Did you plan an experiment similar to any of those shown?
Which of the three experiments above will best show what diastase does?

## A Bacterium and Its Food

A bacterium digests food in much the same way as a mold plant. It produces enzymes which break down food substances into simple compounds, such as sugar. These simple compounds dissolve in water. Then they can pass through the cell membrane into the cell.

A mold plant can grow and produce spores, and each spore produces another mold plant. A bacterium, on the other hand, grows and divides into two. ■ Bacteria multiply very quickly, sometimes as fast as once every 20 minutes. So a single bacterium falling on the food mixture (bouillon in gelatin), described on page 101, divides into two, the two divide to make four, the four to make eight, and so on. Suppose the number doubled every 20 minutes. How many bacteria would there be at the end of 24 hours? The answer should explain why it does not take long to produce a colony.

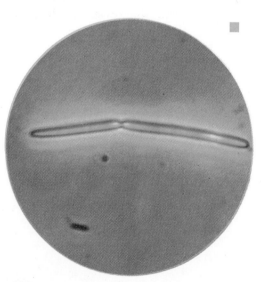

When decay bacteria or molds collect and grow on a dead tree, the wood soon begins to rot or decay. The molds and bacteria secrete enzymes which break down the wood of the tree. They use the digested wood as food. They feed, and grow, and reproduce; and, in time, there are enough of them to consume the entire tree.

Bacteria occur in countless numbers and are found almost everywhere—in air, water, and soil. Individually they are so small as to be invisible to the unaided eye, but they are of very great practical importance. In the soil they make nitrogen available to plants. They are the chief agents of decay of dead plants and animals. They are essential in many industrial processes and are the source of many valuable substances. But bacteria are often harmful, too. They are responsible for the spoilage and loss of vast amounts of foods and are the cause of many serious diseases.

Sometimes harmful bacteria fall on an open wound and begin to feed on the cells inside the cut. They grow and multiply very rapidly and soon begin to spread around the entire area. **Infection** occurs. The infection may even invade the blood stream. How could you prevent the growth of bacteria in a wound? How could you stop it?

Various sanitary practices, such as cleanliness, disinfection, and sterilization are common aids in preventing infection; and even your body has ways of defending itself.

A. Study the statements below and choose the correct responses. They will help you fix in mind the concepts of this section.

1. Unlike geraniums, bacteria have
   a. no chlorophyll        b. chlorophyll

2. Bacteria are very much like
   a. animals        b. molds

3. Most bacteria grow well at
   a. the temperature of ice        b. room temperature

4. Before food can pass through the cell membrane of a bacterium, it must be
   a. digested        b. starchy

5. To digest food outside its cell membrane, a bacterium uses
   a. enzymes        b. roots

B. Write a paragraph or two on this topic: How a Bacterium Gets Its Food.

1. How do bacteria break down a dead tree?

2. How do bacteria reproduce?

3. What may happen when certain bacteria get into a wound?

Suppose a bacterium divides in a half hour. Then the two resulting bacteria divide in a half hour. At this rate, how many bacteria would there be in 72 hours?

At this rate, why do bacteria not keep on dividing and cover the earth?

# 3. Your Body's Defenses

There are bacteria everywhere, or so it seems. Why are you not ill all the time? Why is not everyone ill? One reason is that the body is on the defense all the time.

## The First Line of Defense

How is the inside of a house protected from the rain? By its roof and walls, of course. When there is a break in the window or a hole in the roof, the rain gets in; so can certain living things, insects, for instance.

How is your body protected against invasion by bacteria or other infectious organisms? You are protected by a covering of skin. The skin is the first line of defense on the outside of your body and is made up of layers of cells. It is almost waterproof; and unless it is broken, it is practically germproof.

There is a layer of flat cells on the outside of the skin. This layer is not dry but is almost always covered by a thin layer of moisture from perspiration. Perspiration helps also to protect the body against bacteria. Bacteria that stick to the moist skin are removed when you bathe. You wash away many of the bacteria with soap and warm water.

What about the inside of your body? How is it protected? There, too, you will find cells that hold the line of defense against bacteria. The **covering cells** line the inside cavities of the body. These areas could be reached easily by **infectious** bacteria, but the protective cells have an extra way to defend the body. You can investigate this personally.

Wash your hands until they are quite clean and feel the inside of your cheek. The covering cells inside your mouth are moistened with saliva—a substance containing much water and a sticky fluid. That sticky fluid is important.

These covering cells inside the body have another kind of moistness from a substance called **mucus** (myōō′kəs), as shown in the picture.■ Mucus is **secreted** from the cells which line certain cavities inside the body, such as the mouth, throat, nose, food tube, and tubes which lead to the lungs. When a substance is produced *inside* the cells and used *outside* the cells, we say it is secreted by the cells.

Some covering cells secrete mucus which forms a protective coating. Certain other cells secrete other substances, such as the digestive juices. Digestive juices kill many bacteria that are swallowed with our food.

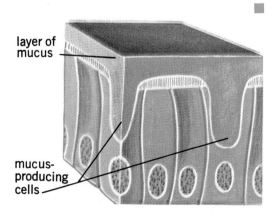

layer of mucus

mucus-producing cells

How does mucus help defend the body against bacteria? If you were to shake some ground pepper on a moist plate, the idea would be clearer to you. Just as pepper sticks to the film of water on the plate, the bacteria stick to the mucus. Does this help to explain what happens to bacteria which get into your nose and throat?

Do you ever sneeze or cough? Sneezing and coughing are reflexes that help get rid of bacteria. When you breathe, bacteria and other harmful substances are caught in the mucus of the nose and throat. They are removed from the body by sneezing and coughing.

If you were to use a microscope to look at the cells which line the wall of the windpipe, you would see special kinds of cells like the ones in the picture. 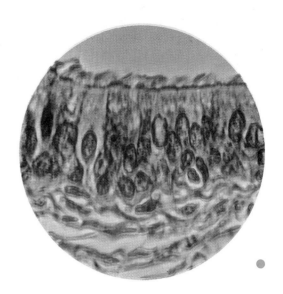 These cells have tiny hairlike parts, called **cilia** (sil′ē·ə). The cilia move the way oars move when you row a boat. They push bacteria that are caught in the mucus back up into the throat. Then a sneeze or a cough sends them out of the body. This should explain why you should use a handkerchief when you sneeze or cough.

### Getting Rid of Bacteria

You breathe in bacteria. You swallow them with your food; but it is hard for them to get past the cells that line the inside of your body. There are lining cells that secrete mucus to catch the bacteria. Cells lining your windpipe have cilia which push back the bacteria. Then, of course, sneezing and coughing, two reflexes, help to throw many of the invading bacteria out of your body.

But suppose the skin, the mucus, and your body reflexes fail to get rid of the bacteria. What then?

Suppose bacteria get past the windpipe and into the stomach. What protection do you have? The investigation on the next page will help you to find the answer to that question. Be sure to control all the variables.

Sometimes you may scrape or cut yourself and break the skin. This gives the bacteria a chance to get past the first line of defense. Suppose you do not wash the cut thoroughly with soap and water. Suppose you do not use an **antiseptic** (an′tə·sep′tik). Antiseptics are substances that stop the action of bacteria or kill them completely. What happens to the cut? What can you do about infection? What can your body do?

# AN INVESTIGATION into What Happens to Bacteria in the Stomach

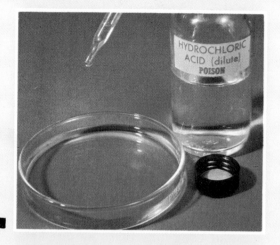

**Needed:** weak hydrochloric acid; gelatin for growing bacteria (such as you made on page 101); four dishes

Stomach cells secrete a digestive juice that contains an **acid.** It contains weak hydrochloric acid (hī′drə-klôr′ik as′id), a solution of hydrogen chloride.

Make enough of the gelatin mixture to pour about an inch into each of the four dishes. When the gelatin has congealed in each dish, put a quarter inch of water over the top of the gelatin. Add ten drops of weak hydrochloric acid, which your teacher will give you, to two of the dishes; add ten drops of water to the other two dishes. ■ These are the controls. You can use them to compare your results.

Now let the bacteria grow. Cover the dishes and put them in a warm place, a closet perhaps.● In which dishes do you expect to find large colonies?▲ In the ones with acid?

What *do* you find? (If your results are not as you expected, what might be the explanation?)

Were all the variables controlled?

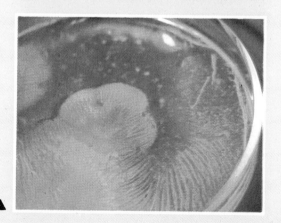

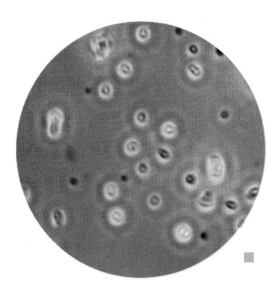

## Fighting Infection

A cut that becomes infected is white or yellowish in color, in addition to being surrounded by an inflamed red area. What gives an infected cut its color?

Under the microscope, the material in an infected cut looks like that shown in the picture. ■ Notice the tiny bunches of black dots. These are

a special kind of bacteria, which cause many common infections and can be very resistant to treatment. The name for this bacterium is *Staphylococcus* (staf′ə·lō·kok′əs), staph, for short. Recall that all ball-shaped bacteria are called cocci.

The larger cells in the picture are special ones that are found in the blood, the **white blood cells.** They are easy to recognize in a drop of blood when viewed through a microscope. They move in a strange way. They move by extending what are called false feet, but which are really more like false fingers.

Look at the pictures of a white blood cell that were made using a camera attached to a microscope. ● ▲ It was photographed as it was moving. It seems as if a white blood cell extends a part of itself as a kind of finger in one direction, and another part of itself as a second finger in another direction. The white cell

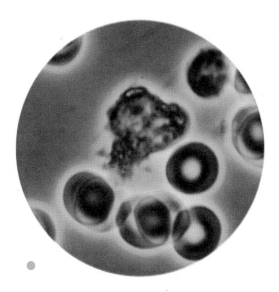

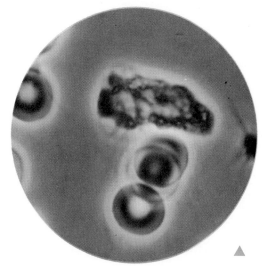

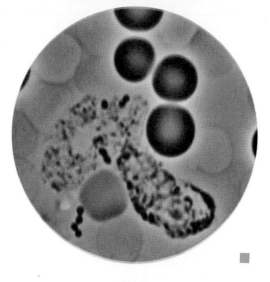

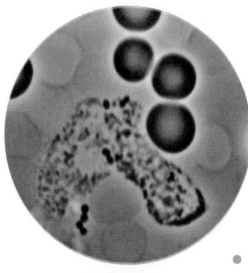

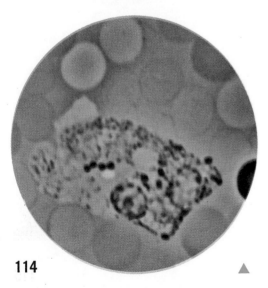

moves along in this manner and surrounds the bacteria. The bacteria are absorbed into the body of the white blood cell.

The pictures show how a white cell takes in bacteria. ■ ● When it does so, the white cell engulfs, or surrounds, the bacteria with its body and then digests them. The bacteria are destroyed. ▲

Sometimes it is possible to prevent harmful bacteria from entering the blood through an open cut. What can you do to keep bacteria out?

What should you do when you cut yourself? Wash the wound with soap and water, of course. Doctors recommend washing the cut carefully and, perhaps, adding a drop or two of antiseptic. (Whenever it is possible, show the cut to your parents or your teacher before treating it yourself.) Your doctor or your school nurse can give you the names of some good antiseptics.

What does an antiseptic really do? To find out try the investigation on the opposite page.

## When Body Defenses Fail

Suppose you do not wash a cut or use an antiseptic in time or suppose the antiseptic does not work.

Suppose the white blood cells are unable to kill all of the harmful bacteria. Sometimes the white blood cells are overcome by poisons produced by the bacteria. What then? Is the battle lost? Not necessarily, in modern times, as you will discover.

# AN INVESTIGATION into How to Keep Bacteria from Growing

**Needed:** a few flat dishes (Petri dishes); some antiseptics, such as Isodine (your druggist can supply several different kinds of antiseptics); food-gelatin mixture (p. 101)

Pour the food-gelatin mixture into the dishes. Allow it to cool (exposed to the air) for several hours as you did in the investigation on page 101. To one dish, add enough water (boiled and then cooled) to cover about half of the gelatin. This first dish is your control. All of the others should test for one variable each. They can be compared to the control.

Add a few drops of a different antiseptic to one of each of the other dishes. 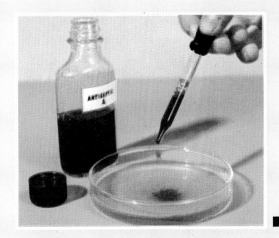 With the boiled water, cover the gelatin in each dish about halfway to the top of the dish, as you did before. Place all the dishes in a warm place.

What is the result after one day? after two days? after several days?

Did you get the results shown in the pictures?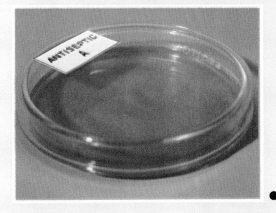

Most microorganisms do not grow when an antiseptic is used on them. The same thing happens when an antiseptic is applied to a cut.

**A.** Study the statements below and choose the correct responses. They will help you fix in mind the concepts of this section.

1. The first line of defense that the body has against infectious bacteria is the
   a. skin cells          b. blood cells

2. The covering cells inside the body produce and secrete a fluid called
   a. mucus          b. Staphylococci

3. In the stomach, a defense against bacteria is
   a. acid          b. food

4. Which one of these reflexes helps to get rid of bacteria?
   a. yawning          b. sneezing

5. When the skin is broken, we can defend the body against infection by applying
   a. enzymes          b. antiseptics

6. In the blood, the cells which destroy bacteria are the
   a. red cells          b. white cells

**B.** Write a paragraph or two on this topic: The Body's Defenses. Explore sources other than your textbook for additional information.

1. Why is it important to keep the skin clean?

2. Why is it important to wash a bruise clean with mild soap and water?

3. Why is mucus more effective than water in catching bacteria?

4. Not all bacteria are harmful. What useful purposes do they serve?

5. In what ways are molds and bacteria related? In what ways are they different?

**A.** Design an experiment that will answer the following questions:

Do antiseptics destroy molds?

How can you be sure that the mold would not die even without the antiseptic?

How can you be sure that it is the antiseptic that keeps the mold from growing?

Grow some bread mold, as you did on page 105. Then design an investigation to determine whether an antiseptic (one of the iodine products, for example) will kill the mold. You may want to get samples of some of the many advertised brands of antiseptics and mouth washes to find out how effective they are. Design your experiment so that all of the variables are controlled.

**B.** Get a copy of the *American Red Cross First Aid Textbook*, and study it carefully. Find the best methods for treating injuries.

## 4. Molds to the Rescue

In the year 1928, one day began like any other day, but it did not end that way. It became a "red letter" day for Dr. Alexander Fleming (later knighted as Sir Alexander Fleming). He had gone to work in his laboratory. Sir Alexander was a bacteriologist (bak·tir′ē·ol′ə·jist). Bacteriologists study the structure and behavior of bacteria.

He grew colonies of bacteria in much the same way as you grew them in the investigation on page 101. As a bacteriologist, he tried to isolate pure colonies of bacteria. (A pure colony contains only one kind of bacterium.) That is, he tried to study only one kind of bacterium at a time, perhaps a kind that caused a certain disease, for instance. To do this, he used a special type of broth or gelatin which he put into a culture dish. He had to work with great care to keep all other organisms, except the kind he was studying, out of the dish. Sometimes, no matter how careful he was, organisms that did not interest him got into the dishes. Many of these unwelcome visitors were molds.

Several days before this special day in 1928, Dr. Fleming opened the lids of some culture dishes containing a certain kind of bacterium. He prepared a slide with some of the bacteria to observe with the microscope. For a few moments while he prepared the slide, the gelatin mixture in the dishes was exposed to the air.

When Dr. Fleming examined another sample of bacteria later, on this special day in 1928, he became very curious. One of the culture dishes had a growth of *Penicillium* (pen'ə-sil'ē·əm), a bluish-green mold; but the thing that Dr. Fleming became excited about was this: Around the growth of mold there was a clear space. *Almost no bacteria grew in this space.* Why?

For a long time, scientists had suspected that some plants secrete substances that can be used to kill bacteria in the human body. This was an exciting idea: that some plants can secrete substances that can be used against other plants like bacteria. Sir Alexander's observation of the growth of *Penicillium* (a plant) and the clear space around it led him to wonder whether *Penicillium* was producing such a substance.

Dr. Fleming observed that the *Penicillium* mold *seemed* to make a substance that destroyed bacteria. He found it easy to grow *Penicillium;* it is also easy to grow bacteria. He should find it easy to test his idea. How could he *prove* that *Penicillium* produces a substance that kills certain kinds of bacteria? How could he prove that such a substance would not harm the human body?

### Sir Alexander's Investigation

It is important to know what Sir Alexander *did not do,* as well as what he *did do.* He *did not* take his first observation as proof that *Penicillium* produced a substance which stopped the growth of bacteria. He *did not* come to a conclusion from only one observation.

Recall the situation: One day in 1928, Sir Alexander Fleming observed what had happened to some of his colonies of bacteria. He saw the mold *Penicillium* growing in one of his dishes; and there was a clear ring around the mold. Almost no bacteria were growing in that clear ring.

Sir Alexander made a sketch of the dish, and wrote down his observation. He must have hoped that his interpretation of what he saw was correct, because if what he saw were true, it would have great usefulness. Any man would have been excited at such a great discovery.

Whatever he might have thought, Sir Alexander decided to try to find out whether or not *Penicillium* produces a substance which destroys certain kinds of bacteria. He set about designing an **experiment.**

The *experiment* is a great tool of the scientist. In an experiment, the scientist tries to set up the conditions in the laboratory in such a way that he can *control* what happens. Outside, there are too many things happening at once to isolate one specific cause and effect. If he designs his experiment carefully enough, it may yield data which will help him to find the answers to his questions. However, his experiment may not yield the results he expects; it may only indicate the need for further experiments.

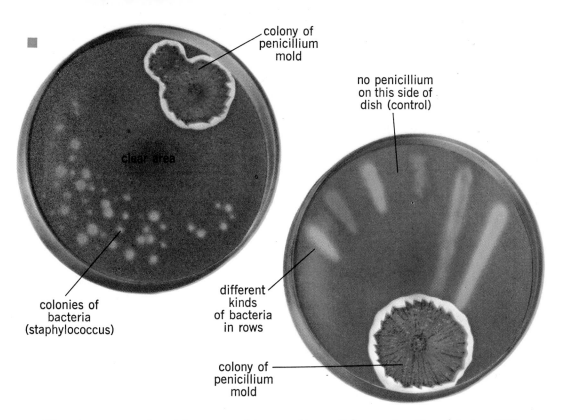

colony of penicillium mold

no penicillium on this side of dish (control)

clear area

colonies of bacteria (staphylococcus)

different kinds of bacteria in rows

colony of penicillium mold

Fleming started with a working idea based on what he had seen. He was not working in the "dark," as we say. A working idea that helps a scientist plan, or design, an experiment is called a **hypothesis** (hī·poth′ə·sis). Fleming's hypothesis may have been: *Penicillium* produces a substance which destroys some kinds of bacteria. The experiment I need to design should provide conditions that show, without doubt, that certain bacteria do *not* grow where *Penicillium* grows.

His *experiment was therefore designed* to: ■

1. *Grow different kinds of bacteria* in pure culture in lines on plates.

2. *Grow Penicillium* in pure culture.

3. Introduce *Penicillium* on one side of the plate at one end of each line of bacteria. Do this on 100—or perhaps even 1,000 plates; *one* investigation is not enough.

4. Do *not* place *Penicillium* on the *other* end of each line of bacteria. This is the **control.** In a control, the *thing the scientist wants to study* is usually left out.

5. Allow the bacteria to grow in exactly the same surroundings, except that some bacteria are near the *Penicillium*, and others are not.

If Dr. Fleming's hypothesis was correct, and if his experiment was designed correctly, then:

1. The bacteria in contact with the *Penicillium* should not grow.

2. At the ends of the rows of bacteria where there was *no Penicillium* growing, the bacteria should grow.

This is exactly the result Sir Alexander Fleming found in some of the rows. He repeated the experiment in *many different ways* and at *many different times*. He kept careful written records and photographed his results. ■ *Other scientists repeated his experiment.*

He finally was able to show conclusively that *Penicillium* does produce a substance which destroys *certain kinds* of dangerous bacteria. He also performed other experiments that showed that **penicillin** (the substance derived from *Penicillium*) was not harmful to higher animals.

Other scientists, before Sir Alexander, had suspected that molds produced such substances. Some had even written about their ideas; but Sir Alexander designed the experiment which *proved* that these substances secreted by molds would destroy certain bacteria.

## A Successful Experiment

When Sir Alexander Fleming proved that *Penicillium* produces a substance that kills some kinds of bacteria, he called it penicillin. He also found, by injecting it into animals, that penicillin is generally harmless to higher animals; but it took many years and the help of many scientists to find a way to produce large amounts at a reasonable cost.

Penicillin kills many kinds of harmful bacteria. Should your body, with its natural defenses, be unable to throw off any of these kinds of bacteria, your doctor may give you penicillin to help control them.

Two other scientists, Dr. Howard Florey and Dr. Ernst Chain, aided Dr. Fleming; they found a way to purify penicillin to make it safe for man to use. For their great contribution, the three scientists were awarded the Nobel prize. The Nobel prize is perhaps the greatest prize that scientists can receive for their work—except, perhaps, the personal satisfaction which they get from doing the work.

Penicillin, however, is not effective against *all* kinds of bacteria, so the search for other beneficial molds began. Soon Dr. Selman Waksman, an American scientist, extracted another substance from a mold.● He called it **streptomycin** (strep′tō·mī′sin). It is more effective for killing certain types of bacteria than is penicillin.

That is especially true when streptomycin is used to destroy the bacteria that cause tuberculosis.

Today there are many different substances extracted from molds which help kill bacteria. These substances are called **antibiotics** (an′ti·bī·ot′iks). Antibiotics are not the same as antiseptics. Antibiotics are chemical substances which are secreted by living things. Many diseases and common infections are now being conquered by antibiotics. ▲

Scientists have discovered how to make the body a poor environment for bacteria by introducing antibiotics. Because of the work of scientists like Sir Alexander Fleming, it is very likely that you will live longer than your ancestors did.

▲

| SOME COMMON ANTIBIOTICS | |
| --- | --- |
| Name of Antibiotic | Helps destroy disease germs causing |
| Achromycin | Ear, sinus, and throat infections, bone infections, pneumonia, scarlet fever, meningitis, undulant fever |
| Aureomycin | Virus pneumonia, typhus fever, Rocky Mountain spotted fever |
| Chloromycetin | Parrot fever, rabbit fever, typhus fever, one kind of pneumonia, smallpox, and many more bacterial and virus diseases |
| Erythromycin | Certain diseases such as typhus, virus diseases, and others |
| Penicillin | Pneumonia, colds, boils, gas gangrene, epidemic meningitis, kidney and bladder infections, and many more bacterial diseases |
| Streptomycin | Tuberculosis, rabbit fever |

## Your Own Investigation

Sir Alexander Fleming wondered why there was a clear area around a mold. Because he was a *trained* scientist, he not only wondered, but took the question to the laboratory. There he worked very long and very patiently, until he had the evidence he was looking for. In planning your investigation into what diastase does (suggested on p. 107), did you have a *hypothesis?* and a *control?*

Did you begin to design your experiment around a clearly stated hypothesis? Sir Alexander's was: *Penicillium* produces a substance which destroys some kinds of bacteria. What was your hypothesis?

How close was the plan of your experiment to that of Sir Alexander's?

BEFORE YOU GO ON

A. Study the statements below and choose the correct responses. They will help you fix in mind the concepts of this section.

1. Sir Alexander Fleming discovered an
   a. antiseptic
   b. antibiotic

2. Penicillin is produced by
   a. a plant
   b. an animal

3. Penicillin was first tested on
   a. men and women
   b. rabbits

4. In designing his investigation, Fleming planned an experiment. In an experiment a scientist tries to
   a. control the conditions
   b. let many things happen

5. The working idea that helps a scientist plan or design an experiment is his
   a. hypothesis
   b. experimental design

6. When a scientist sets up an experiment to include a situation where the one thing he wishes to study is left out, that part of the experiment is the
   a. proof
   b. control

7. Before scientists accept the result of an experiment, the experiment is
   a. repeated many times
   b. published

8. Like penicillin, streptomycin is an
   a. antibiotic          b. antiseptic

B. Write several paragraphs on one of these topics:
   Sir Alexander Fleming          Penicillin
   The Importance of a Controlled Experiment

USING WHAT YOU KNOW

1. Iodine has been used for many years as an antiseptic that quickly kills bacteria. With antiseptics available, why did scientists find it necessary to search for antibiotics?

2. A girl found some green mold growing on a piece of bread. She wanted to find out whether the green mold grew best in a moist or a dry environment. She divided the piece of bread so that there was about the same amount of mold on each piece. Then she put one piece of bread in a moist environment, the other in a dry environment. Both of the pieces had a good growth of mold. Was she justified in reaching the conclusion that bread mold grows equally well in both a moist and a dry environment?

ON YOUR OWN

There are a good number of antibiotics in use today. You know a little about penicillin and streptomycin.

Do some additional research in the library to find the answer to this question: *Which antibiotics are used against the major diseases?* Put your findings in a table, as shown. ■

| Antibiotic | Discoverer | Uses |
|---|---|---|
| Penicillin | Alexander Fleming | |
| Streptomycin | Selman Waksman | Mainly against tuberculosis |

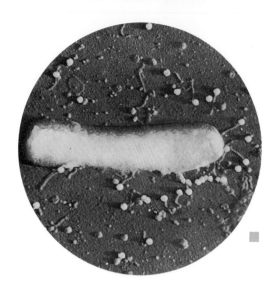

way that bacteria can live inside people. You can see most bacteria under a good ordinary microscope; but viruses are so small that they had never been seen until a special kind of microscope, an electron microscope, was invented.

Joseph Meister, whom you read about on page 99, was suffering from a virus. Rabies is caused by one of many viruses.

Among the many different kinds of viruses are those that can cause influenza.● Many viruses look like tiny spheres, as shown in the pictures.

## 5. Another Battle: Another Victory

The *enemy* in this story is a **virus** (vī′rəs), not a bacterium. Viruses are still another type of invisible killer. A virus is even smaller than a bacterium, as the picture shows.■ Some viruses are so small that they can live inside bacteria, in somewhat the same

### Polio Virus—The Enemy

This time the enemy is the virus which causes infantile paralysis (in′-fən·tĭl pə·ral′ə·sis), or **polio** (pō′-lē·ō), as the disease is called. Look at a picture of the villain.▲

What does the polio virus do? First of all, it multiplies. Second, in large numbers, it attacks the nerves which

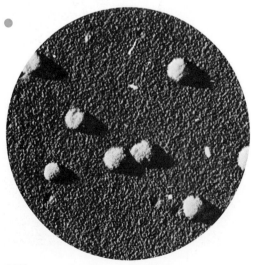

124

lead to the muscles. The nerves carry impulses to the muscles from the brain and spinal cord. When the nerves are affected so that impulses do not reach the muscles, the muscles cannot move. The picture shows a healthy nerve cell and one which has been attacked by the polio virus. ◆ The polio virus thus strikes at the nervous system. The result is that the muscles cannot function properly. When the muscles do not function or are paralyzed, they become useless. The virus attacks young people as well as adults. Franklin Delano Roosevelt, a former President of the United States (1933–45), was crippled by polio when he was a young man. He fulfilled his duties as President in a wheelchair.

Sometimes the virus attacks the nerve cells leading to the leg muscles. Sometimes it attacks nerves leading to the muscles which control breathing. Then the victim must be placed in an iron lung.★ The iron lung serves as an artificial means of breathing; the change in air pressure is regulated by a kind of pumping action. It causes the victim's ribs and lungs to expand and contract—to take in air and to push out air.

Polio is now on the way out. It will go down in history as another disease which is no longer a menace to man— another example of man's control of his environment.

The virus of smallpox and the bacterium of diphtheria belong in the same category. They can be kept

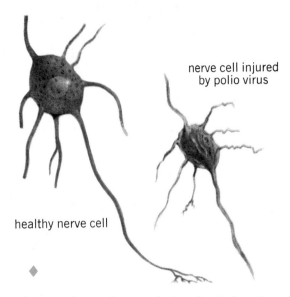

nerve cell injured by polio virus

healthy nerve cell

there only with your help, the help of your parents, and the help of departments of public health.

Why is this so? Read on to see how scientists battle a disease like polio.

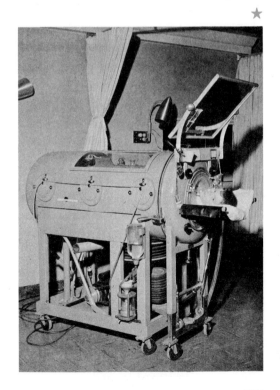

## The Battle Against Polio

What happens when bacteria or viruses invade your body? They attack in weak moments (when your resistance is low) or in weak places (where a break occurs in the lines of defense). They must get through your first lines of defense, the skin, the film of mucus, and the digestive juices in your stomach. If the bacteria or viruses get through your skin, then the white blood cells attack them; but suppose all these fail. What then? There is, of course, the chemical defense of antibiotics; but that is not all. There is still another chemical defense which scientists have developed to help your body fight disease.

Do you remember being **vaccinated** (vak′sə·nāt·ed) for smallpox? Probably not. Most children are vaccinated against smallpox, a virus disease, when they are very young.

What does the doctor do when he vaccinates against smallpox? He breaks the skin on your arm or leg; then he introduces a bit of cowpox virus into the break. The body reacts to the cowpox virus by producing substances called **antibodies** (an′ti·bod′ēz). Antibodies then destroy the cowpox virus. The antibodies remain in the blood; and because the cowpox virus is very similar to the smallpox virus, the antibodies also destroy smallpox viruses. The illustration shows an artist's view of the conquest of disease. Of course you know that antibodies cannot be seen. ■

Do not confuse *antibodies* with *antibiotics*. Antibiotics are substances produced by molds; they are chemical substances *made outside* the human body but *used within* to fight some kinds of organisms. Antibodies are produced by cells in the human body. When your body makes antibodies to combat a disease, you are said to be **immune** (i·myoōn′) to that disease. This means that the environment is unfavorable for the growth of the viruses or bacteria that cause the disease. They cannot live when the antibodies are present. Antibodies are specific; that means that a different type of antibody is usually needed to fight each different kind of disease. Antibodies are formed in the body of a person who has had a disease. After the person recovers from the disease, the antibodies usually remain in the blood. Then we say the person has developed immunity against that particular disease, or say he is immune to the disease.

A person who has had typhoid, and recovered, has the antibodies against typhoid in his blood. He is immune to typhoid. If typhoid bacteria enter his body again, the typhoid antibodies destroy them. He does not get typhoid again. This is called *natural immunity*. The same is true of smallpox; but having a disease to achieve immunity is too dangerous. It may even be fatal.

Vaccination is a safer way to produce immunity. Vaccination against smallpox stimulates the body to produce the antibodies to smallpox. After

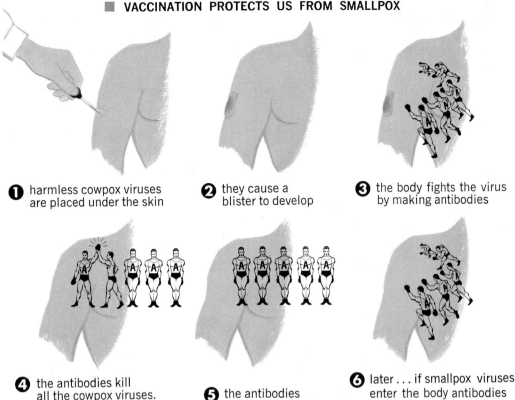

**①** harmless cowpox viruses are placed under the skin

**②** they cause a blister to develop

**③** the body fights the virus by making antibodies

**④** the antibodies kill all the cowpox viruses. the blister goes away

**⑤** the antibodies stay in the blood

**⑥** later . . . if smallpox viruses enter the body antibodies will kill them immediately

this, the viruses of smallpox which may enter your body are destroyed by the antibodies. You are then immune to smallpox. This is called *acquired immunity.*

The scientist is faced with the problem of finding a way to give a person enough of the disease-producing organisms for his body to produce antibodies; without giving him enough so that he gets the disease. Usually, weakened or dead microorganisms of a specific disease are injected in small doses into a person.

Recall that the **serum** given to Joseph Meister by Pasteur (page 99) already contained antibodies. The serum came from the spines of rabbits that were infected with rabies. It contained antibodies that were produced in the rabbits as they fought the disease. The antibodies in the rabbits' serum saved Meister's life.

Many scientists fought in the battle against polio, but three men led the fight. To win the battle, it was necessary to produce a **vaccine** (vak'-sēn). The first step advanced when Dr. John Enders learned how to grow the polio virus outside a living organism. He was then able to study its development. He found that a virus becomes weaker if it is grown under certain conditions.

**127**

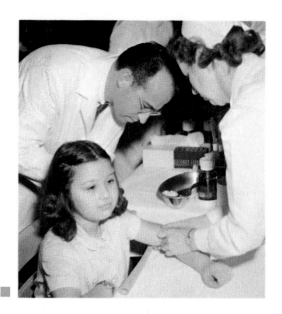

As a beginning in making polio vaccine, Jonas Salk looked for a way to weaken the polio virus so that it could be injected into the body without causing illness. If strong polio viruses were injected into the body, the per-

son might get the disease. Finally, after many years, Dr. Salk discovered that even when the *dead* virus was injected into the body, the body responded by producing antibodies against polio. Many careful tests were made; the Salk vaccine was successful. ■ Polio was on its way out.

The Salk vaccine requires injections by a doctor; but another vaccine, produced by Dr. Albert Sabin and his team of scientists, can be taken by mouth. The Sabin vaccine contains weakened *live* viruses. Both types of vaccine, the Salk and the Sabin, have been thoroughly tested. Both are completely safe. Both enable the body to develop antibodies in the cells. You have probably taken the Salk or the Sabin vaccine. If so, you have antibodies which will kill polio viruses that get into your body. You are immune to polio.

Only half the battle is won in the laboratory. How can the battle against polio virus, or any other germ, be won for all time? First, scientists and doctors fight the battle in the laboratory. The concepts of science are used in the development of an antibiotic or an antibody, but this is not enough. Everyone must cooperate. For instance, once a vaccine has been tested and found safe, the battle is up to us; we must make use of the vaccine.

In the fight against polio, we must all do what the people in the picture are doing: We should take the vaccine. ● Have you taken it?

## A Record of Victories

Look at the table below. Study it carefully; it tells an important story. ▲ The scientists, whose names are listed, worked long and hard. Because they did, the bacteria and viruses that are listed in the table can be controlled. The diseases they cause can be controlled by substances that are produced in your body. You develop immunity. Notice how little space the table takes; but it represents the work of many people over a long period of time. What will be next on the list?

Study the table again. How long did it take to bring these diseases under control?

The table tells another very important story. It tells how man, as a scientist, has learned to control another area of his environment. He is able to control many of the invisible organisms which would otherwise make him ill or cause death. He used his ideas; but he also needed such tools as compound and electron microscopes—another example of the partnership of science and technology.

▲

### SOME DISEASE GERMS WE CAN CONTROL

| Name of disease | Method used | Scientist(s) who discovered method of control | When |
|---|---|---|---|
| smallpox | vaccination with cowpox virus | Edward Jenner | 1796 |
| typhoid | avoiding contaminated milk and water | William Budd<br>C. J. Eberth<br>G. Gaffky | 1856<br>1880<br>1884 |
| yellow fever | control of mosquito found to spread the disease | Carlos Finlay<br>Walter Reed and others | 1881<br>1900 |
| cholera | avoiding contaminated water and food | Robert Koch | 1883 |
| hydrophobia (rabies) | vaccination with antibodies from rabbits | Louis Pasteur | 1885 |
| diphtheria | inoculation with antibodies from immune animals | Emil von Behring | 1890 |
| malaria | control of mosquito that spreads the disease | Ronald Ross<br>Battista Grassi | 1898 |
| bubonic plague | destroying rats which carried fleas that spread the bacteria | Plague Research Commission, India | 1905 |
| polio | vaccination with weakened or killed polio virus | John Enders<br>Jonas Salk<br>Albert Sabin | 1949<br>1954<br>1960 |

**A.** Study the statements below and choose the correct responses. They will help you fix in mind the concepts of this section.

    **1.** Substances produced by an animal inside its body that can destroy bacteria or viruses that get into the body are
        a. antibiotics             b. antibodies

    **2.** If a person is vaccinated with the cowpox virus, his body produces substances which can destroy
        a. the smallpox virus       b. typhoid bacteria

    **3.** The serum given to Joseph Meister contained
        a. antiseptics             b. antibodies

    **4.** Jonas Salk proceeded with the work begun by John Enders to combat
        a. polio                b. tuberculosis

    **5.** The difference between the Salk and Sabin vaccines is that the Sabin vaccine uses
        a. weakened, live         b. dead viruses
           viruses

**B.** Write several paragraphs on this topic: Antibodies.

**1.** What are the differences in these three defenses against bacteria:
    antiseptics        antibiotics        antibodies

    **2.** What is the difference between natural immunity and acquired immunity?

**1.** Do some investigating in the library. Find out what you can about the lives of
    —Louis Pasteur          —Albert Sabin
    —Jonas Salk

    **2.** What kind of polio vaccine is used in your town?

## 6. Health—A Public Concern

You drink water every day with no concern about getting diseases from bacteria in the water. Yet, there was a time when cholera (kol′ər·ə) and typhoid, two diseases which are carried by water, killed many people.

You drink milk without the slightest worry. Yet, milk was once the carrier of many diseases, among them tuberculosis. Today, it would be unusual to find diseases spread by milk; milk is safe to drink.

Safe drinking water and pasteurized milk are things we take for granted. Who is responsible for your protection, and how?

You turn a faucet and water pours out. Where does the water come from, and how do most cities make sure the water is safe to drink?

The glass of water you drink probably came from a cloud. When the water vapor in a cloud condenses, it falls to earth as raindrops and finally reaches a stream. The stream may lead to a **reservoir** (rez′ər·vwôr). Reservoirs are large lakes used for storing water. Water used by most large cities collects in reservoirs.

A reservoir should be located in clean surroundings, away from the city, where the water is not contaminated with wastes from factories, garbage, and sewage. Why is it important for the reservoir shown in the illustration to be fenced in? ■

Even under the best conditions, however, lake water or river water is not free from harmful microorganisms. As water flows along the ground, it can pick up many impurities. Water can pick up all kinds of bacteria and other organisms from its surroundings. How can it be purified so that it is fit to drink? How can *harmful* bacteria be removed or destroyed?

Water can be made safe to drink by boiling it for ten minutes. Of course, you could boil all your drinking water; but would everyone in a city do it? Is there another way to rid drinking water of harmful microorganisms?

There are several ways to make water fit to drink. One method that helps to remove germs is called **filtration** (fil·trā′shən). In many cities the water flows through a filtering plant before it gets to the faucet. In the filtering plant the water passes through layers of sand and gravel. As the picture shows, much of the dirt in the water does not pass through. ■ The particles are too large to go through the layers of fine sand. Since bacteria frequently cling to particles of dirt, many of them do not pass through the filter either. They remain behind with the particles of mud or dirt.

## Purifying Water for a Big City

A filter can remove many, but not all, of the microorganisms from the water supply. Some smaller bacteria and viruses pass right through. What can be done to stop them from getting through the filter and into your drinking water?

The bacteria can be killed by some substances. In many places a chemical is added to the water. This may be chlorine gas, which is added in small amounts. Chlorine kills bacteria and other microorganisms. In large amounts, chlorine gas is poisonous to people; however, the small quantity needed to kill most microorganisms is harmless to us. The picture shows the chlorination apparatus used for purifying water. The gas is added as the water flows past the gas jet in the pipe. ● The amount of chlorine used is regulated very carefully.

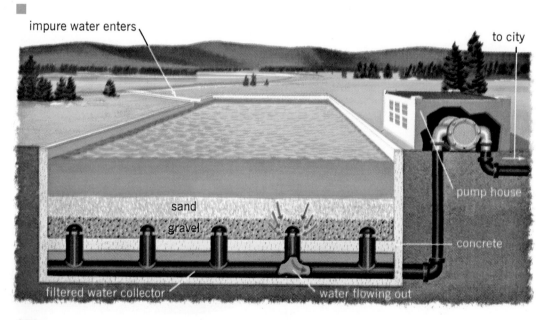

impure water enters

to city

sand

gravel

pump house

concrete

filtered water collector

water flowing out

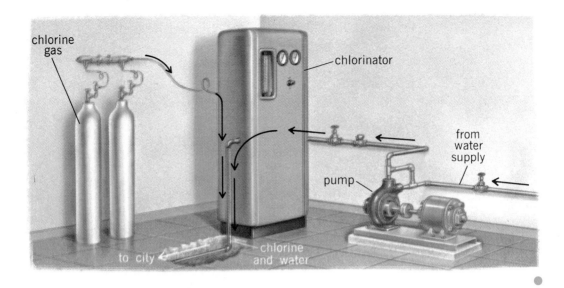

chlorine gas

chlorinator

from water supply

pump

to city

chlorine and water

Sometimes other substances, such as sodium hypochlorite (sō′dē·əm hī′pə·klôr′īt), are used to purify water, instead of chlorine gas. Substances, such as chlorine and sodium hypochlorite, can make the water a poor place for bacteria to live. See this for yourself by doing the investigation on the next page.

### Safe Drinking Water

Your glass of water starts in the clouds. It falls as rain and is gathered in the **watershed**. A watershed includes all the streams that run into a lake or reservoir. Your glass of water finds its way into the reservoir. Sooner or later, most of the dirt settles and the water is clear. If the water is not clear, it may be filtered in order to rid it of soil particles and some bacteria. Clear water, however, may *not* be completely free from bacteria; so it must be treated with substances, such as chlorine, to rid it of

harmful bacteria. The glass of water you finally get *is* fit to drink.

### Water on a Farm

In the city, the turn of a faucet brings you water. The water is pumped in from a reservoir. On a farm, the turn of a faucet brings you water, but the water is often pumped into the house from a well. A well is really a kind of reservoir under the ground. Where does the water in a well come from? How does it get into the well?

Have you ever dug a hole in the sand near the seashore? Or in the soil near the shore of a lake? Soon the hole fills with water. ▲

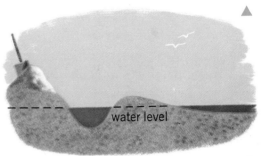

water level

# AN INVESTIGATION into Purifying Water with Chemicals

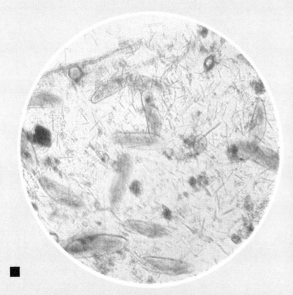

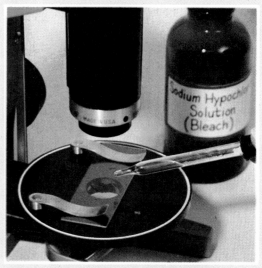

**Needed:** a microscope; a culture of some microorganisms (see below); some chlorine bleach (sodium hypochlorite); medicine droppers; and microscope slides. WARNING: BLEACH IS A POISON. KEEP IT AWAY FROM YOUR MOUTH AND SKIN.

First, prepare a culture of microorganisms. Obtain several pint jars of pond water, each from a different place. Crumble a piece of yolk (about the size of a pea) from a hard-boiled egg into each of the jars of pond water. Keep the jars away from the sun, but keep them in a warm (but not hot) place. After a few days or a week or two, the culture will probably swarm with tiny bacteria and other microorganisms. Use the culture for your investigation.

Examine several samples of the culture under the microscope until you find one containing a large number of living microorganisms. ■ As you watch them moving under the microscope, add a drop of liquid bleach to the water on the slide.● How long does it take the bleach (sodium hypochlorite) to kill all the organisms you see?

Investigate further to find out how much bleach is really necessary to kill the bacteria (or other organisms) in a drop of water.

**Additional Investigation:** Perhaps you have been on a hike. Did you get water for drinking from streams or mountain lakes? Today hike leaders carry Halazone pills, which are dissolved in the water before it is used. Investigate to find out how effective they are.

On a farm, a well may be dug where the ground has water in it. The well may be lined with rocks or concrete. ■ Some modern wells are simply a long pipe connected to a point that is forced into the ground, as shown. ■ To get into the well, the water must soak through the soil; thus, the water is filtered naturally by the soil. This filtering is often all that is needed to remove small particles and to keep out bacteria and other impurities.

It is important that the well be dug far from a barn or pasture. Animal wastes, garbage, and sewage are fine places for bacteria to grow; but they make the water unfit to drink. Which farm well shown in the illustration is in the best location? ●

When there is not enough water near the surface, a well is driven deep into the layers of rock in order to get

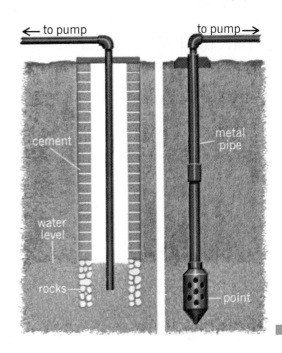

water. Wells driven through porous rock found deep in the ground usually supply water that is safe to use. By the time the water has filtered through rock to such a depth, most of the impurities have been removed.

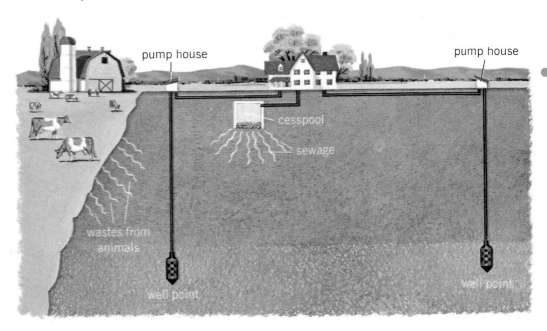

If the water is not clear, if it is even a bit cloudy, it is best to boil it. Boiling for ten minutes will kill most bacteria. Well water must be tested often for bacteria.

When necessary, well water can be chlorinated by using a small device for adding chlorine gas to the water as it comes from a farm well. Chlorine is a purifier.

## Health—A Personal Concern

Keeping well depends a great deal on *you* and *your family.* Ask yourself these questions. If your answer is "yes" to each of them, you are helping to keep dangerous bacteria out of your body and away from your friends.

1. Do I wash my hands before every meal?
2. Do I bathe regularly to keep my body clean?
3. Do I brush my teeth at least after breakfast and after dinner?
4. Do I keep my nails cut and clean?
5. Do I wash my hair at least once a week?
6. Do I always wash my hands after going to the bathroom?
7. Do I get proper care for cuts and bruises?
8. Do I show my teacher or parents a cut that is bleeding?
9. If I have a cold, do I stay away from other people until the cold is under control?
10. Do I stay away from people who have colds or other contagious (kən·tā′jəs) diseases?

You should answer "yes" to all the questions and know the reasons why. If you said "no" to any question, plan to practice doing that one thing until you do it almost without thinking.

Up to now, your health has been the concern of your parents. They have planned your diet, attended to your aches and pains, and been concerned with your growth. They are the ones who have seen that you had regular medical and dental checkups. Your school, too, has been interested in your health. Schools furnish many services, such as a visiting nurse, dentist, or doctor.

Soon your health will be your own responsibility. You must be ready to take over as an adult. You should do everything possible to keep yourself in the finest health. The human body is a marvelous machine. Its care and upkeep are not difficult—if you know what you are doing. Be sure you do.

## Your Government Helps

In your community, much is being done to keep you well. You are required by law to be vaccinated against many diseases. You will not get smallpox or diphtheria, and the chances are very good that you will not get polio.

Water and food supplies are inspected. Laws requiring inspection reduce the chances that impure food or water will ever get to you.

Find out more about how your health is protected by doing the investigation on the opposite page.

# AN INVESTIGATION into Keeping Water and Food Free from Bacteria

**Needed:** you and your imagination

This is a **research** problem. Research is, in a way, another term for investigating.

Research can be carried on in many places. It may take place in the library. It may take place in the laboratory or in the field. It may take place when you talk to an expert.

Wherever research is taking place, an attempt is being made to find out something.

Through research, try to find the answers to the four questions below. Where will you go for your research? to the library? to the laboratory? to an expert? Here are the questions:

a. How is water purified in your village, town, or city? ■

b. How is milk freed from most harmful (called **pathogenic**) bacteria, mainly those of typhoid and tuberculosis?

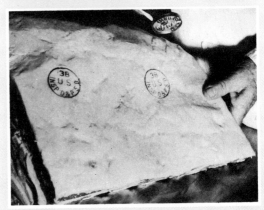

c. What does the purple stamp on meat (Inspected U.S.) mean? ●

d. How is bottled food kept free from bacteria? ▲

Notice that the four questions have to do with the technology of controlling disease.

Write the results of your research in a notebook. Your teacher may want you to report your results to the class.

**A.** Study the statements below and choose the correct responses. They will help you fix in mind the concepts of this section.

1. When on a hike it is easiest to purify water by adding
   a. chlorine                    b. Halazone pills

2. Dirt and mud can be removed from water by
   a. filtration                   b. chlorination

3. Impure milk or water is known to be a carrier of
   a. polio                        b. typhoid

**B.** Score yourself on the questions asked on page 136. Give yourself a mark of 2 for any question you answer "All the time." A mark of 1 goes for any question you answer "Some of the time." Give yourself a mark of zero for any answer like "None of the time" or "Never."

What is your score? Did you score below 20? If so, which health practice needs correcting?

1. With the help of your mother or father, check your medicine cabinet. Is everything labeled? Are all antiseptics and drugs out of the reach of young children?

2. How does a deep well help in the maintenance of a safe water supply?

What is the source of your water supply? If you live in a city, find the area where the source is and where the reservoirs are. Find out what method is used to protect your water supply.

This too is a kind of research problem—a way of investigating. Research may take place in the laboratory, in the library, or in the field. The scientist uses many approaches in seeking the answers to his questions. Probably the most important skill that he uses is that of careful observation; but accurate measurements may be considered equally important.

## 7. The Main Concept: Controlling the Environment

All living things depend on their environment for food, water, and shelter. ■ Without the sun's energy, green plants do not make food and cannot live; without green plants, animals cannot live. They depend on green plants not only for food but also for oxygen.

We depend on our environment; but the environment is not always friendly. The tiger feeds on the deer. Some snakes feed on mice. Animals feed on each other, as well as on plants. Some animals and plants are dangerous to humans, too.

Some bacteria would kill us if we let them; others would make us sick. Over the years there have been many diseases which were caused by microorganisms. Such diseases have killed many men and there are many other diseases that still do.

Before the microscope was invented, man did not know about microorganisms. A tool had to be invented before he could discover the cause of many diseases. Without the microscope we could not have known about microorganisms, the invisible enemies against which we must always be on guard. These invisible enemies killed many people and made many others very ill.

For example, the Black Death, a disease caused by bacteria, killed one-fourth of all the people in Europe about 600 years ago. The disease is caused by a specific kind of bacterium, but the concept that bacteria and other microorganisms cause disease was not known 600 years ago.

Tuberculosis killed many and still does; cholera and typhoid were common too. Before 1900, smallpox was a disease that caused many deaths. Today, smallpox is almost unknown; an epidemic unheard of.

water-purifying plant

modern hospital

refrigerated truck

modern supermarket

Even today, in the warmer climates of the world, malaria, caused by a microscopic protozoan, kills many people—too many.

Through science and technology, however, man has learned to control, and even to wipe out, many diseases. He has learned to do a very important thing, to control and change his environment. ■ He has learned also to change the environment of some microorganisms, so they cannot survive. Now man purifies water to kill the microorganisms in it; the government inspects meat and fish to get rid of any infected food; people are vaccinated against smallpox, diphtheria, or polio.

Man controls his environment. He has learned to control it in many ways. He makes laws, for instance. There are laws against stealing. There are safety laws. Drivers obey safety laws when they drive within speed limits or stop at red lights. There are also laws which apply to contagious diseases. Persons who have diseases that spread easily to other people must be isolated—by law. They are placed under **quarantine.** Quarantine thus protects other people's lives.

In addition to controlling his own environment, man tries to control other living things which could destroy him. What must he know in order to control the microorganisms which could kill us? Man had first to discover what germs are and how and where to find them. To do this, he needed many new inventions: the

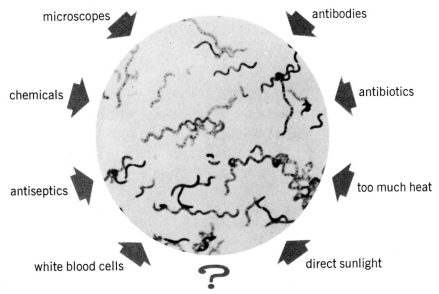

microscopes

antibodies

chemicals

antibiotics

antiseptics

too much heat

white blood cells

direct sunlight

**?**

can you think of more?

microscope, stains to color the bacteria so that they might be examined, ways of growing bacteria, ways of collecting them. To get rid of the bacteria, for instance, he needed to know how to produce antiseptics, to know how the body produces antibodies, and to know how molds produce antibiotics.

Scientists learned to control the environment so that it is not safe for many organisms that cause disease, but is safe for us. ● This is one aim of medical research. Medical-research scientists seek the causes of disease. Just as Louis Pasteur did, or as Sir Alexander Fleming and Jonas Salk did, scientists learn to control certain organisms in our environment, particularly the ones that cause disease. In so doing they prevent disease.

Animals and plants live together in their environment. Man lives in the environment as well. He breathes the air and drinks the water. He feeds on plants and animals; and, in turn, certain organisms (like bacteria and viruses) feed on him—if they can. By learning how to control such organisms, man controls his environment—and in so doing, *improves* and *lengthens* his life.

Man, as a scientist, has learned to control his environment mainly by investigation. By controlling the variables in his experiments, his conclusions are more accurate. Accurate observation and measurement are two of the most important skills that man, as a scientist, has acquired. But that is also true in all walks of life—not just in science.

# Fixing the Main Concepts

Test your understanding of the important concepts of this unit by doing these problems.

**1.** A farmer examined the water in his well and found it cloudy. He sent the water for examination to the Health Department in a nearby city. The Health Department found that the water was full of microorganisms like those shown. ■

a. What was in the water?
b. Are these microorganisms dangerous? Why?
c. What do you suggest could be done?
d. How can well water be purified?

**2.** In 1900, diphtheria and typhoid were common diseases. Now they occur very rarely in the United States. What reasons can you give for this?

**3.** What services does the government provide to protect our health and welfare?

**4.** What reasons would you give for doing the following:
a. A group of hikers boils the water from a stream before they drink it.
b. A housewife puts meat in the refrigerator.
c. Water entering a reservoir goes through a filtration plant.
d. Water entering a big city from a reservoir is chlorinated.

**5.** An antibiotic can be taken (or injected) into the body; so can an antibody. An antiseptic can be used externally but is poisonous when taken into the body. Why?

6. Use each of these key words or terms in a sentence.

| | |
|---|---|
| antiseptic | spirillum |
| antibody | virus |
| antibiotic | vaccine |
| immunity | enzyme |
| coccus | spore |
| bacillus | bacterium |
| covering cell | white blood cell |
| hypothesis | experimental design |
| control experiment | microorganism |

**QUICK TEST**     Study the statements below and choose the correct responses. They will help you fix in mind the concepts of this unit.

1. One of the following is *not* a bacterium. Which is it?
   a. coccus
   b. bacillus
   c. virus
   d. spirillum

2. Certain iodine products are used as
   a. antiseptics
   b. antibodies
   c. antibiotics
   d. enzymes

3. Streptomycin is an
   a. antiseptic
   b. antibody
   c. antibiotic
   d. enzyme

4. Diastase is an
   a. antiseptic
   b. antibody
   c. antibiotic
   d. enzyme

5. A polio vaccine was developed by Jonas Salk. In addition, another vaccine for polio was developed by
   a. Selman Waksman
   b. Albert Sabin
   c. Alexander Fleming
   d. Howard Florey and Ernst Chain

**FOR YOUR READING**     1. *The Wonderful World of Medicine*, by Ritchie Calder, published by Doubleday, Garden City, 1958.

This book describes the story of how man began to control the microorganisms in his environment. It describes the history of medicine from the witch doctor to modern times. Many colored photographs illustrate this book.

**2.** *Miracle Drugs and the New Age of Medicine,* by Fred Reinfeld, published by Sterling, New York, 1962.

This book tells in detail the story of the discovery and production of the modern "wonder drugs."

**3.** *The Story of Microbes,* by Albert Schatz and Sarah Riedman, published by Harper and Row, New York, 1952.

This interesting book tells the ways in which bacteria are used in making such products as cheese and sauerkraut.

**4.** *The Microscope, and How to Use It,* by Georg Stehli, published by Sterling, New York, 1961.

This is a book for beginners; it is especially good for those who own a microscope. If you are interested in using a microscope, you will want to learn many of the technical terms used.

ON YOUR OWN

**1.** Yeasts are fungi. Recall that fungi are plants without chlorophyll. Bacteria are also plants without chlorophyll. In many ways, the yeast cell works like the bacterial cell. The working of a cell is called its metabolism (me·tab′ə·liz′əm). The way a cell makes use of its food is part of its metabolism.

For instance, when your cells use a food they combine it with oxygen to yield energy. Thus, if your cells were to use sugar and oxygen, they would combine them to form water and carbon dioxide.

Yeast cells use sugar, too. What do yeast cells produce when they use sugar? Do they produce carbon dioxide, just as your cells do? As bacterial cells do? Or do they produce oxygen (in the presence of light) as green plant cells do?

Yeast cells can be grown in a solution of sugar. Add about a teaspoon of sugar to half a glass of water. Add to the sugar solution $\frac{1}{2}$ teaspoon of powdered yeast. How can you collect the gas which is given off? How can you find out whether it is carbon dioxide? It is easy to test for carbon dioxide in the air you breathe out; but it is not so easy to do this for yeast.

Test your ability to use your ideas to find or to invent a tool.

**2.** Do some research in the library about the development of an antibiotic to combat the staphylococcus—a bacterium which is very resistant to most antibiotics.

PROJECTS

**1.** Grow a mold garden.

On a paper plate put some scraps of food from the table— a piece of orange, apple, white bread, whole wheat bread, and a grape, if you can. You may want to use foods other than those mentioned.

Leave scraps of food on the plate, open to the air over night. Spores of different molds may be present in the air.

Cover the paper plate with a piece of plastic. This will keep the moisture in. Examine the plate each day.

How many different kinds of molds have you grown? Compare yours with those grown by your classmates.

If you have a microscope examine each sample in a drop of water. To do this, pick up a bit of mold with a toothpick. Put the bit of mold in a drop of water on a slide and cover it with a cover glass. Does it look like one of those shown in the illustration? ■

**2.** Plan an investigation to determine whether molds grow better on carbohydrate foods (starches and sugars) than they do on protein foods (meats, cheeses, etc.). Try to control the different variables.

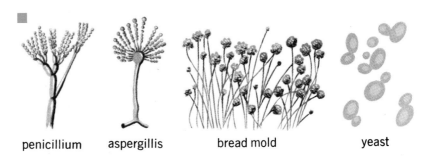

penicillium     aspergillis     bread mold     yeast

# A Concept of Interdependence: A New View

Everyone learns; indeed, everyone must learn in one way or another. The *way* the scientist learns is one of the great designs of man. He is constantly searching for a better understanding of the objects and events in the world around him. Most of his searching takes place in libraries, laboratories, and research centers. He is uncovering a vast reserve of new knowledge that was formerly out of reach. Currently, this new knowledge is being published at the rate of 60 million pages a year. At this rate, it would take a fast-reading scientist eight hours a day (with no time off for lunch), until the year 3363, to finish reading a year's discovery of new knowledge.

Look around you. In this modern age it is hard to find one substance that has not been affected by the knowledge that scientists have discovered; but above and beyond uncovering new knowledge, *what are scientists really searching for?* Let us use a particular example to find one answer to that question.

When you go into the woods or into any environment where you can observe living things, you will find a vast number of plants and animals. In just one environment you may find an odd assortment of such things as dogs and daisies, rabbits and roses, frogs and salamanders, many kinds of fishes, mosses, ferns, and seed plants.

What a vast number of plants and animals there are! The number is so vast that one wonders how anyone can learn all about them. Fortunately, there exists among all these different living things certain likenesses or relationships; but you may ask why they are important. Well, let's see if we can find out.

Look at the chart on the opposite page. It shows one way that scientists group, or **classify**, animals. Animals in certain groups seem to be closely related to each other. ■ Mammals are related. They have much the same structure. The muscles, bones, and nerves of a dog are much like those of a cat, an elephant, a horse, or a tiger. They all have hair. If we were to look at the skeletons of each of these animals (all mammals), we would find that their skeletons are similar.

Birds are related to each other. They all have feathers. In addition to being related to each other, they have a structure which is similar to that of the amphibians and reptiles. The fishes too, as well as the mammals, have something in common with the birds, amphibians, and reptiles. They are all **vertebrate** animals. Their backbone is made up of sections called **vertebrae.**

**Invertebrates** are animals without backbones. The number of invertebrates is vast and includes such ani-

# CLASSIFICATION OF SOME ANIMALS

**invertebrates**
(animals without backbones)

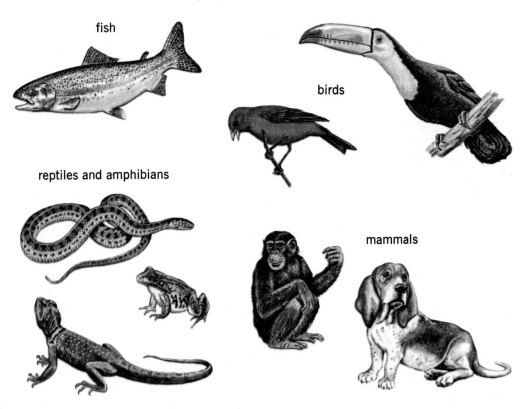

hydra

crustaceans

mollusks

insects

**vertebrates**
(animals with backbones)

fish

birds

reptiles and amphibians

mammals

## ■ CLASSIFICATION OF SOME PLANTS

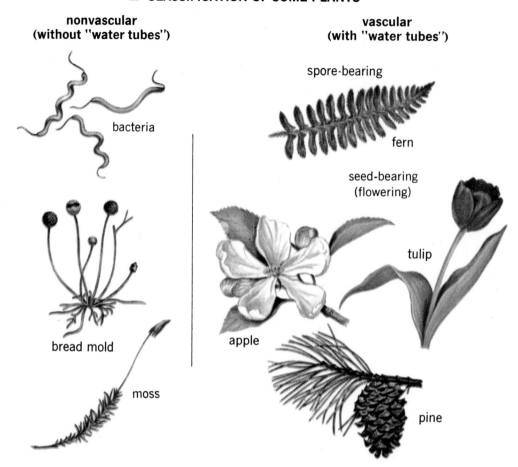

**nonvascular**
**(without "water tubes")**

bacteria

bread mold

moss

**vascular**
**(with "water tubes")**

spore-bearing

fern

seed-bearing
(flowering)

tulip

apple

pine

mals as worms, insects, and shellfish. Can likenesses also be found among invertebrates?

Look at the chart which shows one way that scientists classify plants. ■ Flowering plants seem much like each other; they have the same structure. If you look inside their stems and examine their flowers, you will find that flowering plants are related. Mosses, ferns, and molds are different from flowering plants. Do they have likenesses to each other? Careful examination will show that they do.

Plants and animals, then, can be grouped, or classified, according to their likenesses or relationships. Understanding their likenesses makes their differences easier to understand. In addition then to uncovering new knowledge, the scientist is constantly searching for relationships, the *concepts of science*.

Now focus your attention on one of the major concepts in this section: *Interdependence*. Everywhere you look, you can observe that living things are dependent on their environment.

Cattle cannot live without grass. Grasses are other living organisms. They depend on and use light energy from the sun, 93,000,000 miles away, to make their food. Both cattle and grasses depend on their environment for the matter and energy to keep them alive.

This is true for other living things as well. The robin feeds on the earthworm; the earthworm feeds on decayed leaves that are found in the soil. The decayed leaves were once the *green* leaves of the plants which got their energy from the sun. A mouse feeds on wheat; the wheat got its energy from the sun. In turn, the mouse may become food for a cat or a hawk. Each animal obtains matter and energy from its food. The carbon in food combines with oxygen from the air that an animal breathes in. The animal breathes out carbon dioxide.

There even seems to be a kind of order in the feeding habits of animals, as shown in the diagram of the pyramid of life. It is another way of showing how living things depend

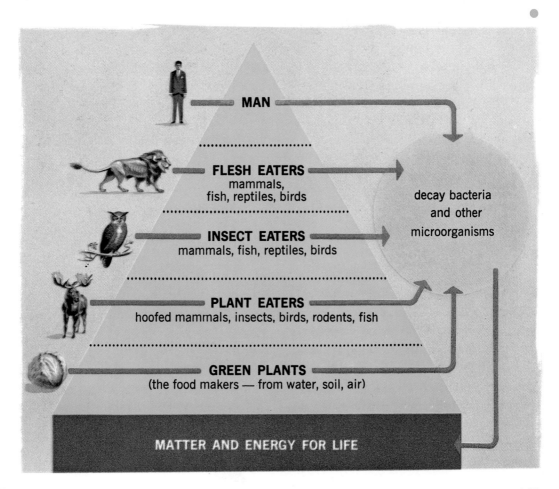

MAN

FLESH EATERS
mammals,
fish, reptiles, birds

decay bacteria
and other
microorganisms

INSECT EATERS
mammals, fish, reptiles, birds

PLANT EATERS
hoofed mammals, insects, birds, rodents, fish

GREEN PLANTS
(the food makers — from water, soil, air)

MATTER AND ENERGY FOR LIFE

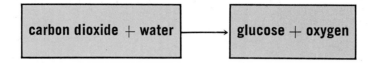

| carbon dioxide + water | → | glucose + oxygen |

upon one another. The animals near the top of the pyramid get most of their food by eating other living things which are lower down on the pyramid. This is not always true. Can you think of some exceptions?

A scientist once made the statement: "Every living thing is useful because it provides food for some other living thing." Can you explain what the scientist meant by that statement? Do you think he was correct? Does this statement apply to man as well? Under what conditions do you think it applies to man? Give reasons for your answer.

Animals get food and oxygen from plants. What do plants get from animals? They get carbon dioxide gas, which supplies some of the matter needed by green plants for the process of foodmaking. ■ In the green plant a chemical reaction takes place to produce glucose, a kind of sugar. In the reaction, oxygen is given off. A word equation for the reaction is shown above. ●

Plants cannot live without carbon dioxide; animals cannot live without oxygen. Neither plants nor animals can live without the sun's energy; it sustains all life.

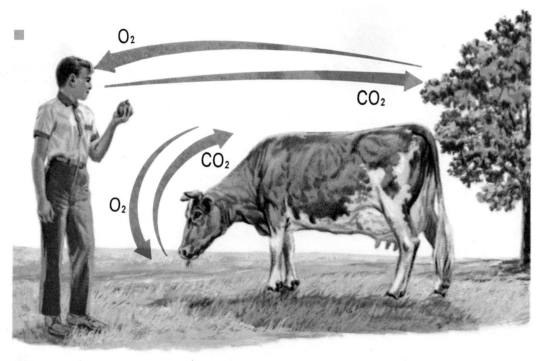

This brief survey about plants and animals points out one great concept: *Plants and animals are interdependent with one another and with their environment.* Both plants and animals get the matter and energy for growth *from* their environment. As plants die, they return matter and energy *to* their environment. So do animals. Plants and animals are constantly exchanging materials.

Man too depends on his environment and on plants and animals. If you visit a supermarket, you will see how dependent you are on plants and animals for food. As a matter of fact, you don't even need to go to the supermarket to find out. Just ask yourself this question: How many different kinds of plants and animals did I eat today? What products did I use that came from plants or animals?

Besides using plants and animals for food, man uses the hides of animals for shoes, the wood from trees to build houses, the fiber from the cotton plant to make his shirts, and the wool from sheep to make his suits and coats. Even the synthetic fibers that man uses are made from matter found in the environment.

Man is interdependent with his environment but that is not the whole story. Modern man can do much more; he uses science and technology to *change* his environment. Because of his brain man can investigate his environment and change it in such a way that men who lived 10,000 years ago would not recognize it.

Man, as a scientist, has learned *to observe* and *to investigate* his environment. He searches for relationships which help him *to understand* his environment. From the relationships he develops concepts which enable him *to change* his environment. He is always looking for new and better ideas to create new and better products.

For example, the concept that matter is made up of particles provides the basis for rearranging the particles (the atoms and molecules) to form new substances. Man takes from his environment

—iron ore and makes iron;

—iron and makes steel;

—coal, air, and water, and makes nylon.

What concepts does man use when he

—makes antibiotics to combat disease?

—makes rockets to conquer space?

—makes refrigerators, furnaces, and houses to combat weather?

—builds schools and writes books so that what he has learned is available to others?

Man is the dominant organism on the earth. He is learning how important the environment is to him. He is learning also, even if slowly, to use it wisely.

Science is a part of your world. Just as you have learned to use words and numbers, you are now learning to use the concepts and tools of science. Will you use them wisely?

# UNIT FOUR

# MACHINES
# IN ACTION

Look at the picture. It is a scene of a favorite sport of many people all over the world. Study the picture carefully and then see if you can answer this question: Would you say that work is being done? A scientist would, but he has a special reason for describing the action as work. Do you know the reason? How many things can you identify as machines? When you have finished studying this unit, look back to this introduction and once again list all the machines that you find in the picture. You may be surprised.

Machines are a part of our daily life. Today, we could not get along without them; but in the beginning, they all started as extensions of the human body—to assist in the action of the muscles in your arms and legs. For example:

Suppose you tried to lift your father with one hand. Could you do it? Perhaps you are not strong enough, but the picture on top of the next page shows how you might do it by using a machine to multiply the force of your muscles.

From the Stone Age cave dweller's first attempts to make tools to man's fantastic success in the technology of today, man has applied his mind to invention. This unit explains how man uses his brain and hands, his imagination and skill, to change his environment and let machines do his work.

**MULTIPLYING A FORCE**

# 1. Multiplying the Force of Your Muscles

Andrew had hurt his leg and had to use a wheelchair to move about. The door to his home, however, was two steps up from the sidewalk. Andrew's muscles could not supply enough force to lift him and the wheelchair up the steps together; so how could Andrew get up the steps in his wheelchair?

Andrew's father laid boards over the steps to make an **inclined plane** (in·klīnd′ plān).■ Then Andrew could move from the bottom of the first step into the house. Andrew was using a **simple machine,** an inclined plane, to help him get up the steps.

An inclined plane is a simple machine, but what makes an inclined plane a simple machine? The investigation on the opposite page will help make the concept of a simple machine easier to understand.

## An Explanation

When you lifted the skate straight up with your hand and arm alone, the entire weight of the skate was recorded by the spring balance. You were using only the force of the muscle in your arm to hold up the skate.

When you rolled the skate up the inclined plane, the plane itself supported part of the weight. The rest of the weight was still supported by your arm. The scale on the spring balance recorded less weight (force), because the inclined plane was helping your arm to support the skate. The inclined plane therefore increased the smaller force you were applying so

■

**154**

# AN INVESTIGATION into an Inclined Plane as a Simple Machine

**Needed:** a roller skate; some books; a spring balance; and a board about 2 feet long

Stack several books to about 1 foot high on a table. Slowly and smoothly, lift the skate with the spring balance from the table to the top of the pile of books. The indicator on the spring balance shows how much **force** is applied to lift the skate. ■

How much force does it take to lift the skate to the top of the books?

Now place the board so that it slopes upward from the top of the table to the top of the pile of books, making an inclined plane, as shown.● Slowly and smoothly pull the skate with the spring balance up the inclined plane to the top of the pile of books.

Does it feel as if you are using more force or less force than when you lifted the skate straight up to the top of the books?

The spring balance again shows how much force is needed to raise the skate to the top of the pile of books.

Now how much force does it take? Repeat the investigation to make sure your results are correct. Does it take more force, the same force, or less force to get the skate to the top of the pile of books, when using the inclined plane? How does this show that the inclined plane is a simple machine?

■

**Additional Investigation:** Make the inclined plane steeper by putting more books on the pile. How do you think this will affect the force needed to raise the skate to the top? With the spring balance, measure the force to see if you have predicted correctly.

●

← fulcrum

that you could lift the same weight as before. This is one of the things that simple machines can do; they can *multiply force*.

If you were to lift your father on a jack, the force of your muscles would be *multiplied*. It might take *four* of you to lift a grown man without the help of a simple machine. With a jack, however, one of you can do it alone. There are different kinds of jacks. Each one is made up of simple machines that can multiply force.

You could lift a grown man another way. Look at the picture. ■ The board acts as a simple machine called a **lever** (lev′ər). The log underneath the board is called a **fulcrum** (fŏŏl′-krəm). If you push the lever down on one side of the fulcrum, the other side goes up. ● ▲ The fulcrum is the support on which a lever rests and turns. Find out more about a lever as a simple machine by doing the investigation on the opposite page.

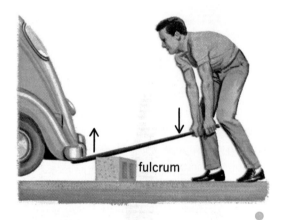

fulcrum

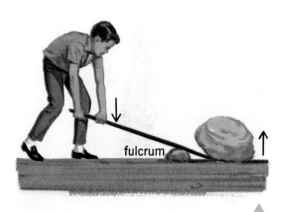

fulcrum

156

# AN INVESTIGATION into Another Simple Machine, a Lever

**Needed:** several books; a 12-inch ruler; the back of a chair; a piece of string; and a spring balance

Lift a book using the spring balance, as shown in the picture.■ How much force must you apply to lift the book?

Now use the ruler as a lever with the back of the chair being used as the fulcrum. Fasten the spring balance to the ruler, as shown, and lift the book.● What does the spring balance read? Are you now applying a smaller force to lift the same book?

Tie another book to the first one, and lift the two books.▲ Does the lever help you to multiply your force? One person found that the spring balance read about the same when he lifted two books with the lever as when he lifted just one book without the lever. The force of his muscles was doubled because of the action of the lever.

**Additional Investigation:** Try using the lever to lift several different known weights. For instance, try lifting a weight of 1 pound, 2 pounds, or even 10 pounds. Make a chart and record the amount of force needed to lift each weight. Be sure to keep the fulcrum in the same place.

Before you do the investigation, predict how many times the lever will multiply the force.

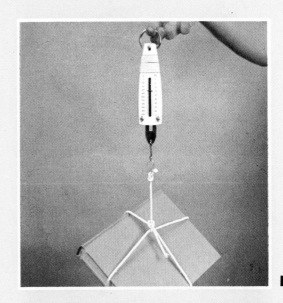

■

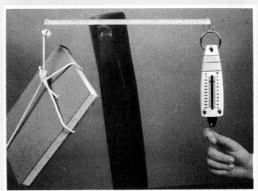

●

▲

157

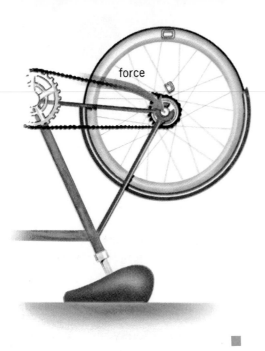

force

## The Ways of a Simple Machine

A lever is a simple machine; so is an inclined plane. *Both can increase or multiply force;* but some simple machines can be used for other purposes. Let us study two more simple machines. One of them is the rear wheel of a bicycle or automobile; the other is the pulley used on a flagpole.

Turn a bicycle upside down and examine the rear wheel. ■ It is fastened to a small shaft called an axle. Together they make another type of simple machine called a **wheel and axle.** Turn the pedals slowly, and watch the wheel as it moves. Can you see where the force is being applied to the wheel? Look at the picture. You will see that the force coming from the drive chain is being applied to the axle. Turn the pedals once again. Be sure you know where the force is being applied.

Now place a sticker or a piece of tape on one of the spokes near the axle, and another sticker on the tire at the wheel's outer edge, as shown in the illustration. Turn the wheel again and watch carefully to see which sticker is moving faster, the one nearer the axle or the one on the edge of the wheel. If you are not sure, ask yourself which sticker is moving a greater distance. The sticker on the edge of the wheel moves at a greater speed than the one near the center because it covers more distance in the same amount of time. A simple machine such as the wheel and axle, then, can be used to *multiply speed.*

There is another kind of machine that you have probably seen often, even though you may not have thought of it as a simple machine. Watch a flag being raised. How is it done?

At the top of the flagpole, there is a kind of grooved wheel with a rope around it called a **pulley.** ● The type used on a flagpole is a **fixed pulley,** because it is fastened to the top of the pole. It is not like the wheels of a bicycle, which take you from place to place. Without the help of the pulley and the rope it would be difficult to raise the flag to the top of the pole. It would be necessary for someone to climb the pole each day.

With a pulley, the flag goes up, as the rope is pulled down. The fixed pulley, then, is a simple machine which *changes the direction of a force.*

Look at the picture. The force is in a downward direction while the flag (the load) is going up.

Fixed pulleys are used for many purposes. They are used to hoist a load aboard a large ship, to raise or open the curtain on a stage, and in some schools, to open and close the high windows of the auditorium or gymnasium. Can you think of any other uses for which fixed pulleys may be used about your school or home? Wherever a single fixed pulley is used, the direction of the force is changed by the pulley. Changing direction is another possible use for a simple machine.

Now it would be useful to review what you have learned about the use of simple machines.

*Simple machines can increase or multiply a force.* You can lift a heavier weight with a smaller force. A lever and an inclined plane are good examples of machines that multiply force. What examples of levers or inclined planes have you used?

*Simple machines can increase or multiply speed.* Drive wheels on bicycles and automobiles are good examples of machines that multiply speed. In cars, trucks, locomotives, and buses, a force from the engine is applied to an axle and thereby turns a wheel. In each of these vehicles the wheel and axle is used to multiply speed.

*Simple machines can change the direction of a force.* A fixed pulley is a good example of this kind of machine.

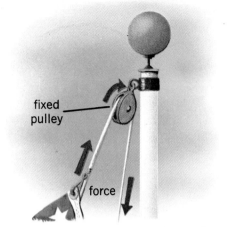

fixed pulley

force

You have found out, then, that a simple machine is a tool which can *multiply a force, multiply speed,* and *change the direction of a force.*

You must have used at least one simple machine today. Perhaps it was a lever, an inclined plane, a wheel and axle, or maybe it was a pulley.

Have you used a doorknob? a faucet? some scissors? shop tools? steps? a window shade? a light switch? a radio knob? or even your arms and legs? Do any of these contain simple machines? Yes, they all do, but this is just the beginning.

You probably realize by now that simple machines can also be found in larger, more complicated machines, such as the automobile or bicycle. On the automobile, for example, the door handles, accelerator pedal, window cranks, gear shift, and directional signal switch are all forms of simple machines. As you read on, you will see why.

But first, what about your bicycle? How many simple machines does it contain? You already know about the wheels. What about the pedals? or the handlebar?

**A.** Study the statements below and choose the correct responses. They will help you fix in mind the concepts of this section.

**1.** A simple machine can
    a. multiply a force            b. make a force

**2.** A single fixed pulley is a simple machine that can do which one of these things:
    a. multiply force
    b. move from place to place
    c. change the direction of a force

**3.** The rear wheel of a bicycle is a simple machine that can do which two of these three things:
    a. multiply a force
    b. multiply speed
    c. move from place to place

**B.** Write a paragraph or two on this topic: How Can Simple Machines Help Us to Do Work?

**1.** In your home, you probably have either window shades or venetian blinds. Can you think of any simple machines that would be used with either? A careful investigation should give you a clue.

**2.** What kind of machine is being used in the picture? ■

Set up an inclined plane, as you did in the investigation on page 155; but move the board so that about one-fourth of it is sticking up over the books.

Will you need to apply more force to pull the skate up the board in this new position?

## 2. The Levers You Use

Today, you may have used a pair of scissors, pried open a can with a screwdriver, or opened a big packing box with a crowbar. You may have cracked a nut or pruned a branch from a tree.

If you have ever pried the lid from a paint can with a screwdriver, you probably gave no thought to the matter. You just put one end of the screwdriver under the lid, pushed down on the other end, and up came the lid. Have you ever wondered why you used the screwdriver in the first place? Think about it now and see if you know the advantage in using one.

In each case, you would have used a lever. A lever is an important simple machine. How you use it is even more important. Knowing where to put the fulcrum is most important of all.

Look at the diagram below. ● Notice the position of the fulcrum. The distance from the **effort** to the fulcrum is much greater than the distance from the fulcrum to the **load.** What is the advantage of this arrangement? Suppose the load and effort were reversed. Do you know any situations in which it would be an advantage to have the effort nearer the fulcrum?

It is easy to recognize that a see-saw is a kind of lever. The smaller child is using one to help him lift the larger boy. ▲ If he is to succeed, where should the fulcrum be placed? Where in the pictures is the effort being applied? Which of the boys is the load?

We live with and use many kinds of levers every day and there are basic principles or rules that all levers follow. For instance, there are only three things to consider—the load, the effort, and the fulcrum, and there are only three different ways they can be arranged. To understand why this is true, start with the investigation on the next page. From there you can look next at all levers.

# AN INVESTIGATION into the Location of the Fulcrum

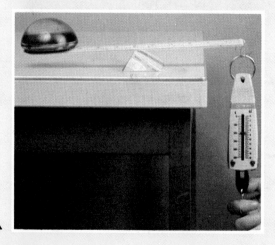

**Needed:** a weight to be lifted (a paper-weight will do); a ruler or yardstick; a support to act as a fulcrum; and a spring balance

Since there are so many levers everywhere, you can investigate them either at home or at school.

Make a fulcrum by cutting a small box top diagonally, as shown in the picture; use a ruler or yardstick as the lever itself.

Place the weight to be lifted on the lever with the fulcrum placed first in the position shown. ■ Notice that the fulcrum is near the point where you apply the force, as you pull down on the ruler (the lever). Lift the weight on the lever, using the spring balance, as shown. Then find out what the difference will be if the fulcrum is placed somewhere else. Try placing the fulcrum under the ruler in a position near the object to be lifted. ● The object to be lifted by the lever is called the load. Now lift the load again. Are the results the same as they were the first time? Are they the same as those in the picture? How do you account for the difference?

Try lifting the load with the fulcrum placed near the middle of the lever. ▲ What are your results?

In which of the positions of the fulcrum did it take the least effort to lift the load?

## A Problem—Finding the Fulcrum

Scientists use a special name for the force applied to a simple machine; it is called the **effort.** The place where you push or pull on a lever is the point where the effort is applied.

A load can be moved most easily when the fulcrum is *farthest* from the place where the effort is applied. A lever set up this way is the best for multiplying a force.

Examine two types of pruning shears, one with long handles, the other with short handles. Examine different kinds of scissors. In what ways are they different? Why do you think they are different? How are shears and scissors alike? Shears and scissors contain two levers that are fastened together and share a single fulcrum. Which kind of shears would be best for cutting a thick twig, the one with long handles or the one with short handles? Can you explain your answer in terms of levers?

Clearly a lever can be very useful to us if we know where to place the fulcrum and where to apply the effort. Study each one of the levers in the picture, and for each one find the following three things: ■

a. the load
b. the fulcrum
c. the best point to apply effort

**163**

**A.** Study the statements below and choose the correct responses. They will help you fix in mind the concepts of this section.

**1.** One of the following is not likely to be used as a lever. It is a

a. seesaw          b. screw          c. crowbar

**2.** A load can be moved most easily when the fulcrum is located at a certain point in relation to where the effort is applied. That point is

a. nearest to the effort      b. farthest from the effort

**3.** Where should the fulcrum be placed for ease in lifting the load in the picture? ■ How does the position of the fulcrum affect the usefulness of a lever?

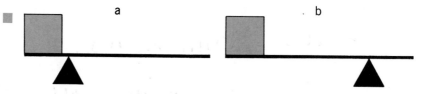

**B.** Write a paragraph or two on this topic: How Levers Help to Do Work.

**A. Try This Investigation**

Set up a lever like the one shown in the diagram. ● You will need a pint milk carton, some sand or soil, a wide ruler to be used as a lever, a spring balance, and perhaps a wooden block as the fulcrum. Use the carton filled with sand as your load. You can apply an effort to lift the load by pulling down on the lever.

If you change the weight of the load by adding or pouring out sand, there will also be a change in the amount of effort you have to use.

Try to find out whether the change in effort corresponds in any way to the change in load. You can weigh the load each time by using your spring balance. Write down your results after each trial.

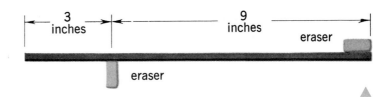

|← 3 inches →|← ——— 9 inches ——— →|
eraser

eraser

## B. Try This Investigation

Make a catapult (kat′ə·pult) with a ruler and two erasers. ▲
When you pound your fist down on the short end of the lever,
the load shoots up with great speed. ◆ Can you explain why?
Which force do you think is greater, the effort or the load?

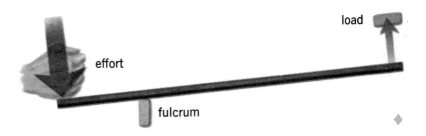

effort

load

fulcrum

## 3. Uses of Pulleys

Perhaps your classroom has shades which can be pulled up and down with a cord or it may have venetian blinds. You may have wondered how they are moved up or down. If you could look inside the box at the top of the blinds, you would find a pulley. ★

If you have ever lived on a farm or visited one you may have seen pulleys being used. Imagine carrying a large

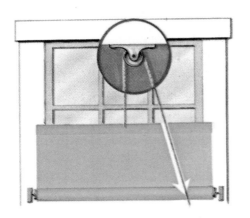

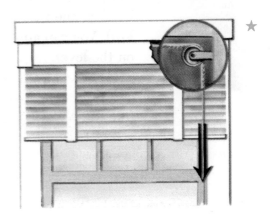

bag of feed up a ladder into the loft. It would be difficult to do without help, and the best help is from a machine.

Bags of feed are often lifted as shown in the picture. ■ The load moves *up* as the effort is applied *downward*. The effort applied must be as great as the weight of the feed. The fixed pulley changes *only* the direction of the effort, making it more convenient for the person who is doing the work. It does not multiply the effort he applies.

Fixed pulleys make it more convenient to do many tasks. You can use them to help hang out the wash or to lift the sail on a sailboat. A fixed pulley changes the direction of the pull; but this is not all that pulleys can do. The investigation on the opposite page shows more about the uses of pulleys.

### Lifting an Iron Beam or Piano

It is not easy to lift a piano to the top floor of a building, but there are several ways that it can be done. The piano can be carried up in an elevator, if the elevator is large enough; or it can be lifted up with a combination of fixed and movable pulleys. When fixed and movable pulleys are used together, the system is called a **block and tackle.** What is the advantage of combining pulleys in this way? A single fixed pulley only changes the direction of the effort. What does a movable pulley do? Investigate to find out the purpose of a block and tackle.

# AN INVESTIGATION into the Use of a Pulley

**Needed:** some heavy cord; several bricks; some small pulleys

Tie a heavy cord around a brick, and lift it with one finger. It is not very easy to do. *Be careful not to lift the brick directly above anyone's feet, in case it should fall.* The cord will probably squeeze your finger.

Obtain some small pulleys or make them out of empty thread spools, wire, and nails. Fasten one of the pulleys to a solid support, such as an overhead bar, or to a hook on the wall. Place the string over the pulley and lift the brick. ■ Is it easier this way? Or is it really true that a fixed pulley only changes the direction of a force?

Another type of pulley you can try is called a **movable pulley.** Attach a movable pulley, like the one shown in the picture, to your load. ● Tie one end of the cord to the fixed support and lift the same load by pulling up on the other end of the string. Does lifting the brick seem any easier now? Is a movable pulley another simple machine that can multiply the effort you apply?

**Additional Investigation:** Repeat the investigation above, but this time use a smaller weight and a spring balance to measure the effort. How many times does the movable pulley multiply the effort?

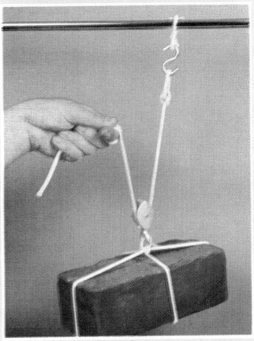

Examine the block and tackle in the picture.■ A block consists of a pulley wheel or of several pulley wheels in a frame. Each of the blocks shown in the illustration contains two pulley wheels. Notice that one block is fixed, while the other is movable. A block and tackle is usually a pair of pulley blocks.

The number of lines running through the pulleys is very important. In the block and tackle shown in the illustration there are four such lines. It is possible for one man to lift a heavy beam with a block and tackle of this type. How can he do it? You can find out by doing the investigation on the opposite page. It shows

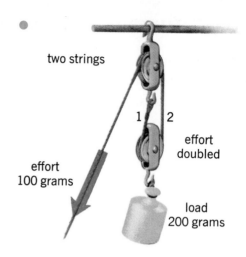

two strings

effort
100 grams

1  2

effort
doubled

load
200 grams

how to make and use a small model of the larger block and tackle used by workmen.

## An Explanation

What is the difference between the two pulley systems shown on this page? Study them carefully. Observe that one has two strings supporting the movable pulley; the other has four.

With two strings, an effort of only 100 grams was applied to lift a load of 200 grams.● Each string supported 100 grams, or one-half the load of 200 grams. Therefore with two strings, you could lift 200 grams ($2 \times 100$) with only 100 grams of effort. The third string coming off the fixed pulley merely changed the direction of the effort.

With four strings supporting the movable pulley block, an effort of only 50 grams can be applied to lift a load of 200 grams. Each string supports a weight of 50 grams. The fifth string changes the direction. ■

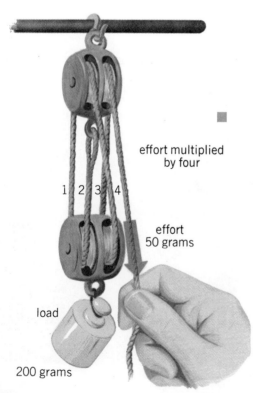

effort multiplied
by four

1  2  3  4

effort
50 grams

load

200 grams

# AN INVESTIGATION into Using a Block and Tackle

**Needed:** a set of small weights; a spring balance; two single and two double pulley blocks; several feet of string

If you cannot obtain a set of small weights, you can make your own by pouring different amounts of sand into several small jars or plastic bags. Weigh them with your spring balance, and label each one with its correct weight. ■ The group of students that did this investigation weighed their sand in **grams,** which is the basic unit of weight in the **metric system** (454 grams are equal to one pound). You may use the system you prefer, the English or the metric.

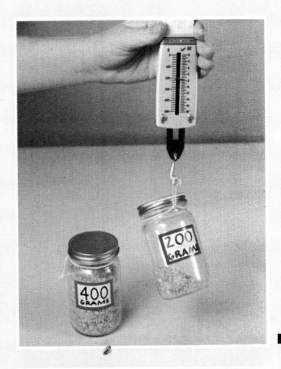

Set up the two single pulley blocks, as shown on the opposite page. This makes a block and tackle with one fixed pulley and one movable pulley.

How many grams of effort are needed to lift a 200-gram load with this block and tackle?

Now set up the double pulley blocks, as shown.● The block and tackle in the picture is a model of the one the worker used to lift the steel beam. Lift the same 200-gram load with the double pulleys. How many grams of effort do you need now? (The students found they needed only 50 grams.) Why is less effort needed with the second pulley than with the first? After all, the load is the same in each case. What makes the difference?

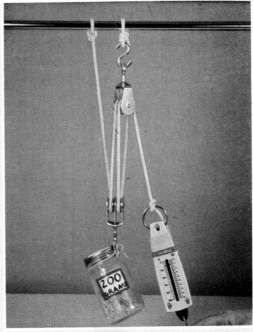

Study the results of your investigation once again and see if you can answer this question: Which of these three statements is correct?

1. The fewer the number of strings used, the greater must be the effort applied.

2. The fewer the number of strings lifting the load, the more the effort is multiplied.

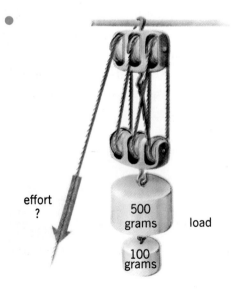

3. The greater the number of strings lifting the load, the more the effort is multiplied.

Which of these is true? The group of students performing the investigation marked 1 and 3. Do you agree?

## A Problem

You might see a block and tackle like that in the picture almost any place where construction is going on. Study the block and tackle shown lifting the beam. ■ How many ropes are between the pulleys? If the beam weighs 1,000 pounds, how many pounds of effort must be applied to lift the beam?

Since the four ropes together support a load of 1,000 pounds, each rope, by itself, supports 250 pounds, or one-fourth of the load. A force of 250 pounds then could be used to lift the weight. The simple machine therefore multiplied the effort by 4 (250 pounds × 4 = 1,000 pounds.)

Here is a problem which you can now figure out for yourself. See if you can find out why the effort in the picture should be 100 grams. ● Ask yourself these questions:

What is the load?
(500 grams + 100 grams = 600 grams)

How many ropes support the load?
(six ropes)

What is the effort? Why?

How many times did the machine multiply the effort?

**A.** Study the statements below and choose the correct responses. They will help you fix in mind the concepts of this section.

All of the statements below are made about pulleys.

**1.** When the number of strings lifting a load is decreased, the load is

    a. lifted more easily          b. harder to lift

**2.** When the number of strings lifting the same load is increased, the effort needed is

    a. less                 b. greater

**3.** To lift a greater load with the same amount of effort, we would

    a. increase the number          b. decrease the number
         of strings                    of strings

**B.** Write a paragraph or two on this topic: Pulleys.

**A.** Using a weight, a spring balance, and pulleys, like those in the investigation on page 169, see if you can find the answer to this question:

What distance must you pull the string as you lift a load with a block and tackle?

You can start with a block and tackle with four strings to lift the load. Measure the length of string you must pull in order to raise the load a distance of 1 foot.

Then use a block and tackle with two strings between the pulleys. Again lift the weight 1 foot. What length of string must you pull to lift the load now?

What is your conclusion?

**B. In the Library**

$$1 \text{ pound} = 454 \text{ grams}$$
$$? \quad = 1{,}000 \text{ grams (1 kilogram)}$$

Finish the table. Then consult a dictionary or encyclopedia to find out about the metric system.

## 4. Other Machines You Use

Do you recognize a simple machine in the picture below? ■ Can you tell what kind it is?

First imagine a road going up a hill. It is the same as the ramp that Andrew's father built for him, so that he could wheel the chair up into the house with less effort. Since a road up a hill is really an inclined plane, part of the weight of the object being moved up the hill will be supported by the sloping road.

A road going up a hill multiplies the effort applied to move the load to the top of the hill. The principle is the same as that found in the investigation on page 155.

The ramp shown in the picture below winds around and around. It goes up and around to the observation tower. The winding ramp is an in-clined plane also. It is a winding, or spiral, inclined plane. A road winding up the side of a mountain is also.

It is possible for heavy-duty trucks to move up the side of a mountain on a winding road. The more times the road winds around the mountain, the more gradual is the slope, or incline. The gentler the slope, the less effort it takes to get up the mountain. But, remember one thing, the distance that the truck travels is increased as the effort is decreased. This is an important principle of simple machines. What other kinds of winding inclined planes do you know about?

There is another kind of winding inclined plane that is used very often in your home. Can you guess what it is? It is the screw. You can find out more about the screw as a simple machine by doing the investigation on the opposite page.

# AN INVESTIGATION into a Winding Inclined Plane

**Needed:** a sheet of paper; a pair of scissors; a pencil; a piece of wood; a screw; a screwdriver

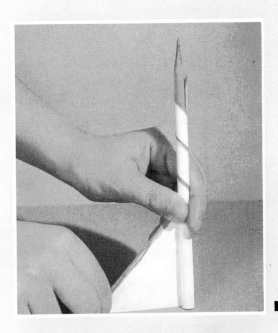

Cut an inclined plane out of paper. Make it 12 inches long and 6 inches high (as in the photograph) and wind it around a pencil. ■ Does it remind you of the **threads** on a screw?

Examine a screw closely, perhaps with a magnifying glass. ● Trace the winding plane around the screw and up to the pointed tip.

Turn the screw into a piece of wood with a screwdriver. When the screw is half way into the wood, stop turning and try to push it in the rest of the way with the screwdriver. Is it easier to push the screw straight in or is it easier to turn the screw into the wood? When the screw is turned, its point is pushed ahead with greater force.

Has the turning screw helped to increase the force of your wrist? The screw is another simple machine that can multiply a force.

Is the screwdriver also a simple machine? If so, what kind?

Fasten two pieces of wood together with a screw and then try to pry them apart. You will probably find this difficult to do, much more so than if the pieces were held together only by a nail. The screw multiplies the force which binds the pieces of wood together.

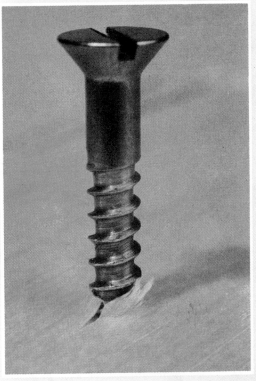

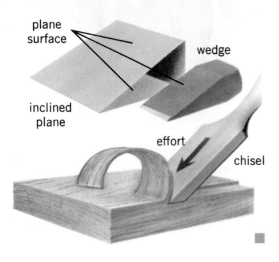

plane surface

wedge

inclined plane

effort

chisel

## Still Another Simple Machine

An inclined plane slants up from a point. Cut two long planes, such as those shown in the diagram, and put them together. ■ By doing so, you have made another form of inclined plane called a **wedge.**

If you have a chisel or a screwdriver, look at the tip where two plane surfaces come together, forming a wedge. When a chisel is forced into a piece of wood, its sharp edge goes between the grains of wood easily and pries the wood apart.

Once the sharp edge of a wedge is forced into any object, it can split the object apart.

As the effort moves the wedge forward it pushes sideways against the grain of the wood. This happens because the greater thickness of the wedge exerts greater force as it moves into the grain. The wedge therefore changes the direction of motion. In what other way does the wedge act as a simple machine? Does it multiply effort? Does it multiply speed?

A wedge greatly multiplies force. It can do work that might be impossible if you used only your muscle. A wedge is one more simple machine which multiplies force.

What other wedges have you used? Have you used a hatchet to split wood? A snowplow is also a wedge, as is a plow that turns over the soil.

If you look about your home, you should find many kinds of inclined planes. How about the knives in the kitchen? Are they inclined planes?

Can you think of a wedge that is a different shape? Some wedges do not have a straight edge at all. Instead they are round and have a sharp point. Think of a nail, for example. Does it act like a wedge? When a nail is forced into a piece of wood, the effort (which is forward) causes the nail to push sideways, separating the wood so it can enter.

There are many other round wedges. A needle is a round wedge, is it not? What about a pin, or a knitting needle, or a bullet, or the nose cone of a rocket? Perhaps you can think of some more.

Since round wedges are very much like screws, many people have trouble telling them apart. How is a round wedge different from a screw? Think about the way in which the effort is applied. A nail, or round wedge, is pushed forward into a piece of wood. The direction of the effort is straight and forward. A screw, remember, is turned. The effort rotates the screw as it moves forward into the wood.

## Doorknobs as Simple Machines

Every time you open a door you use a simple machine. Remove the knob from a door, as shown in the picture, and try to open the door. ● It is not easy to turn the axle without the help of the knob.

The doorknob is another example of a wheel and axle. ● The knob, really a kind of wheel, is attached to a rod or axle. When you turn the wheel fixed to the axle, you increase (or multiply) your effort greatly. The wheel and axle is a simple machine that multiplies effort when the effort is applied to the wheel. For instance, the steering wheel of an automobile is a wheel-and-axle machine. It multiplies the driver's effort so much that he can turn a car or a huge truck with very little effort.

The bicycle wheel, discussed on page 158, is also a wheel and axle; but it is not used to multiply effort as is the doorknob or steering wheel. Instead, it multiplies speed. How is the bicycle wheel different? Why does it multiply speed rather than effort? Where is the effort applied?

wheel

wheel

axle

The crank on a pencil sharpener is also considered a wheel and axle; it can also multiply effort. Have you noticed that whenever you turn the crank around completely, it really outlines the shape of a wheel?

Without the machine, you might find it just as inconvenient to sharpen a pencil as to open a door.

The wheel and axle has many uses. Some examples are shown in the picture. ▲ Look at them carefully. Which are used to multiply force? Which are used to multiply speed?

▲

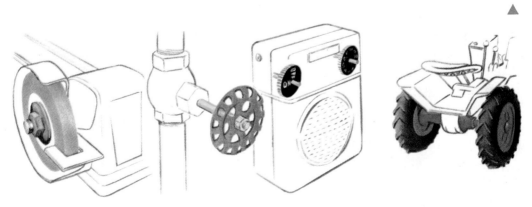

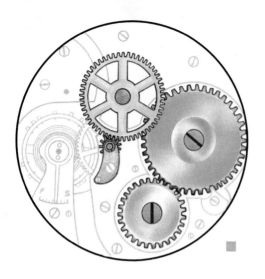

## The Uses of Gears

A special form of the wheel and axle can be found inside of a watch. ■ It is the toothed wheel, commonly called a **gear** wheel. The teeth on a gear wheel make it possible for one wheel to turn another.

Study the picture to see how gear wheels can multiply speed. ● The larger gear, with 24 teeth, turns a smaller wheel which has only 12 teeth, or only half as many. The teeth of the larger gear fit into the teeth of the smaller gear, so that when the larger gear turns, the smaller gear must turn as well. For each turn of the larger gear wheel, the smaller gear wheel must turn *two* times, so the smaller gear turns *twice* as fast.

Examine an eggbeater by turning the handle around once, slowly. ▲ How many times does the beater turn? Ask two classmates to count the number of turns that the beater makes while you count how many times you turn the handle. You may find that the beater makes about four turns while the handle is turned only once. Since the beaters turn more often than the handle in the same time, they are moving at a greater speed.

Count the teeth on each of the gear wheels of the eggbeater. ◆ Suppose the larger wheel has 40 teeth, and the smaller wheel has 10 teeth, or one-fourth the number of the teeth on the larger wheel. For each turn of the larger gear, how many times would the smaller gear turn? Would the answer be four?

The smaller gear turns the beater. Why does the beater turn four times faster than the handle? Do all eggbeaters have the same gear ratio?

Gears are machines that can multiply speed, but they can be used in other ways, too. The picture shows a model of a hand-operated crane. ★ When a force is applied to the smaller wheel, the larger wheel is able to lift a greater load. Gear wheels, then, can also be used to multiply effort. They are a special kind of wheel and axle. Can they also be used to change the direction of a force?

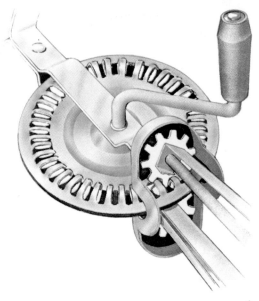

## Compound Machines

Many machines are made up of more than one kind of simple machine. Recall that the kinds we have been studying are: lever, pulley, wheel and axle, inclined plane, wedge, and screw. Machines containing more than one kind of simple machine are called **compound machines.**

A pair of scissors is a compound machine. It has two levers fastened together at the fulcrum, and the cutting edge on each of the blades is a wedge. Therefore all scissors, shears, and the like, are compound machines containing levers and wedges. Both the lever and the wedge are simple machines which may multiply effort.

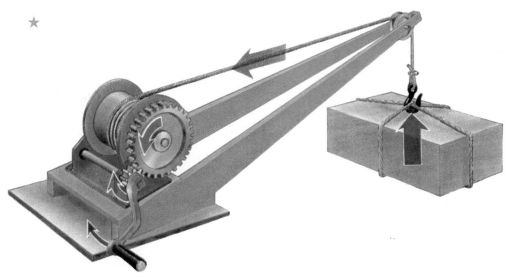

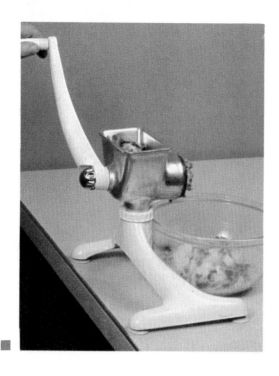 

Another compound machine is the meat grinder. The handle of a meat grinder is really part of a wheel and axle. ■ Look inside and you will find that the handle is attached to a kind of screw.● The meat grinder, then, contains a wheel and axle that turns a screw.

Below is a list of the six basic simple machines that can be combined to form compound machines. Which of them are combined in a jack?

lever                  inclined plane
pulley                 wedge
wheel and axle    screw

BEFORE YOU GO ON A. Study the statements below and choose the correct responses. They will help you fix in mind the concepts of this section.

1. Two of the following which act like an inclined plane are a

a. steep road                    c. nutcracker
b. ramp

2. One of the following contains a winding inclined plane. It is a

a. hammer                         b. meat grinder

**3.** A wedge acts like
a. a pulley                 c. a lever
b. an inclined plane

**4.** Two of these which have gears as part of them are
a. a bicycle          c. a doorknob
b. an eggbeater

**B.** Write a paragraph or two on this topic: The Uses of Gears.

USING WHAT
YOU KNOW
**1.** If you wanted to bind two pieces of wood together tightly, you would use a
a. nail                b. screw
Why?

**2.** Which of these have wedges as part of them?
a. screw          d. knife
b. chisel         e. axe
c. pole          f. nail

ON YOUR OWN
**In the Laboratory**

Cut two gears out of cardboard which have the same number of teeth as those shown in the picture. ▲ Be certain to fix the gears so that the teeth fit each other (that is, so that they mesh).

Suppose the smaller of the gears is connected to an axle that is connected to a wheel, as shown in the picture. Then answer the following questions:

**1.** For each complete movement of the larger gear, how many times does the smaller gear move?

**2.** If the small gear were made even smaller, would the wheel attached to it move faster or slower? Why?

**3.** Make several other combinations of gear wheels, for example, one that multiplies speed by 3, or multiplies force by $2\frac{1}{2}$.

# 5. A Resisting Force

Do you live in a part of the country where you can ice-skate? If so, you may have sometimes wished that the ice were not so smooth, so that you could glide more slowly. Why do you glide so smoothly on ice?

The sharp edges of the skate blade are really wedges, simple machines. This kind of machine bites into the ice and helps to keep you from skidding sideways, yet a push sends you forward. If you were to spread sand on the ice, what would be the action of the sand? The investigation on the opposite page will give you some clues.

## The Force of Friction

Why is it harder to pull the block over the rough surface of the sandpaper? Each time you pull the piece of wood across the table, your work is made harder by **friction.** Friction is a force that resists motion. It is caused by two surfaces rubbing against each other. *The amount of friction depends on the types of surfaces that are rubbing against each other.* Since the surface of the sandpaper is rougher than the surface of the tabletop, it causes more friction. It is harder to pull the piece of wood across the sandpaper because the force of friction is greater.

Why is it harder to pull two blocks across the top of the table than to pull just one? It takes more force because the extra weight makes the bottom piece of wood press harder against the surface of the table. The force of friction is greater.

Why does the can move farther when it is rolling than when it is sliding? It moves farther because there is less friction to slow it down. Remember, friction is caused by two surfaces rubbing against each other. When surfaces are rolling they do not rub against each other as much. Let us see why.

Place a finger into the open end of a juice can (be sure there are no sharp edges) and rest it gently on the palm of your hand. Move the hand under the can forward, as shown. ■ Look at the two touching surfaces. Notice that the surface of the can moves in the same direction as the surface of your hand. Now move the hand under the can back toward you. The surface of the can moves with your hand. The surface of the can always moves in the same direction as the surface of your hand. The surfaces are *moving with* each other more than they are *rubbing against* each other.

This is similar to what happened when the can rolled along the tabletop. There is less friction because

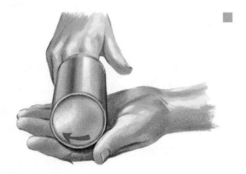

# AN INVESTIGATION into the Force of Friction

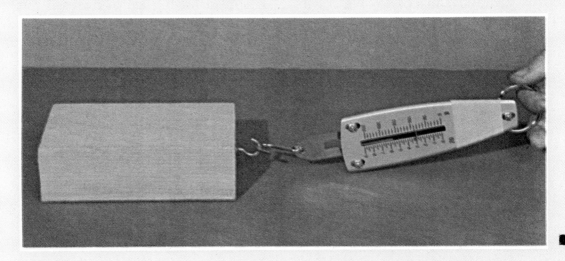

**Needed:** a piece of wood; a spring balance; several sheets of sandpaper; some wax paper; machine oil; a sheet of aluminum foil; an empty juice can

Pull a piece of wood across the top of a table with a spring balance, as shown. ■ What does the scale read?

Now place another piece of wood on top of the first and pull both pieces across with the spring balance. What does the scale read now? Is a greater force needed? Why?

Place several sheets of sandpaper on the table, with the rough surface up. Pull the piece of wood across the sandpaper. What does the scale read?

Now, put some wax paper or a sheet of aluminum foil on the table. Spread some oil on the paper or on the aluminum foil. Pull the single piece of wood across again. Does this take more or less force than at first?

Place an empty tin can upright on the tabletop. A juice can will be fine. Give it a push. How far does it slide? Turn it on its side and push it again, so that it rolls across the tabletop. Does the can go farther when it is rolling than it did when it was sliding? Why?

**Additional Investigation:** A transfer of energy takes place as a result of friction. Several kinds of energy, such as heat energy, light energy, and sound energy can result from the mechanical energy involved in friction.

Try rubbing your hands together rapidly. What kind of energy results? What kind of energy results from rubbing a violin bow against the strings or by striking a piece of flint against a steel file?

there is less rubbing of the two surfaces against each other. Friction can be greatly reduced by using rollers.

One of man's inventions takes advantage of a rolling surface to reduce friction. Some people think it is man's greatest invention. It is the wheel, of course! Friction increases the amount of effort needed, but the wheel reduces friction.

Strangely enough, we sometimes do not want to reduce friction. There are even times when we want to increase it. Often we do not want wheels to move easily. Can you think of such a case?

Imagine an icy road. What can be done to make it less hazardous? Sand is spread on the ice to increase the friction as wheels press on the road. Sometimes it is important to increase friction to prevent accidents.

What happens when ice freezes on a sidewalk? Sand and gravel are spread to increase friction; otherwise, someone may slip and get hurt when he falls. What happens when one walks on a waxed floor? A waxed floor decreases friction. A heavy rug on a waxed floor increases friction.

Friction retards motion; in so doing, it sometimes saves lives.

BEFORE YOU GO ON **A.** Study the statements below and choose the correct responses. They will help you fix in mind the concepts of this section.

**1.** Of the following two surfaces, the one which increases friction is a

a. wet road               b. dry road

**2.** Of the two surfaces named below, the one which decreases friction is a

a. linoleum floor         b. cement floor

**3.** Which of the three things listed below would reduce friction most on a dry road?

a. a sled                 c. a flat board
b. a wagon

**4.** The friction produced by pulling a wooden box across a floor is greater when the box is

a. full                   b. empty

**B.** Write a paragraph or two on this topic: The Importance of Friction.

Some colonists wanted to move some large logs. They had no wagons or animals. They had the large logs (which could be lifted only with great difficulty), and they also had some small logs.

Invent a way the large logs could be moved with the help of the small logs, if only for a short distance.

**In the Classroom or Laboratory**

**A.** You can show (as in the investigation on page 181) that force is needed to overcome the force of friction.

**B.** Plan a demonstration to show others in the class that friction between two surfaces produces heat. Then determine a way to show that the greater the friction between two surfaces, the greater is the heat produced.

## 6. Is More Work Done?

Can a simple machine help you to do more work? This is a very important question. What is your answer now, before reading ahead?

Recall that simple machines may be used to multiply force. They can also multiply speed or change the direction of a force. From this you might reason that a simple machine can decrease the amount of work to be done. Before you decide, you will need to do some more investigating.

### A New Concept of Work

Pick up a book from the table and lift it about a foot or more.■ The scientist would say you have done some **work.** You have lifted an object through a distance. If you push the book across the table, you have also done work. *You have moved an object through a distance.*

When you push a lawn mower, you are doing work. When you walk, you are still doing work. When you lift anything or move anything, you are doing work.

Look up the word "work" in the dictionary. You will find many meanings listed for this important word. A scientist, however, is very careful to use a word in *one* way only. He must be sure that when he uses the

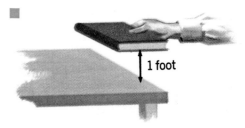

1 foot

word, it will mean the same thing to any other scientist, anywhere in the world. To the scientist, then, the word "work" means only one thing. Its meaning remains the same whether the scientist is German, French, Russian, Italian, or Rhodesian.

Suppose you were to push on the wall of the classroom or of your home. ■ Even if you pushed as hard as you could, and even though pushing against the wall might have made you very tired, the wall would not budge. A scientist would say you have done no work at all.

In order to do work, *you must move an object through a distance.* ●

If the object does not move, no matter how much force you use on it, you are not doing work. The object must move if work is done.

Recall that scientists deal with both concepts and tools. All concepts in science must be clearly stated and understood if they are to be used.

The scientist's concept of work is: *When an object is moved through a distance, work is done.* The scientist then uses the term "work" only as it applies to moving objects

Man is able to do many things with the use of simple machines that he could not do without them. He can substitute the power he gets from wind, water, and other sources, for his muscle power. If you look at pictures of the pyramids of Egypt, the Grand Coulee Dam, or the skyscrapers in a city, you can see the results of using machinery.

With all the work that is being done, we are apt to think we can get more energy or work out of a machine than is put into it. What do you think?

Try the investigation on the opposite page to find out whether the simple machine, a tool, really helps you to do more work, in the way a scientist understands the concept of work. See if you can keep an accurate account of the work done as the energy is transferred from one place to another.

●

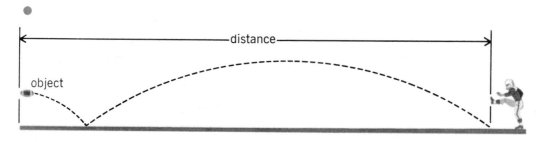

distance

object

# AN INVESTIGATION into How a Simple Machine Multiplies Force

**Needed:** a board, 2 feet long; several books; a skate; a spring balance

Prop one end of a board about 2 feet long on top of a stack of books. The elevated end should be about 1 foot above the tabletop. This simple machine was used in the investigation on page 155.

This time, lift the skate a distance of just 1 foot, as shown in the picture. ■ Look at the scale to see how much force is needed to lift the skate. Now pull the skate up the whole length of the inclined plane. You have pulled it a distance of 2 feet. ●

Does the scale read less when you pull the skate up the plane than when you lift it? Are the results about the same as before (page 155)? If so, you have confirmed your results by trying the investigation a second time. This is an important procedure in any investigation. One student found that when he lifted the skate without using the machine, the effort was 2 pounds. When he pulled the skate up the inclined plane, the effort was 1 pound.

He wrote his results in his notebook. Study them carefully.

Distance skate was lifted: 1 foot

Force needed: 2 pounds (32 ounces)

Distance skate was pulled up inclined plane: 2 feet

Force needed: 1 pound (16 ounces)

Are these results similar to your own? How does the slope of the plane affect the amount of effort needed?

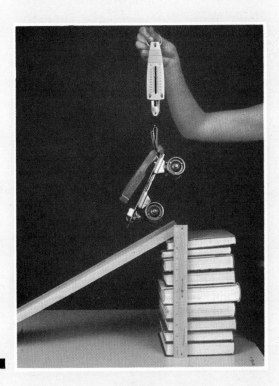

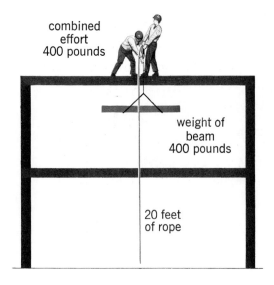

combined effort 400 pounds

weight of beam 400 pounds

20 feet of rope

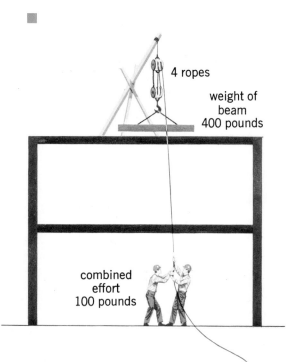

4 ropes

weight of beam 400 pounds

combined effort 100 pounds

80 feet of rope

## Something for Nothing?

The student found that it took less effort to pull the skate up the inclined plane than to lift it straight up. Although it took less effort to pull the skate up the inclined plane, he pulled the skate a longer distance (2 feet) than when he lifted it (1 foot). The work done was the same in each case.

Yes, it took more effort to lift the same skate straight up; but in lifting the skate straight up, he lifted it a shorter distance (1 foot) than when he pulled it along the inclined plane (2 feet).

In other words, the student moved the skate a longer distance with the machine. The machine multiplied his smaller force, but the machine did not multiply the amount of work that was done. Why? He moved the same object (the skate) a longer distance on the inclined plane than when he lifted it straight up; but the final result was that he lifted the same weight the same height. The work done was the same in each case.

*He* raised a weight of 2 pounds to a height of 1 foot each time. On the inclined plane, he pulled the same object twice the distance. The force (effort) was multiplied by using the inclined plane, but the student had to move the object a greater distance. The work done was the same in each case.

## Another Example

Look at the picture on the opposite page of the men lifting a beam weighing 400 pounds. Suppose the men were to lift the beam straight up with just one rope. ■ Each man would then use about 200 pounds of effort. Together they would be using 400 pounds of effort.

Instead, the men decided to use a block and tackle, a simple machine. The block and tackle had four ropes, as in the picture. ■ The machine made their work much easier. Their combined effort was 100 pounds.

4 ropes × 100 pounds = 400 pounds
(weight of the beam)

When the men lifted the beam straight up, they applied their effort through a distance of 20 feet. With the block and tackle, they had to move their effort through a distance of 80 feet. The distances were determined by the lengths of rope used in each case.

The machine multiplied the men's force four times, but they had to pull the rope a longer distance—four times longer than before. Their force was multiplied, but their force was applied through a greater distance. They used a smaller force over a longer distance by using the machine. They accomplished no more or less work; their work was just easier at any given moment.

The men put the same amount of work into the machine that they got out of it. They did not get something for nothing and that's a very important concept to remember.

**BEFORE YOU GO ON**

**A.** Study the statements below and choose the correct responses. They will help you fix in mind the main concepts of this section.

**1.** A piano weighs 500 pounds. To lift it, four men would each need to use a force of at least
  a. 125 pounds    b. 500 pounds

**2.** If one man used a pulley arrangement with four ropes to lift the 500-pound piano, he would need to use a force of
  a. 500 pounds    b. 125 pounds

**3.** Suppose a man could lift about 200 pounds. Using a four-rope block and tackle, he is just barely able to lift a large piano. How much must the piano weigh?
  a. 800 pounds    b. 1,000 pounds

**4.** In using a simple machine to lift the piano a man

    a. would multiply force      b. would multiply the amount of work done

**B.** Write a paragraph or two on this topic: Machines and Work.

A roofer wants to lift 100 pounds of shingles to a roof 20 feet above the ground. He is using a two-rope pulley, so his effort must be 50 pounds (2 ropes × 50 pounds = 100 pounds).

In lifting the shingles 20 feet, however, he uses 40 feet of rope. He pulls a length of rope (40 feet) to reach the distance (20 feet). One of the following explanations of why the roofer needs to pull 40 feet of rope is correct. Which is it?

a. A simple machine multiplies the amount of work done; therefore, the roofer should not have needed to pull twice the length of the rope. He did not know how to use the machine.

b. A machine does not multiply the amount of work done. If the machine multiplies effort, it is necessary for the effort to move through a greater distance. Since his effort was multiplied by two, he had to pull twice the distance.

Archimedes, a Greek (born about 287 B.C.), was probably the first person to study the mathematics of simple machines. He once boasted to his king that he could pull the biggest ship afloat into shore single-handed with the help of some simple machines.

**1.** Suppose Archimedes could only apply an effort of 100 pounds, while a force of 1,000 pounds was needed to move the ship. Draw a picture of a possible combination of simple machines he might have used to do this.

**2.** On such a machine, how far must the effort move to make the load move 10 feet?

## 7. The Main Concept: Energy, Machines, and Work

Most of you can lift 50 pounds but with a great deal of effort. With the help of a simple machine you can lift much more. Apply a force of 50 pounds to a block and tackle with four ropes between the pulleys, and what weight can you lift? Each rope supports 50 pounds, making a total lifting force of 200 pounds—enough to lift a small piano! The block and tackle helps you multiply the force of your muscles; but have you done more work? No. Although you have used a machine to multiply the force of your muscles, the force must be applied through a longer distance. The distance is four times as far.

We must put just as much work into a simple machine as we get out of it. Machines may multiply force, but they do not increase the total amount of work done.

In order to do work, we must have a source of energy. Our energy comes from the food we eat. The energy in food supplies our muscles with the force to push against an object. No matter what kind of work is being done, energy is needed. Using a machine does not eliminate the need for energy. A machine only transfers the energy from one place to another.

In any study of science much time is given over to the study of energy. Energy can be changed from one form to another. Steam from boiling water can turn a turbine. ■ The heat energy changes the water into steam, and the energy in steam becomes mechanical energy in a turbine. Mechanical energy can be transformed into electric energy by a generator and used for many purposes.

■ **ENERGY CHANGES**

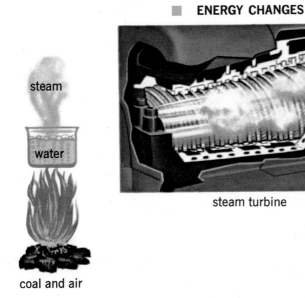

steam

water

coal and air

steam turbine

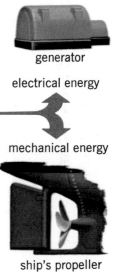

generator

electrical energy

mechanical energy

ship's propeller

We do not gain energy or lose energy when we change it from one form to another. Neither do we gain or lose energy by using a simple machine. We get no more *energy* out of a machine than we put into it. We get no more *work* out of a machine than we put into it.

This is also true of matter. Matter can be changed from one form to another, but matter is neither gained nor lost when it is changed in a chemical reaction.

For example, iron combines with oxygen to form a new compound, iron oxide (rust). Suppose you try to make some iron oxide by exposing a certain amount of pure iron to the oxygen in the air. To make 40 grams of iron oxide, you must use a total of 40 grams of oxygen and iron. In this chemical reaction, no new matter is made; no matter is destroyed. The matter is only changed in form. This is true of all chemical reactions on earth. Would it be true of chemical reactions taking place elsewhere in the universe?

When we multiply a force with a simple or compound machine, no energy is gained—no more work is done; but we are using the force to greater advantage.

Man has learned to use machines to do work. He has learned to use force wisely because he has learned to use it to greater advantage in doing work. The word *work* is used here in the scientific sense. Clearly, science demands that we use our concepts accurately.

# Fixing the Main Concepts

Test your understanding of the important concepts of this unit by doing these problems.

**1.** A man is applying 100 pounds of effort to the pulley machine at the left. ■ The weight he is lifting must be

    a. 100 pounds          b. 200 pounds

**2.** To raise a barrel to the rear of a car, it would be best to use

    a. an inclined plane          b. a lever

**3.** To stop accidents on a slippery road, it is best to use sand to

    a. increase friction          b. decrease friction

**4.** Which of these statements are true? (All may be true. None may be true. Some may be true and some may be false.)

a. A simple machine may multiply force, but it does not increase work done.

b. A simple machine does not produce more work than is put into it.

c. A simple machine does not produce more energy than is put into it.

**5.** Test your understanding of the main concepts in this unit by using each of these key words in a sentence.

| | | |
|---|---|---|
| work | inclined plane | winding inclined plane |
| pulley | wedge | multiply force |
| gears | force | increase work done |
| save force | simple machine | compound machine |
| wheel and axle | lever | multiply speed |

QUICK TEST    **1.** Name the simple machines shown in the illustration below: ●

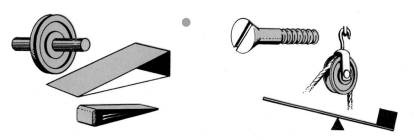

**2.** Below are four compound machines which are operated by hand. Of which simple machines are they made?

a. juice-can opener     c. meat grinder

b. scissors     d. fork

**3.** Name one compound machine that contains all of the simple machines listed below.

a. lever     c. wheel and axle

b. wedge     d. screw

**FOR YOUR READING**

If you are interested in machines and engines, then you might want to read:

**1.** *Machines That Built America,* by Roger Burlingame, published by Harcourt, Brace & World, New York, 1953.

This is the story of the inventors who built the machines that helped make our nation great.

**2.** *Machines,* by Robert O'Brien, published by Time, Inc., New York, 1964.

This is an interesting book with some good pictures of the machines that make your life easier.

**ON YOUR OWN**

There are two additional investigations in this part.

One is on a machine called a perpetual motion machine.

**1. A machine that works forever (a perpetual motion machine).**

Here is an example of a perpetual motion machine called a perpetual rocker. ■ It looks like a kind of lever, with the fulcrum (the point on which it rests) exactly in the center.

It works like this: the heavy rubber ball is started rolling with a good push (at A). It rolls down the hill and up. As it hits the other end (marked B), it bounces off and starts rolling back. It hits the end again and starts rolling.

The machine rocks back and forth, back and forth, back and forth *perpetually* (forever). What is your hypothesis?

Will it work?

If yes, why?

If not, why not?

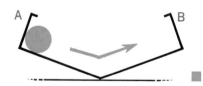

**2. Balancing a seesaw.**

A boy and his father were walking in a park when they saw a seesaw, which is really a simple machine, a lever. It is a board which is balanced on a fulcrum. (See below.)

In any event, the boy wanted to get on the seesaw and *to balance his weight against his father's.* He persuaded his father, as boys sometimes can, to get on the board with him.

It just happened that the boy weighed 80 pounds, and that his father weighed 160 pounds, twice the boy's weight. Below is shown how they finally balanced themselves.

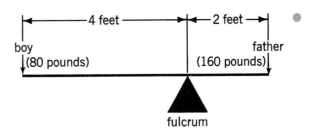

fulcrum

Do you see why they could balance? Try the investigation below.

Take a yardstick and hang it in the middle with a string, as shown below. ▲

Use two weights, one twice the weight of another. Try to balance them on a measuring stick, as shown. ♦ One way of balancing these weights is shown. Try several others to find the concept that explains the balancing of weights.

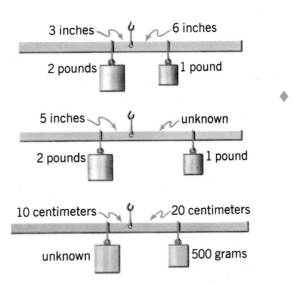

# UNIT FIVE

# MOLECULES IN ACTION

On a hot summer day the concrete pavement may expand and buckle, creating a serious bump in the road.

On a cold winter day water may freeze and expand, causing a pipe to burst and creating a serious water problem.

In late summer, storm warnings are up and small craft take to the safety of a harbor. A hurricane rages unchecked, leaving a path of destruction in its wake.

You cannot see the action which caused the highway to buckle or the pipe to burst, nor can you see the wind that caused so much damage. You can only see the effect of the force and the *action.* In each case, the effect came from the motion of molecules. You cannot see them; but moving molecules can exert tremendous force.

For example, moving molecules in an engine can send a train speeding along its track, or an automobile speeding along a freeway, or a missile soaring through the air. Can you explain how the motion of invisible particles can do so much work?

Perhaps you would like to know how anything too small to be seen can do work. This unit will help you. It explains how man, as scientist and engineer, uses his brain and hands, imagination and skill, to change his environment with the force of moving molecules.

# 1. A Modern Genie

Do you remember the story of Aladdin and his magic lamp? When Aladdin rubbed the lamp, the genie came forth to do Aladdin's bidding. He had tremendous energy; he could do anything Aladdin demanded, no matter how difficult.

Of course, this is only a story, and we do not really believe such things can happen; but man has learned to control a "genie" or two that will rival Aladdin's. Suppose we try to imprison a genie of our own. Let us begin with a small genie; we can imprison a larger one later.

Suppose we bottle up a "modern genie" in a balloon machine like the one shown in the picture. ■ What can this machine do? What makes it work? It is made of several common items: a balloon, a hot plate, a Pyrex beaker, and some water. What happens to the balloon when the water in the beaker is heated? What makes it happen? What happens to the cube of sugar? Perhaps the ruler will give you a clue.

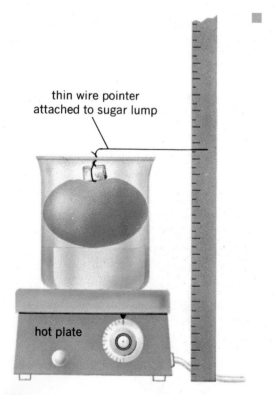

thin wire pointer attached to sugar lump

hot plate

hot water

196

Before you go on, take a deep breath. Breathe out. You cannot see the air you breathe in or the air you breathe out; yet you know that you have breathed in some air.

What is air made of? One explanation is that air is made up of particles, particles too small to be seen. The small particles of air are molecules. Molecules of the gases that make up air are too small to be seen, even with the help of a powerful microscope; yet there is evidence that molecules do make up the matter which surrounds us. Do you know of any such evidence? What do you know already about the nature and behavior of air?

You may recall making these two discoveries about air in earlier science classes:

Air is invisible.

Air takes up space and has mass.

The evidence indicates that air is made up of particles (molecules) of matter which are too small to be seen, and which are constantly moving. What can moving molecules do?

Molecules of air can be our modern genie. They have energy, which means they are able to do work. *Energy is the ability to do work.*

How can the molecules of air inside a balloon do work?

Take a balloon and blow it up. The molecules you cannot see have expanded the rubber balloon. Now take the balloon and use it to make the machine shown in the picture. This may not look like a machine, but it is. It will do work; the molecules of air will do the work. (Refer to the scientist's definition of work on page 184.) The energy of moving molecules in this machine will lift a cube of sugar; it may even lift several cubes of sugar.

This is a very small "genie," and it does very little work; but you will discover later how moving molecules can lift a plane high into the air or send a rocket to the moon.

The balloon "machine" does work as the walls of the balloon stretch and lift the cube of sugar. The balloon stretches as the volume of air inside expands. The air expands because the molecules are moving faster; they have gained kinetic energy. As we found earlier, kinetic energy is the energy of motion. A bowling ball rolling toward the pins has kinetic energy.● A moving locomotive has kinetic energy. Water turning the generators in

**197**

a huge dam has kinetic energy. Molecules in the air have kinetic energy; they are always in motion.

*Heat* increases the kinetic energy of the molecules, so that they move farther apart. In that way, the molecules tend to occupy more space. Whenever the molecules of a gas are heated, the motion of the molecules is increased; the gas expands.

As the kinetic energy of a gas increases, its *force* against the walls of the container increases. In your small "genie" the molecules of air push against the inside of the balloon and expand the balloon. Recall the scientist's concept of work: *Work is done whenever an object is moved through a distance or whenever a force acts through a distance.* The piece of sugar is moved as the balloon expands. The expanding air stretches the sides of the balloon and lifts the cube of sugar. ■

The molecules of air could do work because they have kinetic energy.

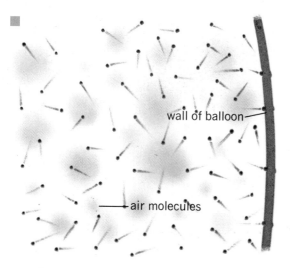

wall of balloon

air molecules

This is an important concept: When matter (solid, liquid, or gas) expands, it can exert a force on anything nearby. A force is a push or pull that can change motion. Expanding matter can do work because of the force exerted by its moving molecules. If we can harness the energy of moving molecules, that energy can be transferred to do useful work. That is, *force* is used to move an object. *Work is done as the force moves the object through a distance.*

Let us put some energy to work. The energy comes from matter in motion. By the word "matter," we really mean the molecules, or invisible particles, of which visible matter is made. How can we do it? Simple! We must get the matter to expand, as it will do in the investigation on the opposite page. Try it.

### An Explanation: Moving Molecules

As heat is applied to water, the molecules of water move faster and farther apart. As they move faster, many of them escape into the air at the top of the tube. Because kinetic energy increases at a higher temperature, the molecules of both water and air push harder when they hit the cork at the top of the tube.

The water in the Pyrex tube, which you used in your investigation, expanded as it became steam. The force of the moving molecules (of both the steam and air) pushed against the cork. The cork flew out as the gases suddenly expanded. Work was done

# AN INVESTIGATION into How an Expanding Liquid Can Do Work

**Needed:** a Pyrex test tube; a cork stopper to fit; Vaseline; an alcohol lamp or Bunsen burner; a toy steam engine

Fix a Pyrex tube in a clamp, as you see in the picture. Be sure to use a clamp that can be tightened, one that screws together. Pour about an inch of water into the tube. Rub a little Vaseline onto the stopper and fit it into the Pyrex tube. *(Be careful not to point the stopper toward anyone.)* Heat the tube gently, moving it back and forth over the flame. Watch to see what happens. Suddenly, the stopper flies out of the tube. ■ Why?

Now examine the toy steam engine. As you do so, compare it with the diagram of a toy engine on the next page. To operate the engine, heat the water in the boiler. Soon the wheel begins to turn; it turns faster and faster.● How is the energy of the expanding water being used? Could this kind of energy be used to do work in a large machine—for example, in a factory or on a ship? How?

**Additional Investigation:** Can you find a way to make the toy steam engine do some *useful* work? If you have an Erector set, or if you are good at building things, try to construct a machine that can use your engine for some useful purpose.

199

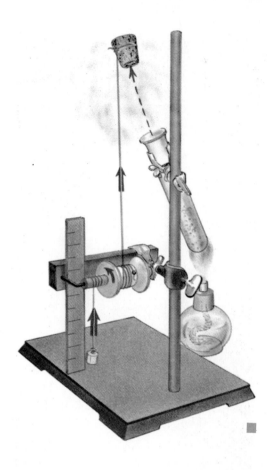

round, something like the cork, and can slide back and forth. The force of the piston, sliding back and forth, is used to turn the wheel.● The energy of expanding steam is thereby transferred to the turning wheel.

How can a piston-operated steam engine do useful work? In a factory, the piston turns a wheel which, in turn, can turn other wheels of other machines. A century ago the piston steam engine, as shown in the picture, was used to run the machinery in many factories.▲

The wheel attached to the steam engine had a flat belt around it. The belt turned a shaft which transferred the energy from the steam engine to other wheels of other machines throughout the factory.▲ These machines did the work of many men, all because the force of expanding steam can be transferred to turn a wheel. In

by the moving molecules. The work was not very useful, was it? If you had been able to tie the cork to a shaft and to a wheel, the molecules of the gases might have done useful work as they expanded.■ The wheel would have turned and lifted the weight for you.

Blowing the cork from a test tube is used as a model of the idea behind the work of a steam engine. In the model steam engine, water is boiled. It is changed from liquid to steam (which is a gas). The force of the steam does useful work by pushing the **piston.** The illustration shows the piston of a toy steam engine.● It is

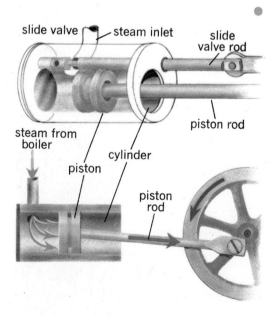

slide valve — steam inlet — slide valve rod

steam from boiler

piston rod

piston

cylinder

piston rod

a steam locomotive there are two or four pistons. Each one turns a wheel.

The piston steam engine was at one time the most important kind of engine we had. It was used in factories, mines, ships, locomotives, and pumping stations; but it is not often used any more. It has been replaced by more modern engines. Read on to find out about a more modern type of steam engine.

## Instead of a Piston

You have seen pinwheels and windmills. The energy of moving air (wind) turns them. Windmills can do useful work such as pumping water or grinding grain into flour. Moving steam can also turn a special kind of wheel. This special kind of wheel is called a **turbine** (tùr′bin).

Make a small turbine out of aluminum foil, shaped like the one in the picture. ◆ If you have no aluminum foil, shape your turbine from heavy paper cut from a milk carton. Place about 1 inch of water in a Pyrex test tube and plug the opening with a one-holed stopper or modeling clay with a hole through it, as shown. ◆ Heat cautiously over a flame and direct the jet of steam against the turbine. Note how it turns. This arrangement concentrates the fast-moving jet of steam against the pinwheel turbine, so that it turns. ◆

In a modern steamship, the steam from a boiler turns a turbine, a bigger one, of course. The steam is directed against the blades of the turbine; the turbine turns a shaft, which is connected to the propeller. The shaft turns the propeller, and the propeller pushes the ship through the water. Study the diagram which shows how a turbine turns a ship's propeller. ■

The energy of burning fuel, such as coal or oil, heats water in a boiler. The water makes steam. The expanding steam turns a turbine instead of pushing a piston. Steam turbines are better for many purposes than are piston engines. They do not wear out as fast because there are fewer moving parts; friction is less.

Also, because they have fewer moving parts, steam turbines do not waste as much energy as a piston engine. Some of the energy of the fuel must be used to work each moving part of an engine. Since the turbine and shaft are turned by the steam directly, much more of the fuel's energy is used to push the ship. Machines that convert the greatest amount of the fuel's energy to do useful work are said to be the most efficient.

Steam turbines are used to run many of the largest ocean liners, and they also are often used in running electric power plants. The turbines turn huge generators, which provide electricity to light our homes. Turbines can be turned by other things as well as by steam; they can be turned by moving water, by the explosive power of gasoline, or by moving air. Do you think that particles of sand sliding down a chute could turn a turbine?

The steam engine is nothing really new. On a map of Egypt, you will find the city of Alexandria, where, about 1,600 years ago, a young Greek named

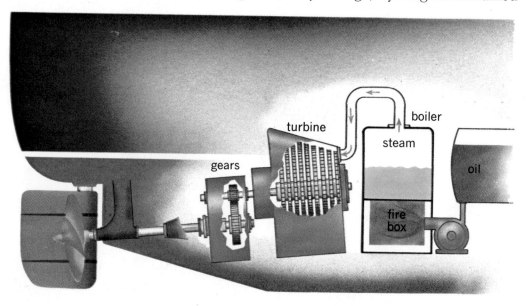

Hero made a steam engine that worked! Look at the picture of Hero's engine. ● What made it spin around?

Hero's engine worked because the heat energy from burning wood makes the molecules of water move faster; the kinetic energy of the molecules is increased. As the kinetic energy of the molecules of water increases, the water begins to boil. Then the water molecules escape from the surface to become steam. When water expands to form steam, the molecules of water can exert enough force to do a great deal of work.

How did the steam make Hero's engine move? **Clue:** Why does a jet plane move? Why does a rocket move?

BEFORE YOU GO ON **A.** Study the statements below and choose the correct responses. They will help you fix in mind the concepts of this section.

**1.** If the movement of molecules could be stopped, the molecules would no longer have

    a. kinetic energy          b. weight

**2.** One way of increasing the energy of molecules is to

    a. apply heat to them          b. remove heat from them

**3.** When a closed balloon is made to expand, the number of molecules of air in the balloon

    a. increases          b. remains the same

**4.** As a closed balloon expands, the molecules of air in it

    a. increase in size          b. move farther apart

**B.** Write a paragraph or two on this topic: One Way of Putting Molecules to Work.

USING WHAT
YOU KNOW
**A.** A stone lying on top of a hill has stored energy, or **potential energy,** as it is called. An electric battery has potential energy; so does the wound spring in a toy car or a tankful of gasoline. When an object has potential energy, it means that it has the capacity to do work.

It can do work, however, only when the potential energy becomes the energy of motion. The rock's potential energy will be changed to kinetic energy if it starts rolling down the hill.

How can the wound spring's potential energy be changed into kinetic energy?

How would you change the potential energy in the water behind this small dam into kinetic energy? ■

**B. In the Library**

An important invention that uses the energy of moving molecules was the Pelton wheel. Do some research in the library to find out about this wheel and about the man who invented it. In what ways is the Pelton wheel similar to the steam turbine?

## 2. An Explosive Genie

According to an old story, James Watt conceived the idea for *his* steam engine from watching a boiling kettle when he was a small boy. What do you expect to happen to the kettle shown in the picture, which has a potato closing its spout?● The water in the kettle is just starting to boil.

The cover on the kettle will bounce and rattle as the steam pushes it up. The steam exerts pressure on the lid of the kettle. What really happens is this: Heat from burning fuel increases the kinetic energy of the water molecules. The pressure or force on the inside area of the lid also increases. The rapidly moving molecules bump up and down against the cover of the kettle. Work is done as the kettle cover is forced to move. Remember the scientist's meaning for the word work (page 184).

The energy of moving molecules can be harnessed to run a locomotive or any machine that can use the rapidly moving molecules of expanding steam.▲ Expanding steam can do

●

work. Steam to be used in a large engine is produced in a boiler, but such a boiler takes up a lot of space. Perhaps there is another way to get large amounts of work done and to do so by using a source of energy which does not take up too much space.

### A Useful Explosion

When a substance explodes, its molecules of waste gases spread out extremely fast. The substance *suddenly* takes up a great deal more space, or at least tries to. The sudden expansion of some exploding substances can push walls aside and

▲

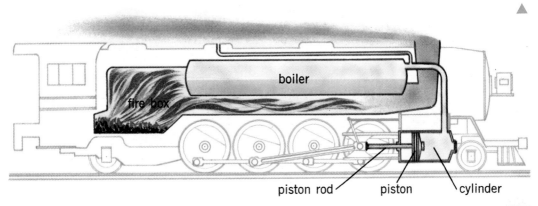

boiler

fire box

piston rod    piston    cylinder

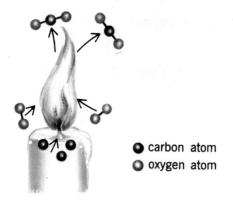

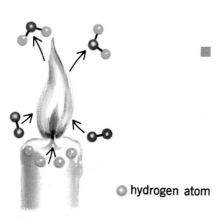

● carbon atom
○ oxygen atom

● hydrogen atom

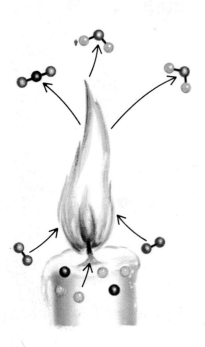

splinter glass; but such an explosion can be controlled to do useful work.

There are some compounds that explode easily and the explosions can be controlled. One is gasoline for the family car. Gasoline is *very dangerous* when near a flame, but it can be exploded safely inside an automobile engine.

When gasoline explodes, it is burning very rapidly in a closed space.

What really happens when gasoline burns, or explodes? You can get the answer by watching the burning candle in the investigation on the opposite page.

### Energy from Burning Fuel

Candle wax is a **fuel** containing carbon and hydrogen. When the candle burns, carbon from the wax combines with oxygen from the air to form carbon dioxide gas. ■

**carbon + oxygen → carbon dioxide ($CO_2$)**

At the same time hydrogen from the fuel (wax) also combines with oxygen from the air to form water vapor ($H_2O$). ■

**hydrogen + oxygen → water ($H_2O$)**

Fuels contain hydrogen and carbon; so, whenever a fuel burns, carbon dioxide and water vapor are produced. Both carbon dioxide and water vapor are gases. Gasoline, or wood, or coal, when burned, will produce these two gases.

**fuels + oxygen → carbon dioxide**
**+ water**

206

# AN INVESTIGATION into What Happens When a Fuel Burns

**Needed:** a candle; a pie plate; a quart jar; limewater; a small glass

Light the candle and carefully drop some wax on the pie plate. *Be careful to keep your hand away from the flame.* After several drops of wax have fallen, quickly blow out the flame and set the bottom of the candle on the soft wax. Hold the candle in place until the wax hardens. Then place a small glass of limewater near the candle.

Without lighting the candle, place the quart jar over the candle and limewater for a short time. Are there any changes in the limewater?

Remove the jar and light the candle. Then replace the jar over the candle and glass of limewater. ■

Watch closely as the candle burns. Can you see droplets of water forming on the inside of the jar? Where does the water come from?

After the flame goes out, let the jar stand in place and watch the limewater for several minutes. Move the pie plate gently back and forth as you watch. What happens? ● What do you think is present to change the limewater?

**Additional Investigation:** Are carbon dioxide and water produced when other fuels burn? Try burning some wood shavings on the pie plate to find out whether they do or not.

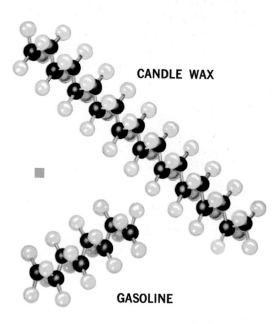

CANDLE WAX

GASOLINE

Candle wax and gasoline both contain carbon and hydrogen. But a molecule of gasoline is different from a molecule of candle wax. The picture of *models* of molecules shows you the difference between a molecule of candle wax and one of gasoline. ■

Gasoline burns much faster than candle wax. Yet when a molecule of gasoline or a molecule of wax burns, the same two gases are formed:

carbon dioxide (**$CO_2$**)
water vapor (**$H_2O$**)

These gases are formed when any molecule containing carbon and hydrogen is burned. Oxygen combines with the carbon and hydrogen to form $CO_2$ and $H_2O$.

Gasoline has potential energy, another name for stored-up energy. When gasoline explodes, its potential energy is changed into kinetic energy, the energy of motion. The kinetic energy of moving molecules can be used to do work.

When gasoline burns, the molecules of gasoline suddenly burst apart and the pieces rapidly combine with oxygen. The reaction is an explosion. The molecules from the suddenly exploded gasoline (mainly, gases) push outward. The pressure increases as the gases try to expand. Expanding gases can do a great deal of useful work. How?

### Exploding Gasoline in a Tube

In most automobiles, liquid gasoline is changed into a vapor (a gas) in the **carburetor** (kär′bə·rā′tər). Here, as the gasoline evaporates, the vapor is mixed with air. The mixture of gasoline vapor and air then goes into a closed metal tube called a **cylinder** (sil′in·dər). ● Inside the cylinder is a piston. Gasoline vapor in the cylinder is ignited with a *spark*, which jumps across a gap on the **spark plug.**

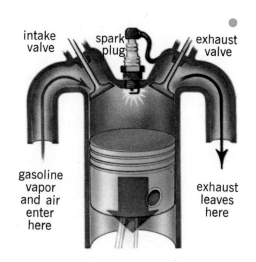

intake valve

spark plug

exhaust valve

gasoline vapor and air enter here

exhaust leaves here

The spark explodes the mixture of gasoline vapor and air. Hot exhaust gases expand and exert a force that pushes the piston. The piston turns a wheel, as shown in the picture, and does work by moving a car, a truck, or a machine. ▲

Next time you have a chance, ask an adult to show you what is under the hood of a car. Look for the spark plugs on the engine. How many cylinders does an automobile engine have? You can tell by counting the number of spark plugs.

You cannot see the cylinders, because they are inside the engine. There are usually four or more in cars, buses, or trucks. ◆ The gasoline engine works because gasoline vapor and air are exploded in the cylinders. The resulting gases expand from the rapid increase in kinetic energy and are used to move the pistons.

By learning how to use the kinetic energy in expanding gases, scientists have harnessed a powerful "genie."

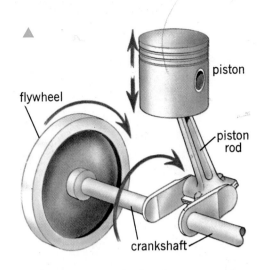

The concept behind our modern genie is simply stated: *Energy can be changed from one kind to another* and *transferred from one place to another.*

### Two Kinds of Change and One Goal

The idea behind the work of a steam or gasoline engine has been to get the molecules of a substance to move very fast. They produce a force, a push. The force moves the wheels of an automobile, a locomotive, or a factory machine. Work is done when

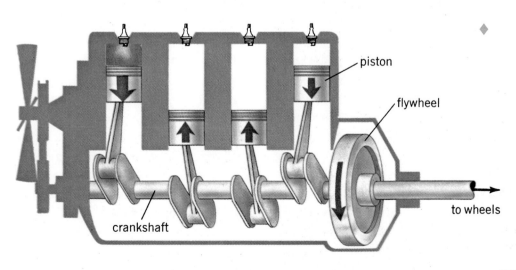

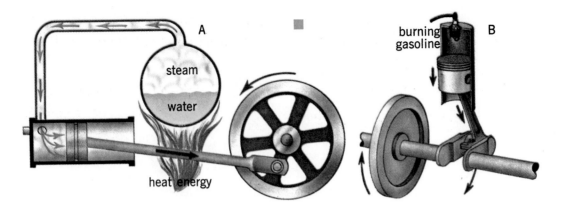

the force of moving molecules moves an object (a car, a locomotive) through a distance.

The molecules in the steam and the molecules in the gasoline explosion were caused to move by different methods even though the outcome was the same—to exert a force. Really, two kinds of change took place.

In one kind of change, water was heated and changed into steam; but water and steam are the same substance. ■ Both are forms of water. (The formula is $H_2O$.) The difference between water and steam is a difference in *form* or *state*. Molecules of steam are farther apart and thus take up more space than molecules of water. Steam can be changed back into water by cooling it. This kind of change is a **physical change,** or what is called a change of state of the same substance. The rapid change from a liquid (water) to steam, a gas, causes the substances to expand and by expansion, to exert a force.

When gasoline burns, however, different substances are produced; the molecules themselves are changed.

Molecules of carbon dioxide and water vapor are formed. This is not a physical change but a **chemical change.** In a chemical change the molecules themselves are changed. Molecules of carbon dioxide and water vapor are not the same as molecules of gasoline and oxygen.

A chemical change takes place when coal or oil is burned to furnish heat to boil water; but this takes place outside the engine itself, in a firebox, perhaps. The only change inside the steam engine is a *physical change*—water to steam. On the other hand, a *chemical change* takes place inside the gasoline engine.

Either physical changes or chemical changes can cause particles to move. The physical change from water to steam increases the kinetic energy of the water molecules. The chemical change, in gasoline vapor and air, also causes an increase in the kinetic energy of the molecules. Physical and chemical changes can cause molecules to do work as they push against objects and make them move.

BEFORE
YOU GO ON **A.** Study the statements below and choose the correct responses. They will help you fix in mind the concepts of this section.

  **1.** A steam locomotive can harness the kinetic energy of
     a. molecules of water      b. hydrogen and oxygen
                                        gases

  **2.** When gasoline explodes, its molecules
     a. remain the same      b. break apart

  **3.** When water boils, the change is a
     a. physical change      b. chemical change

  **4.** When gasoline explodes, the change in its molecules is a
     a. physical change      b. chemical change

  **5.** Gasoline and candle wax both contain
     a. carbon      b. oxygen

**B.** Write a paragraph or two on this topic: Putting Molecules to Work.

USING WHAT
YOU KNOW Below is a puzzle box made of strong steel. Fuel oil is being poured into the funnel. Water vapor (a gas) and carbon dioxide (a gas) are coming out the other side.

What must be happening inside the box? Do you have a "machine" at home that operates in a manner similar to this? Do not say "no" until you have given it some thought.

oil can                                     hot
gases

## 3. Balloons and Planes— Going Up

Fill a balloon with helium, and it will rise. If it is large enough, it can even carry a man with it. Do you know why? Helium is lighter than air. A balloon full of helium weighs less than an equal volume of air. The lighter balloon rises and floats on the heavier air. Will a balloon filled with ordinary air rise?

Fill a balloon with the air exhaled from your lungs. Will the balloon rise or not?

One thing is sure, however; a balloon filled with air will rise in and float on water. The reason is that the gas (air) is lighter than the liquid (water).

The principle of balloon flight is fairly simple. Fill the balloon with a gas lighter than air, and it will rise and float on the heavier air. (At some point, the balloon may reach a height where it weighs the same as the same volume of air outside and the balloon will not rise any higher.) The larger the balloon, the more men and objects it will be able to carry aloft.

An airplane with an engine is different from a balloon filled with helium; it is heavier than air. What makes it possible, then, for a plane to rise in the air? The engine, which moves the plane forward, makes it possible. On planes with propellers, the gasoline engine turns the propeller, which moves the plane forward. The backward motion of the air from the propeller produces a forward motion of the airplane. In jet engines the thrust of the engine moves the plane forward. As the plane moves forward, the air molecules flow past the wings. Most of the **lift** on a plane is caused by reduced pressure on top of the wing as air travels over the curved upper surface. The increase in speed of the molecules of air results in a loss of pressure. The lower pressure above the wing and the higher pressure underneath makes the plane rise. To understand how this may happen, do the investigation on the opposite page.

### An Explanation

Did it seem strange to you that the apples moved together instead of moving apart when you blew air between them? The result with the Ping-Pong ball seems even more unusual. The force of gravitation is pulling down on it and the air blast from above seems to be pushing down on it as well. Was the air really pushing down on the ball? It is important to understand just what forces were acting upon the apples and the ball.

A *force* is a push or pull that can change motion. A force must be applied to move a stationary object. When you blew between the apples, what force pushed them together? What force pushed the Ping-Pong ball against the inside of the funnel?

One substance surrounded the apples and that substance is air. Before you blew on the air between the

# AN INVESTIGATION into a Mysterious Push

**Needed:** two apples; a bar, or rod, from which to suspend them; books or some object to hold the bar up

a. Hang two apples on pieces of string, each about 2 feet long. Be sure to suspend the apples on the strings so that they are no farther than an inch or so apart. When the apples are hanging without movement, blow hard on the air between them. ■

Do you get the same result as is shown in the photograph? How far apart can you move the apples and still get this result?

b. On the basis of what you have done with the apples, can you guess what will happen as you try to blow a Ping-Pong ball out of the funnel, as shown? ●
Hold the Ping-Pong ball inside the upside-down funnel and blow hard through the spout. As you are blowing, take your hand away suddenly.

Try it.

What happens? Will blowing harder force the ball out of the funnel? Will blowing easier do it?

How do you explain your results? What have these results to do with the flight of an airplane?

apples, they hung straight down from the bar. This means that the air around them was pushing on them *equally* from all directions. ■ That is, the *pressure of air* around the apples was the same in all directions.

Blowing air between the apples caused them to move toward each other. This happened because the pressure between the apples was lowered. ■

The air pressure was lowered between the apples, but remained the same on the outside of the apples. The unequal pressure, the higher pressure on the outside of the apples and the lower pressure between them, pushed the apples together. In other words, the air around the outside of the apples was still. The air between the apples was moving because you blew on it. Because it was moving, the air between the apples had a lower pressure.

*The pressure inside a region of air is lower when the air is moving than when it is standing still.*

The scientist, Daniel Bernoulli, spent many years studying the effects of moving **fluids,** such as water. A fluid is any substance that flows easily. Liquids and gases are fluids. Air is a mixture of gases and thus is fluid. He found that the faster a fluid moves, the lower is its pressure. Bernoulli's discovery is very important. What does it have to do with the flight of an airplane?● A great deal, but Bernoulli's principle is by no means the whole story. The investigation on the opposite page will tell more of the story.

### An Airplane Flies

Examine the diagram of the airplane wing.● Notice that the upper part, or surface, is curved, and that

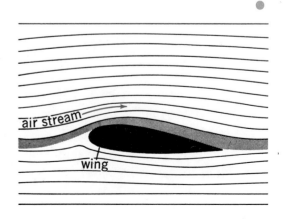

# AN INVESTIGATION into Flight from Da Vinci to Goddard

**Needed:** an adequate library

The pictures show two interesting moments in the history of flight. The top picture shows an early balloon made by the Montgolfier brothers in France. ■ The picture on the bottom shows an early airplane flight made by Claude Grahame-White on October 14, 1910. ● Men have dreamed of flying for a very long time. Even the Greeks had a myth about a father, Daedalus, and his son, Icarus, who flew with the wings they had made. Do you know the legend of Icarus? Look for it in an encyclopedia or other reference book.

This investigation is one into the way men's minds work. Start with the legend of Icarus and continue by investigating some of the real contributions that were made toward an understanding of flight by the following:

Leonardo da Vinci
Joseph and Jacques Montgolfier ■
Claude Grahame-White ●
Samuel Langley
Wilbur and Orville Wright
Robert Goddard

If possible, do the investigation in a library. Consult as many reference books as you can. Perhaps your teacher will want you to work with others in your class. Then you can share your findings.

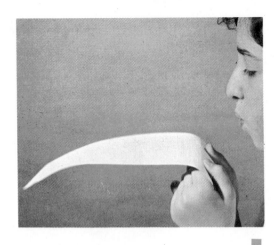

the lower surface is nearly flat. The air passing over the wing is squeezed between the wing and the air above. As a result, the air speeds up in order to get through the narrowed space. According to Bernoulli's principle, this increase in speed causes the air pressure above the wing to become less than the pressure below the wing.

In flight the wing also is tilted to point slightly upward (what might be called a climbing attitude or "angle of attack"). As the air flows under the wing, it strikes against the bottom surface of the wing that is in the way. This tends to force the wing upward, so the pressure on the bottom is greater. The difference in pressure is the lift; but remember that it is the forward motion of the plane that causes the air to rush over and under the wing. You will learn more about what causes the forward motion of a plane in the next section.

Try lifting the paper with your breath as the girl is doing. ■ Why does the paper fly up? Try explaining it any way you wish; but then try using Bernoulli's principle, which is: *The faster a fluid moves, the lower is its pressure.*

**BEFORE YOU GO ON** **A.** Study the statements below and choose the correct responses. They will help you fix in mind the concepts of this section.

**1.** When you blew between the two apples hanging from a bar, the air pressure between the apples was

    a. lowered      b. raised

**2.** The air pressure on top of the wing of a moving airplane is

    a. lowered      b. raised

**3.** It is difficult to blow the Ping-Pong ball out of the funnel because the air pressure on top of the ball is ●

    a. greater than that on the bottom
    b. lower than that on the bottom

air

**B.** Write a paragraph or two on this topic: How Can a Heavy Airplane Rise into the Air?

USING WHAT YOU KNOW Try this investigation to test Bernoulli's principle:

Place a pin through a small card about 2 inches square. Hold the card and pin under an empty spool, as shown, and blow through the hole in the spool. While blowing, remove your hand from the card. ▲

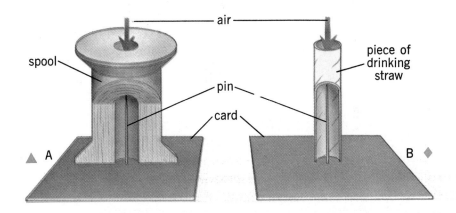

Repeat the same investigation using a short drinking straw instead of the spool. ◆

The problems posed by this investigation are:

**1.** How will the card react each time a fast current of air passes over it?

**2.** Will it react differently when placed under the straw than when it is under the spool?

Before you do the investigation develop a hypothesis about what will happen when the card is placed under the spool and air is blown through the hole. Will this result be different from what happens when the card is placed under an air blast from the straw?

In forming your hypothesis you can draw on the knowledge of Bernoulli's principle you now have gained through the investigations with the apples and the Ping-Pong ball. You can also draw on your knowledge, gained from reading the text, of what makes an airplane fly.

## 4. Jets and Rockets

Look again at the picture of Hero's engine on page 203. Notice that it was turned by two jets. In addition to being the first steam engine, it was also the first jet engine.

Hero was far ahead of his time. If he could visit us today, he would see the principle of his engine in wide use.

Blow up a balloon and then let it go. It flies. It is a kind of jet engine. A stream of moving air molecules rushes out of the neck, and the balloon flies in the opposite direction. An action in one direction (the push of the jet) causes a movement in the opposite direction. This is an example of the application of another great concept, Newton's Law of Action and Reaction. It states: *Every action has an equal and opposite reaction.* Let us examine how this concept is applied in space flight. ■

Imagine yourself out in space, perfectly safe in a pressurized suit. Suppose you want to move to your right. Then you must send a jet of moving particles to the left. Any **action** in space will produce an equal and opposite **reaction.** You may not recall how a space capsule is turned. Look at the picture. ■ The astronaut fires some small jets. Suppose he fires the jets toward the left (of the page). In which direction would his capsule go?

### A Jet Plane Takes Off

Most of the high-speed planes of today are propelled by powerful jet engines. In addition to being powerful, the jet engine is so efficient that engineers are now designing smaller ones to replace the piston engine in automobiles.

A jet engine has no cylinders and no pistons. Think of it as a tube. At one end, air mixes with a fuel, such as kerosene. The fuel and air mixture burns and expands inside the tube. Fast-moving molecules blast out the rear (action), and the plane moves forward (reaction).

What is inside a jet engine? The picture shows one type.● Study it carefully. Notice this one has two wheels with many blades, similar to the blades on an electric fan. The first wheel acts like a pump; it is called a **compressor.** The compressor forces air from the front toward the back of the tube. That is, it compresses the air. Kerosene is squirted into the com-

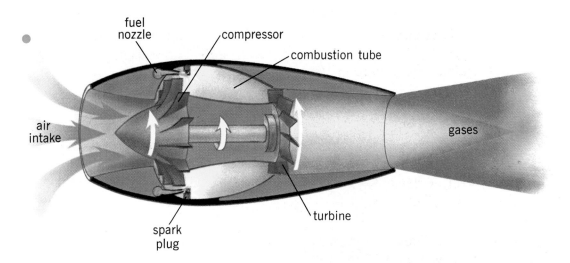

fuel nozzle · compressor · combustion tube · air intake · gases · spark plug · turbine

pressed air, and a spark plug ignites the mixture. It burns very rapidly with a roaring flame. Heat increases the kinetic energy of the molecules. As the kinetic energy increases, the gases expand and exert a force.

The moving molecules cannot shoot out the front of the jet because the compressor keeps pushing air in. They shoot out the rear of the engine (action); and the jet moves forward (reaction). The fast-moving gases also turn a bladed wheel as they flow toward the rear. The second wheel in the picture is a turbine. A shaft is attached to the turbine. It turns the first wheel, which compresses the air.

The air must be compressed if the burning of the kerosene is to produce enough force to move the plane. The kerosene keeps squirting in and burns, and the exhaust gases blast out the rear. The turbine keeps turning, and with it, the shaft. The shaft turns the compressor which keeps forcing air in, and the blast of hot gases from the rear forces the jet forward.

The explanation of how a jet engine works seems simple enough, but if you read it carefully you may have become aware of one problem. If the air must be compressed before the engine will work, and the engine must be moving to work the compressor, how does a jet engine get started? The answer is that a jet engine cannot start by itself. A small electric starter engine turns the compressor before the fuel is ignited.

As the jet plane moves forward, molecules of air rush rapidly over the upper surface and under the lower surface of the wing. With the wing tilted slightly upward, the air pressure on the upper surface of the wing is reduced, and the greater air pressure striking the lower surface of the wing lifts the plane up. The jet plane rises. Bernoulli's principle may be used to explain this action.

Jet engines need oxygen to combine with the kerosene for the kerosene to burn. Those that use the oxygen in air are useless out in space.

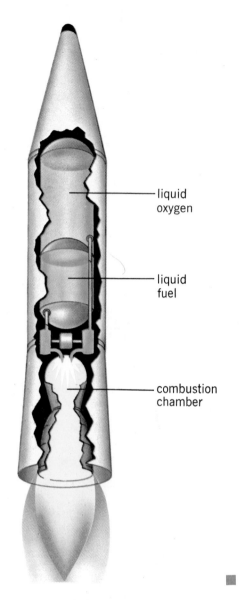

liquid oxygen

liquid fuel

combustion chamber

Rocket engines, however, carry their own supply of oxygen with them. They can go out into space where there is no air. ■ The *action* of the blast of moving molecules from the rapidly burning fuel causes a *reaction* that pushes the rocket through space. Note that the jet blast of burning fuel moves the rocket ahead in a straight line.● The *action* of the

burning fuel in one direction creates an equal *reaction* that moves the rocket in an opposite direction.

### A Rocket Blasts Off

Every action has an equal and opposite reaction. The blast from a rocket is downward (action). The rocket goes up (reaction).

Suppose the rocket has four stages, like the one on the opposite page. ▲ The load (sometimes called the payload) of instruments or passengers is carried in the fourth stage. The first stage carries enough fuel to move the rocket high into the atmosphere. It drops off to reduce weight. Then the second stage, the booster, takes over.

After the fuel in the second stage is used up, the booster drops off and the third stage takes over. The blast from each stage gives the rocket still more speed and boosts the rocket still farther into space.

The fourth stage of the rocket may have instruments in it. It may be a man-made satellite designed to revolve around the earth or it may be a spaceship with a pilot inside.

The rocket might carry a liquid fuel and liquid oxygen. The fuel and the oxygen combine to give the rocket a powerful thrust *forward* as the blast of moving molecules of gas roars *backward* out of the rocket tube. Rockets may use different kinds of fuels. Some rockets use a solid fuel.

Suppose a spaceship has a pilot in it or, perhaps, an entire crew. Suppose they are on their way to the moon. When the rocket leaves the earth's atmosphere and gets into outer space, the pilot must be able to control his spaceship. This is important in case something goes wrong with the automatic control system.

As the rocket approaches the moon, it will be pulled by the moon's force of gravitation. What will happen? At the tremendous speed of the rocket, the pilot could crash into the moon.

How will it be possible for astronauts to land safely on the moon and later be able to return to earth?

The explorations are being carried on now. You may wish to keep a notebook on each exploration (Apollo, Gemini, and others) as they are carried out. Many experiments are planned before a man can land on the moon.

One plan is to use a landing capsule carried to the moon by an Apollo spacecraft. This plan is called LOR (Lunar Orbital Rendezvous). When the spacecraft comes close to the moon (100 miles above the surface), it releases a small landing craft. The landing capsule curves closer and

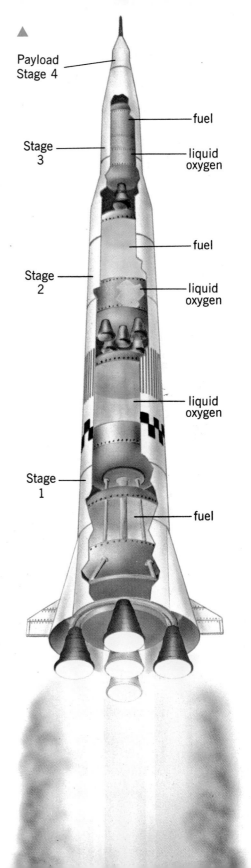

Payload
Stage 4

fuel

liquid oxygen

Stage 3

fuel

liquid oxygen

Stage 2

liquid oxygen

liquid oxygen

Stage 1

fuel

closer to the moon's surface, while the Apollo continues to orbit. To keep from crashing into the moon, the astronaut in the landing craft fires a rocket so that the blast pushes against the moon's gravity. This should slow the capsule down so that it will "soft-land" easily on the moon's surface. To return to the earth, the landing capsule will take off and rejoin the Apollo still in orbit around the moon.

To understand each step, study the diagram carefully. ■ Be sure to notice the color and shape of each part of the giant spaceship and to follow the numbers in their exact order. The symbols show you which part of the spaceship is participating in each step. The colored arrows show the various courses that will be taken. The red arrows show the course from earth to the moon. The purple arrows show the course of the craft that lands on the moon; the orange arrows show the orbit of the Apollo around the moon; and last, the green arrows show the Apollo's course back to earth.

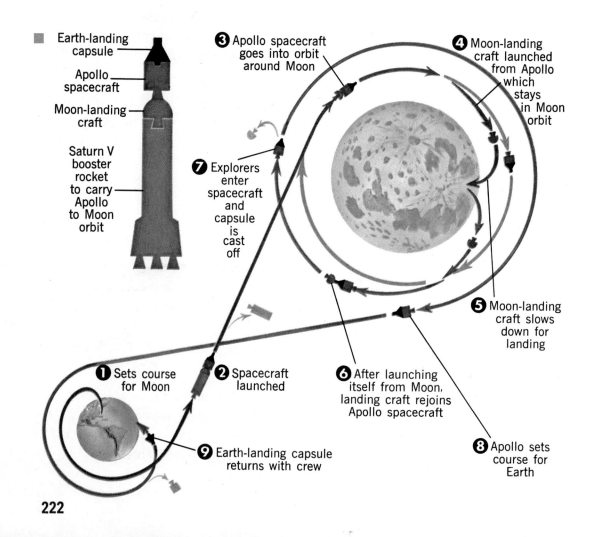

Earth-landing capsule

Apollo spacecraft

Moon-landing craft

Saturn V booster rocket to carry Apollo to Moon orbit

❸ Apollo spacecraft goes into orbit around Moon

❹ Moon-landing craft launched from Apollo which stays in Moon orbit

❼ Explorers enter spacecraft and capsule is cast off

❺ Moon-landing craft slows down for landing

❶ Sets course for Moon

❷ Spacecraft launched

❻ After launching itself from Moon, landing craft rejoins Apollo spacecraft

❽ Apollo sets course for Earth

❾ Earth-landing capsule returns with crew

**A.** Study the statements below and choose the correct responses. They will help you fix in mind the concepts of this section.

**1.** The motion of Hero's jet engine may be explained by means of
  a. Bernoulli's principle of reduced pressure
  b. Newton's law of action and reaction

**2.** The flight of rockets in space can best be explained by
  a. Newton's law of action and reaction
  b. Bernoulli's principle of reduced pressure

**3.** Rockets are different from jet planes because they
  a. need oxygen for flight
  b. carry their own oxygen

**4.** When a jet engine is operating at full speed, the
  a. turbine is turning the compressor
  b. compressor is turning the turbine

**5.** A spaceman, dressed in a pressure suit, steps out of his spaceship into space. He shoots his jet gun to the right. A stream of molecules rushes in that direction. The spaceman moves to the
  a. left                              b. right

**B.** Write a paragraph or two on this topic: Jets and Rockets.

**1.** Suppose one of your friends made this statement: "Let some of our rockets carry jet planes to the moon. Other rockets could carry the fuel. Then our jets could take off from the moon."

Would this be possible? What is the reasoning behind your answer?

**2.** A squid (a relative of the octopus) is able to move quickly through the water. It squirts a jet of water into the water around it. Describe how a squid could move with this method. Suppose it squirted water directly behind it, where would it go?

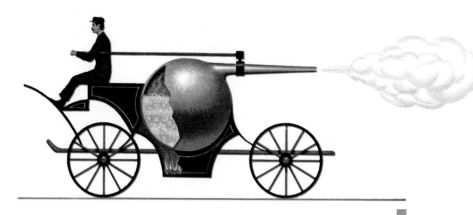

ON YOUR OWN Many years ago, Sir Isaac Newton designed this car (see the illustration) to demonstrate the law of action and reaction. ■ The car did not work.

Could you design a car or cart that does work by jet propulsion? Try it! One girl mounted the nozzle of her garden hose on the back of an old doll carriage. A boy made another model cart using tiny $CO_2$ cylinders that he was able to purchase at a hobby shop.

## 5. The Main Concept: The Use of Moving Molecules

Long ago man could do only as much work as his muscles allowed; they were his source of "push and pull." He could lift and tug and haul. The energy from the food in his body was the only energy he could use. Later he learned to use animals to work for him. He began to modify and improve his environment by inventing new things.

Still later, he learned to use simple machines: the lever, the pulley, the wheel and axle, the inclined plane, the wedge, and the screw. With simple machines he could multiply force; but he could get no more work out of a simple machine than he put into it. He needed a source of power. To add to his own power man needed new sources of energy. He first learned to use the energy of wind and water and, still later, fuels.

Man learned to use fuel as a source of energy to do work. In burning, the fuel combines with oxygen. The *heat* of the burning fuel was used to increase the motion of the molecules of water. The result was that the water expanded—and became steam. Gasoline and kerosene, too, combine with oxygen to produce gases that expand suddenly. Expansion furnishes the force to do work.

The energy in fuels can be traced back to the molecules in the fuel, in gasoline, for instance. When these molecules burn, heat is produced which causes gases to expand rapidly. When burning gases are trapped in a cylinder that has a movable piston, they can do work. They can push a piston or push a jet. By putting them to use, man has increased the energy available at his command.

Once he had learned to use the force of moving molecules, he was able to do much more work.

The concept is simple: moving molecules in expanding gases can be used to do work. They can push a piston; they can turn a turbine. Finally, man learned that moving molecules forced out the back of a jet plane could push the plane forward at a high speed or could push a rocket into space! The concept behind this phenomenon is that *for every action there is an equal and opposite reaction.* By understanding the concept man moves forward in his effort to control his environment and to reduce his limitations—especially those of ignorance.

Man learned that the kinetic energy of molecules increases as they are heated; they tend to move farther apart. With this understanding of the kinetic energy of molecules, man is now able to move into space.

He can do so because he has discovered, for one thing, that matter can release energy, energy that has been stored in the matter. Energy can be changed from one kind to another. *Potential* (stored-up) *energy* in matter can be changed into *kinetic energy* (the energy of moving objects or particles). The *kinetic energy* of molecules of a gas can push a piston or turn a wheel.

As man learned to release the stored-up energy in fuels, he learned to get more work done in much less time. He could use the time saved from human labor to do other things, things that he enjoyed doing. He found time to read, to write, and to think. He was able to give more time to art, to music, to literature, and to science.

There is a great need for scientists, as there is a great need for engineers. But there is not only a need for scientists and engineers; there is a great need, as well, for artists, for musicians, for writers, for teachers. There is a need, too, for carpenters, lawyers, doctors, and laborers to accomplish all the work that men and women must do.

The world is so full of a number of things that it needs the cooperation of men and women of all abilities and skills; there is a need for everyone. What do you hope to be or do?

There is no need to rush to make up your mind. As you go on in school, look about you. Find out what you like to do and what you can do best. This is a world in which science plays a great part. No matter what your interests may be, you will find your place in it.

# Fixing the Main Concepts

Test your understanding of the important concepts in this unit by doing these problems.

**1.** In the summer, especially on a hot day, the air inside the tires of automobiles expands. Some air has to be let out. In the winter, they go down a bit; so air has to be added.
How would you explain this?

**2.** a. A turbine, in a steam turbine engine, whirls as the molecules of hot steam hit it.
   b. A turbine, in a jet plane engine, whirls as the molecules of exhaust gases from burning kerosene hit it.
What is the difference in the kinds of changes the molecules undergo in (a) and in (b)?

**3.** Bob noticed that the shower curtain on a stall shower moved in when the water was turned on hard. How would you explain this?

**4.** Joan threw a basketball while she was standing on roller skates. She noticed that, as she threw the ball forward, she moved backward slightly.
How would you explain this?

**5.** Below is a list of some well-known kinds of engines. Try to determine which are *internal combustion engines* (fuel burned inside the engine) and which are *external combustion engines* (fuel burned outside the engine).

jet engine        auto engine
Hero's engine    piston steam engine

**6.** Which of these items are examples of *kinetic energy?*

a wound clock spring
logs rolling down a hill
an unexploded stick of dynamite
a high fly to left field

**7.** Check your understanding of the main concepts in this unit by using each of these key terms in a sentence that makes sense.

molecules
potential energy
kinetic energy
physical change

chemical change
Bernoulli's principle of reduced pressure
Newton's law of action and reaction
energy or force

**A PROJECT TO DO**

In the next ten years men will try to reach the moon.

Keep a notebook entitled: *Operation Moon*. In a sense you will be writing your own book.

Keep a record of each stage in the project. For instance,

a. The development of a powerful rocket

b. The first flights to explore the moon (Ranger, and others)

c. The first flights of Gemini, the spaceship that can carry two astronauts.

Keep maps of flights, especially of the orbits of the rockets and spaceships.

**FOR YOUR READING**

**1.** *Spaceflight and How It Works*, by William P. Gottlieb, published by Doubleday & Co., Garden City, 1964.

There are good photographs by the author in this book and good explanations of why aircraft fly.

**2.** *Rockets Into Space*, by Alexander Crosby and Nancy Larrick, published by Random House, New York, 1959.

The authors discuss rockets, satellites, spaceships, space stations—and getting a man to the moon.

**3.** *Off Into Space!* by Margaret Hyde, published by Mc-Graw-Hill, New York, 1959.

The principles behind space travel are discussed. The place of gravity, atmosphere, and the principles of rocket travel are among the important topics in this book.

**4.** *Jets*, by Charles Verral, published by Prentice-Hall, Englewood Cliffs, New Jersey.

This book is about jets and the principles of jet propulsion.

**A.** Over two hundred years ago when men were still crossing the ocean in sailing ships, Sir Isaac Newton was developing formulas that had to do with rockets traveling in space. He was truly a man living ahead of his time. He was so far ahead of his time that he found it necessary to develop a new kind of mathematics in order to complete his calculations. He called his new mathematics *calculus*.

On the basis of his results, Sir Isaac made these predictions.

1. In order to stay in orbit around the earth a satellite would have to achieve a speed of 5 miles a second.

How many miles per hour would this be?

2. In order to escape the earth's gravitational pull altogether, a rocket must achieve a speed of 7 miles per second.

How many miles an hour would this be?

Were his predictions correct? Investigate by visiting the library and looking through some up-to-date books on space travel.

**B.** Try to invent a mathematical formula for measuring the amount of work you do. A mathematical formula is a short and simple way to explain something. It is shorter than a sentence.

For example, let us express this next sentence in a mathematical formula. *To find the area of a rectangle, multiply the length by the width.*

First choose a symbol or letter to stand for each part of the statement. A can stand for *area*, L for *length*, W for *width*. The above sentence can now be written as a mathematical formula $A = L \times W$, or area equals length times width.

To find the area of any rectangle, use this formula. If $L$ equals 4 inches, and $W$ equals 2 inches, what is $A$ (the area)? Did you say 8 square inches?

Now, how can you develop a formula for *work?*

To do *work*, you must move an object through a *distance*. To move an object, you must apply a *force*.

Suppose you lift a pound of sugar to a height of 1 foot. The force you apply is 1 pound. Suppose you lift the same pound of sugar to a height of 2 feet. You would still apply the same force (1 pound). But you would be doing more work. How much more work? You are lifting the sugar *twice* the distance.

If you lift the pound of sugar to a height of 3 feet you are lifting it 3 *times* the distance. You are doing 3 *times* the work.

Does the term "3 *times*" give you a clue? What does "*times*" mean in arithmetic?

Try to fill in the blanks in the sentence below. If you can, you should have no trouble making a mathematical formula for *work done.*

To find how much *work* is *done,* __?__ the *force* needed to lift an object __?__ the *distance* it is being lifted.

What unit is used to measure *work done?* A combination of the units in the formula is used. For example, if you lift an object to a height of 1 *foot,* and apply a force of 1 *pound,* you are doing 1 *foot-pound* of work.

Derive a formula for *work.*

**Clue:** The formula will use three quantities:

> work
> force
> distance

Now you are on your own.

# UNIT SIX

# ELECTRONS IN ACTION

Lightning flashes across the sky and a tree is split in half. A few days later, the tree shows signs of dying. Another flash and a fire is started in a forest and rages uncontrolled. Lightning is a natural, observable phenomenon, yet we consider it an extraordinary event and watch it in wonder.

We flick a switch and banish the darkness, yet we consider the use of electricity to light our homes an ordinary event. We take electricity for granted and hardly wonder about it at all.

We answer the telephone and talk to a friend many miles away. We spend an evening watching television, and these events are so common that we never stop to consider how they are possible. Do you ever wonder? Suppose no one had ever wondered!

Look at the skyline of a city where electricity means survival for millions of people. Look at a giant dam where the forces of nature are transferred to the wires of a power line and into your home. Look and wonder, for electricity is the energy of moving electrons.

This unit explains how man, as scientist and engineer, uses his brain and his hands, his imagination and skill, to change his environment and his way of life with electrons in action.

## 1. "Rubbing" Off Parts of Atoms

Have you ever scuffed across a wool rug and felt a small shock when you touched another person or a piece of metal? If it was dark, you may even have seen a spark. Also, when you combed your hair on the same day you may have heard a crackling sound.

What do these observations—the shock, the spark, the crackling— mean? By doing the investigation on the opposite page, you will add to these observations and be able to make sense of them.

### One Explanation

Look around you. *All* the things you see are made of atoms. The atom shown in the diagram is an atom of carbon, greatly enlarged. ■ The real carbon atom is very small; it is so small that it would take millions of carbon atoms to make a piece of carbon big enough for you to see.

■

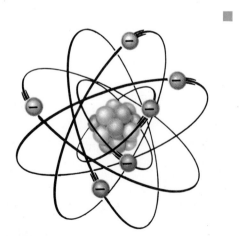

In the center of the atom is the **nucleus** (noo'klē·əs) and revolving around it are **electrons** (i·lek'tronz). Electrons are tiny electrically charged particles. They are *negative* charges of electricity.

The electrons "rub off" onto the plastic rod or the comb. The term "rub off," however, is not accurate. It is better to say that the electrons in certain substances (for example, wool) are easily transferred to other substances such as hard rubber (vulcanite) or plastic. The rubbing helps to transfer the electrons.

Electrons can be transferred from many substances to other substances by rubbing. The plastic rod seems to collect the electrons from the wool.

A negative charge is usually written as *minus* charge or just plain "—". The more electrons the rod collects, the stronger the negative charge becomes. Each electron is really a single unit of negative electric charge.

The rod has a negative charge because it has collected extra electrons. On the other hand, the bits of paper or the stream of water have *not* collected extra electrons. If they had, they would have a negative charge also. Clearly the negative charge on the rod is different from the *neutral* state of the bits of paper or the stream of water. In fact, the paper and water have no charge; that is the meaning of the word "neutral." When there is a difference in charge on two substances, the substances attract

# AN INVESTIGATION into a Force of Attraction

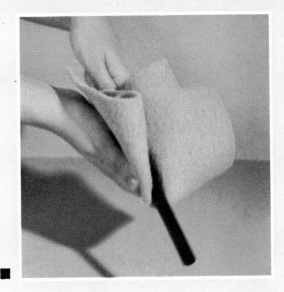

**Needed:** a plastic, or vulcanite, rod or comb; a piece of wool or fur; a balloon; tissue paper

First, tear up bits of tissue paper. Hold the rubber rod or the comb near them for a moment, then remove it. Were the bits of paper attracted to the rod?

Rub the rod or the comb briskly with a piece of wool or fur.■ Again bring the rod near the bits of paper.● Does the rod attract the bits of paper now?

Bring the rod near a stream of water.▲ Does the stream bend toward the rod?

Now briskly rub the wool or fur against the side of an inflated balloon. Throw the balloon to the ceiling or place it against the wall. Does the balloon stay there?

**Additional Investigation:** Sometimes, however hard you try, the balloon does not stay on the ceiling or on the wall. What kind of day is best for this investigation?

233

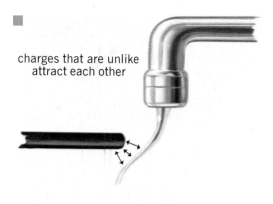

charges that are unlike attract each other

each other; thus the paper and the water are attracted to the rod. ■

The opposite of a "negative" charge is a *positive* or *plus* ("+") charge. A substance develops a positive (+) charge when it loses electrons. The piece of wool, for example, developed a positive charge when it lost some electrons to the rod.

When a substance with a positive ("+") charge is brought near a substance with a negative (—) charge, the force of attraction is strong.

Again, rub the piece of wool against the rod, and then pass the rod back and forth about ¼-inch above the part of the cloth you just rubbed.● Do you find that the small fibers of wool are attracted to the rod? They are attracted because the charges are different. The part of the wool cloth that was rubbed is positive (+), the rod is negative (—).

The bits of paper are neutral; they have no charge (neither negative, nor positive), but they are attracted to the negative rod because there is a charge difference between the paper and the rod.

Would the pieces of paper also be attracted to the positively charged part of the wool cloth? Test your answer.

### Static and Current Electricity

Electricity that is not moving is called **static electricity.** When the

electrons collected on the rod, the rod had a charge of static (not moving) electricity. A charge of static electricity can be removed, or discharged, by bringing the substance near a good **conductor** of electricity. A conductor is any substance, such as metal, through which electrons can flow easily.

Recall your experience when you walked on a wool carpet. You were charged with electrons as you scuffed across the wool carpet, but you discharged the electrons when you put your finger close to something made of metal.

In a thunderstorm, great amounts of static electricity are discharged. Clouds moving in the atmosphere can collect a charge of electrons. When the charge becomes great enough, lightning flashes through the sky. Lightning is a discharge of static electricity. The electrons may be attracted to a metal lightning rod or even to a tree. ▲ Even though a tree will not conduct small charges of electrons, a flash of lightning is powerful enough to pass through it. Lightning, then, is a huge number of electrons that move fast—suddenly, with a flash of light. The sound of thunder follows.

You can move electrons in another way. Of course you have turned on the electric light, or television, or radio. With a flick of the switch electrons flow along a wire. Electricity moving through a wire is called **current electricity**.

When you flick a switch, you do not use static (nonmoving) electricity, but current (moving) electricity. In other words, a light bulb glows when electrons are moving in a wire (current electricity). See for yourself by doing the investigation on the opposite page.

## From Muscular Energy to Electric Energy

There are many forms of energy. When you lit the bulb by means of the hand generator you changed energy from one form to another. The chemical energy from food in your body was changed to mechanical energy (movement of the arm). The mechanical energy was changed to electric energy and then to light energy.

When you cranked the generator, then, the chemical energy from the food in your body was changed into electric energy, the energy of moving electrons. Now let us search further into the way electrons can be made to move.

**BEFORE YOU GO ON**

**A.** Study the statements below and choose the correct responses. They will help you fix in mind the concepts of this section.

1. All the things around us are made up of
   a. compounds        b. atoms

2. When a plastic rod is rubbed with wool or fur, it collects
   a. protons        b. electrons

3. The sign which would show the charge of an electron is
   a. "—"        b. "+"

4. When there is a difference in charge on two substances, the substances which are differently charged
   a. attract each other        b. repel each other

5. Electricity that is not moving is called
   a. static electricity        b. current electricity

**B.** Write a paragraph or two on this topic: Two Kinds of Electricity.

**USING WHAT YOU KNOW**

In the diagrams on page 238, you will find what are called *pith balls* hanging from strings.

# AN INVESTIGATION into Lighting a Bulb with an Electric Current

**Needed:** a small hand generator; a socket, as shown; and a small bulb

If your school has a small hand generator like the one shown, examine it carefully. ■ The purpose of this investigation is to see what it does and how it works.

Place a small bulb in the socket of the generator, and turn the crank quickly. ■ Does the bulb light up? It should light up as electrons move through it. You have generated an electric current, or a stream of electrons moving through a wire, to light the bulb.

Current electricity is lighting the bulb. Where did the electric energy to light the bulb come from? What energy changes took place?

Ask your teacher to help you take the generator apart.● What are the U-shaped pieces of metal, and what are they used for? What turns inside these metal "U's"?

In diagram 1, the pith balls have been charged with electricity. ■ In diagram 2, the pith balls also have an electric charge. ●

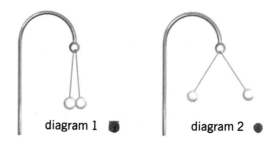

diagram 1 ■          diagram 2 ●

1. Which diagram shows pith balls charged with unlike charges of electricity?

2. Which diagram shows pith balls charged with like charges of electricity?

Explain your answer.

## 2. Generating an Electric Current

When you turned the crank of a generator, you did some work to produce the electric current. Recall from Unit Four the scientist's concept of the word *work*. Whenever an object is moved through a distance, *work* is done. In the hand generator, which object was moved through a distance? The crank moved as you turned it, and the coil inside the magnet moved as well. As it spun around, somehow an electric current was produced.

Let us look further into the way an electric current may be produced by doing the investigation on the opposite page.

## Electric Current— An Explanation

What happened when you stopped moving the magnet; in other words, what happened when you stopped doing work? The needle stopped moving as well; there was no flow of electrons.

The chemical energy in your muscle cells is changed into the mechanical energy which moves the magnet. The mechanical energy of the moving magnet was changed to electric energy in the coil. In order to change one form of energy to another, work was done. You worked to move the magnet through the coil. Electric energy in the coil moved the needle. When you stopped, the needle stopped.

# AN INVESTIGATION into an Electric Current

**Needed:** a meter, a **galvanometer** (gal′və·nom′ə·tər), as in the picture; ■ about 50 feet of insulated bell wire; a strong magnet; a cardboard tube

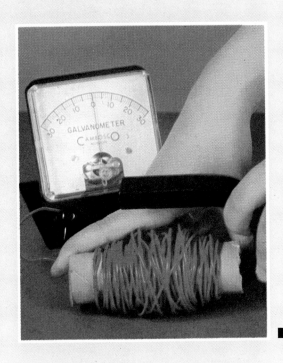

The meter measures the flow of electrons so that each time the needle swings, it is an indication that electrons are flowing.

Did you notice the two knobs on the meter? These are the terminals, the places where the two ends of the wire are attached.

Now make a coil by winding about 75 turns of wire around the cardboard tube. Insert one pole of the magnet into the coil. Pull and push it back and forth inside the tube. ■

Does the needle move? If so, you have produced an electric current.

What happens when you hold the magnet inside the coil but do not move it back and forth? ●

What must happen if an electric current is to be produced?

**Additional Investigation:** What happens if the magnet is held still while the coil around the magnet is moved back and forth?

Try to develop a hypothesis of what might happen. Then find out by investigation if your hypothesis correctly explains what happened.

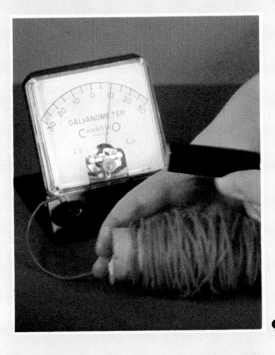

Does a greater amount of work result in a greater flow of electrons? The investigation on the opposite page will help you to answer this question.

## The Ideas Behind Electricity

The ideas behind electricity are simple. One way to produce a small electric current (flow of electrons) is to move a magnet in a coil of wire, so that it quickly passes each of the turns in the coil. Can you guess how it is possible to make the flow of electrons great enough to light a factory or a home or to run a machine? The investigation you just completed on the opposite page provides several important clues.

To help you remember, let us review some of these clues. When an electric current is produced by a magnet in a coil, the flow of electrons can be increased by:

1. moving the magnet faster;
2. using a stronger magnet;
3. increasing the number of turns of wire on the coil.

You can make a good guess about what is needed in a generator. Recall the way you made electrons flow in the wire (page 237). Then look at the drawing which shows the inside of one kind of small generator. ■ Do you see a magnet? Do you see the coil of wire? *When the magnet is moved inside the turns of wire in a coil*, electrons flow.

In another type of generator (such as the one shown in the investigation on page 237), electrons flow *when the coil of wire turns between the poles of a magnet.*● With either generator work must be done to light the bulb.

240

# AN INVESTIGATION into the Flow of Electrons

**Needed:** a homemade coil on a cardboard tube; an electric meter (galvanometer); a strong and a weak magnet

Attach the coil to the meter, as shown in the investigation on page 239. Insert the strong magnet into the coil and move it back and forth very slowly. Record the highest reading.

After you have recorded how much the needle moved, insert the magnet again. This time move it back and forth rapidly.  Do you notice a higher reading on the meter? Was a greater flow of electrons produced by moving the magnet faster?

Now insert the pole of a weaker magnet into the coil. Move it back and forth rapidly. Record the reading. 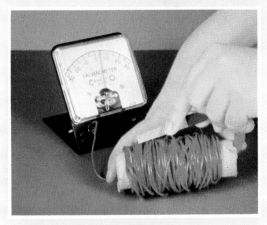 Which magnet gives a higher reading, the stronger or the weaker magnet? Which produces a greater flow of electrons?

Remember the last reading on the meter when you inserted the strong magnet. Begin to unwind the coil of wire. Take off about half the loops, then cut the wire and attach the smaller coil to the meter as before. Again insert the strong magnet into the coil, and move it back and forth at the same speed as before.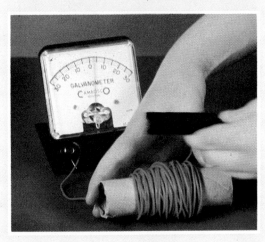

Does the meter read less? Does the number of turns of wire affect the flow of electrons?

For a small generator, the muscle of your arm does the work to move the magnet or to move the coil. The small hand generator changes the mechanical energy of your muscles into electric energy; yet it can light only one small bulb. At this rate, a large number of people would be required to turn many generators in order to light even one small house. How then are commercial, large-scale generators turned? One way utilizes the energy of water falling through a dam. This energy can be used to turn a turbine, as shown. ■ Then the turbine does the work of turning the magnets or coils of wire. Another method utilizes the force of expanding steam to turn the turbine, which then moves a generator.

The next part of this section explains how moving magnets within a coil of wire or moving coils of wire between the poles of magnets can generate great amounts of electric current. Without electricity our modern way of life would not be possible. Did you ever think how much you depend on a moving coil or a magnet? Can you imagine what it would be like if there were no electric current to serve you? Can you remember a time when the electricity went off in your home?

### Producing Powerful Electric Currents

If you did the investigation on page 239, you produced enough electricity to move a tiny needle back and forth or to light a small bulb, and

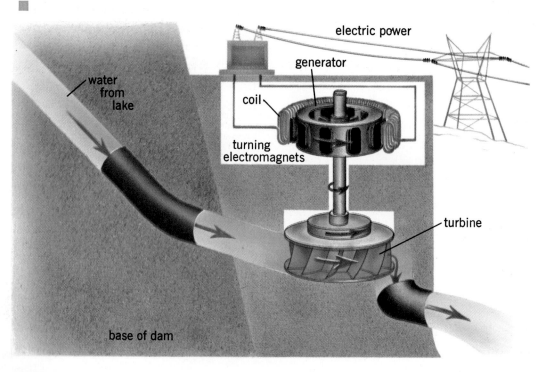

water from lake

electric power

generator

coil

turning electromagnets

turbine

base of dam

you know that the force of a magnet has something to do with the production of an electric current.

Perhaps you also have an idea of what is meant by a **magnetic field.** If not, you can observe the way magnetic force acts by using a magnet, some iron filings, and a piece of glass or plastic. Place the glass on top of the magnet, as shown.● Sprinkle some of the filings carefully on top of the glass. Tap it gently. The iron filings collect along the **lines of force** of the magnet. They give you a visual image of a magnetic field (as shown in the picture).

Notice that the strongest lines of force seem to be between the poles of the horseshoe magnet. Perhaps this explains why it is easy to produce an electric current by moving a wire between the poles. You are then moving it across the strongest part of the magnetic field.▲

If you move a wire across a magnetic field, it seems as if the electrons in the wire are given a push; they flow through the wire and can move the needle on a meter. In order to keep the electrons flowing, however, the wire must be kept moving through the magnetic field. If the wire stops moving, the electrons stop moving. *If no work is done, electric current is not produced.* Of course, you could do it another way, as in the investigation on page 239. You could hold the wire steady, but what then would be required to move in order to move the electrons?

With a moving magnet and a wire, you have made a tiny generator produce a tiny current.

How can a larger current be produced? How can a current large enough to run an electric train or to light a city be produced? The results of the investigation on page 241 should give you a clue. When you think you have the answer, read on to find out how large electric currents are generated and to learn about one of the world's greatest dams.

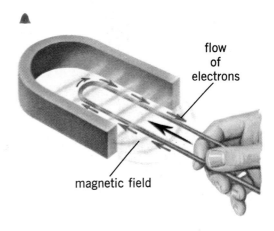

flow
of
electrons

magnetic field

## A Visit to Hoover Dam

As you stand on the dam and look back, you see water trapped in a huge lake. Then as you look down on the front of the dam, you see the water flowing from openings near the base of the dam into the river below. ■

Inside you are standing beside a big generator; you cannot miss its loud and steady hum. Let us find out what is causing the hum.

The water of the lake rushes through the dam in large runways. This falling water is turning wheels, or turbines, in a way much like that shown on page 242. As each turbine turns, strong magnets that are inside huge coils of wire turn also. The stored energy, or potential energy, in the water behind the dam is turned into energy of motion—or kinetic energy. This energy turns the turbines which turn the generators and cause electrons to flow through large wires (cables) for hundreds of miles.

The magnets in the generator do not look like the metal magnets you have seen. Look at those in the picture. ● They are not shaped like a common horseshoe magnet. They have coils of wire wrapped tightly around them. They are, as you probably have guessed, **electromagnets.**

Look at the simple electromagnet shown on the opposite page. Notice that the wire is connected in a **circuit** (sûr′kit) going from one terminal of the dry cell to the other. Between the two terminals, the wire is wound into a coil around a soft iron bolt, as shown in the picture. ▲ The bolt is the core of the electromagnet. The magnetic force around the coil of wire, through which a current is flowing, makes the soft iron core act as a magnet. This bolt, wrapped with turns of wire, becomes an electromagnet when an electric current is flowing through the wire.

An electromagnet can only work while a current is passing through the coil. For this to happen there must be a *complete circuit*, or path, through which the electrons can move. ◆ When either terminal is disconnected, as shown, the circuit is broken, and electrons will not move along the wire. ★

An ordinary magnet will pick up nails, or tacks, or paper clips, or other objects made of iron or steel. An electromagnet will do the same. How can you make an electromagnet pick up objects heavier than paper clips? That is, how can you make it stronger? Of course, you can increase the number of dry cells or you can wind more turns of wire around the bolt. Try it and see.

In the generators at Hoover Dam, the magnets used are electromagnets. They, too, have many turns of wire around pieces of iron to make very strong magnets. Because of this, the electromagnets have a very strong magnetic field.

In most power plants, flowing water or steam turns a turbine; the turbine turns a generator and an electric current is produced. That is, a large number of electrons flow through the coils near the poles of the electromagnets, and out along cables to homes, schools, and factories. Electricity lights each home, runs the radio or the television, toasts bread, and cooks food.

The electromagnet shown on this page works only when it is connected to the dry cell. If the circuit is broken, no electrons flow through the wire. Since an electromagnet works

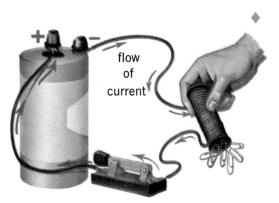

flow of current

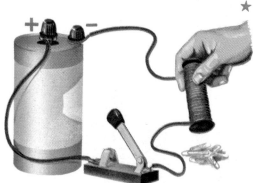

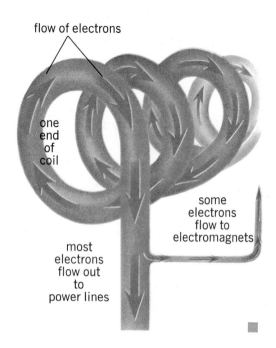

flow of electrons

one
end
of
coil

some
electrons
flow to
electromagnets

most
electrons
flow out
to
power lines

only when a current flows through the coil, where does the electromagnet in a generator get the electricity to make it work?

At Boulder Dam, some of the current produced in the coil of the generator is shunted to the wires of the electromagnets, as shown in the diagram. ■ This keeps the magnetic field around the electromagnet quite strong. As the electromagnet spins, the electrons within the stationary coils flow out through wires in great quantities to supply the country with electrical energy to light homes and run machines.

■

**BEFORE YOU GO ON**

**A.** Study the statements below and choose the correct responses. They will help you fix in mind the concepts of this section.

1. When a magnet is moved in a coil of wire
   a. an electric current is produced
   b. static electricity is produced

2. In order to generate electricity, work
   a. must be done
   b. need not be done

3. A greater flow of current is produced in *all but one* of these conditions. Give the one condition.
   a. A magnet is moved faster in a coil of wire.
   b. A stronger magnet is used.
   c. A larger coil of wire is used.
   d. A rubber rod is rubbed faster with a piece of wool.

**B.** Write a paragraph or two on this topic: Generating an Electric Current.

**USING WHAT YOU KNOW**

1. To make a small generator of electricity, you need a magnet and a coil of wire. What else is needed?

**2.** Below is a diagram of iron filings. ● What is responsible for the pattern of the filings? How would you change the pattern?

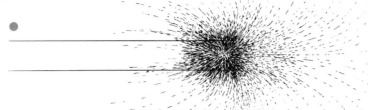

**3.** What is the difference between potential energy and kinetic energy?

ON YOUR OWN **In the Laboratory**

Get a bar magnet. Test its strength by using it to lift paper clips or nails.

Now make an electromagnet which is twice as strong as the bar magnet. How can you do it? How will you know the electromagnet is twice as strong as the bar magnet?

## 3. Electric Bells and Electric Motors

If you visit any factory, you will find some power-driven machines. Perhaps you will find some that push pieces of ore along by means of a screw or winding inclined plane. Perhaps you will find a machine with gears to separate fibers, as shown in the picture. ▲

These machines may be simple or compound, but the force which makes them work is not supplied by muscles as it was years ago. Perhaps the earliest factory machines were operated by muscle power. Men worked them, or else the force of animals walking on huge treadmills was used.

But muscle power was too limited; it took too long to get a job done.

Still later, the force of wind or the force of moving water turned wheels that operated machinery. As man gained more knowledge, he found newer and better sources of energy.

He learned to use steam engines to turn long shafts, as described in Unit Five. Today, however, most of the energy used to run machines in a factory is supplied in a different way. The energy is transferred from one place to another through wires. It is the energy of moving electrons.

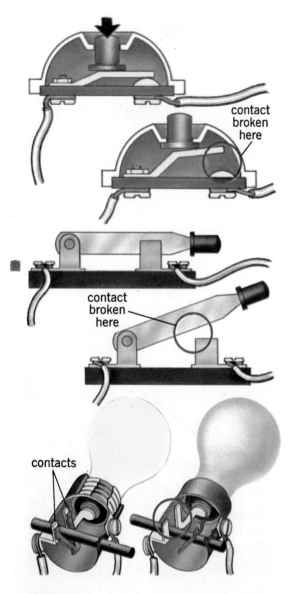

contact broken here

contact broken here

contacts

By pushing a switch, man can unleash this energy. When he pushes the switch he starts millions of tiny electrons moving through a circuit to do work for him. In our discussion of electric bells and motors, let us start with electrical switches. How do switches help man control the great energy of moving electrons?

## The Purpose of Switches

The push button or switch on a lamp serves the same purpose as a knife switch. Look at the pictures of a doorbell button. ■ Compare them with the knife switch. Can you determine how the doorbell button works? When the button is pushed, the current flows through the circuit to ring the bell. When the button is released the circuit is broken, and the current stops. The electrons cease to move through the wires.

The next pictures show how a lamp switch works. ■ There are many different types of switches, but they all do the same thing. They make and break an electric circuit.

The moving electrons (current electricity) run motors. The motors operate the machinery of the factory or the simple and compound machines found in your home. Moving electrons make machines work. How do moving electrons move the parts of an electric bell or an electric motor? How are electric bells and electric motors similar? See for yourself by doing the investigations on the next three pages.

# AN INVESTIGATION into the Similarity of Electric Bells and Electric Motors

**Needed:** an electric bell; a small electric motor

Take the cover off the front of an electric bell. ■ Look inside an electric motor. ● The pictures will give you an idea of how they are built.

Look for something that is similar in both of them. Do you find an electromagnet in each? Sometimes there are several. They may have different shapes, but they each have a metal core with wire wound around it. You may recognize that the metal core is iron and that the pieces of iron with wire wound around them *are* electromagnets.

How are electromagnets used to ring a bell or to run an electric motor?

If you do not know, why not make a bell of your own, as shown on the next two pages? You will find it interesting, and you can use it to test how well you can put ideas and tools together.

**Additional Investigation:** Is the motor in the picture different from an electric generator? Do they both contain the same basic arrangement of parts?

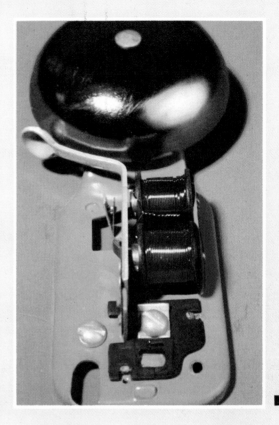

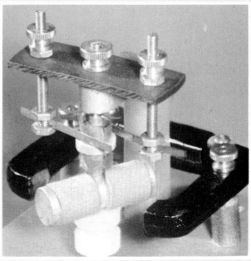

249

# MAKING A MODEL: An Electric Bell

**Needed:** three pieces of board—one for the base, about 5 x 7 inches; one to hold the electromagnet, and another, about 2 x 2 inches, to hold the clapper; insulated bell wire; two washers on a 3-inch bolt; a clock spring; a hammer; nails; a 1-inch angle iron; a small bolt ($\frac{3}{4}$-inch) and two nuts; a 2-inch bolt and three nuts; a knife switch

Make and operate your own electric bell. ■ For the electromagnet, wind at least 100 turns of insulated bell wire between two washers, on a 3-inch bolt. Leave several inches of free wire at both ends. Fasten the electromagnet to a block, as shown, and mount the block on the baseboard by driving nails through from the bottom of the board.

For the clapper, use a 7-inch piece of softened clock spring, not less than $\frac{1}{2}$-inch wide. (Your teacher can soften a clock spring for you by heating it gently over a Bunsen burner or gas stove until the spring can be straightened easily. While heating the clock spring, it is best to hold it with two pairs of tongs or pliers.) The spring from a broken alarm clock or kitchen timer is fine, or the clock repairman in your town may be willing to give you an old spring. After the piece of spring has cooled, punch a hole with a hammer and a nail near one end of the piece of spring, and two holes, about 1 inch apart, at the other end. Fasten, mount, and bend the clapper, as shown. The clapper should be about $\frac{1}{8}$-inch from the end of the magnet. Place a small bolt with two nuts through the hole on the top.

For the contact point, use a 1-inch angle iron and a small bolt about $\frac{3}{4}$-inch long. Fasten the bolt with two nuts, as shown. Set the bolt so that it is pressing firmly against the clapper, and connect the wires.

Close the knife switch in the circuit before mounting the gong. (Do you see why the switch is called a knife switch?) Adjust the contact point by turning the bolt slowly until the clapper vibrates back and forth. Tighten the two nuts. This position of the clapper indicates where you should mount the gong so that it will be in range of the bolt at the end of the clapper. Mount the gong with a 2-inch bolt and three nuts. Drill a hole through the base large enough for the 2-inch bolt to fit through. Now your bell is complete.

When you are ready to ring the bell, close the knife switch.

What happens when you close it? If the clapper misses the gong, you can make the necessary adjustment by slightly bending the clock spring. How does the bell work? Compare your model of an electric bell with a commercial one.

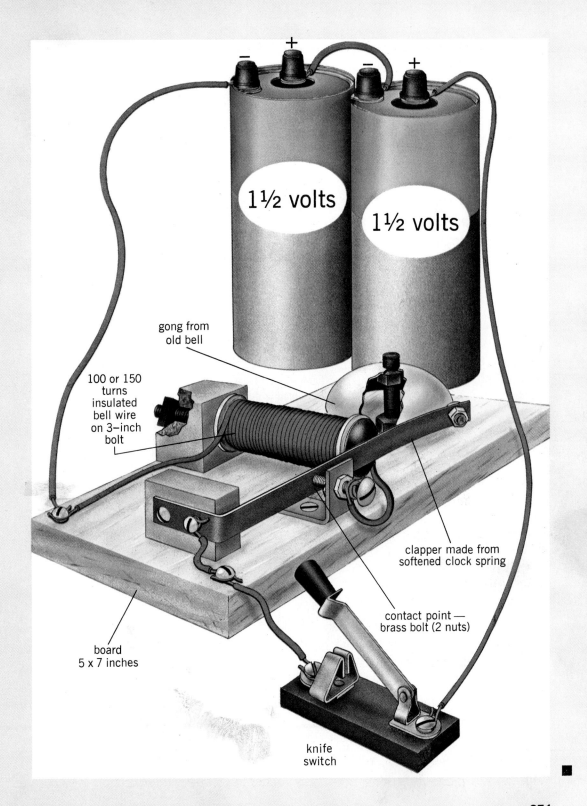

- **+**
- **−**
- **+**
- **−**

1½ volts

1½ volts

gong from
old bell

100 or 150
turns
insulated
bell wire
on 3–inch
bolt

clapper made from
softened clock spring

contact point —
brass bolt (2 nuts)

board
5 x 7 inches

knife
switch

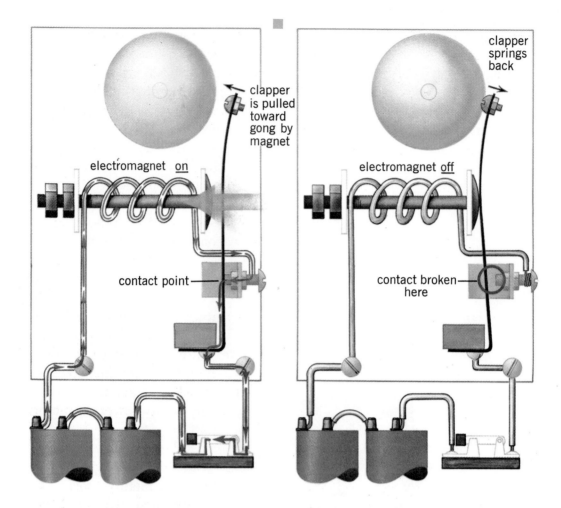

electromagnet <u>on</u>

clapper is pulled toward gong by magnet

contact point

clapper springs back

electromagnet <u>off</u>

contact broken here

## An Explanation of an Electric Bell

With a source of electric energy, we can move electrons. We can direct the path of electrons to flow where we need electric energy to do work. Recall this basic concept: Work is done when an object is moved through a distance. Take a moment to think about this question: Is work done when an electric bell rings? What object is moved?

In the bell, electric energy produces a magnetic force in an electromagnet that attracts the bell clapper.

The current flows through the coils of the electromagnet and the electromagnet pulls the clapper. Then the clapper hits the gong. What happens to make the clapper move back and forth again, and again, and again, to make the bell continue ringing?

When the current is off, the electromagnet does not attract the clapper. (The soft iron stays magnetized *only* as long as the current is moving in the coil.) The clapper springs away from the gong. When the clapper springs away, the current goes on again and the electromagnet attracts the clapper again. The clapper hits the gong again. This happens over and over. But why does the current keep turning ON and OFF?

Study the picture. ■ Do you see how the electromagnet pulls the clapper away from the contact point and breaks the circuit? When the circuit is broken, the electrons stop flowing. When the clapper touches the contact point again, it completes, or closes, the circuit. Once again electrons move through the circuit, and the electromagnet is on again.

The knife switch opens and closes the circuit. It allows the current to pass through or cuts the current off when you want the bell to stop ringing.

Now go on to examine an electric motor.

## Electric Motors

Electromagnets perform an important role in electric motors. You can discover a great deal about how an electric motor works by making your own model. Follow the directions on the next two pages.

## Motors—An Explanation

Large electric motors work on the same principle as the model motor shown on page 255 and also the model electric bell. In each case, the energy of moving electrons produces a magnetic force in an electromagnet. In the bell, the clapper moves because it is attracted to the electromagnet. In the electric motor, the armature spins around because it is attracted by the poles of electromagnets.

In the model motor an electric current is sent through the electromagnets, under the blades of the armature. The stationary electromagnets attract the poles of the crosspieces on the armature only when the brush is touching the bottom of the armature. (See page 255.) When the armature contacts the brush, the circuit is complete, and current flows to the electromagnet. The electromagnet attracts the blades of the armature and the armature moves away from the brush, allowing the blades to coast until they are attracted to the electromagnet on the other side. Soon the armature is whirling about.

In larger, more powerful motors the armature may turn the blades of a fan or of other machines, such as washing machines, electric mixers, power saws, and factory tools.

More complicated electric motors use electromagnets *on* the spinning armature, as shown on page 249. Most of them use a more complicated electric circuit and a different arrangement of parts for more efficient operation.

Make a list of all the appliances that you can think of which use electric motors. It will probably fill several pages. Each year more new ones are produced. The electric can opener, the electric blender, and the electric shoe buffer all do jobs that were once done by muscles alone.

# MAKING A MODEL: An Electric Motor

**Needed:** a piece of pegboard about 4 x 6 inches; a thin sheet of iron or steel (about 4 x 4 inches), perhaps cut from a can; two bolts, which fit the holes in the pegboard, about $1\frac{1}{4}$-inch long; four nuts and four washers to fit the bolts; a strip of clean metal about $\frac{1}{2}$-inch wide and 3 inches long; a spool of insulated bell wire; a piece of copper wire 4 inches long, bare at the end; four short bolts to fit the pegboard; six nuts to fit these bolts; a 6-inch metal strip; a pointed tool; metal shears

Study again the diagram of the bell on page 251. Recall that the electromagnet attracts the clapper, making it move. Now look at the diagram of a simple electric motor. ■ Electric motors are turned by electromagnets. You can make this simplified motor with the materials listed above.

Wind at least a hundred turns of the bell wire around each of the $1\frac{1}{4}$-inch bolts, between two washers, as shown; the more windings the better. Use tape to keep the coils from unwinding. Leave about 6 inches of wire at each end for making connections.

Use the four nuts to attach both electromagnets to the strip of clean metal (cut 4 inches long) and to the pegboard, as shown. Attach the wires, as shown.

Use metal shears to cut the **armature** (är'mə·chŏŏr) from the piece of 4 x 4 thin steel. Watch out for sharp edges on the metal. Measure carefully so that it will clear the tops of the bolts. Bend one flap forward and the other backward, as shown. (It may be wise to get an adult to help you with this procedure.)

Use a pointed tool to make a small dent or cup in the strip of metal. This cup will serve as the upper pivot for the spinning piece of metal, called the armature. Make a similar pointed cup in the center of the bottom metal strip to serve as the lower pivot point for the armature.

Bend the 6-inch metal strip so that it forms a holder for the armature to spin in an upright position. Fasten it to the pegboard with two small bolts.

Attach the brush (4-inch piece of bare copper wire) to another small bolt, as shown. Connect a piece of insulated wire from the same bolt to the switch or to a dry cell. Adjust the brush so that it just touches the bottom angled part of the armature. It should touch only for a short time as the armature turns and only when the armature is in such a position that the crosspieces are not too close to the electromagnets.

Once the motor has been assembled, it must be connected to a source of electric energy. Dry cells, connected in series, are suitable for this purpose.

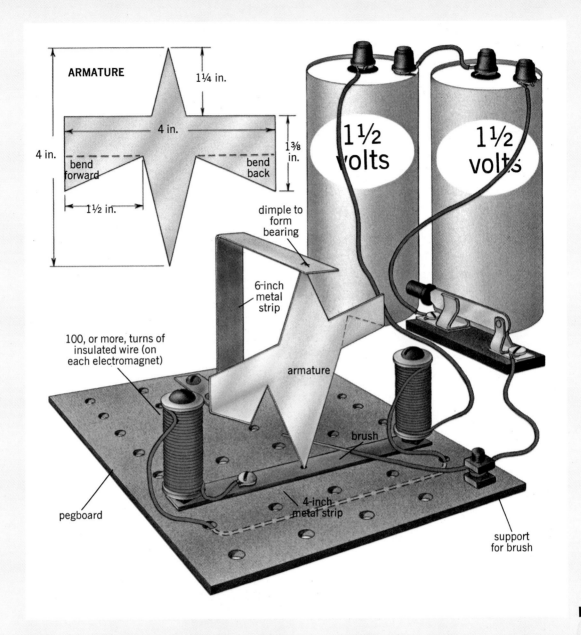

ARMATURE

1¼ in.

4 in.

4 in.

1⅜ in.

bend forward

bend back

1½ in.

1½ volts

1½ volts

dimple to form bearing

6-inch metal strip

100, or more, turns of insulated wire (on each electromagnet)

armature

brush

pegboard

4-inch metal strip

support for brush

Connect the electromagnets and wires to two dry cells and a knife switch, as shown above.

Close the knife switch and give the armature a start in the direction of the points on the blades of the armature.

You may have to adjust the position of contact between the brush and the armature to get it to spin steadily.

Go to the library and get information about other electric motors. Do all motors work on the same principle?

**A.** Study the statements below and choose the correct responses. They will help you fix in mind the concepts of this section.

    **1.** Electric motors and electric bells would not be able to operate without
        a. switches               b. electromagnets

    **2.** Different kinds of electric switches are used to complete an
        a. electric circuit          b. electromagnet

    **3.** The part of an electric motor that acts like the contact point on the electric bell is the
        a. brush                b. electromagnet

**B.** Write a paragraph or two on this topic: How an Electric Motor Works.

**A.** Below are diagrams of an electric bell and an electric motor. Note the numbers which lead to different parts of each. Name each part and write what each part does. ■ ●

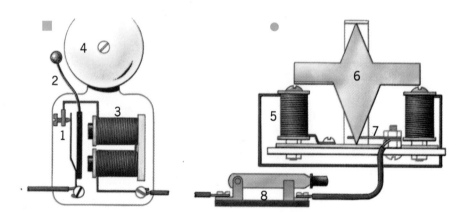

**B.** Compare the electric motor (page 249) with the generators (page 240).

    **1.** How are they similar?

    **2.** How are they different?

## 4. Electric Signals

At the top of this page are shown ways people have used to communicate with others some distance away. ▲ What are some other ways to communicate quickly at even greater distances, such as with other countries throughout the world?

We can, of course, send letters by jet plane. A jet plane crosses the continent in 4 hours, reaches France (from New York) in 7 hours, or approaches Hawaii (from San Francisco) in 8 hours; but there is a way to send a message much faster than this. In fact, you can send a message with the speed of light, about 186,000 miles per second.

In your school, how many different ways are used to send messages? Are they conveyed by direct speech, by delivery of a hand-written note, by electric energy through a wire, or by radio waves?

Have you ever made an announcement on a loudspeaker or called a friend on the playground?

Have you ever carried a written message from your teacher to the teacher in another classroom?

Does your classroom have a telephone or an "intercom" system?

Is there a radio or a television set in your school? These can carry voice messages over a long distance. The first electrical devices for carrying long-distance messages, however, could not transmit the human voice. They carried messages in code.

### Messages by Code

A telegraph sends messages by a code. Are code messages used in your school? Here is a clue: What is the signal for dismissal? for a fire drill? It is probably a gong or a bell which conveys a message by a kind of code. A button is pressed in the office, and the gong rings. One ring may mean dismissal; two rings may mean a fire drill. Three rings may mean something else—what do they mean in your school?

Today a message can be sent by telegraph across the country faster than you can say "one." In fact, a message sent at a speed of 186,000 miles per second (the speed of light) could go around the earth in about one-seventh of a second. How does the telegraph work?

Study the telegraph shown. ■ Notice that there are really three separate parts:

1. A *telegraph key* that opens and closes an electric circuit to control the electric current.

2. A *sounder bar* that produces a clicking noise each time the circuit is closed by the key. The time lapse between clicks establishes the code.

3. A *source of electricity* (in this case, two dry cells) that provides an electric current.

Does the key remind you of a switch (page 248)? Each time the key is pressed down, the electric current flows in a circuit. When the key is released, the current stops flowing.

Now look at the sounder. The metal bar moves up and down and makes a sound.

What makes the metal sounder move up and down? Notice the electromagnets below the sounder bar. Each time the key is pressed down, electric current flows through the electromagnets, and they attract the iron crosspiece on the sounder bar. As the sounder moves up and down, it makes a clicking sound as it hits the screw above or the frame below. These clicks are the code for a message, as you can find out if you make your own simple telegraph.

### A Model Telegraph

Why not make your own model of a telegraph? You can use it to send messages to your friend across the yard or to your brother or sister upstairs. Directions for making the telegraph are on the opposite page.

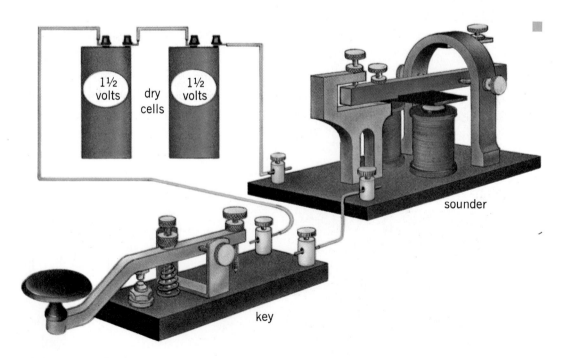

dry cells

1½ volts   1½ volts

sounder

key

# MAKING A MODEL: A Telegraph

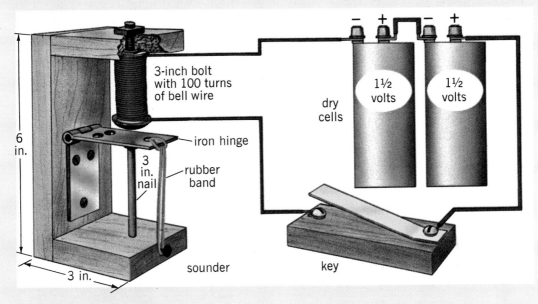

6 in.

3 in.

3-inch bolt with 100 turns of bell wire

iron hinge

3 in. nail

rubber band

sounder

dry cells

1½ volts

1½ volts

key

**Needed:** all the materials shown in the diagram of a hinge telegraph ■

Construct a telegraph sounder, using the simple materials shown in the diagram. By turning the nut at the top, you can adjust the height of the electromagnet so that the hinge is in range.

If the hinge sticks to the bottom of the bolt when the current is turned off, place a thin rubber band between the hinge and the base, as shown.

Make the key by using shears to cut a strip of metal from a tin can. You can protect yourself from the sharp edges on the metal strip by putting tape on the edges.

If you make two telegraph sets, you will be able to communicate with a friend some distance away. The diagram shows how the two sets should be wired ● Remember, the key closes and opens the circuit. The person receiving the message always holds his key down.

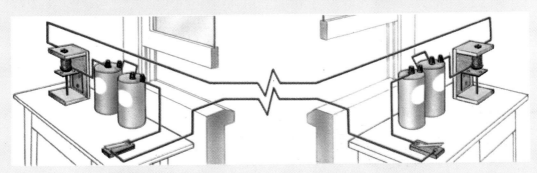

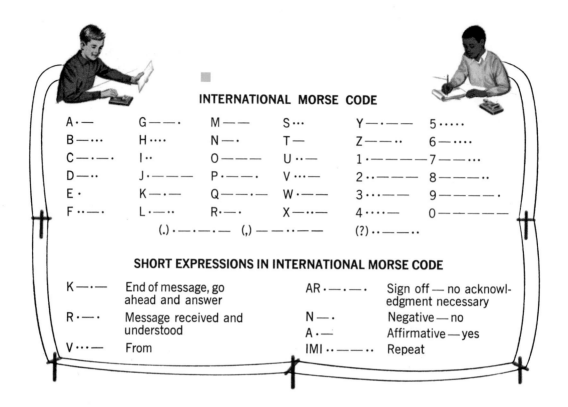

### INTERNATIONAL MORSE CODE

| | | | | | |
|---|---|---|---|---|---|
| A ·— | G ——· | M —— | S ··· | Y —·—— | 5 ····· |
| B —··· | H ···· | N —· | T — | Z ——·· | 6 —···· |
| C —·—· | I ·· | O ——— | U ··— | 1 ·———— | 7 ——··· |
| D —·· | J ·——— | P ·——· | V ···— | 2 ··——— | 8 ———·· |
| E · | K —·— | Q ——·— | W ·—— | 3 ···—— | 9 ————· |
| F ··—· | L ·—·· | R ·—· | X —··— | 4 ····— | 0 ————— |

(.) —·—·—    (,) ——··——    (?) ··——··

### SHORT EXPRESSIONS IN INTERNATIONAL MORSE CODE

| | | | | |
|---|---|---|---|---|
| K —·— | End of message, go ahead and answer | AR ·—·—· | Sign off — no acknowledgment necessary |
| R ·—· | Message received and understood | N —· | Negative — no |
| | | A ·— | Affirmative — yes |
| V ···— | From | IMI ··——·· | Repeat |

## Using a Telegraph

If there were two telegraph sets in separate rooms, how would you send a message from one set to the other? You would need a code. Of course, you could make up your own, but why not use the International Morse Code, which most telegraphers use and which is shown on the top of this page. ■ The letters are represented by various combinations of dots ( · ) and dashes ( — ). To send a "dot," press the key and let go immediately. To send a "dash," press the key and hold it for about the time it takes to say "dash." You may think of a dot as a short interval between clicks and a dash as a longer interval between clicks (about three times longer). You read the code by listening to short and long intervals between clicks. After some practice you should be able to recognize the different combinations of dots and dashes easily.

Translate a word message into code and send it with your telegraph. Perhaps you might send this one:

"Well done, well done."

Check with one of your classmates. How successful were you in sending the code, and how successful was he in "reading" it? Try other messages until each of you can understand the messages sent in the dots and dashes of the Morse code. After you have practiced for a while you will be able to gain speed when sending and receiving. Some of the short expressions at the bottom of the code will also help you to gain speed.

Suppose you were to receive this message in code. Can you translate it?

/•--/••••/•-/-/ /••-/•--/•/
/•----/---/•••/ /•-••/---/••/-•/--•/
/•-/•••-/-/•/•--•/
/•••/-••-/••••/---/--/•-••/••••-•/

The telegraph was invented by Samuel F. B. Morse. Sending code messages over wires was a great improvement in communications, but it is much better to hear the actual *voice* of a friend. Many scientists considered the idea, but Alexander Graham Bell made it happen.

/--•/---/ /---/-•/ /-/---/

/-/••••/•/ /-••/•/---•/-/

/•••/•/-••-/-/-•/---/-•/•--••-/

### Voices from Afar

Long-distance telephone calls can be made very rapidly on the special telephone shown in the picture. This particular telephone is similar to the one on the desk of the President of the United States.

By inserting a particular card into a slot, the President is able, in an instant, to talk to leaders in London, or Paris, or Rome, or Moscow.

Many more of these modern telephones will be in use during the next few years. Some business organizations are now using them as a rapid method of contacting branch offices around the world. Notice the slot for inserting prepared cards to get the numbers most often called, and the pushbuttons that have replaced the round dial.

Think of the many ways in which the speed of communicating by telephone can help us. It can be used to report an accident, to call the doctor, to report a fire, to order groceries, to catch a criminal, or to save a life.

How does the telephone system relay a message such a long distance in such a short time?

First, let us look at a telephone; it has three important parts.

1. A *transmitter* (trans·mit′ər) that picks up your voice and then translates the sound into **electric impulses** (the message).

2. A *wire* that carries the message.

3. A *receiver* that receives the electric impulses (message) and translates them back into sound for someone else's ear.

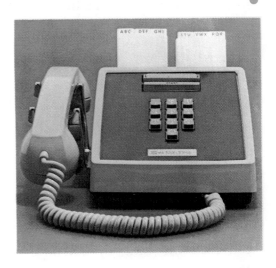

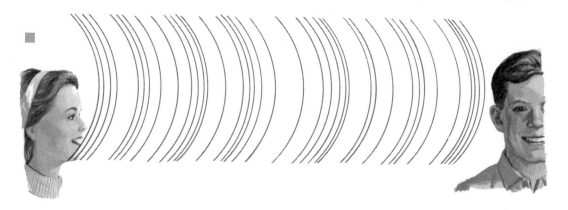

## What Happens to Your Voice

In order to produce the sound of speech, you must cause particles in the air to move in wave patterns called sound waves. ■

These sound waves cause a small thin disk in the transmitter of the telephone to vibrate. The vibrations have the same pattern as the sound waves produced by your voice, and the "message" of your voice is transmitted along a wire but not as sound. Sound vibrations can travel along a solid wire for only a short distance, whereas an electric current can travel a very long distance through a wire. The object then is to change the sound waves into electric impulses, which then travel through the wire in the same pattern as that of the sounds produced by your voice. ●

When the electric impulses reach the receiver, a thin metal plate vibrates to produce the same pattern of sound waves as the ones spoken. Your friend's ear then receives the sound.

To find out how a telephone transmitter works, make a simple one of your own. Perhaps the directions on the opposite page will suit you. If not, invent your own ideas and tools.

## Changes in the Word "Hello"

When you call a friend and say "hello" into the transmitter of the sugar-box telephone, what happens? Can you explain how the message travels from your vocal cords to the transmitter, over the wire to the receiver, and from the receiver to your friend's ear? Perhaps your explanation might be as follows on page 264.

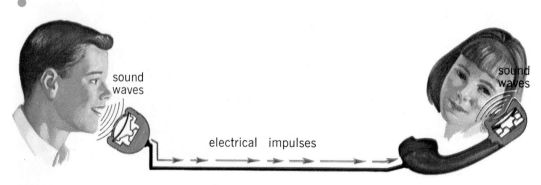

sound waves

electrical impulses

sound waves

## MAKING A MODEL: A Simple Telephone

**Needed:** 2-pound sugar box, and other materials shown in the diagram

Cut two small pieces from the bottom of the aluminum-foil pie plate. Bend each piece near one end, and fasten it to the front surface of the box by inserting paper clips, as shown. Place the two or three pieces of pencil "lead" (really, graphite which is a form of carbon) across the tops of the aluminum strips, as shown. ■ This completes the telephone transmitter.

For a receiver, use an amateur's radio headphone or a discarded telephone receiver. ■ Use four 1½-volt dry cells connected in series or one 6-volt cell in the circuit.

After you have attached all of the wires and batteries as shown, test your "telephone." Ask a friend to take the receiver some distance away and to listen while you talk into the open pouring spout. Try changing the number of pencil carbons, and the distance between your mouth and the spout, until you get good results. Does the telephone transmit your voice? What happens to the pencil carbons when you talk into the spout? What happens to the electric current in the circuit?

Unscrew the plastic cover of your headphone and examine the inside carefully. ■ Do you find an electromagnet? What do you think is the purpose of the electromagnet?

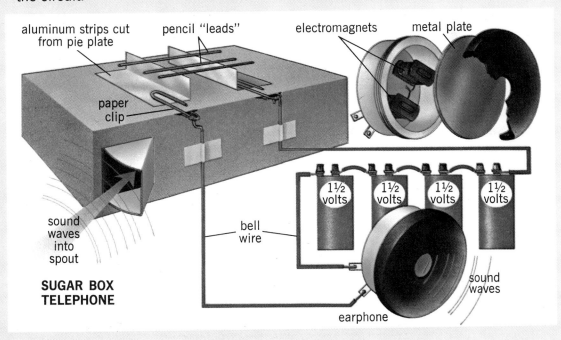

aluminum strips cut from pie plate

pencil "leads"

electromagnets

metal plate

paper clip

sound waves into spout

**SUGAR BOX TELEPHONE**

1½ volts

1½ volts

1½ volts

1½ volts

bell wire

sound waves

earphone

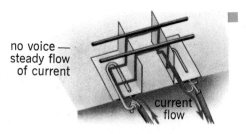

no voice — steady flow of current

current flow

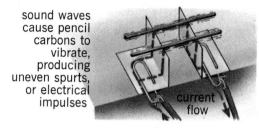

sound waves cause pencil carbons to vibrate, producing uneven spurts, or electrical impulses

current flow

Vibrations set up by your vocal cords caused the sugar box, aluminum strips, and pencil carbons to vibrate. As the pieces of carbon vibrated, they "danced" up and down on top of the aluminum strips "in time" to the pattern of vibrations produced by the sound of your voice. As the carbons moved, they changed the steady flow of electrons through the circuit into strong and weak spurts of electricity, or electric impulses. ■ These electric impulses move along the wire to the receiver where they cause the electromagnet to become stronger or weaker, in patterns which match perfectly the sound waves produced by your voice. As the strength of the electric impulse varies, the strength of the electromagnet varies. The pull of the electromagnet on the thin metal disks varies as well.

In this way, the disk in the receiver vibrates back and forth "in time" (in the same pattern) with the sound waves which began in your voice box. Your friend hears your "hello."

What happens when you say "hello" to your friend over a modern telephone, like the one at home or in the school office? Is it the same as the sugar-box telephone?

Look at the diagram of a modern telephone shown below. ● The transmitter and receiver are both in the part that is lifted up by the hand. Compare the receiver unit with the diagram of the headphone on page 263. To what part of the diagram on the same page would you compare the transmitter below? You can find out more about the modern telephone by doing the investigation on the opposite page.

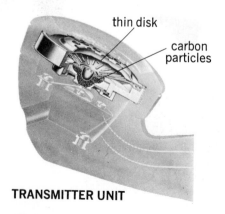

thin disk

carbon particles

**TRANSMITTER UNIT**

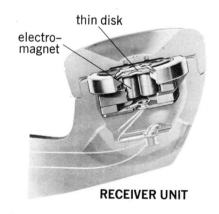

electro-magnet

thin disk

**RECEIVER UNIT**

# AN INVESTIGATION into a Modern Telephone

**Needed:** a modern telephone. DO NOT TAKE APART A TELEPHONE THAT IS IN SERVICE. Your teacher may be able to borrow one for this purpose by calling the local telephone business office

First, lift the receiver of the telephone from the cradle, and unscrew the cover from the mouthpiece. Take out the small unit just inside, as shown. ■ If the unit is stuck inside the mouthpiece cap, ease it out gently with a small screwdriver. This piece, about the size of a cookie, is the transmitter; and, of course, it works more efficiently than the sugar box, aluminum strips, and carbons that you used in making a model telephone. Examine the holes on top. Do you see anything inside that might vibrate? Look at the bottom of the tiny transmitter, and notice the small piece that is sticking out.

Now, in the same way, open the receiver. ● Tilt the receiver down so that the small unit falls into your hand. On some models, the unit is attached to a wire and cannot be taken out very far. Again, look into the holes. Do you find a plate that could be made to vibrate? Touch a steel paper clip to the side of the receiver. ▲ What happens?

The receiver is very much like the headphone that you used with the simple telephone model.

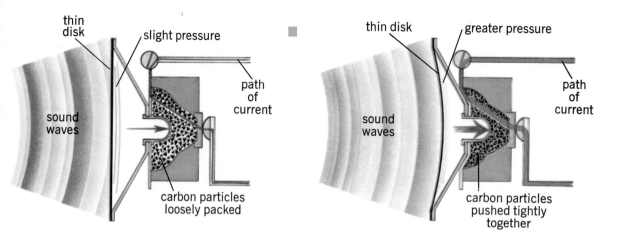

thin disk

slight pressure

path of current

sound waves

carbon particles loosely packed

thin disk

greater pressure

path of current

sound waves

carbon particles pushed tightly together

## The Modern Telephone

The transmitter and receiver of a modern telephone are sealed units, and they cannot be taken apart easily. Use your imagination to visualize, with the help of the diagrams, what is on the inside of the transmitter. ■ You can also refer to the diagram on page 264. Notice the thin metal plate, or disk, inside the holes, which vibrates with the same pattern as your voice waves. Behind this disk are fine particles of carbon. These particles are equivalent to the two pencil carbons on the pieces of aluminum. As the disk vibrates, the carbon particles move closer together and then farther apart.

In the diagram on the left, for example, a fairly weak sound wave is hitting the thin disk, and because of its small force, is not causing the disk to move very much. ■ Therefore, very little pressure is being applied to the carbon particles; they remain loosely packed. It is not possible for a very large electric current to pass through

them. On the other hand, in the diagram on the right, a stronger sound wave is hitting the disk, pushing it inward with greater force. ■ Since they are under much greater pressure, the carbon particles are pushed closer together. When they become more tightly packed, they become a better conductor of electric current, as shown. A stronger electric impulse is therefore allowed to pass through the wire.

When the particles are closer together, they are said to be compressed. When they are farther apart, the volume of carbon particles expands. This compression and release of the carbon particles changes a steady current to electric impulses that travel along the wire. The telephone receiver changes the impulses back into sound waves that the listener can hear.

The telephone is a valuable aid. Raise the receiver and dial a number. Almost in an instant the connection is made, and your voice is transmitted with the speed of light to your friend.

**A.** Below are diagrams of a telegraph set, and a telephone transmitter and receiver. ● ▲

**1.** Note the numbers which lead to different parts of the telegraph set. In your notebook name each part and write what each part does.

**2.** Name each numbered part of the telephone transmitter and receiver and write what it does, in your notebook.

**B.** Write a paragraph or two on this topic: How a Telephone Works.

Look again at the diagrams of a telephone transmitter and receiver. ● ▲

**1.** How are the transmitter and receiver similar?

**2.** How are they different?

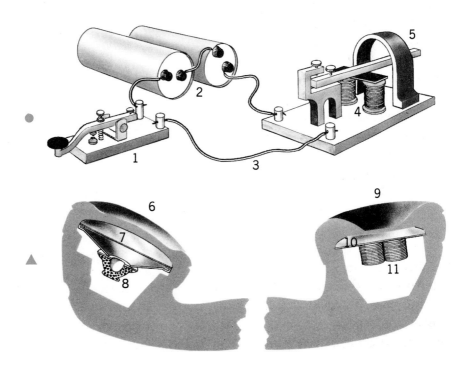

## 5. Relays Without Wires

High in a space capsule, an astronaut talks to his ground crew. 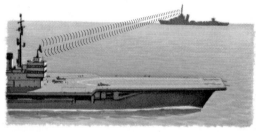 Aboard a destroyer, the captain reports to his admiral on the flagship, many miles away. He turns a knob, speaks into a kind of transmitter, and the admiral hears the captain's voice. At home you turn a knob and listen to the news the same way.

The development of the radio was one of the greatest advances in technology. The first long-distance radio transmitter was built by Guglielmo Marconi. In 1901 Marconi constructed a sending station at Cornwall, England. He then sailed to Newfoundland and set up a receiving station where he received the first transatlantic signal, the letter "S" in Morse code. From that time on radio has steadily improved.

How does a radio work? How can the pattern of a human voice be carried without wires for long distances?

Marconi and other engineers might never have invented radio communication had it not been for the discovery by another great scientist of the force around a wire. See for yourself what this force can do by doing the investigation on the opposite page.

### A New Kind of Wave

A compass needle is really a tiny magnet. The needle moves when an electric current flows through a nearby wire.

Iron filings are attracted by magnetic lines of force, but they can also be lined up by electric current flowing through a nearby wire. When the electric current flows through the wire, what is produced around the wire?

The Danish scientist Hans Oersted (ûr'sted) observed the action of a compass which lay near a wire through which an electric current was flowing. After repeating his observation many times, he concluded that: *Whenever a current flows through a wire, a magnetic force is produced around the wire.* The magnetic *force field* can cause iron filings to line up. A wire with an electric current flowing through it acts like a magnet; it can move the magnetic needle of a compass even though there is only air between. Notice then that the

# AN INVESTIGATION into a Force from a Wire

**Needed:** insulated bell wire; a dry cell; a plastic lid; iron filings; a small compass

Attach one end of a 2-foot piece of insulated bell wire to one of the poles of a dry cell. Place the plastic lid over part of the wire, so that an air space is left between the wire and most of the surface of the lid. Sprinkle some iron filings onto the lid near the wire, and tap the lid several times. Notice what happens to the iron filings.

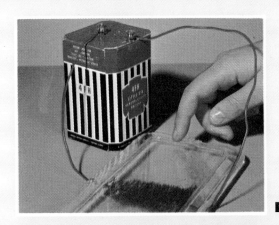

Now attach the other end of the wire to the other pole of the dry cell (as shown), making a complete circuit, so that an electric current travels through the wire. Again tap the lid several times. ■ What happens to the iron filings? What force is present in the air space between the wire and the filings? Disconnect the wire to save your dry cell and remove the lid and filings.

Make a single coil with the same wire, and hold a small compass in the middle of the coil, as shown.● Again connect the wire.▲ What happens to the compass needle? Try this several times, placing the coil so that it forms different angles with the needle. What happens?

Does it happen all the time?

What kind of force makes the needle move?

Does the force extend through the air? How do you know?

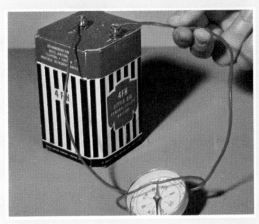

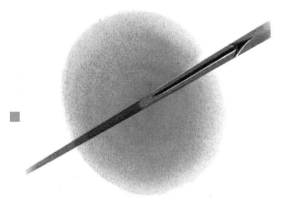

Electric current moving along
a wire in one direction sets up
a magnetic field around the wire

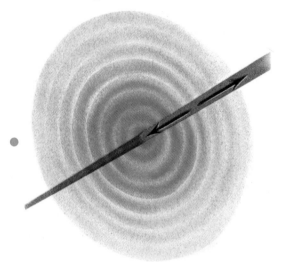

Electric current moving quickly
back and forth along a wire sends
out electromagnetic waves
in all directions

rent moves *back and forth* in a wire, as in the bottom diagram. ● The current must move back and forth (must change direction) in the wire very fast, as often as one-half to one million times a second.

Once the concept of how radio waves are produced was understood, it was possible to learn how to relay a "voice pattern" with radio waves.

## Patterns of Sound

The sound of your voice does not go through the wires of a telephone; the vibrations of your voice are changed into electric impulses and are transmitted in patterns of strong and weak impulses that match the patterns of vibration of your vocal cords. In transmitting by radio, the pattern of vibrations is carried by electromagnetic waves. The pattern is transferred to the electromagnetic waves (radio waves) by the action of sound waves on the microphone.

Look at the diagram of the electromagnetic waves which do not carry a voice pattern. ▲

▲

When electromagnetic waves carry the pattern of your voice, they are changed to resemble those shown in the next diagram. ◆

◆

magnetic force can extend through air or through a vacuum. The diagram at the top shows part of the magnetic force field that occurs when an electric current moves through the wire in one direction, as in the investigation on page 269. ■

You may think of radio waves as *waves through a magnetic force field.* Radio waves are **electromagnetic waves** produced when an electric cur-

How are radio waves transmitted and received? What must be done to make the waves strong enough to travel a long distance?

In transmitting by radio, you talk into a microphone. The vibrations of your vocal cords set up vibrations, in the microphone, which produce electric impulses. There is little difference between the microphone and the telephone transmitter. The diagram on the right shows one kind of microphone which you can compare with the telephone transmitter.★ (See page 264.) In the telephone, electric impulses move through wires. In radio transmission, the pattern is transferred to the electromagnetic waves.

How are radio waves transmitted and received over long distances?

The electromagnetic waves are sent out by the radio transmitter which can produce waves powerful enough to travel many miles. These waves

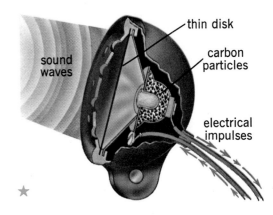

★

spread out in all directions from a wire called the **antenna,** which is situated high on a tower. In the illustration at the bottom of the page, you can see the important steps in sending strong radio (electromagnetic) waves. ◈

Where do these strong electromagnetic waves go?

### Radio Reception

Perhaps your parents have described an old-style radio to you. If

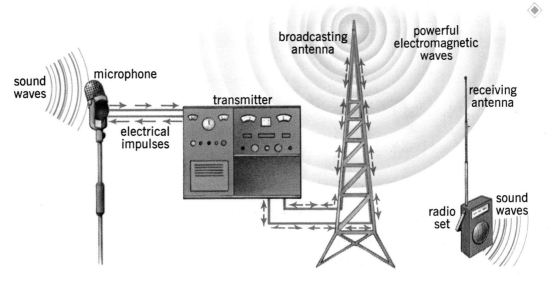

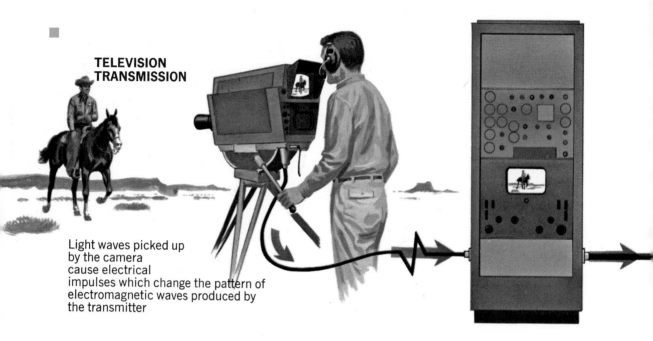

**TELEVISION TRANSMISSION**

Light waves picked up by the camera cause electrical impulses which change the pattern of electromagnetic waves produced by the transmitter

they have, you may have heard about the wires which acted as the receiving antenna. The radios found in homes today still act as a receiver; they receive with an antenna the electromagnetic waves sent out by a transmitter, but the antennas of today are much smaller and more compact.

The pattern of these waves is transferred to sound waves by the speaker in your radio.

A television set also has a radio receiver built into it which produces the sound to go with the picture.

## Saving Life by Wireless

Unless you have a special kind of radio, you do not usually hear police signals. Many police cars now have "radio telephones" that enable them to receive messages from the police station or from other police cars.

Most homes do not yet have radio telephones, but the time may come when they will be very common—in homes, and in most cars. Their use has already saved many lives.

There are other ways in which radio waves can be used to save lives. If a ship is in trouble at sea, an S O S is broadcast by the ship's radio. Warnings of storms, tornadoes, hurricanes, and floods are broadcast by radio. Right now, we are receiving messages from space by means of radio transmitters in satellites. They send us information about the conditions in space—the temperature, the amount of light, and the amount of radiation. Why is such information of value? First, we always need to know more about the world in which we live. Second, astronauts are already going into outer space, and they need

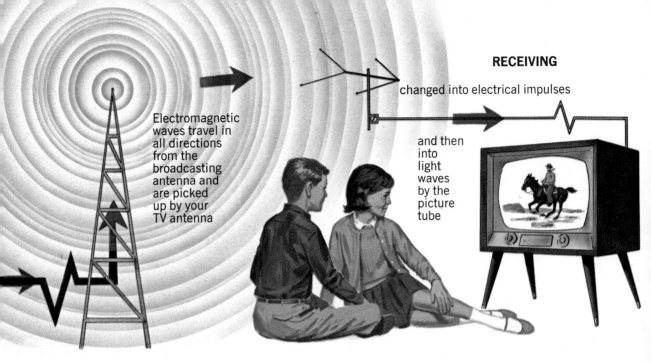

Electromagnetic waves travel in all directions from the broadcasting antenna and are picked up by your TV antenna

**RECEIVING**

changed into electrical impulses

and then into light waves by the picture tube

to know as much as possible about the different environments they will encounter.

### Transmitting Pictures

How did the pictures of the latest American space flight reach you? How will pictures of the first American to land on the moon reach you? How do pictures of a baseball game and the words of the announcer reach your television set from the ball park? One good way to start to answer questions is to use what you know.

You have learned something of the way the spoken word is transmitted by radio waves. What then can be used to send pictures through space? You will be correct if you say that electromagnetic waves can transmit pictures (patterns of light), as well as words (patterns of sound).

### Comparing Radio with Television

In radio transmission, sound vibrations go first into the microphone where they are changed into electric impulses. The resulting radio (electromagnetic) waves travel from the antenna outward in all directions. They are received by the antenna of a radio where they are changed back to electric impulses. The speaker changes these impulses into vibrations which cause sound.

Study the diagram (page 271) which shows the way a radio works. Compare this diagram with the one showing how a television picture is transmitted. ■ How do radio and television compare with each other?

In sending a television picture, light must be used. After all, an object is seen only when light waves are reflected from it.

Let us think of the way a picture, of a horse perhaps, is taken by a camera. ■ The light is reflected from the horse and is focused on the film by the lens of the camera. Since light affects certain sensitive substances on the film, the film is changed chemically by light.

The television camera is also sensitive to light. Study the illustration of a television camera, and, as you do, think of the film in your camera. ■ Notice that the television camera has a screen which is coated with a material that is sensitive to light. When light waves reflected from the horse strike this coating, the pattern of the picture is transferred, by means of a very complicated process, into a pattern of electric impulses. In the television station, the pattern of these impulses is transferred to the electromagnetic waves and is broadcast in all directions from the television station's antenna. Television waves are similar to radio waves but are much shorter in length.

At home, you "tune in" a "channel." Your television set, or receiver, has an antenna that collects the electromagnetic waves. The type of antenna you use depends on how far you are from the transmitter. ● The pattern of these waves is reproduced by electric impulses, which are, in turn, changed into an image on your television screen. The result: you see the horse.

## The Story Is Not So Simple

The story of television is not so simple as that given here, however. For instance, the way a picture tube reproduces the picture is quite complicated. Of course, the transmission of color television is even more complicated than the transmission of a black-and-white picture. You will learn more about this amazing story in future science classes.

For a clue now, however, adjust your television picture to get it slightly out of focus. Is it really one solid picture, or is it made up of many small lines, as shown?

The picture is divided into these fine lines before it is transmitted and is then reproduced as a complete picture on your screen.

## Messages from Space

Have you seen movies of the pony express in the early days of the West? Then you know that the riders had stations where they could get fresh horses. At some of the stations, called relay stations, new riders would take

over the job of delivering the mail. Today we use relay stations in space to expand the efficiency of our communications. The relay stations make it possible to transmit certain types of electromagnetic waves over a much greater distance. Someday, many of these relay stations will be permanently placed in space.

Echo I was the first of the communications satellites to be sent out into space. Then came Telstar, which could relay live television broadcasts across the Atlantic. These have been followed by several others. Echo and Telstar are really relay stations; they were the first to be used to bounce

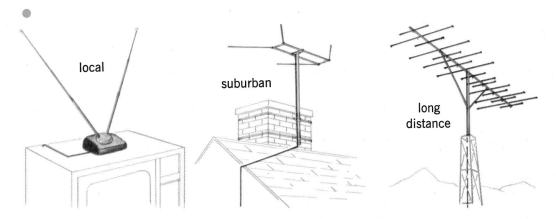

local

suburban

long distance

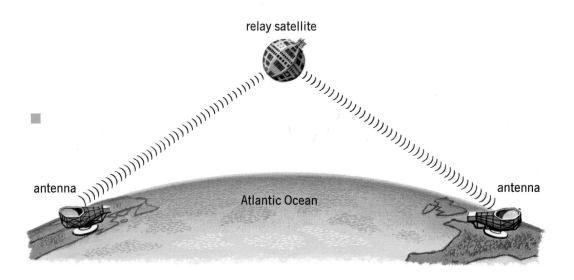

relay satellite

antenna

Atlantic Ocean

antenna

messages back to earth. Since television waves travel only in straight lines, they cannot go around the curve of the earth. The relay satellites receive messages from one point on the earth, and *reflect* the messages to a point on earth a long distance away from the original point of transmission. ■ A relay satellite in space makes it possible, then, to send television pictures much farther.

In addition to sending electromagnetic waves farther on the earth itself, scientists are trying to discover whether the electromagnetic waves that reach us from other stars and planets throughout space can indicate whether there is some kind of life elsewhere in the universe.

Scientists know that there are many kinds of electromagnetic waves traveling through space. The problem has been to collect these and to analyze them to see what conditions caused them to be produced.

Of course, these waves *can* come from stars, meteors, comets, or planets, which are always giving off some kind of waves.

Electromagnetic waves of some type are usually produced whenever energy is released. This can be heat energy, nuclear energy, or light energy. For example, scientists have been able to determine the temperature of Mars by analyzing light waves from that planet.

To find out what kinds of objects in space give off all these waves is one problem, and another is to discover whether any of the waves might be carrying messages.

Is it possible to collect electromagnetic waves coming to us from outer space? Yes.

How are electromagnetic waves from outer space collected? They are collected with the dish-shaped antenna of a radio telescope and also with special relay satellites, such as

Ariel II. The satellite collects all kinds of electromagnetic waves which reach us from outer space and relays them to huge antennas on the ground, as shown in the picture. ●

It would be exciting to find that somewhere out in space there are other planets on which intelligent life exists, and that individuals on one of those planets are trying to send messages to us here on earth. How exciting it would be to try to find out.

Do you think that life on other planets is possible? Is there any available evidence that life exists on other planets? What hypotheses have been developed?

Why not consider this problem for a while? Perhaps you would like to do some research in the library to find what information is available about the possibility of life on other planets. Then perhaps you can do some speculating on your own.

**A.** Study the statements below and choose the correct responses. They will help you fix in mind the concepts of this
section.

    **1.** Radio waves are
       a. electromagnetic waves     b. sound waves

    **2.** Vibrations of the vocal cords set up
       a. sound waves         b. electromagnetic waves

    **3.** In the radio receiver, electromagnetic waves are first
changed into
       a. electric impulses       b. sound waves

    **4.** In the television receiver, the electromagnetic waves are
first changed into
       a. light waves        b. electric impulses

**B.** Write two or more paragraphs on either of these two
topics: How a Radio Works; How Television Works.

**1.** Voice patterns can be transmitted by means of the radio,
as well as by means of the telephone.
    a. How is a radio similar to a telephone?
    b. How is it different?

    **2.** Below is a diagram of a radio telephone. ■ What is the
difference between it and an ordinary telephone?

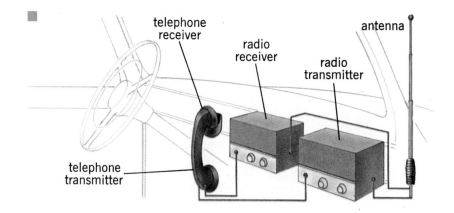

## 6. The Main Concept: Changing and Transferring Energy

From 93,000,000 miles away, energy from the sun runs your television set. Do you think that this is a ridiculous statement? That there is no evidence for such a statement? If so, follow this energy chain. ●

The sun's energy heats water, which evaporates to form water vapor. The water vapor rises into the atmosphere; and, sooner or later, it cools. As the water vapor cools, it condenses to form clouds from which fall rain, snow, and sleet.

The rain flows into rivers or lakes and may be stored behind dams. At the bottom of a dam, the force of falling water can turn a turbine and run a generator. The generator produces an electric current, which travels along wires to your house. There it runs the television set and many other appliances.

Even when the turbines are turned by steam, the energy may have come from the sun. Steam comes from boiling water. What supplies the heat to boil the water? It may still be the sun.

Heat must be used to change the water into steam, and the heat required may be supplied by burning coal. Where did the coal come from? It came from ancient plant life, from huge forests buried deep in the earth where pressure and heat turned the plants and trees into coal. The plants used the energy of the sun to make food. The food was then converted into the plant body for growth.

While they were growing, the plants stored up some of the sun's energy. Later, when they became coal deposits, the sun's energy was still stored in them. Today, the coal is used in many power stations for generating electricity. We use electric energy, the flow of electrons, to speed communications.

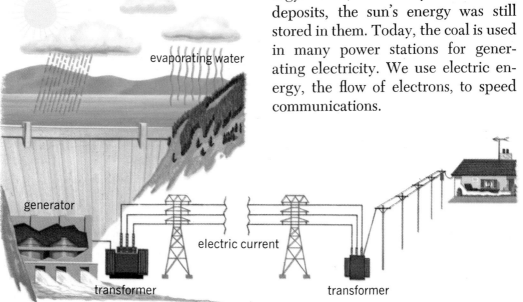

evaporating water

generator

electric current

transformer

transformer

As long as men could only communicate face to face, their world was very small. When scientists learned how to control electricity, communication became faster. Wherever wires could go, man could communicate with words or codes.

Then came the discovery of electromagnetic waves. Man was no longer limited to the use of wires. Electromagnetic waves travel in all directions at the speed of light.

We can hear a voice from Rome, or Paris, or London, by radio the moment the first word is spoken. Moreover, electromagnetic waves can also be used to send pictures. Not only do we hear the sound of voices or music by radio, but we can also see announcers, or musicians, or actors, on television screens.

These are some of the uses of moving electrons. The world has been made smaller by the use of electro-magnetic waves, and this is another example of how science and technology, working together, change the world. (See Unit Two.)

Scientists study the *phenomena* of the world—for instance, the phenomenon of moving electrons. On the basis of their study of phenomena, scientists develop concepts. Engineers use the concepts to invent tools and machines to improve man's environment. As a result, we have light bulbs, electric engines, radio, television, telephones, and many other products that would not exist without the combined efforts of science and technology.

This is not the end of the partnership of science and technology, of ideas and tools, however. We are beginning to use not only the outer parts of the atom, its electrons, but also its nucleus. The uses of the atomic nucleus are discussed next in your study of the environment in which you live.

# Fixing the Main Concepts

TESTING YOURSELF

Test your understanding of the important concepts in this unit by doing these problems.

1. Have you ever observed a car pass a tollbooth on a bridge or a highway? Next time you are near a tollbooth, notice the wire that sticks up from the road near the booth. It is long enough to touch the bottom of a car or a truck.

Why is the wire there?

**2.** What you see in the figure was removed from an electric bell. ■ Will the bell still work? If not, why not?

**3.** What you see in the figure was removed from the transmitter of a telephone. ● Will the transmitter still work? If not, why not?

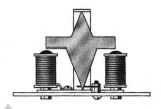

**4.** What you see in the figure was removed from the receiver of a telephone. ▲ Will the receiver still work? If not, why not?

**5.** Should the motor shown in the illustration work? ◆ If your answer is "yes," why? If your answer is "no," why not?

**QUICK TEST**  Study the statements below and choose the correct responses. They will help you fix in mind the concepts of this unit.

**1.** Your table lamp has a wire ending in a plug. When you put this plug into the wall socket, you connect the lamp to a source of

    a. current electricity      b. static electricity

**2.** Current electricity moves in a
    a. nucleus      b. circuit

**3.** Both current electricity and static electricity consist of
    a. neutrons      b. electrons

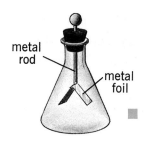

metal
rod

metal
foil

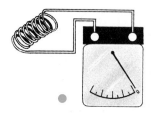

**4.** The two metal leaves in the jar (called an electroscope) have moved apart, as shown. ■ They are charged with

    a. like charges          b. unlike charges

**5.** A coil of wire is connected to the meter. ● To make the needle of the meter move, we should move, back and forth in the coil, a

    a. plastic rod          b. magnet

**6.** When a current passes through a wire, it produces

    a. static electricity          b. magnetic force

**7.** In radio transmission the pattern of a sound wave is carried by

    a. electromagnetic          b. sound waves
       waves

**8.** On a television screen, the picture is reproduced from

    a. electromagnetic          b. sound waves
       waves

**9.** When coal or oil is burned to generate electricity, chemical energy is used to produce electric energy. In this process energy is

    a. created          b. transformed

**10.** In generating electricity, the mechanical energy of falling water can be used to turn the generator. In producing electric energy from mechanical energy, energy is

    a. destroyed          b. transformed

**11.** When energy is changed from one form to another, work

    a. must be done          b. is not needed

**FOR YOUR READING**    This book is useful for a further study of electricity. Even *before* you go to other books, however, why not examine the section ON YOUR OWN, which follows this one.

*Experiments with Electricity,* by Nelson F. Beeler and Franklyn M. Branley, published by the Thomas Y. Crowell Co., New York, 1949.

**1.** An electric circuit is illustrated below. The electricity flows in something like a circle from the dry cells to the lamp. ▲ As long as it does, the bulb lights. In the figure on the right, why is the bulb not lit? ◆

**2.** Now an open switch is placed in the circuit. ◆ How would you get the bulb to light?

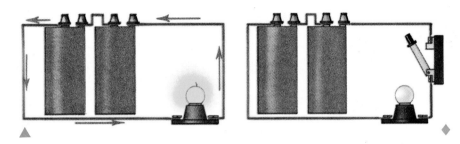

**3.** Switches may be made of different kinds of metals. One kind is the mercury switch. Since mercury is a liquid metal, it is a good conductor of electricity.

Is the current on when the mercury switch is in position "a" or when it is in position "b"? ★ ◈

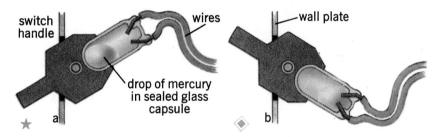

switch handle    wires    wall plate

drop of mercury in sealed glass capsule

★  a    ◈  b

The following American scientists did work in the field of electricity. What discoveries did they make?
1. Benjamin Franklin
2. Josiah Willard Gibbs
3. Thomas Edison
4. Alexander Graham Bell
5. Lee De Forest
6. Allen B. Du Mont

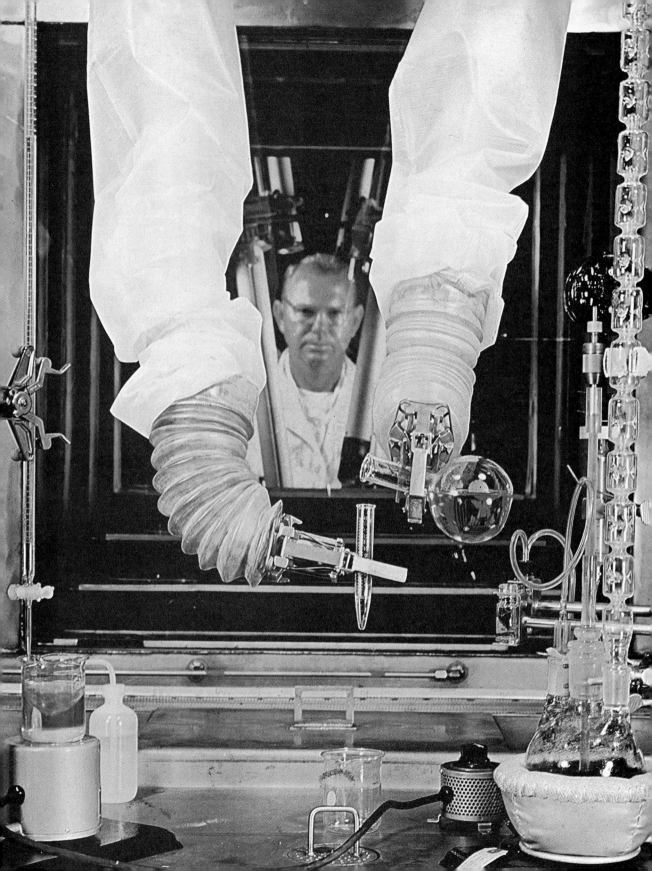

# UNIT SEVEN

# MATTER
# INTO ENERGY

The discovery of atomic particles and the power they contain is one of the new pages in the history of mankind. Left free, this power brings destruction and death, but modern technology enables man to set up protective measures against harmful influences. For example: If you worked in an atomic energy installation, you would carry your own pen-sized radiation monitor in your pocket. When the radiation level gets "hot," the monitor flashes its neon bulb and buzzes a warning tone.

The picture on the opposite page is another example. It shows a device for extending the reach and power of the human hand. Such devices have been developed for very specialized purposes. The one shown is used to handle radioactive materials inside a nuclear reactor and to perform operations in a "hot chemistry" laboratory. In fact, the need for handling radioactive materials by remote control has been mainly responsible for the invention and design of artificial manipulators.

In the world of atomic particles, in a few hundred-thousandths of a second, a frightening quantity of energy can be released. In a nuclear reactor this energy is controlled. In an atomic bomb it is not. Where does the energy come from?

# 1. Inside an Atom

Before the time of Marie and Pierre Curie, atoms were believed to be the smallest particles of matter, much too small to be seen. It was thought that they were *invisible* and *indivisible.*

The idea that the atom was indivisible was held for a long time. This idea dates back to the Greeks, in particular, to Leucippus and his pupil Democritus, who lived about 400 B.C. Their ideas were purely imaginary and not based on investigation.

Here is what they believed: Take a piece of a substance, such as copper. Cut it in half, then in half again, in half again, and in half again. ■ If you continue this "cutting in half," the theory was, and still is, that you would finally have the tiniest piece of copper that could exist and still be copper. This would be an *atom* of copper. The atom of copper was considered to be invisible and indivisible. This was thought to be true of the atoms of substances, such as copper, iron, sulfur, zinc, oxygen, carbon, and all of the other elements.

The atom seemed to be the smallest particle of which matter was made.

Much later, John Dalton (who lived from 1766 to 1844) did experiments which seemed to strengthen this idea. To Dalton, too, atoms were like tiny spheres, solid and indivisible. ● They seemed to act as wholes, that is, they could not be divided. This seemed true of all atoms.

Today, we still hold that an atom is the smallest part of copper that can exist and still be copper; but the atom is no longer considered to be the smallest particle of which matter is made. That atom of copper is itself made of something else. Now we know that atoms can be divided.

The Curies discovered that this was true of radium atoms, at least. Their important discovery gave scientists a new idea, or concept, of the atom and with that, a new concept of matter.

## Radium—And a New Concept of Matter

As the Curies worked to get a supply of pure radium, they found that this particular element was giving off

**■ THE CONCEPT OF DEMOCRITUS**

| a piece of copper | is cut in half | the halves are cut | again and again | into smaller and smaller pieces |

finally the smallest pieces that are still copper are called     atoms

energy in the form of *rays*. Careful experiments showed that one of these so-called "rays" was really made up of particles. These tiny particles, later called **alpha particles,** were found to be very small—much smaller than a radium atom. In other words, it was found that atoms of radium were *not* solid spheres at all. They were not indivisible. Radium atoms gave off smaller particles!▲ Therefore the idea evolved that perhaps some atoms, or even all kinds of atoms, might consist of even smaller particles.

Soon other scientists began to discover alpha particles, particularly when they worked with elements such as radium and uranium. Elements that give off particles spontaneously are called **radioactive** (rā′dē·ō·ak′tiv). They give off energy as well as particles. Notice that the word *radi*oactive relates especially to the word *radi*um; but uranium was found to be radioactive also.

Experiments with atoms of other elements showed that even though they were not radioactive, they too were made up of smaller particles. Such scientists as Ernest Rutherford (New Zealand) and Niels Bohr (Denmark) showed that *all* atoms were made up of particles. Bohr gave us a new "model" of the atom, showing the atom as made of smaller particles.

### A Newer Model of the Atom

The drawing of the carbon atom on this page shows the kind of model made by Niels Bohr. ◆ Atoms of all

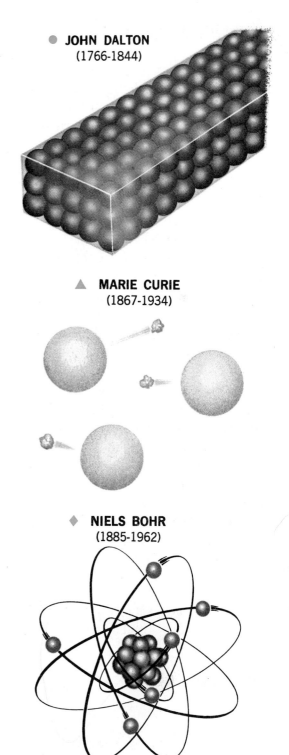

● **JOHN DALTON**
(1766-1844)

▲ **MARIE CURIE**
(1867-1934)

◆ **NIELS BOHR**
(1885-1962)

**287**

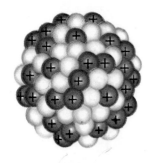

the elements can be modeled in the same manner. Although each of the atoms is different from every other, they all contain the same kinds of particles.

Now investigate the models of atoms on the opposite page. See what is similar, and also what is different, about the four atoms.

### Removing Particles from an Atom

Electrons are tiny particles with *negative* (—) electric charges. Suppose the electrons were removed from the atom of lithium pictured on this page. ■ What would be left? The *nucleus* of the lithium atom (with its **protons** and **neutrons**) would be left.

The symbols (+, —, n) on the model stand for the electric charge of

the particle. The protons in the nucleus have a positive (+) charge of electricity. The neutrons (n) in the nucleus have no charge; they are neither positive nor negative, but are neutral. Although the nucleus of an atom consists of neutrons and protons, the nucleus has a positive charge because of the protons. If any of the electrons of an atom are removed, and only the nucleus is left, the atom will have a positive charge. ● Now it is easy to understand why a substance was left with a positive charge when electrons were "rubbed off," as shown in Unit Six.

Suppose no electrons are removed from an atom. What charge would the atom have?

Study again the diagrams of the atoms of carbon, oxygen, nitrogen, and iron. How many electrons and how many protons does each of the atoms have?

To have a positive charge, an atom must have more protons than electrons. To have a negative charge, an atom must have more electrons than protons. The positive (+) charge of one proton and the negative (—) charge of one electron neutralize each other.

Each kind of atom normally has an equal number of protons and electrons. Check the diagram to see if this is correct. In an atom, the positive charge of each proton balances the equal but opposite negative charge of each electron. The charge, then, of an atom is neutral.

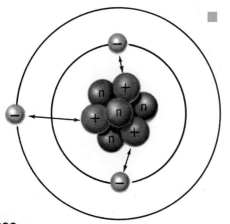

# AN INVESTIGATION into Models of Atoms

**Needed:** physical models as well as diagram models of atoms

Here are models of four atoms drawn flattened out to give you a clearer idea of the number and kinds of particles they contain. The models are of carbon, oxygen, nitrogen, and iron. ■

Three kinds of particles are shown. The neutrons are green, the protons red, the electrons yellow.

Where are the protons and neutrons located in an atom?

Where are the electrons located?

In what ways are these atoms different from each other? similar?

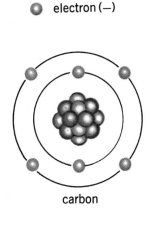

- ● neutron (n)
- ● proton (+)
- ● electron (−)

carbon

oxygen

nitrogen

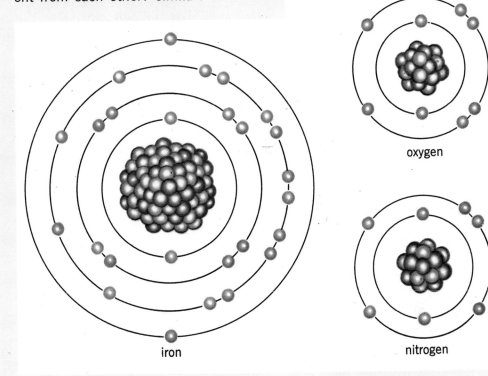

iron

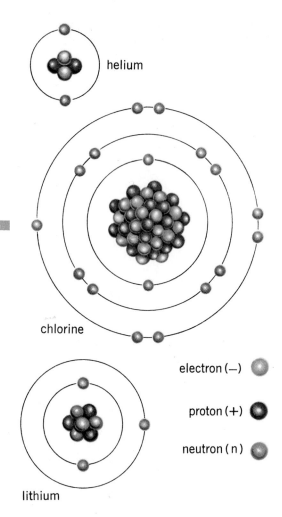

helium

chlorine

electron (−) 

proton (+) 

neutron (n) 

lithium

Now look at the diagrams of three other atoms—helium, chlorine, and lithium. ■ Try to find the number of protons and electrons in each atom. How many do you find in each of these three atoms?

### The Structure of an Atom

Complete the table to show the atomic structure of some familiar elements. ● Copy the table on a separate piece of paper and fill in the numbers of protons and electrons

which are missing from each of the atoms. Remember that all of the atoms are *neutral*. For the moment, however, do not fill in the number of neutrons.

Were you able to fill in the table properly? All normal atoms have equal numbers of protons and electrons. Except for the lightest-weight hydrogen atom, all atoms have neutrons as well. Neutrons have no electric charge. An atom has, therefore, equal numbers of (+) and (−) charges.

Is there any way of determining the number of neutrons in an atom? Study the table of common elements on the opposite page and then try to determine a method for finding the number of neutrons in an atom. ▲ Try to determine this before you read ahead. If you find it difficult, go on to the next page.

●

| | Protons | Electrons | Neutrons |
|---|---|---|---|
| hydrogen | 1 | | |
| helium | | | |
| lithium | | | |
| carbon | | | |
| oxygen | | | |
| nitrogen | | | |
| sodium | | 11 | |
| potassium | 19 | | |
| silver | 47 | | |
| gold | | 79 | |
| calcium | 20 | 20 | |
| iron | | | |
| phosphorus | | 15 | |
| uranium | 92 | 92 | |
| chlorine | | | |
| sulfur | | 16 | |

| NAME OF ELEMENT | APPROXIMATE ATOMIC WEIGHT | NUMBER OF PROTONS (ATOMIC NUMBER) |
|---|---|---|
| aluminum | 27 | 13 |
| antimony | 122 | 51 |
| argon | 40 | 18 |
| arsenic | 75 | 33 |
| barium | 137 | 56 |
| beryllium | 9 | 4 |
| bismuth | 209 | 83 |
| boron | 11 | 5 |
| bromine | 80 | 35 |
| cadmium | 112 | 48 |
| calcium | 40 | 20 |
| carbon | 12 | 6 |
| cesium | 133 | 55 |
| chlorine | 35 | 17 |
| chromium | 52 | 24 |
| cobalt | 59 | 27 |
| copper | 64 | 29 |
| fluorine | 19 | 9 |
| germanium | 73 | 32 |
| gold | 197 | 79 |
| helium | 4 | 2 |
| hydrogen | 1 | 1 |
| iodine | 127 | 53 |
| iron | 56 | 26 |
| krypton | 84 | 36 |
| lead | 207 | 82 |
| lithium | 7 | 3 |
| magnesium | 24 | 12 |
| manganese | 55 | 25 |
| mercury | 201 | 80 |
| neon | 20 | 10 |
| nickel | 59 | 28 |
| nitrogen | 14 | 7 |
| oxygen | 16 | 8 |
| palladium | 106 | 46 |
| phosphorus | 31 | 15 |
| platinum | 195 | 78 |
| potassium | 39 | 19 |
| radium | 226 | 88 |
| radon | 222 | 86 |
| rubidium | 85 | 37 |
| selenium | 79 | 34 |
| silicon | 28 | 14 |
| silver | 108 | 47 |
| sodium | 23 | 11 |
| strontium | 88 | 38 |
| sulfur | 32 | 16 |
| tin | 119 | 50 |
| titanium | 48 | 22 |
| tungsten | 184 | 74 |
| uranium | 238 | 92 |
| xenon | 131 | 54 |
| zinc | 65 | 30 |
| zirconium | 91 | 40 |

Once you know the atomic weight of an atom and the number of protons in an atom, you can determine the number of neutrons. Here is the formula:

**neutrons + protons = atomic weight**

The atomic weight given in the table is accurate enough to help you compare the weights of the different atoms. The atomic weight does not include the weight of the electrons. Electrons do not seriously affect the weight of the atom, because they are so very light. It takes 1,836 electrons to equal the weight of 1 proton.

Now use the table of atomic weights and see if you can determine the number of neutrons for each of the atoms listed on page 290.

## A Look Ahead

Now that you know what is inside an atom, let us split one kind of atom to see what happens. What happens when the nuclei (plural of nucleus) of uranium atoms are split?

Before going ahead, fix the structure of an atom more clearly in your mind. Make your own models of atoms as in the investigation on the opposite page.

**BEFORE YOU GO ON** **A.** Study the statements below and choose the correct responses. They will help you fix in mind the concepts of this section.

**1.** An atom has 11 protons in its nucleus. Outside its nucleus, there are

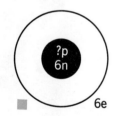

    a. 22 electrons          b. 11 electrons

**2.** The atom mentioned in **1** has an atomic weight of 23. It has in its nucleus

    a. 12 neutrons          b. 11 neutrons

**3.** In your notebook finish the drawings of the two "models" of atoms shown in the margin.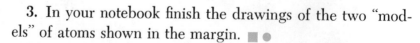

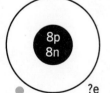

**4.** The electric charge of a single atom is usually

    a. positive          b. neutral

**5.** The belief that atoms are indivisible was held by

    a. Bohr          b. Dalton

**B.** Write a paragraph or two on this topic: A Model of the Atom—Today.

## MAKING MODELS: The Atom

**Needed:** materials from which to invent and construct models of sodium, carbon, or oxygen atoms

Only one clue is needed at this time. Notice in the atom models here, and on earlier pages, that electrons revolve around the nucleus on different shells. In the oxygen atom, the shell nearest the nucleus has only two electrons. ■

Invent your own model. ■ ● ▲ What material will you use for the nucleus: clay, perhaps? for the electrons: beads, perhaps? Can you think of a way to make the electrons actually revolve?

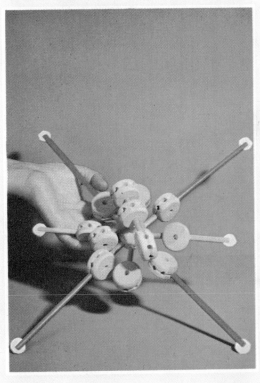

1. Copy the following table in your notebook and try to complete it. ■

| Element | Atomic weight | Number of neutrons | Number of protons | Number of electrons |
|---------|---------------|--------------------|--------------------|---------------------|
| oxygen | 16 | 8 | | 8 |
| nitrogen | 14 | | 7 | |
| chlorine | 35 | 18 | | 17 |
| sodium | 23 | | | 11 |

2. In your notebook, draw a model of an atom with 10 neutrons and 10 protons. How many electrons would it have? What is the name of the element?

One of the great scientists who did much to discover the structure of the atom was Ernest Rutherford, a British scientist. Perhaps you will want to do research in the library to find out more about him.

# 2. Splitting the Nucleus

When scientists use the phrase "to split the atom," they really mean "to split the nucleus." Splitting of the nucleus of an atom such as the uranium atom is called **fission** (fish′ən). What happens when the nucleus of an atom undergoes fission?

## Bullets to Split an Atom

Let us make a model of an atomic nucleus, using a collection of marbles. Arrange the marbles as shown in the illustration. Now, how can we split up this model of an atomic nucleus? We can shoot a single marble into its midst and scatter the marbles in all directions. ●

This model gives you the general idea behind the splitting of atomic nuclei. An entire nucleus is very small; but the protons and neutrons are smaller still. Exactly what force binds the protons and the neutrons tightly together in the nucleus is not known; but it is known that tremendous energy is required to separate them.

If the marbles were glued together into a spherical shape, the single marble would have to be hurled with tremendous force to break them apart. What could be used as an atomic "bullet" to be hurled at the target, the atomic nucleus? Moreover, how could this bullet be given enough force to split a nucleus?

Scientists have found that a neutron, the tiny particle with no electric charge found in the nucleus, can be used to split atoms. ▲ Certain unstable atoms can be made to give up neutrons from their nuclei. These neutrons can be shot into the target nuclei of other large atoms and cause them to split apart into several pieces. ▲

Scientists have also found that certain nuclei, the nuclei of some of the heavier atoms, are easier to split. For instance, the nuclei of uranium atoms break apart much more easily than the nuclei of most other atoms. You

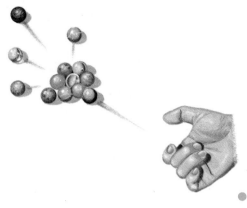

can see from the table on page 293 that the uranium atom is a very heavy atom. How many protons does it have in its nucleus?

Neutron bullets have been used to split uranium atoms. The uranium nuclei undergo fission. Each nucleus

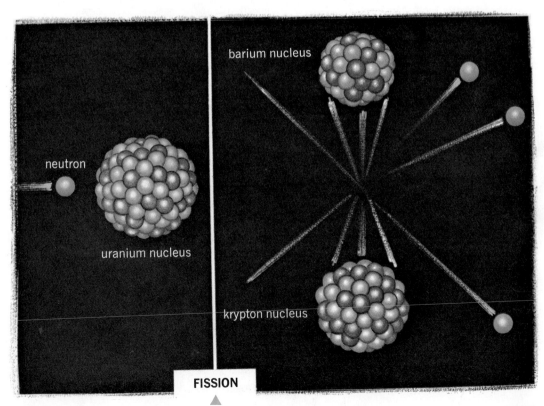

barium nucleus

neutron

uranium nucleus

krypton nucleus

**FISSION**
▲

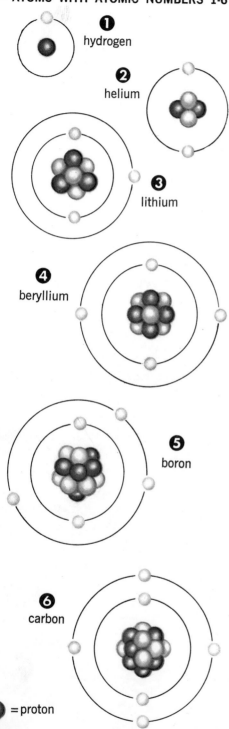

❶ hydrogen

❷ helium

❸ lithium

❹ beryllium

❺ boron

❻ carbon

● = proton

breaks into two or more smaller nuclei, thus creating different elements. Completely different elements may be formed. Some of the elements that are produced when the nuclei of uranium atoms fission are barium, krypton, cesium, and rubidium.

The previous page shows nuclei formed from fission of a uranium nucleus. From the table on page 291, find the number of protons in a uranium nucleus. Compare this to the number of protons in a barium nucleus and in a krypton nucleus. Were any protons lost?

### An Important Number

Look at the list of important elements in the table on page 291. Notice again the *number* of protons found in each element. This is called the **atomic number.** Look at the illustration which shows the atoms with atomic numbers 1 to 6. ■ Do you see that each element has a different atomic number? It is the number of protons (atomic number) which determines the characteristics of the atom.

Notice that the atomic number of carbon is 6; that is, carbon has 6 protons. If one proton were added to the nucleus of carbon, it would have 7 protons, and the atom would no longer be carbon. What would it be? Look in the table and find the atom with 7 protons (an atomic number of 7). That atom is nitrogen. By adding one proton to the nucleus of a carbon atom, it can be changed to a nitrogen nucleus.

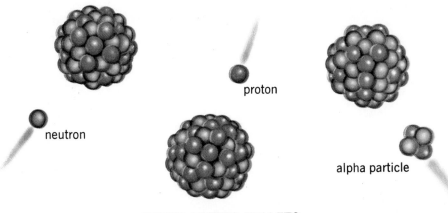

neutron

proton

alpha particle

● THREE ATOMIC BULLETS

The neutron then is not the only kind of "bullet" that can cause changes in the nucleus of an atom. Read on to find out about other kinds of atomic bullets—kinds that must be shot from a kind of "atomic gun."

### Bullets from an "Atomic Gun"

The neutron, a tiny particle with no electric charge, can be shot into the nuclei of certain kinds of atoms to cause fission. Suppose a "charged bullet," an electrically charged particle, were to be shot into the nucleus of an atom. What would happen? The proton, which has a positive (+) charge, can be used. You can get protons by using the nucleus of a hydrogen atom which has one proton.

The nucleus of a helium atom, which has two protons and two neutrons, can be used also as an atomic bullet. It has a positive charge and is known as an alpha particle. ● (Remember that alpha particles were given off by the radium samples that were studied by Madame Curie.)

A helium nucleus (with an atomic number of 2) may be used as the bullet to hit a nucleus of lithium (with an atomic number of 3). ▲ A nucleus of boron (with an atomic number of 5) results.

The problem of hitting a nucleus with a single proton or with another charged nucleus, such as an alpha particle, is not easy. What is the electric charge of the nucleus of an atom? It is plus (+), because the neutrons have no charge; the protons do. Particles having like charges repel each other, so the nucleus of an atom would normally repel a proton. Unless a proton moves fast enough to over-

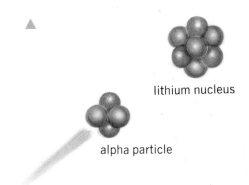

lithium nucleus

alpha particle

come the force of repulsion, it will be pushed away (repelled) by a nucleus. The problem then is to increase the proton's speed.

One way to make protons move fast enough to hit a nucleus is to use an "atomic gun." This is not the kind of gun found in science fiction movies. An atomic gun is a huge structure. One type of atomic gun is the **cyclotron** (sī′klə·tron). ■

The "bullets" used in a cyclotron are either the nuclei of hydrogen atoms (protons) or the nuclei of helium atoms (alpha particles).

In the cyclotron, then, the atomic bullets, the positively charged particles (protons or alpha particles), can be shot at very high speed. The nuclei of different atoms are the targets. When a proton hits a nucleus, the nucleus may change. In this way new atoms may be formed.

In scientific terms, the cyclotron is a nuclear **accelerator.** It *accelerates,* or speeds up, the motion of the nuclear particles. It has helped scientists to learn more about the nature of the atom. The cyclotron was invented by an American, Dr. E. O. Lawrence.

Inside the cyclotron protons are rushed around and around in a circular path, from the center to the outside. ● This speeding up is brought about by adding strong charges of electricity to the two plates called "dees" (each one is shaped like the letter "D"). Huge electromagnets keep the tiny particles in their circular path. They start at the center and travel around and around, faster and faster. Then, finally, these atomic bullets speed out along a straight path to hit the nuclei of other atoms. They often hit their targets and cause the target nuclei to change.

The cyclotron accelerates "bullets" having a positive charge. ● Other types of accelerators may use "bullets" having a negative charge; they may use electrons.

A cyclotron, then, can be used to change the nuclei of atoms. But the nuclei of some kinds of atoms change by themselves.

▲

## Unstable Atoms

Some kinds of atoms, such as the radium and uranium atoms, have a nucleus that does not hold together very well; it is said to be unstable. An unstable nucleus breaks up by itself, giving off tiny particles and energy. No atomic bullets are needed.

Recall that a substance, such as uranium, which has an unstable nucleus, is radioactive. Because some of its nuclei are always breaking up, a lump

of uranium keeps giving off particles and radiant energy. ▲ Heat energy is one form of energy produced.

How is it known that particles and "rays" of energy are being given off? Perhaps your school has the kind of apparatus shown on page 300. If not, one can probably be borrowed from the local Civil Defense headquarters, for use in the investigation outlined on the next page.

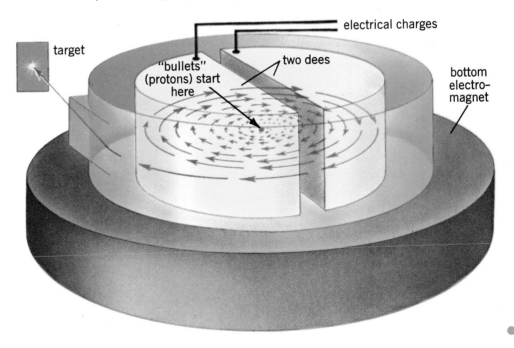

target

"bullets" (protons) start here

electrical charges

two dees

bottom electro-magnet

# AN INVESTIGATION into the Detection of Radioactivity

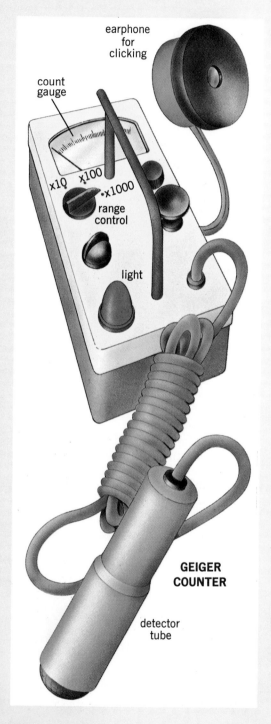

earphone for clicking

count gauge

x10 x100 •x1000
range control

light

**GEIGER COUNTER**

detector tube

**Needed:** a Geiger counter

The apparatus shown is called a Geiger counter. ■

Notice that it consists primarily of a tube. Each time a charged particle enters the tube, it causes a change in the gas inside. An electric current jumps across the tube, causing either a *flash* of light (in a bulb) or a *sound* (a click). The Geiger counter registers, or counts, particles in the surrounding area.

How many clicks or flashes do you observe per minute? The *counts* let you know how much radiation is present. The counter shows that nuclear particles and radiations are all around us, but the normal amount of radiation in the air is not dangerous. Your Civil Defense director can give you more information about radiation and its effects.

If a radioactive ore, or substance, were to be placed near the Geiger counter, would the counts increase? **An adult should always be present when you test a radioactive substance with the counter.** How useful is the Geiger counter to scientists?

**Additional Investigation:** Is there a watch with a luminous dial in the school laboratory? Test the watch with the Geiger counter. What radioactive substance might it contain? What precautions should be exercised?

**A.** Study the statements below and choose the correct responses. They will help you fix in mind the concepts of this section.

**1.** When the nucleus of an atom is split, we say it has undergone

    a. fission   ✓         b. charging

**2.** When an atomic nucleus is split, it gives off particles such as neutrons and

    a. protons   ✓         b. heat

**3.** An atomic bullet which is used by scientists to split an atom is the

    a. cyclotron           b. neutron ✓

**4.** The atomic number of an atom is its number of

    a. neutrons          b. protons ✓

**5.** A cyclotron is an

    a. atomic gun         b. atomic bullet ✓

**B.** Write a paragraph or two on this topic: Splitting an Atom.

To do the following problems, use the table on page 291 and the diagrams of atoms below. ■ ● ▲

**1.** What atom would be formed in each case if a proton were shot into the nucleus of the atom?

**2.** What would happen if, instead of gaining a proton, a nitrogen atom were to lose a proton?

**3.** If the new atoms gained only protons and no electrons, would their charge be positive or negative?

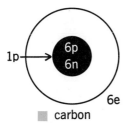

carbon

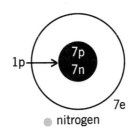

nitrogen

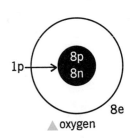

oxygen

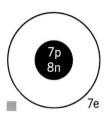

An oxygen atom has 8 protons and 8 neutrons. What if it lost a proton but kept the same number of neutrons, as shown in the diagram? ■ What atom would this be?

It has the atomic number of nitrogen; therefore it is an atom of nitrogen. But it has an atomic weight of 15. Nitrogen atoms normally have an atomic weight of 14.

Atoms with the *same atomic number* but *different atomic weights* are called **isotopes** (ĭ′sə·tōps). Thus nitrogen with an atomic weight of 15 is an *isotope* of nitrogen.

Note that the oxygen atom has also lost an electron. Would you expect this to happen?

Why not go to the library to find out more about isotopes. For instance, find out

    a. how they are made        b. how they are used

Share your knowledge with your class.

## 3. Nuclear Reactions

When an atomic nucleus breaks up, its particles shoot out in all directions and a great deal of heat is produced. Suppose an engineer had the problem of obtaining heat from an element like uranium. He would need to find a way to break up the nuclei of many atoms of uranium—without an explosion. Such a way has been found. It makes use of an invention known as an **atomic pile.**

In an atomic pile many nuclei split, that is, undergo fission, by a process known as a **chain reaction.**● To get an idea of how a chain reaction occurs in an atomic pile, we can use our model nucleus made of marbles and a spring marble launcher. ▲ When we shoot a single marble (atomic bullet) at the bunch of marbles (target nu-

cleus), the marbles from the marble nucleus scatter in many directions.

Suppose that as the marbles from the marble nucleus scatter, some of them hit other bunches of marbles, or nuclei. Then these nuclei would also be split. Their particles would scatter and would, in their turn, break still more nuclei.

In an atomic pile, the atomic bullets are neutrons. A speeding neutron hits a uranium nucleus. The uranium nucleus splits up and sends out other neutrons. These neutrons also hit uranium nuclei and cause *them* to send out neutrons. In a very short time, much less than a second, fission after fission of uranium nuclei takes place. On and on this goes, very steadily—neutrons hitting nuclei and freeing other neutrons to hit more nuclei. This process is the chain reaction.

## Controlling a Chain Reaction

If the chain reaction were to happen too quickly, there would be an explosion. Rapid fission causes an explosion in a nuclear bomb. A nuclear explosion releases a tremendous amount of heat and nuclear radiation.

In an atomic pile, however, the chain reaction proceeds as slowly or as fast as scientists may decide. They control the rate of fission and the amount of radiant energy which will be given off.

In the early days when atoms were first being split, the devices in which the chain reactions were controlled were known as atomic piles. Today they are usually known as **reactors.** (Notice the similarity between the words *reactor* and chain *reaction.*)

The best way discovered, so far, for slowing down the speed of a chain re-

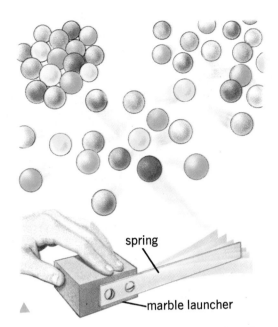

spring

marble launcher

action is to "soak up," or absorb, many of the neutrons before they get a chance to cause fission. This can be done with special **control rods** made of the metal cadmium (kad'mē·əm).

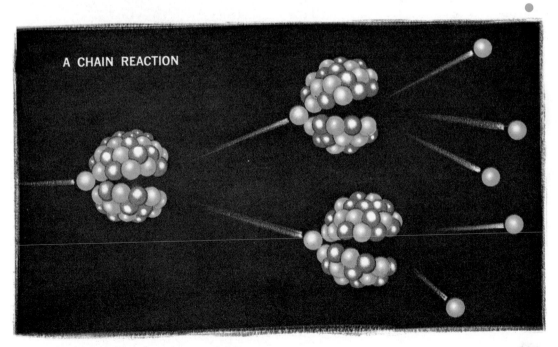

A CHAIN REACTION

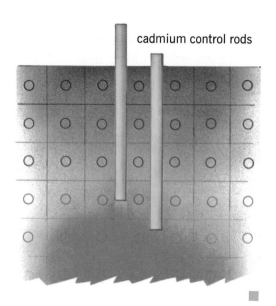

cadmium control rods

The rate of fission is controlled by raising or lowering the cadmium rods into the reactor. ■ The rods absorb many of the free neutrons. This helps the person operating the reactor to control the speed of the reaction. As the rods are lowered even farther, they absorb still more neutrons. The reaction becomes slower and slower

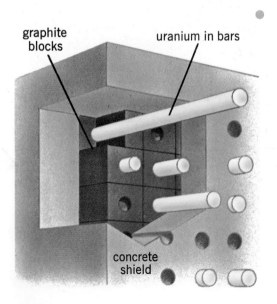

graphite blocks

uranium in bars

concrete shield

since there are then fewer neutrons to act as bullets. When the cadmium rods are lifted, the reaction speeds up. By putting the cadmium rods in certain positions, scientists can cause the chain reaction to proceed at the speed which they want.

### Building a Nuclear Reactor

What is needed to build a nuclear reactor?

*First,* a substance is needed that has nuclei which break up easily to give off free neutrons (atomic bullets). To get a supply of neutrons, scientists use one kind of fissionable uranium called uranium-235. The nuclei of uranium-235 split apart more easily than ordinary uranium nuclei (known as uranium-238). When the nuclei of uranium-235 are hit by neutrons, they split and a chain reaction is started.

*Second,* a substance is needed to slow down the neutrons. Graphite is one such substance. Graphite is a form of carbon, the type used in pencil "lead." In some reactors, the uranium is placed in blocks of graphite. ● As the free neutrons travel through the graphite, they are slowed down. Slower-moving neutrons have a better chance than faster-moving neutrons of hitting the nuclei of uranium-235 and causing them to fission.

*Third,* a material is needed which can act as a "sponge" to soak up excess neutrons, if too many are released. For the "sponge" we may use control rods of cadmium lowered into the center of the reactor.

By means of these three basic substances, a chain reaction for nuclear fission can be controlled. In addition, a shield is needed so that neutrons do not escape from the reactor. They can be very dangerous to people nearby.

This is a diagram of an early reactor.▲ It is the kind of reactor in which the nuclei of uranium undergo fission in a chain reaction.

The speed of the reaction can be controlled by raising or lowering the cadmium rods from the top of the reactor. When a chain reaction proceeds very fast, tremendous heat is produced. When it proceeds more slowly, there is less heat at any given time. The object is to control the rate of fission and thus to control the amount of heat that is produced.

Here is a new source of energy, of heat energy in particular. How this energy may be used is described in the next section. First build a model of an early reactor (as shown in the investigation on the next page).

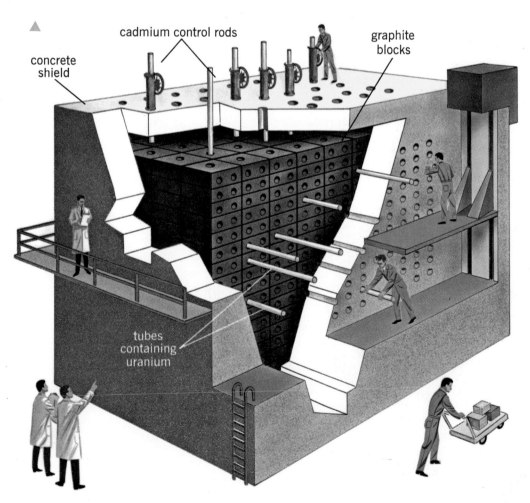

cadmium control rods

graphite blocks

concrete shield

tubes containing uranium

# MAKING A MODEL: A Nuclear Reactor

**Needed:** modeling clay; sugar cubes; toothpicks; shoe box; dominoes and pencils

Now that you have studied the structure and function of a nuclear reactor, design a model of one. In designing your model you must keep in mind the factors involved, for example, the dangers of radioactivity. You will need a structure to guard against dangerous accidents; otherwise, neutrons and other radiations will escape from the reactor into the air. These can be very dangerous to living things, especially in large doses.

Escaping neutrons could hit people near the reactor and could cause changes in the nuclei of the elements and compounds in the human body. Radioactivity may be harmful or even fatal to the human body.

For reasons of safety, then, nuclear reactors are surrounded by a heavy shield to keep neutrons from escaping. The shield may be a thick wall of concrete or of lead. Sometimes it is made of both.

What might you use as a model of the cement shield for your model reactor? A shoe box might be used as a model of these walls. Pencils might be used to show how the control rods are raised and lowered. What would you use as a model for the uranium? for the graphite? Look at the models in the pictures. ■ ● Can you make one that is a better model?

■

●

306

**A.** Study the statements below and choose the correct responses. They will help you fix in mind the concepts of this section.

**1.** In a chain reaction, the particles which act as atomic bullets and cause uranium to undergo fission are
    a. neutrons          b. electrons

**2.** An invention for getting a controlled chain reaction is the
    a. reactor          b. cyclotron

**3.** Another name for an atomic pile is
    a. an atomic gun          b. a nuclear reactor

**4.** To keep a chain reaction going and to increase the chances of neutrons hitting atomic nuclei, neutrons are slowed down by
    a. graphite          b. cadmium rods

**5.** A substance used to control the chain reaction by absorption of neutrons is
    a. graphite          b. cadmium

**B.** Write a paragraph or two on this topic: Controlling a Nuclear Chain Reaction.

**1.** Suppose the control rods (cadmium or some other metal) in an atomic pile were missing, what would go wrong?

**2.** Suppose the heavy shield of cement or lead on the outside of a reactor were missing, what might go wrong?

**3.** Suppose the graphite (or other substance used to slow down the neutrons) were missing, what might go wrong?

In some reactors, "heavy water" has replaced graphite as the material for slowing down neutrons. Find out from research in the library what other materials are being used in reactors today—as shields, atomic bullets, sources of neutrons, or replacements for the cadmium rods.

# 4. Uses of Nuclear Energy

What is the colorful building shown in the picture? ■ Inside the building, huge generators are being turned by steam turbines. They are sending forth great quantities of electricity to the nearby area; but something is missing. Where are the giant smokestacks usually associated with electric power stations? This building does not need smokestacks because it does not use a combustible (burns with a flame) fuel. It has no coal or oil furnaces. Nevertheless, steam is produced easily.

You are looking at a picture of a new kind of power plant, a nuclear power plant. It is the new Yankee Atomic Electric Power Plant in Rowe, Massachusetts. The heat energy used to produce the needed steam does not come from a combustible fuel but from a nuclear reactor.

As we have seen, the nuclei of uranium atoms undergo fission in a nuclear reactor. A chain reaction results. Great amounts of heat energy are produced. How is the heat energy changed into electric energy in a power plant?

## Nuclear Power Plants

Suppose the heat from nuclear fission, instead of from coal or oil, could be transferred to the water in a boiler. It, too, could change the water into steam, steam that could then turn a turbine. The turbine, we know, would turn a generator to produce electricity. The diagram will remind you of the different steps in this process. ●

First, atomic nuclei are split inside the reactor. Uranium atoms are still most commonly used although atoms of other elements are also being used. Great amounts of heat are produced from the fission of the atomic nuclei.

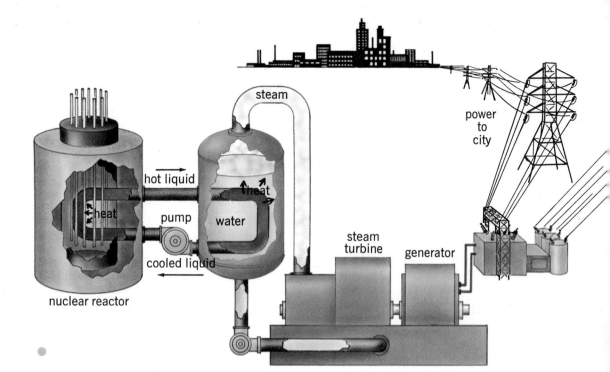

steam

hot liquid

heat

pump

water

heat

cooled liquid

power
to
city

steam
turbine

generator

nuclear reactor

The rate of fission is controlled, or regulated, by the control rods.

Second, the heat is transferred to a pipe containing a liquid (often a liquid metal) under pressure. The liquid is pumped around inside the pipe, as shown. It carries heat energy from the reactor to the boiler. The heat is then transferred from the hot liquid to the water in the boiler, changing it to steam. As the liquid in the pipe gives up heat to the water, it cools, returns to the reactor, and is again heated.

Third, the steam produced is used to turn turbines.

Fourth, these turbines turn a generator that produces electricity.

Fifth, the electricity can run motors or bring light and heat to homes. Small nuclear power plants can also

be used to generate electricity in submarines and for many other purposes.

Thus, in the nuclear power plant, nuclear energy has been changed into electric energy. Nuclear power plants of this type are already in use today to provide electricity to homes and factories in several areas.

The nuclear power plants are very heavily shielded to prevent dangerous radiation from escaping. The people working inside the plants are also protected by careful shielding of equipment, and by other safety measures.

The operation of these plants is proving that the energy locked up inside the atomic nucleus can be used for peaceful purposes with safety.

Energy can be changed from one form to another. In an ordinary power plant, what changes in energy take

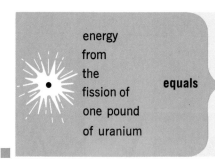

energy
from
the
fission of
one pound
of uranium

**equals**

the energy
from burning
2,300,000 pounds
of coal
(enough to fill
19½ freight cars)

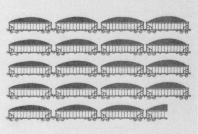

place? First, heat energy may be obtained from burning coal. The heat energy is used to change water to steam. The energy of the steam, which comes from the energy of moving molecules, turns a turbine. The mechanical energy of the turbine drives a generator which transforms mechanical energy into electric energy.

In a nuclear power plant, many of the same changes in energy take place. Moreover, the electric energy produced by using nuclear fission is the same kind as the electric energy produced by the burning of coal. But there is a very important difference between a nuclear power plant and an ordinary power plant. That difference can be seen in the diagram.■ How does the energy obtained from a pound of uranium compare with the energy obtained from over 2 million pounds of coal?

### Reactors in Power Plants

At Shippingport (Pennsylvania), Detroit (Michigan), Indian Point (New York), and Rowe (Massachusetts), reactors are now in use in power plants that produce electricity for factories and homes in nearby cities. It is expected that many other cities will soon be obtaining their power from nuclear energy.

The reactors are, of course, better developed than the atomic pile shown on page 305. For instance, substances other than graphite may be used to slow down the neutrons. The uranium, instead of being placed in blocks of graphite, may be mixed with a liquid which, like graphite, slows the movement of the neutrons. Yet all these reactors still need and use substances which serve the four main purposes with which you are familiar.

1. A substance is needed which gives off neutrons as its nuclei split.

2. A substance is needed which can slow down the neutrons just enough so that they can cause other nuclei to split and give off neutrons.

3. A substance is needed to control the speed of this chain reaction.

4. A substance is needed to act as a shield against escaping neutrons.

### Nuclear Energy for Defense

The great heat that is produced in nuclear reactors is now being used to provide energy to drive submarines and aircraft carriers.

Have you read accounts of the voyages of nuclear submarines, such as the *George Washington* or the *Patrick Henry?* ● Have you perhaps seen pictures of the new nuclear aircraft carriers with room for many, many planes? These nuclear-powered ships are a part of our country's defense.

In a nuclear submarine, a reactor provides the energy needed to turn the turbines, which turn the generators; these then turn the propeller, which drives the submarine through the water. The engine of a nuclear submarine is shown on the next page.

Because a reactor uses so little uranium, the submarine can travel for thousands of miles on one supply.

A submarine which obtains its energy from ordinary fuel, rather than from a nuclear reactor, would have to stop several times to obtain more fuel to travel the same distance. Nuclear submarines have gone around the world, as well as under the ice cap at the North Pole. They can travel great distances under the surface of the ocean.

Some of these nuclear submarines carry rockets that are fitted with nuclear bombs, which can be fired while the submarine is still below the surface. Such rocket missiles are remote-controlled to hit a target many miles away. Nuclear submarines carrying rockets now can travel great distances in defense against attack.

●

In a nuclear reactor, the chain reaction is controlled. Nuclei after nuclei split, but at a controlled rate—that is, only a certain number of nuclei split at a time. In this way fission can go on indefinitely. A nuclear explosion, however, is an expanding chain reaction that happens very fast. When a nuclear bomb hits its target, the entire chain reaction is completed in a small part of a second. An unbelievable amount of energy is given off at one instant. That is why a nuclear bomb causes tremendous damage.

The very power of nuclear energy may keep the world free of war. A nuclear war, with the nuclear power available today, could probably destroy every living thing on the earth. Because total destruction is so unthinkable, it is hoped that war itself will become unthinkable.

## Nuclear Energy Against Disease

The work of Marie and Pierre Curie has had great benefits. It has led, for example, to the control of radium and other radioactive substances, which have since been used in the treatment of cancer.

A cancer is a growth of diseased cells in the body. A cancer gets in the way of the normal functioning of the healthy organs in the body.

Because the radium nucleus is radioactive (unstable), it breaks down. As it does so, it gives off radiations that can destroy some cancers. Nowadays, radium and other radioactive substances are used in such a way that their radioactivity can be directed at any spot in the body.

For instance, the patient shown in the picture is being treated in a hospital. ■ The big machine uses a piece of

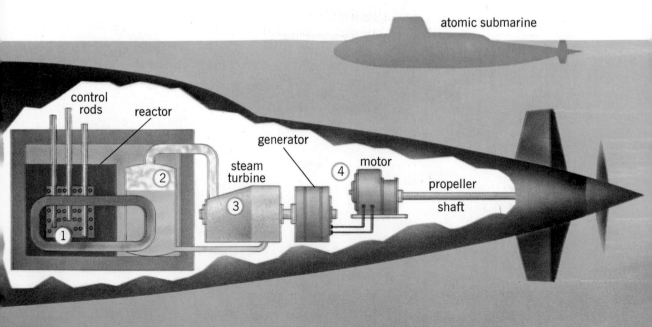

atomic submarine

control rods
reactor
generator
steam turbine
motor
propeller shaft

1 2 3 4

radioactive substance; but in this case, the substance is not radium, but radioactive cobalt. The nuclei of the radioactive substance send out atomic radiations. In other words, the machine is a kind of radioactive gun. When the radiation from this radioactive gun is aimed at a cancer, the radiation can be made strong enough to destroy cancer cells without causing great harm to healthy cells nearby.

Radioactive substances are now being used not only to treat disease but also for many kinds of medical tests. The advantage of using radioactive atoms in testing is that the path of these atoms through the body can easily be traced with the use of a Geiger counter.

Here is how one such test works. Your thyroid gland absorbs iodine from your blood. If this gland becomes diseased it may absorb iodine too slowly or too quickly. To test whether this is so, a person is given a tiny, harmless amount of radioactive iodine. How long it takes for the thyroid gland to absorb the radioactive atoms is determined with a Geiger counter.

More and more often, nuclear reactions are being used. They are being used to give us electric energy for home and industry and to operate ships and submarines for military purposes. As you have seen, they are also being used to treat disease and to make various kinds of medical tests.

Nuclear energy has become one of the most powerful servants to work for us. In nuclear energy there is a great promise for an even more remarkable future—if it is used wisely.

**BEFORE YOU GO ON** This time, to fix the concept of nuclear reactions and the uses of nuclear energy in your mind, begin a book of your own entitled: *The Nuclear Age.* You might use an ordinary loose-leaf notebook. Divide the notebook into at least five parts. You may want to have more parts in it later on. The five parts may be:

    a. The Uses of Nuclear Energy in Health
    b. The Uses of Nuclear Energy in Industry

c. The Uses of the Atom as a Source of Energy (for Heat, Light, Electricity)

d. The Uses of Nuclear Energy in Space Exploration

e. The Uses of Nuclear Energy in Military Operations

Under each section, you can keep records of any new advances in the uses of nuclear energy. Where will you get your material? Here are some possible sources:

1. Newspapers (you may wish to paste in clippings or to write your own reports).

2. Magazines;

3. Reports on television or radio.

You may find many other sources of material as well. New uses of the atom are being developed so fast, it is very helpful to keep an up-to-date record of them.

Perhaps you and your classmates may decide to work on one book together.

## 5. The Main Concept: Particles of Matter

Man's early understanding, or concept, of the composition of matter has changed.

Before the early Greeks (more than 2,500 years ago), people thought that all the things about them were made up of fire, water, air, and earth. Some of the early Greeks thought the same.

The Greeks went further, however. Leucippus and his pupil Democritus developed the idea that all matter was made up of atoms, atoms that were invisible and indivisible. How else, Democritus asked, could we explain what would happen if we kept dividing a piece of copper until we reached the very smallest particle of copper.

That tiny particle he visualized (imagined) as an atom.

However, neither Leucippus nor Democritus investigated atoms. Their idea of the atom was a result of their thinking only, and was not based on any investigations in the laboratory.

Since the time of Democritus, many scientists have searched for a more complete understanding of the composition and behavior of matter. There were many scientists who contributed to this understanding. Among them were Robert Boyle, a Scottish scientist; Joseph Priestley, an English minister; Antoine Lavoisier, a French scientist. There was John Dalton, an English school master, who did his work early in the nineteenth century. He investigated many different compounds, including water. He, too, accepted the concept that the atom was tiny and *invisible* and, furthermore, that it was *indivisible*. His work was based on investigation that was limited by a lack of equipment.

Then came Madame Marie Curie, who found, by investigation, that an atom of radium is not indivisible, that atoms of radium decay (break down), and give off particles smaller than atoms. Other scientists began to find that the same was true of other atoms; in short, they *confirmed the concept* that the atom was made up of smaller particles.

Technologists helped develop ways to investigate atoms and their **subatomic** (smaller than atoms) **particles.**

### "Seeing" Atomic Particles

Have you ever seen a jet airplane flying very high in the sky? It leaves a track of frozen moisture (vapor trails) in the cold atmosphere.

Charged atomic particles leave a kind of cloud in a Wilson cloud chamber, as shown. ■ Particles from an atom pass through invisible vapor, and the vapor condenses to give a cloud-like trail along the path of each particle. In this way, the particles leave a clear record of themselves, as shown in the picture.● The tracks differ for each kind of particle, whether proton, alpha particle, or electron. Scientists have studied the way particles move in this cloud chamber (invented by Charles Wilson in 1911) and have discovered that they can

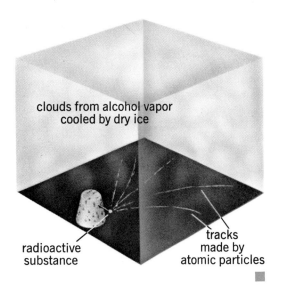

clouds from alcohol vapor cooled by dry ice

radioactive substance

tracks made by atomic particles

name the different particles by the way they move and by the curvature of their paths.

There are other ways of detecting atomic particles. They have been studied as they were hurled at high speeds from a cyclotron and as they were produced in atomic piles and reactors.

The old concept of the atom as invisible and indivisible had to be changed. It has been replaced by the

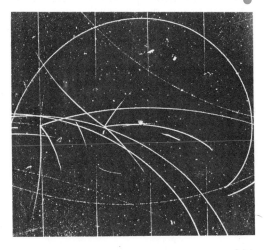

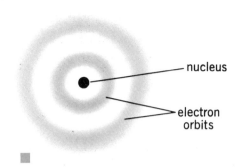

new concept of an atom that is made up of subatomic particles—electrons, protons, and neutrons.

Niels Bohr, a Danish scientist, defined the new concept. This concept describes the atom as having most of its weight concentrated in the nucleus—in its protons and neutrons. Moving around the nucleus are electrons. The electrons are sometimes described as being in orbit around the nucleus, as planets are in orbit around the sun. Some scientists picture the electron orbits as clouds about the nucleus. The darkest areas show where the electrons are most often located.

The atom is a source of tremendous energy. Because the nucleus of the atom is divisible, *fission* can take place. The energy released by nuclear fission of uranium, for example, can be harnessed to serve man.

Energy released by nuclear fission is far greater than energy released by chemical changes in matter, such as the burning of fuels. Man's new concept of the atom as divisible makes it possible for him to control this vast energy from fission for his own uses.

Nuclear energy from another source has been serving man as long as he has been on this earth! This is the energy from nuclear **fusion** (fyōō′zhən) in the sun. Nuclear energy from the sun lights the earth and supplies green plants with the energy they need to make food. That energy supports all forms of life.

You will read more about nuclear fusion in Unit Nine; but first let us find out more about life, and living things, here on earth.

# Fixing the Main Concepts

TESTING YOURSELF    Test your understanding of the important concepts in this unit by doing these problems.

**1.** A theory is a reasonable explanation of the facts. Which of these theories on the structure of the atom would you accept?

a. An atom is indivisible.        b. An atom is divisible.

**2.** Below are two statements on the structure of matter. Which would you accept as being more accurate?

    a. The smallest particles of matter are molecules and atoms.

    b. The smallest particles of matter are protons, neutrons, and electrons.

**3.** What are some of the problems in building a nuclear reactor, and how have they been solved? In your notebook, report how some of these problems have been met.

**4.** Which of the following would you consider to be a correct model of an atom? ● ▲ Can you explain why? Draw the correct atom model in your notebook. Next to the model, explain why its structure seems correct. Explain, also, why you have not chosen the other atom.

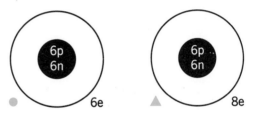

**5.** Which of the following models of an atom is correct? ◆ ★ As in problem 3 above, draw the correct model in your notebook, and give the reasons for your choice.

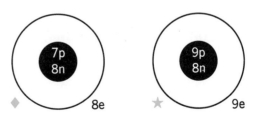

**6.** A sodium atom has an atomic weight of 23. It has an atomic number of 11. In your notebook, draw a model of the sodium atom showing the number of protons, neutrons, and electrons in it. Use the symbols for these particles that are used in the models of the atoms above.

**1.** Copy the following table in your notebook, and fill in the missing information. ■ You should be able to figure out the missing information from the information that is already given. If you need help, read again Section 1 of this unit, which describes the structure of the atom. Compare your figures with those from a reliable source.

■

| Element | Atomic weight | Atomic number | Protons | Electrons | Neutrons |
|---------|---------------|---------------|---------|-----------|----------|
| oxygen | 16 | 8 | | | |
| nitrogen | 14 | 7 | | | |
| sulfur | 32 | 16 | | | |
| aluminum | 27 | 13 | | | |
| copper | 64 | 29 | | | |
| iron | 56 | 26 | | | |
| uranium | 238 | 92 | | | |

**2.** In your notebook, draw a model of one of the last three atoms listed in the table, and show the number of protons, neutrons, and electrons in it.

**3.** Suppose a proton were shot into the nucleus of a sulfur atom, so that its atomic number would be raised by one. What element would be produced? Look for the answer in the table of elements on page 291.

**4.** Suppose the nucleus of an aluminum atom lost a proton, so that its atomic number would be lowered by one. What element would be produced? To answer this, you will again need the table of elements on page 291.

**5.** Some of the statements below are correct, but some are not. When you find a statement that is incorrect, decide how it can be changed to make it correct. Write the correct statement in your notebook.

a. An atom is made up of smaller particles.
b. An electron is heavier than a proton.
c. The atomic weight of an atom is equal to the sum of its protons and neutrons.
d. In an atom the number of electrons is equal to the number of neutrons.
e. In an atomic pile or reactor, fusion takes place.
f. In the sun, fission is the source of energy.

**FOR YOUR READING**

**1.** *Giant of the Atom: Ernest Rutherford,* by Robin McKown, published by Messner, New York, 1962.

Lord Rutherford made many important discoveries about the structure of the atom. For an interesting biography of this famous scientist, read this book.

**2.** *Atoms, Today and Tomorrow,* by Margaret Hyde, published by McGraw-Hill, New York, 1959.

This book tells about the uses of nuclear energy today in medicine, industry, and farming. It also describes plans for future uses of nuclear energy.

**3.** *Atompower,* by Joseph M. Dukert and John T. Gorsuch, published by Coward-McCann, New York, 1962.

For further information about nuclear reactors, this book is helpful. It shows that although new types of reactors are being designed today, all reactors still have certain basic things in common.

**4.** *The Curies and Radium,* by Elizabeth Rubin, published by Watts, New York, 1961.

This is the story of the famous husband and wife team and of their important work with radium. It also tells about the work of their scientist daughter and her husband on radioactive substances.

sodium and chlorine

A crystal of salt consists of the compound sodium chloride. Sodium chloride is made of two different kinds of atoms, as shown in the picture. ■ The larger atoms are chlorine atoms; the smaller atoms are sodium atoms. When combined, these atoms are charged and therefore cling together in an orderly arrangement. Do some research in the library to find out what charged atoms are called.

Suppose each atom of sodium were made as large as the letter "O." What size would you be if you could be made larger in the same proportion? You would be 8,000 miles high. ● You would be about as tall as the diameter of the earth (7,926 miles). A crystal of salt enlarged the same way would be about as tall as a skyscraper (1,200 feet). ■

Does this give you an idea of the size of an atom? It may help you realize how very small it must be.

Suppose a cell in your cheek were enlarged in the same way that the things above were. Recall that the crystal of salt, enlarged, is 1,200 feet high. If the cell were enlarged, it might be 1/100 of that size. What size in feet would the cell then be?

Recall, too, that an atom of sodium enlarged the same way would be only this high: O. Measure the height of the O. Compare it to the height of the enlarged cheek cell. Can you now figure out how much larger a cell in your cheek is than an atom?

Can you think of other ways of describing or showing how very tiny atoms are?

# A Concept of Mass-Energy: A New View

In the world around you are so many different things. In the sea are fish and huge crabs, snails and jellyfish, sand and coral, and mountains poking their heads above the water to make islands. On land there are rocks and houses; rabbits and horses; mountains, hills, and valleys. In the air are airplanes, birds, and clouds. In outer space are stars and planets; moons and other satellites; meteors and dust. In your room are different objects such as paper, paper clips, rubber bands, erasers, chairs, and, perhaps, a desk.

*"The world is so full of a number of things,*
*I'm sure we should all be as happy as kings."*

Our world does have a large number of things, as Robert Louis Stevenson wrote. Are all these things quite different from one another, or are there hidden likenesses, or relationships, among all these objects?

## A New View of the World

You know by now that *all* matter—whether in chairs, canaries, air, water, planets—is made up of particles. A substance such as water, for example, is made up of molecules. A molecule of water is the smallest part of water which is still water. If the molecule is broken down, it divides into atoms of hydrogen and oxygen. A substance such as oxygen, made up of only *one kind of atom*, is an *element*.

Atoms of most elements can combine to form compounds. Atoms of hydrogen and oxygen, for example, combine to form the compound water. Rust, or iron oxide, is a combination of atoms of iron and oxygen. All around you, then, is a world made up of elements and compounds or mixtures of elements and compounds. For instance, seawater is a mixture of the elements and compounds shown in the chart. ▲ Which of these substances are elements?

Everything in the world, living and nonliving, and all the elements and compounds in them are made from some of the 103 different atoms. Impossible? Well, the 500,000 or so words in the English language are

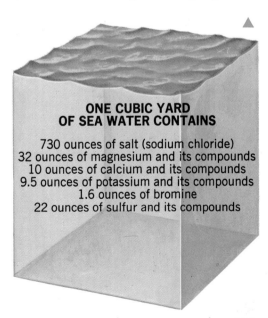

**ONE CUBIC YARD OF SEA WATER CONTAINS**

730 ounces of salt (sodium chloride)
32 ounces of magnesium and its compounds
10 ounces of calcium and its compounds
9.5 ounces of potassium and its compounds
1.6 ounces of bromine
22 ounces of sulfur and its compounds

made from only the 26 letters of the alphabet. With 103 kinds of atoms, then, it is possible to make millions upon millions of compounds.

If we probe further, we find more hidden likenesses in matter. When we study atoms with scientific instruments, we find even smaller particles. On page 289 you saw that the atoms of oxygen, iron, nitrogen, and carbon are all made of the same smaller particles—electrons, protons, neutrons.

All the matter about us, then, whether in the form of rabbits, diamonds, or people is made up mainly of three kinds of particles—*electrons, protons, neutrons.* We can sum up the hidden likenesses in matter in the great concept: *All matter is made up of particles.*

## Changing Matter into Energy

What more do we know about matter? We once thought that matter could be changed from one form to another but could not be created or destroyed. It is true that *in a chemical change, matter is neither created nor destroyed.* This concept holds for any chemical reaction like the reactions that you know about. For instance, when carbon and oxygen combine to form carbon dioxide, the chemist writes:

$$C + O_2 \rightarrow CO_2$$

1 atom + 2 atoms → 3 atoms

3 atoms → 3 atoms

The number of atoms of carbon (C) and oxygen ($O_2$) that go into the re-action is always the same as the number of atoms in the molecule of carbon dioxide that is produced. ■

Whenever substances take part in a *chemical reaction,* their atoms are neither created nor destroyed. The same amount of matter that goes into the reaction comes out of the reaction. *In a chemical reaction, the total amount of matter remains the same.*

A *nuclear reaction,* however, is different from a chemical reaction. In a chemical reaction only the electrons around the nucleus take part. But in a nuclear reaction, the nucleus itself is changed. A nucleus may split, and some of its matter be lost. Or two nuclei may join; again, some matter is lost. The nucleus may lose or gain particles. *In either nuclear reaction, some of the matter from a nucleus may be changed into energy.*

If you burn a log, which is a chemical change, the energy stored in the log is changed into heat energy and light energy. The energy is changed in form, *but the total amount of matter remains the same.*

In a nuclear reaction, on the other hand, some matter is changed to energy. Very careful measurements and experiments have been carried out by teams of scientists. Countless calculations have been done, and, in every case, these show that some of the mass (amount of matter) has "disappeared." This matter is not lost; it is changed into energy. In describing a nuclear reaction, therefore, we introduce a new concept: *In a nu-*

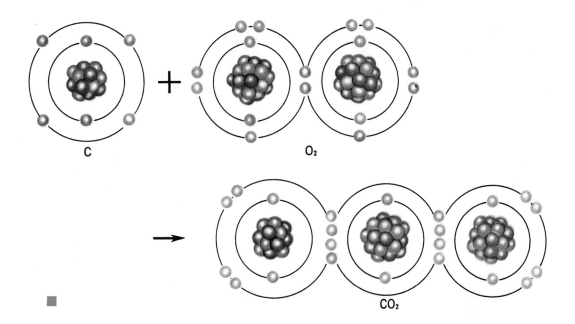

C + O₂

→ CO₂

clear reaction the total amount of matter and energy remains the same. To show that matter (mass) can be changed into energy, scientists now often use the following term for both: **mass-energy.**

In the fission of a uranium nucleus, for example, some matter is changed to energy. When even a tiny bit of matter is changed to energy, huge amounts of energy are produced. This is what Einstein meant when he wrote:

$$E = mc^2$$

Think of this formula as a sentence in which $E$ stands for energy. $m$ stands for mass that is lost. $c$ stands for the speed of light which is, as you know, 186,000 miles per second. $c^2$ is this number multiplied by itself—a tremendous number! In a formula, the two sides balance. Since $c^2$ on the right side is such a huge number, $E$ on the left side must also be huge, even if $m$ is very small.

Our concepts today of the way matter and energy behave may be summed up as follows:

*In a chemical reaction, matter can be changed in form, but the total amount of matter remains the same. Energy can be changed in form and transferred from one place to another, but the total amount of energy remains the same.*

*In a nuclear reaction, matter can be changed into energy, but the total amount of mass-energy remains the same.*

This last important concept of the way matter and energy behave will guide your future work in science.

# UNIT EIGHT

# CODE OF HEREDITY

Visit a ranch. The chromosomes in the nucleus of animal cells are responsible for the characteristics of the animals. Visit a farm. Both the plants and animals owe their characteristics to their chromosomes. Visit a market. The vegetables are a result of the plant breeder's art. Look in a mirror. Your chromosomes are largely responsible for the way you look and, in many ways, for the things you do. In fact, chromosomes are the link between one generation and the next, the reason that each kind of plant or animal produces its own kind. But that is not the whole story.

Long before man understood the concepts underlying heredity, he sought to improve the quality of each succeeding generation of plants and animals. He wanted plants that would produce more food on less land, cows that would produce more milk, chickens that would lay more eggs, cattle and hogs that would have more meat, and plants that would be resistant to disease.

In recent years, armed with more knowledge and techniques, man has applied new tools to old problems. Nowhere has science yielded knowledge of greater importance than in the study of chromosomes. A model of what scientists know about the structure of the chemical substance within the chromosomes is shown on the opposite page. This unit is only a beginning in the study of this substance—the basis of heredity.

## 1. A "Chip off the Old Block"

People sometimes refer to a son as a "chip off the old block," meaning that he is just like his father.

Actually, it is never true that a boy is just like his father or his mother. All boys and girls inherit traits from both parents. The word traits is used to mean many things—eye color, height, hair color, or even intelligence. All the traits that one inherits are called **heredity** (hə·red′ə·tē).

How important is heredity? Can we ever really say that a living thing is a "chip off the old block"? After all, living things that have two parents may inherit traits from each. With some living things, however, the expression "chip off the old block" may really fit.

Take a look at a living thing that starts life as a kind of "chip off the old block." You will make the "chips" yourself in the investigation on these two pages.

### The Results and an Explanation

In several weeks you should begin to get results from your investigation. Do you find that:

1. the bud in the dark closet is pale and thin?

2. the bud which was not watered (after the first watering) has barely managed to sprout at all?

3. the bud with most of its food removed has barely come up and is thin and small?

4. the control is green with a stout stem and several leaves?

# into the Effect of Environment on Living Things

**Needed:** a large white potato with several eyes (buds); four small flower-pots; saucers; some garden soil

Divide your potato into four pieces so that each piece has an "eye." Each "eye" is a bud from which a new potato plant can grow.

Try to divide the potato into four pieces of equal size so that each bud will have as large a piece of potato as the others. After you have done this, trim off almost all the potato from around *one* of the buds.

Now you have several "eyes" with good-sized pieces of potato around them. These untrimmed pieces have a great deal of starch in them. Starch is a food needed to supply the new plant with energy for growth.

One bud was trimmed so that it had only a little supply of starch around it.

Plant one piece of potato in the soil in each of the four pots. Plant the pieces with the eye *up* and water the soil, so that it is moist but not wet.

Place one of the pots containing a large piece of potato in a dark closet. Label this pot #1. ■ Place the other three pots where they will be in the light. Two of these have a large piece of potato. After the first watering, *do not* water *one* of the two pots again. Label this as your second pot. ● The third pot has the small piece of potato (with very little starch around the bud). ▲ The fourth pot (with a large piece of potato) is the control. ◆ All the others can be compared with this one. Keep the soil moist in the first, third, and fourth.

▲

◆

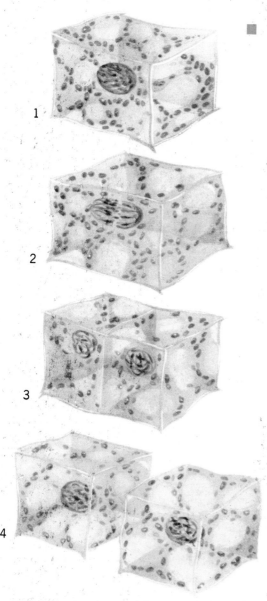

■ Which of the four buds grew to look most like the parent plant? What causes a potato sprout to grow like its parent?

The bud of the potato is made up of cells. As it grows, the cells divide to make new cells. ■ Some of the cells form leaves, others form roots, and still others form the stem.

The potato plant that comes from the bud will be like the parent potato because of its **chromosomes** (krō'mə-sōmz). Chromosomes are found in the nucleus of a cell. They are usually rod-shaped but may be bent in different ways. The cells of the potato bud have the same chromosomes as the parent plant.

Each chromosome is made up of tiny parts called **genes** (jēnz), which are responsible for the traits of plants and animals. The new potato plant will look like the parent plant, because it has the same *genes* as the parent. Genes are the parts of the chromosome which carry the hereditary traits. The genes are believed to be parts of a huge molecule found within the chromosome. A model of a DNA molecule is shown on page 324.

All of the offspring of the potato plant will look like the parent—but *only if* the environment of the offspring is like the environment in which the parent grew.

The genes in the buds of the four pieces of potato were the same, but the environment in which each piece grew was very different. Therefore, the results were different.

Remember that the control is the one which is to be compared with each of the others. Each of the other three plants lacked only one variable (light, water, or food supply). The control did not lack any variable.

How do you explain the results? All were pieces from the same potato. All were "chips off the same block."

*One plant had no sunlight.* The green substance in plants, **chlorophyll** (klôr′ə·fil), needs sunlight to develop. The ability of a plant to make chlorophyll is a trait inherited from the parent plant. This trait was there in the bud of the potato plant. Without sunlight, however, the genes responsible for making chlorophyll were unable to do their work.

*One plant had little water.* Without water the plant roots could not get substances they needed from the soil, and the plant could not make its own food. The genes which are responsible for growth in the plant could not work properly without water.

*One plant had little food at the beginning of its growth.* The genes responsible for growth were present in the potato bud, but the potato bud needed a food supply. Without it, the plant could not grow. The environment which would have supplied food for growth had been removed.

The explanation of the results is plain. A living thing needs a good environment in which to develop. Genes are not enough.

Without a good environment the genes in a seed may not fully develop their traits. The trait of "green color" shows up only when there is enough sunlight. The *ability* to produce chlorophyll is a trait transferred from the parent to the offspring in genes; but the *development* of the trait is determined by certain conditions in the environment. Sunlight is essential for the growth of green plants.

An oak tree is stunted when it grows in sandy soil without enough water. The trait for tallness in the oak is not developed unless the tree is growing in a good environment.

We come then to still another important concept: *A living thing is a product of heredity acting together with the environment.* In other words, heredity, acting in a certain environment, equals the organism.

This concept is true for all living things. Genes from parent plants are passed on to the offspring. You can cut off pieces from other plants, as you did with the potato, and plant them. The offspring are then very much like the parent—*if the environment remains very similar.*

The young potato plants came from *one* parent plant. The genes in the offspring were therefore the same as in the one parent. This is not true of all new plants because some plants, like the tiny lima bean plant in the picture below, start from seeds which result from *two* parent cells. ●

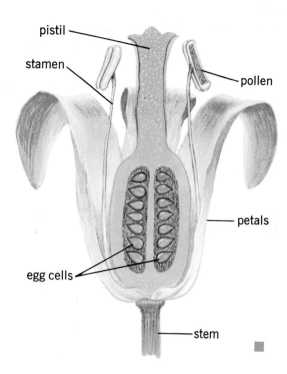

pistil

stamen

pollen

petals

egg cells

stem

## Plants with Two Parents

Certain plants, the seed plants, have flowers. Cut apart a flower as shown in the diagram on this page and find the parts that are labeled. ■ A tulip or a pea flower will do nicely.

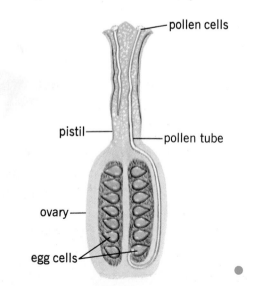

pollen cells

pistil

pollen tube

ovary

egg cells

Before a seed can be formed, the flower must be **pollinated** (pol′ə-nāt·ed); **pollen** (pol′ən) must fall on the **pistil** (pis′til). Tiny grains of pollen are produced by the **stamen** (stā′-mən) of the flower. Each grain contains a living cell called a **sperm cell.** The grains of pollen are sometimes carried to the top of the pistil by the wind or by the feet of insects crawling around the flower. Sometimes pollen from the stamen of one flower is carried to the pistil of another. When the pollen grain lands on the pistil, it grows a long tube.● This tube grows toward the **egg cell** (the part that later becomes the seed), at the base of the pistil. There the sperm cell from the pollen unites with the egg cell. The beginning of a new plant, the **embryo** (em′brē·ō), is produced. The embryonic plant (which is very small) stays in the seed until conditions, such as warmth and moisture, are right for it to grow.

The embryonic plants are so well protected within the seeds that they can survive a cold winter. In the spring, when it is warm and moist, they begin to grow. One or more seeds are formed in the **ovary** at the base of the pistil of each flower. The number of seeds is determined by the kind of flower. Number of seeds is a trait determined by heredity (genes).

In seed plants, the embryo gets chromosomes from *two* parent cells, the sperm cell and the egg cell. The genes in the two parent cells determine the traits of the new plant.

**A.** Study the statements below and choose the correct responses. They will help you fix in mind the concepts of this section.

1. Chromosomes are generally found in
   a. cells                    b. genes

2. Genes are found in
   a. chromosomes              b. chlorophyll

3. Inside the chromosome is a huge molecule known as
   a. the DNA molecule         b. a pollen grain

4. The organism is the product of its heredity and its
   a. genes                    b. environment

5. A plant having only one parent may be reproduced from a part
   a. of itself                b. of a seed

6. When pollination takes place, the pollen grows a long tube which enters the
   a. stamen                   b. pistil

7. A plant which develops from a seed is the product of
   a. one parent               b. two parents

**B.** Write a paragraph or two on this topic: A "Chip off the Old Block."

1. There are many varieties of potatoes, *Idaho, Katahdin,* and others. How can farmers be sure to get the same variety for re-planting as the ones they harvest?

2. The embryo in a seed inherits its traits from two parents. Suppose an embryo came from two parent plants—one was red-flowered, the other white-flowered. Into what kind of plant might the embryo grow?
   a. red-flowered?            c. any other color?
   b. white-flowered?

What is the hypothesis behind your answer?

Some plants can reproduce themselves from their roots, stems, or leaves. The white potato, for instance, is a thick underground stem. Parts of the potato stem can grow into complete plants.

When a plant reproduces itself from its parts, the process is called *vegetative propagation* or sometimes *vegetative reproduction*. Perhaps you would like to see for yourself how vegetative propagation takes place in other plants. Below are two plants which you might want to investigate.

A carrot: its thick orange root will reproduce the entire plant. Plant it and see.

A willow: a twig will grow roots and leaves. (Try this in early spring.)

What other plants undergo vegetative propagation?

To find out, look in an encyclopedia. The answer may be found under any of these topics:

| | |
|---|---|
| plant life | vegetative propagation |
| plant propagation | vegetative reproduction |
| | plants |

## 2. Inheriting Traits

There are garden pea plants that grow tall and some that grow short. What happens when a tall pea plant is pollinated, or crossed, with a short pea plant? For the time being, let us say that a *pure tall plant* crossed with another *pure tall plant* can produce only *pure tall plants*. A *pure short plant* crossed with another *pure short plant* can produce only *pure short plants*. We call a plant **pure** when it has only the genes for a certain trait. For example, a pure tall plant has only genes for tallness. There are no genes for shortness in the plant.

Suppose one of these pure tall plants is crossed with a pure short plant. It can be done this way. Pollen, obtained from the stamen of a flower of one plant, a pure tall one, is placed on the pistil of a pure short plant.

A tall garden pea plant is now crossed with a short garden pea plant. What will the offspring be? Do you understand why? The gene for tallness is represented in the diagram by "T"; the gene for shortness by "s." ■ All the seeds that are produced will grow into tall plants. Although this is true of garden peas, it is not necessarily true when other kinds of plants are crossed.

332

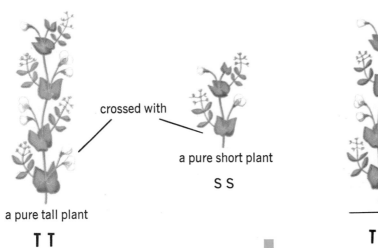

crossed with

a pure short plant

S S

a pure tall plant

T T

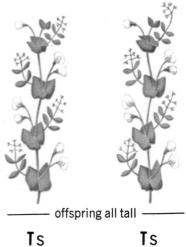

———— offspring all tall ————

T s       T s

Gregor Mendel, an Austrian monk and scientist, first investigated garden peas about 100 years ago. Whenever he crossed pure tall plants with pure short ones, he got offspring which were tall.

He called tallness a **dominant** trait. What does dominant mean? The gene for tallness *seems* to dominate or "rule over" the gene for shortness in garden peas. Mendel called shortness a **recessive** trait because it seems to disappear in the offspring. But the genes for shortness have not disappeared or been destroyed. They are still present in the new plant, the offspring, but only the dominant trait is apparent.

When Mendel crossed pure tall plants with pure short plants, he got only tall plants. Tallness was the dominant trait. The recessive trait (shortness), however, is also in the offspring.

Somehow tallness and shortness are passed on from the parent plants to the offspring.

## The Message in Cells

Scientists think that chromosomes carry a kind of message from the parent to the offspring. You might think of the chromosomes as carrying a kind of *code*. What is a code? It is a shorthand way of giving information. For instance, here are a few lines of the Morse code.

/-/•••/•/ /--•/•/-•/•/•••/ /•-/•••/•/

/-/•••/•/ /-•••/---/-••/•/ /---/•••-/

/••••/•/•--/•/-••/••/-/•-/•••/-•--/

/-/•--/•--/••/-/•••/•----/

Translated it says:

The genes are the code of hereditary traits.

In every organism the genes in all the cells seem to be the same. They seem to duplicate themselves, so that the code is passed on every time the cell divides.

Scientists now believe that the genes are smaller parts of the large molecule called the **DNA molecule,** which was mentioned earlier. In fact, the chromosome contains the large molecule of DNA (short for deoxyribonucleic acid). The genes are thought to be smaller parts of the molecule. When scientists learn more about the nature of DNA, we will have a better understanding of genes. Perhaps they will be able to explain how the genes can determine hereditary traits.

Here is a diagram of the long chromosome of a fruit fly. Some of the tiny lines you see might be the genes for eye color, white eye color. ■ These genes are parts of the chromosome which carry the code for eye color. Each of the two genes was inherited from a different parent. One of the genes for white eye color came from

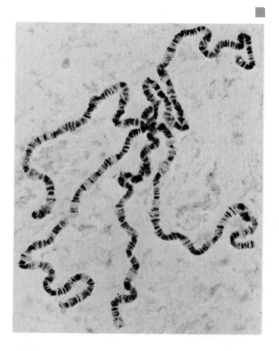

the fly's male parent. The other came from the female parent.

The code in the chromosome or in the long molecules of DNA directs the way a living thing develops. A plant which is pure for tallness carries the code which directs the plant to grow tall. The code in the chromosomes of a certain fruit fly acts on the cells to produce white eyes.

Genes do not act alone, however; the environment plays an important part. Without a good environment, a plant with genes for tallness would not grow as tall as it is capable of growing.

The *DNA code* (the code in the chromosomes) determines the traits; the *environment* helps in determining the development of the traits.

DNA molecules in a hen's cells carry the code which determines whether the hen's eggs will be brown or white. The long DNA molecule in the chromosomes of a red flower determine its red color.

Scientists do not know the whole story yet. They know that the chromosomes contain DNA and that this substance carries a kind of code. This code carries the information, in the genes, which determines which traits will develop.

Look again at the lines and shadings on the chromosome in the picture. Today scientists are not sure what each one stands for. Maybe sometime in the future they will be able to solve the code and solve one of the greatest mysteries of nature.

**A.** Study the statements below and choose the correct responses. They will help you fix in mind the concepts of this section.

**1.** A pure tall plant crossed with a pure tall plant will produce

    a. only tall plants          b. some short plants

**2.** A pure tall plant has at least two genes for tallness. One gene for tallness is received from

    a. each of both parents      b. only one parent

**3.** When a pure tall garden pea plant is crossed with a pure short garden pea plant, all the offspring are

    a. short                 b. tall

**4.** In the garden pea, tallness is

    a. dominant            b. recessive

**5.** The hereditary code of an organism is carried in its

    a. environment         b. chromosomes

**6.** The hereditary code of an organism seems to be in the DNA. DNA is a

    a. long molecule        b. dominant trait

**7.** DNA might be said to be the basis of an organism's

    a. heredity             b. environment

**B.** Write a paragraph or two on this topic: DNA—The Code of Heredity.

**1.** In guinea pigs the genes for black fur are dominant over the genes for white fur. A pure black-furred guinea pig is crossed with a pure white guinea pig. What kind of offspring would be produced? Why?

**2.** In cattle the genes for short horns are dominant over the genes for long horns. A pure shorthorned animal is crossed with a pure longhorned animal. What kind of offspring will be produced? Why?

# 3. Crossing Plants

Look at the picture and study the red- and white-flowering garden peas for a moment. ■

Farmers and plant growers are interested in the colors of the blossoms of garden pea plants, because they are linked with the color of the peas that grow later. White-flowering plants produce the bright green peas that most people buy and eat today. Red-flowering plants, on the other hand, produce a grayish-looking pea that tastes as good as the green pea but is not as attractive. Since the attractive-looking peas are easier to sell, it is natural that most farmers are only interested in obtaining seeds for the white-flowering plants.

Now suppose you were a plant grower, interested in growing only white-flowering garden peas, not red ones. You would want to be sure that your seeds produced only white-flowering plants, *not red ones*. How can you go about getting plants that will produce seeds which will grow into white-flowering plants only?

You might say that you would plant only the seeds that come from white-flowering plants. However, when you plant these seeds, you might be very much surprised. The plants coming from these seeds might produce *either* red *or* white flowers. ● Soon you will discover why.

This is a problem that plant growers are faced with all the time. They want to be sure that the seeds they sell in a seed packet will produce the plants shown on the label. If the label is to say "white-flowering," the plant grower wants to be sure that only

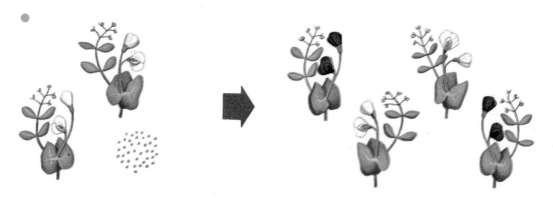

white-flowering pea plants will grow. If a consumer buys the seeds, he also expects to get what the label says.

## Crossing Plants for Color

If the grower wants white-flowering plants, he starts with white-flowering plants. The seeds from the white-flowering plants may produce either red- or white-flowering plants. The reason for this is that a white-flowering plant may have been pollinated by a red-flowering plant.

The grower then makes sure that the white-flowering plants are crossed with other white-flowering plants. He takes the pollen of one white-flowering plant and places it on the pistil of the other white-flowering plant.▲ Then, as in the picture, he puts a bag over the flower. Why? Bees and other insects collect pollen. The insects can carry the pollen to other flowers. That is, insects can **cross-pollinate** (krôs′ pol′ə·nāt) flowers (carry pollen from flower to flower). In this way, it would be possible to produce red-flowering plants. Placing the bag over the flower prevents unwanted cross-pollination.

In this way the plant grower can produce seeds which he is sure of. Whenever he plants seeds labeled "white-flowering peas," he is sure to get white-flowering plants. The seeds for white-flowering garden peas will have genes for producing only white flowers. To keep the plants *pure*, the plant breeder must make sure that red-flowering plants pollinate red-flowering plants and that white ones are crossed only with white ones. Perhaps you would like to try your luck at cross-pollinating flowers. In the investigation on the following pages you will find out how. Try it yourself.

▲

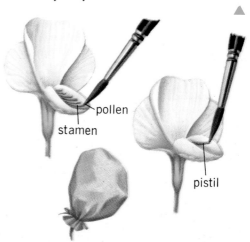

pollen

stamen

pistil

# AN INVESTIGATION into Cross-Pollination of Petunias

**Needed:** tweezers; scissors; plastic bags; red and white petunias; a small brush

Set up your own investigation into cross-pollination. Here is the way one girl tried her luck at crossing red and white petunias.

With a tweezer, she opened the bud of a white petunia plant, and with a pair of small scissors, she cut off all of the stamens to prevent the flower from pollinating itself. ■ Then she covered the bud with a plastic bag and waited for it to reach full bloom. ●

When the white flower was in full bloom, she removed some pollen from the stamen of a red petunia with a small brush, as shown. ▲

She then removed the plastic bag and brushed the pollen onto the pistil of the white flower. ◆ She immediately replaced the bag in order to prevent other pollen from getting onto the pistil.

When the flowers dried out, she removed the seed cases which contained several very tiny seeds from the base of the pistil and saved them all in a dry place until the next spring. ★ Then she planted the seeds and cared for them until they grew into new plants. Which plant (in the picture) did the offspring of the red and the white petunia plant look like? ◈ What is your prediction? Do you need further study?

♦

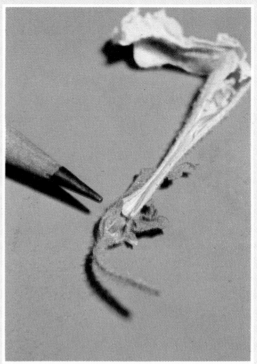

★

◈

## Red Crossed with White

What happens when a red-flowering garden pea plant is crossed with a white-flowering plant?

First, it is important to know which color is *dominant* and which color is *recessive*. Here is one statement that will give you a clue.

*When a pure red-flowering pea plant is crossed with a pure white-flowering plant, the flowers on the offspring will always be red.* This means that in garden peas the trait for red flowers must be dominant, and the trait for white flowers must be recessive.

Let us call the gene for red flowering *R* and the gene for white flowering *w*. A pure red-flowering plant has genes for red flowers only (RR). One gene (R) was inherited from each parent cell. A pure white plant has genes for white flowers only (ww).

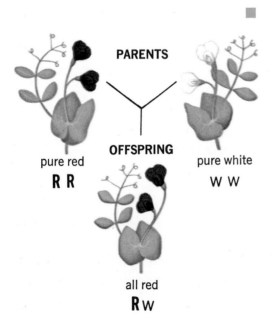

**PARENTS**

pure red
**R R**

**OFFSPRING**

pure white
**W W**

all red
**R** w

The capital letters (RR) show that the genes for red flowering are dominant. The small letters (ww) mean that the genes for white flowering are recessive.

What would the genes be in a plant which was a result of crossing a pure red (RR) with a pure white (ww)?

The pure red (RR) plant would pass on a gene for red (R). The pure white (ww) plant would pass on a gene for white (w). What color would the flowers of the offspring be? *Study the diagram carefully.* ■ Ask yourself this question: When a pure red *dominant* is crossed with a pure white *recessive*, what color will the offspring be?

## A Plant Made to Order

For many kinds of plants, plant growers know how to get the genes they want into a new plant. First, they try to produce a plant pure for the genes they want. Then they must cross the pure plants with each other. Pure red-flowering pea plants crossed with pure red-flowering pea plants will give a pure red-flowering plant.

What you have learned about pea plants is true also of other plants and animals which are bred for a certain trait. The main thing to do is to produce a plant or animal which is pure for the genes that are wanted. Then a cross with another plant or animal that has only the genes that are wanted is needed. In this way, it is possible to be fairly certain of the heredity of the offspring.

**A.** Study the statements below and choose the correct responses. They will help you fix in mind the concepts of this section.

   **1.** To be sure that he will get the kinds of genes he wants, a plant breeder controls
      a. pollination                     b. growth

   **2.** In garden pea plants, red flowering is dominant over white. When a pure red plant is crossed with a pure white plant, the offspring will be
      a. white                          b. red

   **3.** A pure purple-flowering plant is crossed with a pure yellow-flowering plant. All the seeds produce purple flowers, so the purple flowering must be
      a. dominant                       b. recessive

   **4.** A pure black-furred guinea pig is crossed with a pure gray-furred guinea pig. Gray fur is recessive. All the offspring will be
      a. gray-furred                    b. black-furred

**B.** Write a paragraph or two on this topic: Dominance and Recessiveness.

   **1.** A rancher breeds cattle.
      a. Why would he need to know what genes the cattle will inherit?
      b. Suppose he was interested in the way his cattle put on weight. He knows that they have genes for fast growth. Why would he need to be sure that the animals have a good environment as well?

   **2.** Scientists have found that by careful mating, or crossing, of animals or plants, many desirable traits can be carried on to the offspring.
   Why do dog breeders who want pure-bred dogs, such as spaniels, or scotties, mate only pure-bred animals with each other?

dominant                    recessive

## 4. Blending Traits

Scientists learn more and more as they investigate.

After Mendel had written about his experiments in 1859, it was thought that genes were either dominant or recessive. Tallness in garden peas is dominant over shortness. Red flowering in garden pea plants is dominant over white flowering. ▪

Black fur in guinea pigs is dominant over gray fur. When pure black-furred guinea pigs are crossed with pure gray ones, all the offspring are black-furred. ● In chickens the genes for red

feathers are dominant over the genes for white feathers. What color are the offspring of pure red-feathered roosters and pure white-feathered hens? They are red-feathered, of course.

All of this seemed very clear until a German scientist, Carl Correns, began studying another common garden flower. He was interested in how traits in "four-o'clocks" were inherited.

Correns started growing and crossing pure red and pure white four-o'clocks. He did not get the results he had expected.

### A New Concept

When pure red pea plants are crossed with white, all the offspring are red. When Correns crossed pure red four-o'clocks with pure white plants, the offspring were neither red nor white. *The offspring were pink.*

What is the explanation for Correns' results? Obviously, there must be genes which are neither dominant nor recessive. Perhaps the genes act together to produce a **blend** of a certain trait. Perhaps, in four-o'clocks, the gene for red acts with the gene for white to produce pink flowers Correns discovered a blend of flower colors. The results are the same as when an artist mixes red paint with white paint to get pink.

Let us review the facts.

A pure red pea plant is crossed with a white pea plant to give all red pea plants. Red color is a dominant trait in pea plants so the offspring are red.

parents

pure black
**BB**

pure gray
**gg**

offspring
**Bg**

The white plant is recessive. Therefore, it is pure. Do you see why? White plants must have genes only for white (ww). If they had one gene for red (R), they would be red because red is dominant.

A pure tall pea plant crossed with a pure short pea plant gives all tall pea plants. Tallness is a dominant trait in pea plants.

But: A pure red four-o'clock crossed with a pure white four-o'clock produces all pink four-o'clocks.

*Neither red nor white is dominant.* Scientists call this blending.

### The Pink Four-O'Clock

Suppose you could look inside the cells of a pink four-o'clock, the flower that came from the crossing of a red four-o'clock with a white one. What genes would you find in each pink four-o'clock?

You know what the color genes are in a red four-o'clock. These could be written as RR. How will we write those in a white four-o'clock? Write them as WW since they are *neither* dominant *nor* recessive to the red.

A pure red four-o'clock crossed with a pure white four-o'clock results in a pink plant which has the genes RW. One gene (R) must have come from the red plant. One gene (W) must have come from the white plant. The new plant must be RW—*pink.* ▲ Notice that capital letters are used for both red and white genes. Small letters are used only to represent genes that are recessive.

**RR**

**WW**

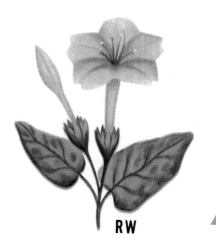

**RW**     ▲

## A Code from Parents

All living things get their DNA code (their genes) from their parents. Geneticists (jə·net′ə·sists), scientists who study heredity, have found this to be true again and again. They have called a living thing with two similar genes for a certain trait (red color, for instance) pure for the trait. When a four-o'clock plant has genes for red color (RR) only, it is pure for this trait.

On the other hand, the offspring, the pink plant, has different genes (RW) for the same trait—color. Geneticists call a living thing with different genes for the same trait a **hybrid** (hī′brid). ■

A pure tall plant (TT) crossed with a pure short (ss) will produce hybrid tall plants (Ts). The hybrid has genes for tallness and genes for shortness. Pure red pea plants (RR) crossed with pure white pea plants (ww) will produce hybrid red plants (Rw). In these hybrids, the gene for red is dominant. The dominant gene seems to cover (or hide) the recessive one.

A pure red four-o'clock (RR) crossed with a pure white four-o'clock (WW) will produce hybrid pink plants. Neither gene is dominant. The genes seem to blend the colors. It seems then that there are two kinds of hybrids. In one kind, one gene seems completely dominant (Rw) and hides the other, the recessive (w). In the other kind, the genes are incompletely dominant (RW).

## Other Hybrids

You may know of some hybrid animals. Texas cattle have long been famous for their beef. Unfortunately, they are highly susceptible to Texas fever, which kills many of them. Brahman cattle are cattle that were developed in India. They are immune to Texas fever.

When a Brahman bull is crossed with a Texas cow, hybrid cattle are produced. The offspring do not get Texas fever. The hybrid is an improved animal that is immune to disease. These animals stay healthier than many other kinds of cattle. Because of this, they are said to have prize genes, and they are very much in demand.

The ears of corn shown in the picture are ears of hybrid corn.● They are much larger ears than those of one of the parent plants and much sweeter tasting.

**HYBRIDS**

T s

R W

R w

What about a mule? A mule, too, is a hybrid. It is the result of crossing a female horse with a male donkey. A mule is stronger than either parent.

Hybrids, such as the offspring of the Brahman bull and the Texas cow, the mule, or hybrid corn, may be prize packages of genes. Geneticists, in breeding plants and animals, try to get the best of all genes into the offspring. Thus, plants and animals can be improved and made more useful.

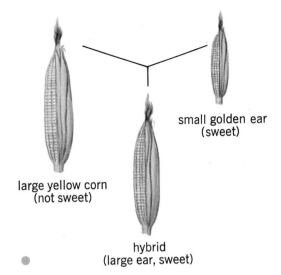

large yellow corn
(not sweet)

small golden ear
(sweet)

hybrid
(large ear, sweet)

BEFORE YOU GO ON **A.** Study the statements below and choose the correct responses. They will help you to fix in mind the concepts of this section.

**1.** The trait for red feathers is dominant over white. When pure red-feathered roosters are mated with white-feathered hens, the result is
    a. only red-feathered chickens
    b. only white-feathered chickens
    c. rust-feathered chickens

**2.** When pure red four-o'clocks are crossed with pure white four-o'clocks, all the offspring are
    a. pink               c. red
    b. white

**3.** When white four-o'clocks are crossed with white four-o'clocks, the offspring are
    a. red               c. pink
    b. white

**4.** Pink four-o'clocks are
    a. hybrids           b. pure

**5.** When pure tall pea plants are crossed with pure short pea plants, all the offspring are
    a. hybrids           b. pure

**B.** Write a paragraph or two on this topic: Heredity and Environment.

1. Hybrid animals and hybrid plants are important to us. Name at least one hybrid animal and one hybrid plant. In what way are they important to us?

2. Why are some hybrids often thought of as prize packages of genes?

Mendel and Correns were scientists who studied the effects of the genes. The findings of such scientists were applied by technologists to make new and improved species of plants and animals.

To find out more about the work of a great plant technologist, look up the life of Luther Burbank in the library. You will be interested in reading about some of his amazing accomplishments—a good example of how science and technology go hand in hand in improving plants and animals.

## 5. Changing the Code

Perhaps you had a fresh orange today. Did it have lots of seeds or was it a seedless orange?

Did you ever ask yourself how a seedless orange came to be? Since it has no seeds, one cannot plant seeds in order to produce more seedless oranges.

How did the first seedless tree come to be? The first one must have come from a tree that produced seeds. It did. Seedless oranges come from oranges with seeds.

The seeded orange must have had genes for producing seeds. Wherever a seed is planted, the tree produces fruit with seeds. One day, however, a tree was found that had good oranges, without seeds. The seedless orange tree must have grown out of a seed from a seeded tree.

One explanation of why this happened makes sense. There must have been some kind of change in the genes. The genetic code must have changed from a code that produced the trait *seeded* to one that produced the trait *seedlessness*.

Scientists now know that genes can change. Genes that change are called **mutant** (myo͞o′tənt) **genes.** Seedlessness in oranges and in grapes was caused by genes that were mutant. In other words, the genes for seeded *mutated* to produce genes for seedlessness. Genes for seedlessness are prize genes. It is much more pleasant to eat a seedless orange.

The picture shows a longhorned Texas steer. ■ The picture is an old one, because the longhorned animals are rapidly dying out. One day a shorthorned animal, a **mutant,** was born. The gene for the characteristic *long horns* had mutated into a gene for *short horns.*

Ranchers find shorthorned cattle easier to handle and easier to ship because they do not hurt each other when loaded into close quarters.

When animal or plant growers decide that a mutant is useful or more desirable, they try to produce more plants or animals with the same mutant genes—if they can.

Most orange growers would like to have many seedless orange trees. A seedless orange is much nicer to eat than an orange with seeds. People are usually willing to pay a higher price for seedless oranges.

Many years ago the first seedless tree was brought here from Brazil. Each year seedless oranges are becoming more and more plentiful, because plant scientists have developed a method for producing new seedless orange trees.

Suppose you wanted to develop such a method; how can it be done with a seedless orange? You have no seeds to plant.

### Propagating a Mutant Plant

Imagine that you are an orange grower and that you find a tree with seedless oranges. How would you produce more seedless orange trees?

You may have taken a twig of a willow and tried to root it in moist sand. This method would work well with begonias, geraniums, and with many other plants. Yet it is not the best method for growing seedless orange trees. The best way of doing this is to make a twig grow on the roots of another tree. For the orange, a twig of the seedless plant is often grown,

branch from seedless orange tree

root
of
lemon
tree

■ plant growers say **grafted,** on the root of a lemon tree. ■ This root is called the root stock. Notice in the top picture a small branch has been cut from a seedless orange tree. The cut was made in the shape of the letter V.

A young lemon tree is cut off at the root in the same manner. The second picture shows how the lemon tree was cut quite close to the ground, leaving only the roots and part of the trunk. The cut on the trunk is like an upside-down V. This prevents rain from getting in later, when the tree is grafted. The branch of the seedless orange tree is then grafted onto the root stock in its place. The graft is sealed, and cloth is wrapped around it to give it

support. This will now grow into a full-sized seedless orange tree. Each branch taken from the seedless tree can also be grafted to a separate root. Each will grow into another seedless tree. Then, later on, branches can be taken from each of these to produce even more seedless trees.

By means of grafting, many seedless trees can be derived from one. Grafting is used to save the traits of a useful mutant and to get many offspring from the original plant. Perhaps you would like to try your hand at grafting by doing the investigation on the opposite page.

### Saving a Mutant Animal

Saving the prize genes of an animal mutant is not so simple. Consider the mutant shorthorned steer as an example.

Genes for shorthorned cattle are prize genes because they produce a desirable trait which the ranchers want. Suppose one offspring of a long-horned steer has short horns. The cattle rancher must wait until it grows up before it can produce offspring. Till then, he feeds it and takes good care of it. At last he crosses the mutant shorthorn with a longhorn. He wonders if the offspring will be a long-horn or a shorthorn. He can only wonder and wait.

Luckily, in this case, the prize genes for short horns are dominant over the genes for long horns. The offspring is another shorthorn. Since one parent was a shorthorn and the other was a

# AN INVESTIGATION into Grafting

**Needed:** a branch to be grafted; a stock root; grafting wax; string or strips of cloth

One method that can be used is to graft a branch onto a stock tree in the early spring when the sap begins to rise in the trees. The branch and the stock tree must be closely related types, such as two kinds of apple, apple and pear, or orange and lemon.

Remove a branch from the mutant tree by cutting diagonally, as shown. ■

Select a branch about the same size as the branch stock to which it is to be grafted. Cut the branch diagonally.

Make a straight cut in the two parts that are to fit together, as shown. ●

Insert the branch so that the letter "N" is formed. ▲ Then wind a string or cloth around the joint several times and tie it tightly. ◆

After the branch is tied, cover the graft with grafting wax or melted paraffin to keep it from drying out. ★

The new branch should become tightly fastened to the tree during the first summer. It should grow leaves and, possibly, fruit. What kind of fruit will it have? Suppose a pear branch is grafted to an apple tree. What will grow on the branch, apples or pears?

On what evidence do you base your answer? What theory explains why grafting is possible?

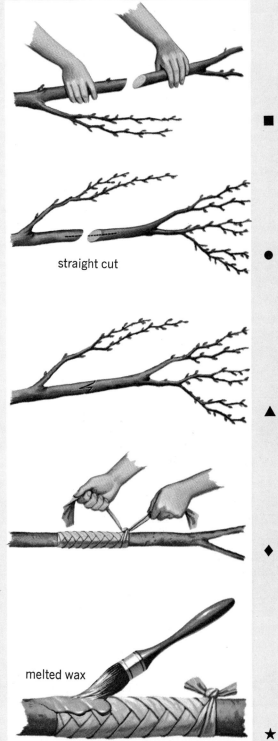

straight cut

melted wax

■

●

▲

◆

★

parents

ll

ss

offspring
Sl

longhorn, the offspring is a hybrid having genes for both long and short. ■ But the cattle rancher wants only shorthorned cattle. To do this, shorthorned cattle are crossed many times with other shorthorns. At last a herd of pure shorthorns is developed.

●

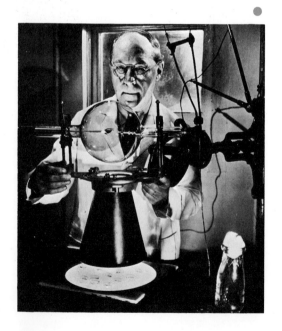

A package of prize genes, then, can be saved in at least two ways. For plants, grafting is used wherever necessary and possible. For animals, the mutants are crossed to produce hybrids until a sufficient number of mutants are born.

### Causing Genes to Mutate

Scientists had been looking for a way to change the genetic code in chromosomes. Dr. Hermann Muller found a way. He changed the genes in an insect, the fruit fly.● Genes in which the code has been changed and inherited by the next generation are called **mutations** (myōō·tā′shənz).

Fruit flies are easy to find indoors and outdoors. They are small enough to pass through most screens.

Collect some fruit flies in the late spring or summer. (The winter season is usually not a good time.) The insects will not hatch until the days are warm. Examine some fruit flies, as in the investigation on the opposite page.

### Mutations in Fruit Flies

The fruit flies used by Dr. Muller were very much like the ones you can collect. They were, however, pure for certain traits.

For instance, some had white eyes and others had red eyes (as shown in the picture). Some had short wings and others had long wings.

White-eyed fruit flies produce white-eyed offspring. What kind of offspring would pure long-winged flies produce?

# AN INVESTIGATION into the Kinds of Fruit Flies You Can Find

**Needed:** some raw fruit (bananas or grapes) or some stewed fruit; a jar; some cotton, cloth, and paper; a magnifying glass

Put some raw or cooked fruit into an open jar. If you do this during the warm season, you may soon find tiny flies swarming around the fruit. Place some soft paper above the fruit to help keep the flies in the jar until you cover it.

Once the fruit flies have begun to collect on the fruit, close the jar with a wad of cotton or cloth. ■ This will allow air to get to the flies. Examine them with a magnifying glass.● Are they all alike? Look at the eye color and the shape of the wings, for example. Perhaps if you keep them long enough, they will lay eggs. Then you may have a swarm of tiny fruit flies. Are they like those shown in the picture?▲

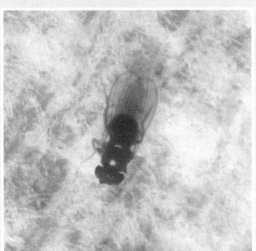

## ■ FRUIT FLIES (highly magnified)

long-winged   short-winged   curly-winged

Remember that Dr. Muller used flies which were pure for a certain trait, for example, for long wings. ■ He bombarded the flies with X rays. Then he examined the offspring. Among the offspring, he found mutants. Flies with genes for *long wings only* had produced offspring with short or even curled wings. The genetic code appeared to have been changed by X rays. Mutants resulted. Dr. Muller proved that X rays could cause mutations, or changes, in the genes. For his discovery, Dr. Muller received a Nobel prize. Since then mutations have been brought about in many experimental animals and plants by the use of X rays and other types of radiations.

## Change Over the Ages

Scientists of today can cause genes to change, or mutate. Can genes change by themselves? Is there a natural change, or mutation, going on in the genes of living things? There is strong evidence that animals and plants have not always been as they appear now. It is believed that the modern horse, for example, came from an animal that was no larger than a fox. ● Slowly, over millions of years the foxlike horse (the "Dawn Horse") changed. Other animals have also changed over millions of years.

Early horses had more than one toe on each foot but the modern horse has only one. How could this change have occurred? The explanation is that the

60 million years ago

today

genetic code for toes changed, that is, the genes mutated. The genes for size of body and skull also mutated. Over millions of years, many mutations resulted in the modern horse. ▲

Ages ago, huge dinosaurs roamed the land. You may have seen pictures of the many kinds. How could so many different kinds of dinosaurs come to be? A good explanation is that they were the result of mutations taking place over millions and millions of years. Then they died out over 60 million years ago.

Scientists believe that many new forms of animals and plants have resulted from mutations in genes. In other words, the changes which have occurred in living things, over millions of years of time, are the result of changes in genes.

Not all mutants survive. In fact, most mutants die out. Why is this so?

## Suited to the Environment

Each kind of animal and plant which exists on earth has lived for a long time in its surroundings. For instance, a fish lives in water. It uses its gills to get the oxygen which is dissolved in water. Suppose the genes which produce the gills mutated, and a fish without gills is born. It will die because it cannot get oxygen. An animal or plant is adapted to live in a certain environment or it will die.

Sometimes a certain environment changes, and the living things are not able to survive in the new environment. One theory that may explain

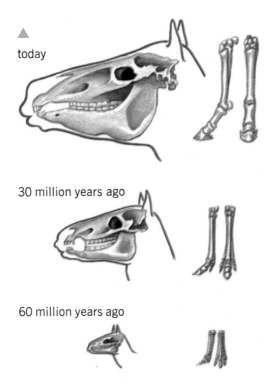

today

30 million years ago

60 million years ago

why the giant reptiles, the dinosaurs, died out is the following. The dinosaurs lived in an environment that was fairly moist. Slowly, over millions of years, the land began to dry out and change in many other ways. The plants changed. The food supply changed. In any event, the dinosaurs died out. It seems as if the changes in the dinosaurs did not keep pace with the changes in environment. Perhaps the genes did mutate but not in a way for dinosaurs to survive.

Some mutations help the animal or plant to live better in the environment, but some do not. Sometimes mutations make it possible for the organism to survive in a changing environment. Perhaps this can explain the changes that have occurred in the horse.

A. Study the statements below and choose the correct responses. They will help you fix in mind the concepts of this section.

    **1.** Shorthorned cattle probably arose as
      a. mutants                    b. hybrids

    **2.** A seedless mutant tree can be saved by
      a. grafting                  b. planting

    **3.** With animals, mutants can be crossed with purebred animals (nonmutants) to produce
      a. pure animals for a trait desired
      b. hybrid animals for a trait desired

    **4.** Mutants in fruit flies were produced by Dr. Hermann Muller by using
      a. X rays                  b. grafting

    **5.** The evidence shows that animals and plants have changed over millions of years. The changes in genes were due to
      a. mutation               b. hybridization

    **6.** When certain kinds of living things like the dinosaurs die out, we say they were
      a. not fitted to the changing environment
      b. a prize package of genes

**B.** Write a paragraph or two on this topic: Mutations.

**1.** Below are pictures of the eyes of fruit flies. ■ The red color is the color most commonly found. What is your explanation of how the other colors of eyes developed?

    **2.** Over 60,000,000 years or so, the feet of horses have changed from those of the three-toed horse to those of the one-toed horse. (The hoof is really the nail of the huge middle toe.) What is your explanation of why the toes of the horse changed over millions of years?

underdeveloped tail  tail cut

fully developed tail

mutant no tail  fully developed tail

offspring no tail
dominant mutant gene

## 6. The Search for Prize Genes

Suppose you are a rancher who wants to improve his herd of Herefords (hûr′fərdz). These are the familiar white-faced cattle which are bred for beef.

Suppose, too, that on your ranch, a new bull calf is born. As he grows, you find that he is different from every other bull in your herd. He is white-faced, and he has a red coat like the other Herefords; but he is hornless or **polled** (pōld), as cattle raisers call it. He is not just shorthorned. He is truly hornless. What a prize! Horns of any kind are troublesome when cattle are being shipped.

You might suspect that he is a mutant and that the genes for *horned* have changed to genes for *hornless*. Does he really have prize genes within him or is his lack of horns the result of his environment? Perhaps he just has not developed like other bulls.

When animals do not develop as they should, they may not have their horns or they may be born without tails (as shown in the picture); but they may still have the genes for the trait which did not develop.

The offspring of the toy bulldogs has a normal tail because his parents' tails were stumped by environmental causes. ● No change in the genes took place. One of the Manx cats, on the other hand had a mutant gene for "no tail," which was inherited by the offspring. ▲

There is only one possible way to make certain that a gene has mutated and that is to look at the offspring of the animal we think is a mutant. If the gene has really changed, then the mutant trait may show up in succeeding generations.

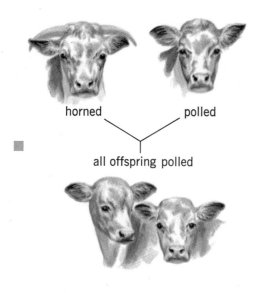

horned     polled

all offspring polled

## A Prize Gene—Hornlessness

Not long ago, a rancher in Iowa found that a prize mutant had been born on his ranch, a polled Hereford bull. He wanted to build an entire herd of polled Hereford cattle. How could he do it? He had only one polled Hereford bull, and he desired to raise an entire herd of polled cattle. He decided that he needed help. He sent out letters to 25,000 ranchers who had been raising Herefords, asking if they had any polled cattle that he could use for breeding. In this way he found four more mutant polled bulls and ten mutant polled cows.

He crossed polled bulls and polled cows. The offspring were all polled. When these offspring grew up, he again crossed them, and again he got polled offspring. Was the gene for polled dominant or recessive? How would you find out? The cattle raiser, or cattle breeder, found out in the following way.

He crossed *polled* cattle with *horned* cattle. All were Herefords. The only difference in them was that some were polled and some were horned.

If the genes for polled (hornless) cattle were dominant over the genes for horned, what would the offspring be? On the other hand, if horned were dominant over polled what would the offspring be? All the offspring developed as shown in the picture—polled. ■ In this way, one rancher developed a herd of polled Herefords.

Today the polled Hereford is one of the most popular kinds of cattle. They range in Canada, South America, Australia, and in other countries. In the United States alone there are over 50,000 registered Herefords. "Registered" means that their breeding (their inheritance with regard to certain genes) is known.

In other words, the genes of registered animals are known. They are prize packages of genes not only for hornlessness but also for good beef production. Today, however, the Herefords are being challenged for beef production by another breed of American cattle. It all began with a bull named Monkey.

## The Story of Monkey

Cattle ranchers have always been searching for ways of improving their cattle—to produce a larger quantity and better quality of beef.

Ever since 1910, ranchers had been crossing American Brahman bulls (shown in the picture) with Texas shorthorned cows. They were trying to produce cattle which not only had better beef but which also were resistant to certain diseases. They also wanted cattle which could stand a hot and dry climate.

In 1920, Monkey was born on the famous King Ranch near Kingsville, Texas. Monkey had prize genes. Monkey was one of the ancestors of the prize bull you see in the picture. ● This bull is one of the Santa Gertrudis (san′tə gər·trud′is) bulls.

The Santa Gertrudis cattle are fast becoming the most important beef-producing cattle in the country. Look at the Santa Gertrudis bull; he is strong and able to endure a dry, hot climate. He is a prize package of genes.

## Prize Genes in Plants

Mutants also occur in plants. The Katahdin potato is the result of crossing many different strains, or kinds, of potatoes. Some strains of potatoes that were crossed had genes that had mutated so that the Katahdin inherited a resistance to some diseases (such as potato blight). Potato blight once wiped out almost the entire crop of potatoes in Ireland.

"Wilt" in tomatoes is a disease which causes the leaves to wilt and the plant to fall over. The leaves of the tomato plant turn brown and can no longer make food. The plant dies before it can produce any tomatoes.

There is a similar disease which causes the cotton plant to wilt. Plant geneticists searched for tomato and

cotton plants which were resistant to wilt disease. They found them. Now there are strains of tomatoes and cotton which are very successful in resisting this disease. Notice that next to a healthy plant, the plant with wilt looks dried out. ■

Resistance to disease often can be traced to genes. For instance, the strain of wheat known as *Rival* wheat has genes for resistance to rust disease. Scientists produced the Rival strain after crossing American and Canadian strains. There are now strains of wheat, corn, and oats that have genes for resistance to rust bred into them.

Desirable plants and animals are prize packages of genes. Next time you go to a food market, take a look at the fruit and vegetable department. You may see boxes of giant red strawberries or blueberries as big as marbles. Look at the bin of large mild Bermuda onions and the firm cabbages. Almost all the fruits and vegetables you see have resulted from cross-breeding of plants with prize genes.

**USING WHAT YOU KNOW**

1. Find as much information as you can on a particular kind of plant or animal. You may wish to choose a kind of animal (Hereford cattle, white leghorn chickens, quarter horses) or plant (potatoes, apples). Perhaps there are new forms of these animals or plants being produced.

How can you find out which kind you are interested in? There are many ways; here are some.

a. If you live on a farm, your parents may suggest an animal or plant. Or perhaps you can talk to the county agent.

b. If you live in the city, try the reference books in the library.

2. Write a report on the plant or animal you have selected. Be sure to organize your report to include: a. the origin of the plant or animal; b. how it was bred; c. the kind of environment it needs; d. its uses to man.

## 7. The Main Concept: The Genetic Code

The seed of an oak tree, the acorn, is planted. When conditions are right, the roots and the stem begin to develop. 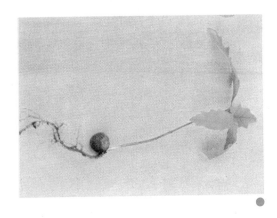 Whether it grows to its full height or is stunted depends on the kind of soil and the minerals in it. It also depends on whether the plant has enough water and sunlight.

Whether the tree is to be a maple or an oak depends on the chromosomes in the nucleus of its cells. More than that, the chromosomes pass on special traits: the shape of the leaves, the color of the bark, or the shape of its seeds and fruits.

The DNA molecule in the chromosomes of the nucleus carries the code, the "message," which determines what traits the organism will have. The environment plays a great part in determining how these traits will develop in the organism. Leaves from any tree may have about the same shape as those from a sassafras tree, shown in the picture. ▲ They may be large or small, deep green or light green. There may be many leaves or few, depending on the soil, water, and sunlight the tree gets. *An organism is the product of its heredity and the environment in which it develops.* Both are important to its growth and appearance. This is a major concept.

The concept just stated is true of oaks, maples, roses, horses, dogs, cats, lions, frogs, kangaroos, and raspberries. It is true of all of us. There is one great difference, however. We can understand that we are the product of our heredity and our environment. We can try, therefore, to provide the best environment. The good traits we have inherited from our parents will then develop to their fullest. It is not

▲ **SASSAFRAS LEAVES**

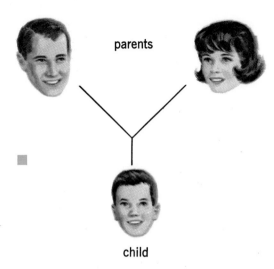

parents

child

much use to inherit genes for a trait, such as height, without also being sure that we eat the right food, so that we can develop as well as possible; nor is it much use to inherit high intelligence without making sure that we use our intelligence through study and learning.

The story is not as simple as it sounds, however. Even the codes in the chromosomes produce different results depending on the combinations of genes which are inherited. A four-o'clock has red flowers only when it is pure for red flowering. It has white flowers only when it is pure for white flowering. It is pink, however, when it is a hybrid—that is, when its inherited code is for both red flowering and white flowering.

Scientists are just beginning to learn of the inheritance of human traits. Physical traits such as eye color, hair color, shape of body, height, features, and skin color are all coded in our chromosomes. The way some of

these traits develop is affected by the environment. Eye color does not change because of environment, but the size of the body depends on what we eat, as well as on heredity. The way we do things depends not only on our intelligence (which is inherited) but also on our education. Thus, what we learn, how we learn, or the way we learn is a result of both our inherited intelligence and our environment working together.

The investigations that scientists have made of the DNA molecule within the chromosomes and their study of the way chromosomes are transmitted from parent to offspring have made it possible for scientists to improve plants and animals. The work of a geneticist takes a long time but can be very successful. Now there are hens which lay an egg a day; there are ears of corn that are twice the size and much sweeter to the taste than those produced by corn plants a few years ago.

A farmer of 100 years ago would be surprised if he were to visit a market today. The changes in the fruits, vegetables and meats sold there are great. The work of the plant grower and of the animal breeder has resulted in more and better food for all of us.

Geneticists began studying heredity only at the beginning of this century. They see, in the code of the genes in the DNA molecule, the clues to questions such as these:

1. *Why is it that the offspring are like the parents?*

Clearly, offspring get their traits from their parents. A dominant gene which both parents have, such as the trait for black hair, is likely to show up in the children. This is shown in the diagram. ■ Do you know any children who seem to be very much like their parents?

2. *Why is it also possible that the offspring can be somewhat different from their parents?*

Suppose that both black-haired parents have inherited the recessive genes for blond hair as well (as in the diagram). ● Then it is possible for their child to have blond hair.

Thus it is possible for a child to show traits different from those of either parent. Do you know any children who have differences from, as well as similarities to, their parents?

3. *How is it possible that living things have changed over the millions of years of the earth's existence?*

We know animals and plants have changed over millions of years. The horse, as you have seen, has changed in many ways. Dogs and cats are very different from their ancestors of long ago. Dinosaurs no longer exist on earth. No one is exactly sure how or why these changes took place.

The scientist's explanation is that the genes must have mutated. Those living things whose mutant genes helped them *adapt better* to their environment survived. Those organisms whose mutant genes did not fit them to their changing environment died out.

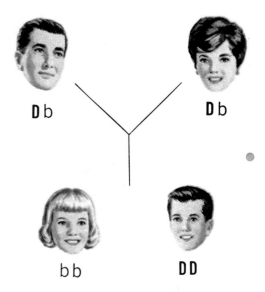

D b      D b

b b      D D

*Over millions upon millions of years organisms have changed.* This is one of the major concepts of science. Everything has changed. The earth has changed. Organisms have changed. Some species of plants and animals have died out. Some have become much stronger and heartier, while others, such as the turtle, seem to have changed more slowly.

The life of the past gave rise to the life of the present. Living things have changed during the millions upon millions of years the earth has been spinning around the sun.

What about the future? Will changes in the universe continue to take place as they have in the past? What is your hypothesis of how living things will have changed 100,000,-000 years from now? Base it upon your knowledge of how they have changed in the past 100,000,000 years. Even if you can develop a sensible hypothesis, are you likely to witness the proof?

# Fixing the Main Concepts

Test your understanding of the important concepts in this unit by doing these problems.

**1.** Recall that a theory is a reasonable explanation of the facts. Which of these theories on the way we inherit our traits would you accept?

    a. Living things inherit their traits through the blood.

    b. Living things inherit traits through chromosomes.

Give reasons for your answer.

**2.** Which of these theories would you accept?

    a. Living things have remained the same over the entire time of the earth's existence.

    b. Living things have changed over the time of the earth's existence.

    Give reasons for your answer.

**3.** A yellow-flowering plant is crossed with another yellow-flowering plant. Only yellow-flowering offspring are produced.

What is your explanation of the results?

**4.** A black-furred guinea pig is crossed with another black-furred guinea pig. The offspring are both black-furred and gray-furred.

What is your explanation of the results?

**5.** The gene for blue eye color is recessive to the gene for brown eye color. Two parents, both with dark brown eyes, have four children: three are brown-eyed, one is blue-eyed.

Explain the results.

**6.** The offspring of a red petunia plant and a white petunia plant are found to have red stripes on white. Which explanation below is more likely to be correct?

    a. red is dominant; white is recessive

    b. neither gene is dominant nor necessive

**1.** Both Mr. and Mrs. Brown are good cooks. Their daughter, however, is not a good cook. Being a good cook is a

    a. trait in the genes        b. part of learning

**2.** When red-eyed fruit flies are crossed with red-eyed fruit flies, all the offspring are red-eyed. For the trait for red eyes, both parents were

    a. pure        b. hybrid

**3.** In another case, red-eyed fruit flies are crossed with red-eyed fruit flies. Some of the offspring are white-eyed, while others are red-eyed. The parents were

    a. pure        b. hybrid

**4.** Experiments on mutation were carried on by

    a. Gregor Mendel        b. Hermann Muller

**FOR YOUR READING**

*The Earth for Sam,* by W. Maxwell Reed, published by Harcourt, Brace & World, New York, 1960.

This is the story of the earth's past life. The book tells how mutations take place and how living things have changed through mutation.

**ON YOUR OWN**

Trace an inherited trait which is characteristic in your own family. For instance, you might trace the trait "dimples," or "red hair color."

Consult with your parents, and make a chart of your "family tree" as far back as they can remember. Indicate by the name of each person on the "tree" whether or not he or she possessed the trait.

Decide now what trait you plan to trace.

Why is it called a "family tree"? The chart really should look like a tree, with you as the trunk. The first two branches are for your parents; the next four are for your grandparents. There are eight branches for your great-grandparents, and so on, and so on.

# UNIT NINE

# STARS AND STARLIGHT

The sun is a star.

It is the center of our solar system and the principal source of heat and light for earth. It is also the source of nearly all the energy used by industrial civilizations, in the form of water power, fuels and wind. It sustains life on earth, disrupts our communications, pours deadly radiation into space, and makes our weather do tricks.

So far our knowledge of the sun has been limited because our atmosphere acts as a barrier. It completely stops most of the sun's radiant energy. In order to learn the how and why and when of the sun's phenomena we need an observatory outside the earth's atmosphere—perhaps on the moon.

Already plans are being developed to launch an orbiting solar observatory. It may not find *all* the answers that physicists and astronomers have sought for about 350 years; but it will collect, store, and transmit data on the sun's radiation. In the process it should pick up some basic facts about the universe.

Man has only begun to gratify his curiosity about the worlds beyond this world. He is looking. He is listening. And he is stretching out long arms with electronic fingers to touch and measure the far reaches of space.

# 1. Energy from a Star

As we begin our study of the universe, we need to understand how stars like our sun give off so much energy.

First, let us try to combine atoms of hydrogen chemically in the classroom. We can combine atoms of hydrogen with atoms of oxygen to form molecules of water. Later, we will compare the way atoms combine chemically with the way nuclei of hydrogen atoms combine with each other. This will help you to understand what is happening in the stars. We can start with an apparatus for taking water apart, as shown in the investigation on the opposite page.

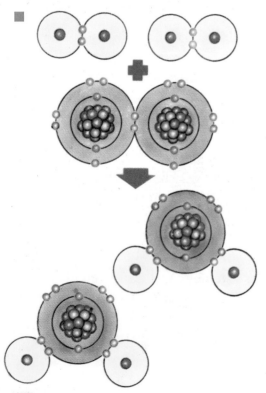

## The Chemistry of Hydrogen— On Earth

Hydrogen is a gas. Only a gas could be collected by bubbling it through water. Because a gas is lighter than a liquid, the gas rises in the water. Hydrogen is also lighter than air. If hydrogen were heavier than air, would it rise in the test tube? How can you be sure hydrogen is in the test tube?

When a flame is brought near the hydrogen gas, a "pop" is heard. The popping sound is caused by the combination of the hydrogen with the oxygen in the air. This combination results in the formation of the compound water. Was there any evidence of water on the inside of the test tube?

The reaction is as follows:

**hydrogen + oxygen → water**

Or to put it in a more exact form: A molecule of hydrogen contains two atoms of hydrogen. The symbol for a molecule of hydrogen is $H_2$. Almost all the hydrogen gas on earth is made up of molecules containing two atoms of hydrogen. The oxygen gas on the earth is also found as molecules consisting of two atoms of oxygen, written $O_2$.

The reaction is as follows:

$$2\,H_2 + O_2 \rightarrow 2\,H_2O$$

Or we could say: Two molecules of hydrogen ($2\,H_2$) plus one molecule of oxygen ($O_2$) will react to form two molecules of water ($2\,H_2O$). ■

When you split the compound $H_2O$ to form hydrogen and oxygen, how

# AN INVESTIGATION into a Chemical Combination of Hydrogen

**Needed:** an apparatus to break up water; dry cells; dilute sulfuric acid

Attach the apparatus that has been set up by your teacher (called a Hoffman apparatus after its inventor), as shown in the picture. ■ The electric current is sent through the water (the formula for water is $H_2O$).

The electric current passing through the water splits the water molecules into hydrogen (gas collecting at the top of one tube) and oxygen (gas collecting at the top of the other). How much hydrogen will be produced as compared with the oxygen? Does the formula $H_2O$ give you a clue?

Examine the apparatus. On which side does the hydrogen gas collect? How much hydrogen collects as compared with the amount of oxygen gas?

Now hold a dry test tube over the side containing hydrogen, as shown.● Release the hydrogen, allowing it to rise into the inverted test tube. Why does hydrogen always rise? Keep the mouth of the tube down until a lighted splint is ready. Then hold it up as your teacher holds the lighted wood splint to the mouth of the tube.

There usually is a "pop" as the hydrogen gas reacts with one of the gases in the air. Is the tube still completely dry after the "pop"? What do you notice inside the tube?

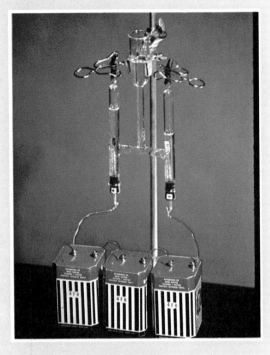

1. Which gas in the air is reacting with the hydrogen? Is it nitrogen? oxygen? carbon dioxide?
2. How can you demonstrate that the gas in the other tube is oxygen?

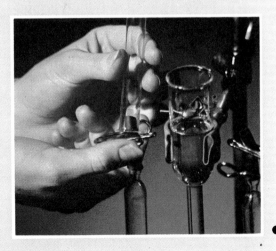

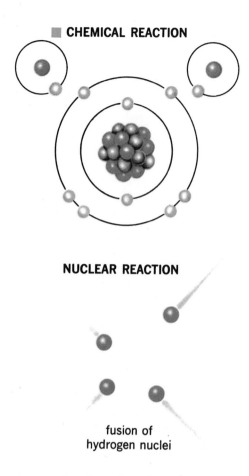

**■ CHEMICAL REACTION**

**NUCLEAR REACTION**

fusion of
hydrogen nuclei

many molecules of each were formed? **Clue:** More than one molecule was split.

In these reactions the hydrogen atom is not changed. It combines chemically with oxygen to form the compound water. With an electric current, water can be split to give hydrogen and oxygen once again.

This is the basis of a **chemical reaction.** Some molecules are formed; others are broken down. Some substances can be combined and then taken apart. But the atoms that make up the molecules are not changed (see page 366).

Hydrogen atoms can also take part in another type of reaction—a nuclear reaction. There is a difference between a chemical reaction and a **nuclear reaction.**

Look at the picture. ■ Notice that in the chemical reaction three atoms are joining to form a molecule. The particles that make up the nuclei (neutrons and protons) of the atoms are not affected by the reaction. In the nuclear reaction shown below, it appears as if the four nuclear particles themselves are going to become joined. Let us now look further into a nuclear reaction before we go 93,000,000 miles away from the earth.

### A Nuclear Reaction

What happens when protons and neutrons are combined to form a nucleus or what happens when the nuclei of hydrogen atoms are *fused?*

Can it be done? Yes. In the hydrogen bomb, the nuclei of hydrogen atoms are fused. There are several different reactions by which hydrogen atoms may fuse.

As shown in the picture, it would take the nuclei of four ordinary hydrogen atoms to form the nucleus of a helium atom. ● The hydrogen nuclei are really single protons. You may wonder then why the helium nucleus has two neutrons and two protons. Two of the protons (hydrogen nuclei) react in some way to produce two neutrons during fusion. All of the particles in the helium nucleus do come from the four hydrogen nuclei.

Hydrogen nuclei can be fused with the nuclei of other elements; but the problem is to cause the nuclei of atoms to combine, or fuse, to form the nucleus of another element. When fusion takes place, there is a great burst of energy. We can therefore get energy from the fusion of atoms.

When the nucleus of an atom is *split*, a burst of energy results. This is the result of *fission* of the nucleus, as shown on pages 294–96. We can get energy from the fission of atoms, and we can also get energy from the fusion of atoms.

In the hydrogen bomb, atoms of hydrogen fuse. In the nuclear bomb, atoms of uranium split. In either case, the result is that a great amount of energy is released. How is a great amount of energy produced in the sun?

**hydrogen + hydrogen + hydrogen + hydrogen → helium + energy**

It is definitely known that the sun has a great amount of hydrogen and helium in it. In fact, 99 percent of the sun is made up of hydrogen and helium. This information has been obtained through careful examination of the sun's light with the spectroscope, and this will be explained later in greater detail.

It appears, from a great deal of study, that the sun gives off energy from the fusion of hydrogen into helium. In a way, the sun is a great big hydrogen bomb, 93,000,000 miles away.

How do we explain the fact that when hydrogen fuses to form helium a great amount of energy is given off? The exact atomic weights of an atom of hydrogen and an atom of helium are given below. These atomic weights have been carefully measured by scientists.

**hydrogen** = 1.008 units of matter
**helium** = 4.003 units of matter

In the example of fusion given in the diagram below, four atoms of hydrogen combine to form one atom of helium. That is:

**4 H → 1 He**

Let us do a bit of arithmetic.

1 atom of **H** = 1.008
1 atom of **H** = 1.008
1 atom of **H** = 1.008
1 atom of **H** = 1.008
_____
4 atoms of **H** = 4.032

But an atom of helium has an atomic weight of only *4.003* units of matter. This is less than the total weight of the four hydrogen atoms. Let us subtract to find how much less.

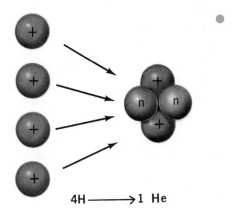

4H ——→ 1 He

$$4.032$$
$$-4.003$$
$$\overline{0.029 \text{ of a unit of matter}}$$ ∎

What happens to the 0.029 of a unit difference?

The fate of the 0.029 of a unit of matter is this: *It is changed to energy.* In other words, little by little, some of the sun's matter is being changed to energy.

Remember that in any nuclear reaction some matter can be changed into energy. The sun's energy, then, is produced because small amounts of the sun's *matter* are constantly being changed into *energy.* In the fusion of four hydrogen atoms into one helium atom, 0.029 of a unit of matter is changed into energy. This amount of matter (or mass) is changed into light, heat, and other forms of energy. Recall, however, the main concept that although mass is changed into energy, the total amount of mass-energy remains the same.

The nuclear energy of the sun (resulting from the breaking down of matter) is tremendously important. It gives us light; it gives us heat. Without the sun the earth would soon be a frozen planet. Even the earth's atmosphere would freeze. All life would end.

The sun's heat energy and light energy are important to us for many reasons. The sun's heat energy evaporates water that later forms clouds and then comes down as rain. The sun's light energy is used by green plants to make food. Without the sun we would starve. There would be no life on earth. Even coal and oil are really chemical stores of energy from the sun that were captured by green plants long, long ago.

This star, 93,000,000 miles away, fusing its hydrogen atoms into helium, gives us the abundant supply of energy that we need to live.

How hot is the sun? This is the story of the next section.

∎

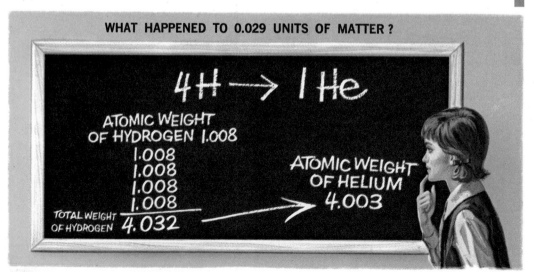

WHAT HAPPENED TO 0.029 UNITS OF MATTER?

4H → 1He

ATOMIC WEIGHT OF HYDROGEN 1.008
1.008
1.008
1.008
1.008
TOTAL WEIGHT OF HYDROGEN 4.032

ATOMIC WEIGHT OF HELIUM → 4.003

**A.** Study the statements below and choose the correct responses. They will help you fix in mind the concepts of this
section.

**1.** In order to split water molecules we use the energy obtained from
    a. heat                      b. electricity

**2.** When we split the compound water into its elements,
the number of hydrogen molecules compared with oxygen
molecules is
    a. two to one            b. one to one

**3.** Finish this reaction: $2\,H_2O \rightarrow 2\,H_2 +$
    a. $O_2$                     b. $2\,O_2$

**4.** In a chemical reaction, the matter taking part may be
changed into energy. This statement is
    a. false                   b. true

**5.** In a nuclear reaction, some of the matter taking part
may be changed into energy. This statement is
    a. true                   b. false

**6.** In the hydrogen bomb and on the sun, atoms of hydrogen fuse to form atoms of
    a. uranium              b. helium

**B.** Write a paragraph or two on this topic: A Nuclear Reaction on the Sun.

**1.** What is the difference between fission and fusion?
    a. Which takes place in the atomic bomb?
    b. Which takes place in the hydrogen bomb?
    c. Which takes place on the sun?

**2.** Which one of the following is a chemical reaction?
Which one is a nuclear reaction? In which one is matter
changed to energy?
    a. $2\,H_2 + O_2 \rightarrow 2\,H_2O$        b. $4\,H \rightarrow 1\,He$

## 2. The Temperature of a Star

Our star, the sun, is a kind of long-lasting nuclear reactor. Hydrogen is being changed into helium, and, in the process, matter is destroyed; or is it? We could more truly say that the matter (0.029 of a unit of matter for every helium nucleus formed) is converted into energy. This energy is in the form of heat, light, and nuclear radiation.

The temperature of the sun at its surface is about 11,000° F. How do scientists determine this? After all, the sun is 93,000,000 miles away, and it is not as if they were taking the temperature of boiling water.

A way of finding the temperature of stars is based on their colors. Steelworkers know that they can deter-mine rather accurately the temperature of glowing hot steel by its color. A *white-hot* piece of steel is hotter than a *red-hot* piece. By determining the exact color of a star, astronomers can determine its temperature. They can do so by means of an instrument called a **spectroscope.**

Light from an object that scientists wish to analyze is broken up by a **prism.** If it is light from a star that the astronomers wish to analyze, they begin by "collecting" the light by means of a lens. Then they analyze the light by using a spectroscope. The light broken up by the prism shows a **spectrum** of color. The spectroscope, as the diagram shows, is really a combination of a prism and certain types of lenses. ◼

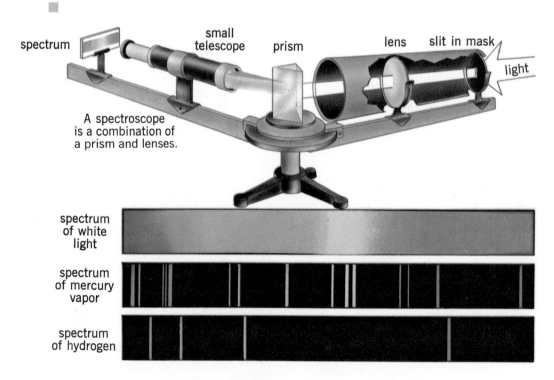

spectrum   small telescope   prism   lens   slit in mask   light

A spectroscope is a combination of a prism and lenses.

spectrum of white light

spectrum of mercury vapor

spectrum of hydrogen

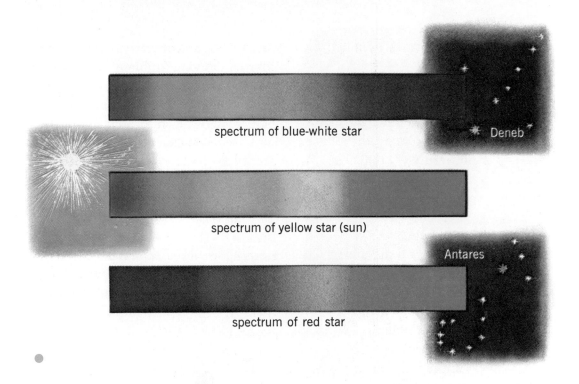

spectrum of blue-white star

Deneb

spectrum of yellow star (sun)

Antares

spectrum of red star

## Spectrum and Temperature

The spectrum from the light given off by a star also tells what kinds of elements are to be found in that star. Each element in the form of a hot gas produces a different pattern on the spectrum. The diagram shows how the spectra of two elements compare with the spectrum of sunlight. ■

The spectrum can also give a clue to the temperature of a star. In the spectrum of a blue-white star, the bluish section of the band of color is much brighter, or more intense, as shown. ● Blue-white stars are very hot. A yellow star, like our sun, has a fairly even spectrum over the whole range from violet to red. ● In the spectrum of a reddish star, the red end is brighter, or more intense. ● By analyzing the spectrum of a star,

astronomers can tell what its surface temperature is. For our purposes, there are four types of stars as far as temperature is concerned—white, yellow, red, and "dark" stars.

What can we learn when we analyze the spectra of different stars? Scientists have discovered that stars differ as to temperature and that a star's color is a definite clue to its temperature. For instance, the yellow-white star (for example, our sun) has a surface temperature of about 11,000° F. Certain blue-white stars, such as Deneb, in the constellation the Swan, have a surface temperature almost twice that of our sun. Yet the huge red star Antares (an·tär′ēz), in the constellation the Scorpion, has a surface temperature of 5,500° F.—only half that of our sun.

Then there are the dark stars, which give no light at all. Their discovery was very strange. Long ago, while tending their sheep, Arab shepherds noticed that a star they called Algol became dark every 2 days and 21 hours. Why did this happen?

Could it be that Algol's light and heat went out every 2 days and 21 hours and then came to life again? No wonder the Arabs called the star "the demon," for that is what Algol means. It took a few thousand years for man to be able to solve the mystery. Why do you think it took so long?

Algol has a twin star, a dark twin, which gives off no light. Can you figure out how the dark star could cause

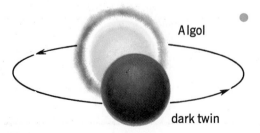

Algol

dark twin

Algol itself to seem to grow dark? The solution to the problem is shown in the diagram.

The discovery of Algol's dark companion showed that some stars—the dark ones—seem to have lost their ability to produce heat and light. Perhaps their hydrogen has been used up.

Have you another explanation?

Algol's dark twin produces little heat. Do stars with higher *temperatures* have more *heat?* What is the difference between temperature and heat? To find the difference between them, try the investigation on the opposite page.

## Heat and Temperature

How did you explain the results of the investigation? What is needed to melt the ice cubes? Heat? Which had more heat, the cupful of cold water or the inch of near-boiling water? Are you surprised to learn that the beaker filled with cold water has more heat in it?

The clue lies in the difference between the amount of water in the full beaker of cold water and the inch of hot water. There was a greater amount of cold water. The cold water had the greater number of molecules.

As you have learned, all molecules are in motion and have kinetic energy. The greater the number of molecules of a substance, the greater is the sum of kinetic energy of all the molecules. The sum of kinetic energy of all the molecules is equal to the heat of the substance. Thus a bathtub full of cold

## AN INVESTIGATION into the Difference Between Heat and Temperature

**Needed:** two Pyrex flasks in which to boil water; eight ice cubes; two Pyrex beakers; a thermometer; a pair of tongs; cold water

Boil the water in one of the flasks. It will soon begin to steam. Now place four ice cubes each into two beakers.

Fill the second flask with cold water (from the faucet). Record the temperature of the water in each flask. Now pour about an inch of boiling water into one of the beakers holding ice cubes and the cold water into the other beaker of ice cubes. ■ ●

Which ice cubes melt faster: the ones over which you poured an inch of near-boiling water or the ones over which you poured a full flask of cold water?

After several trials, compare your results with those shown below.

| | Average Temperature | Average Temperature | Average Time to Melt Ice Cubes | |
| --- | --- | --- | --- | --- |
| | *Hot Water* | *Cold Water* | *in Hot Water* | *in Cold Water* |
| Trial 1 (Ohio) | 181° F | 60° F | 13 min. | 7 min. |
| Trial 2 (Oklahoma) | 187° F | 58° F | 12 min. | 5 min. |
| Trial 3 (New York) | 204° F | 55° F | 17 min. | 6 min. |

water has more heat in it than a glass of cold water at the same temperature. Why? The bathtub has more molecules of water moving about. The greater the amount of the substance the greater is its heat.

The cup of cold water in the investigation had more moving molecules than the inch of hot water. True, the molecules of hot water were moving faster, and a single molecule of hot water had more kinetic energy than a single molecule of cold water. Yet there were many more molecules of cold water, so the sum of kinetic energy was greater for the cold water. The cold water, therefore, had more heat. Suppose you had equal amounts of hot and cold water. Which would have more heat? Why? From your understanding of heat, what do you suppose is the answer to the problem indicated in the picture? ■

nail heated white hot

tub of cold water

■ **WHICH HAS MORE HEAT? WHY?**

Now that you know the definition of heat, why not see if you can find a definition of temperature by doing some research in the library.

A star's *heat* and a star's *temperature*, therefore, give a clue to its size.

### The Sizes of Stars

"Twinkle, twinkle, little star"—so goes the rhyme. But how little *is* little? The star you know most about is 864,-000 miles in diameter. That star is our sun.

If the sun were drawn the size of a half-dollar, how large in relation to the sun would you draw the earth? The earth would be about the size of the period at the end of this sentence. How is it possible to determine the size of a star like our sun, which is 93,000,000 miles away? Perhaps you can find out by doing the same type of problem, using smaller objects and shorter distances. For example, how can you determine the size of a lamp across the room?

Of course, you could measure this distance with a ruler, but you cannot do that with the moon or with a star. Can you measure the size of the lamp from where you sit? One way of doing it is shown in the investigation on the opposite page.

### Giants and Dwarfs

Perhaps you have not yet figured out one of the ways that astronomers can measure the sizes of certain stars.

There are very great differences in the sizes of stars. You already have a

# AN INVESTIGATION into a Way of Measuring Things That Are Very Distant

**Needed:** an object like a lamp or a wall clock; a small card, 1″ × 1″

Close one eye and look at the lamp across the room, as shown in the illustration. ■ Hold the card in front of you so that it just blocks your view of the lampshade. The edge of the card should seem to touch the edges of the shade, as shown. ●

Ask a classmate to measure the distance between your eye and the card. Then ask your classmate to measure the distance from your eye to the lamp. ▲ Also, measure the width of the lampshade. Write the results of each measurement in your notebook.

How many times greater was the distance from your eye to the lamp than to the card? *five times greater?*

How many times wider was the lampshade than the card? *five times wider?*

How wide was the lampshade? How many times wider would you expect the shade to be than the card?

What were the results when *you* used a lampshade or a wall clock?

How can scientists use this method to measure the diameter of the moon or the sun? Astronomers have special equipment for looking at the sun. CAUTION: YOU SHOULD **NEVER** LOOK DIRECTLY AT THE SUN UNDER ANY CIRCUMSTANCES.

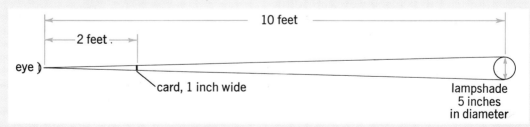

eye ) — 2 feet — card, 1 inch wide — 10 feet — lampshade 5 inches in diameter

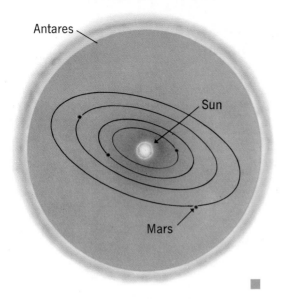

Antares

Sun

Mars

clue to the differences in the temperature of stars from pages 374–76. Some stars are red, others white, others yellow, still others dark. The temperatures of the stars can also give us a clue to their sizes.

By using the spectroscope, astronomers have found that the red star Antares has a surface temperature of about 5,500° F. Our sun has a surface temperature of 11,000° F. Thus for every square inch of surface, the yellow sun is producing more heat and light than the red Antares.

If we measure the *total heat* and light given off by Antares, however, we find that it is giving off more than 2,000 times the heat energy and light energy of the sun. How can we relate these two observations?

OBSERVATION 1:
*Each square inch* of the surface of Antares is giving off *less* energy than each square inch of the sun's surface.

OBSERVATION 2:
The *entire* red star is producing *more* energy than the entire sun.

One explanation of these observations is that Antares, although cooler than the sun, is bigger. This would explain why the entire red star produces so much more energy than the entire sun. In fact, the diameter of Antares is about 320 times greater than the diameter of the sun. Thus, if the diameter of Antares were about the same as that shown in the picture, the sun would be about the size of the head of a nail. ■

To understand the idea of relative size in a different way, examine the orbits of the planets shown in the diagrams. The diameter of the star Antares would be greater than the diameter of the *orbit* of the planet Mars. ■

Antares is a red giant. There are a few other red giants as large or larger than Antares. Most stars, however, are medium-sized like the sun. Compared with the huge red stars, the sun is not very large.

Nevertheless, the sun is our star. We depend upon it for our light energy and, therefore, for our food, for without light energy, green plants would not be able to make sugars, starches, and other types of food. All animals depend on this food whether they feed on plants directly or feed on plant-eating animals.

Even at a distance of 93 million miles, the sun is large enough and near enough to support life on earth.

**A.** Study the statements below and choose the correct responses. They will help you fix in mind the concepts of this section.

1. Of these two, one is hotter. That one is a
   a. white-hot piece of steel   b. red-hot piece of steel

2. Of these two, one has more heat. That one is a
   a. large red star   c. small white star
   b. small yellow star

3. To determine the temperature of a star, scientists use a
   a. thermometer   b. spectroscope

4. The brighter portion of the spectrum of a blue-white star is the
   a. red section   b. blue section

5. A yellow star (the size of our sun) as compared with a red star (the size of Antares)
   a. has more heat   b. has less heat

6. A quart of water at 60° F has more heat than
   a. a pint of water at 60° F
   b. two quarts of water at 60° F

7. The molecules in a glass of hot water, as compared with those in a glass of cold water, are moving
   a. faster   c. slower
   b. at about the same speed

**B.** Write a paragraph or two on this topic: Colors of Stars.

1. What is the source of the heat and light of some stars?

2. What is the explanation of Algol's regular appearance and disappearance?

3. What is your "educated guess" as to why certain stars are dark?

1. Study once again the investigation on page 379. In it you used a card 1″ × 1″ to blot out an object (a lampshade) on the opposite side of the room. Two measurements were necessary.

    a. distance from the eye to the card

    b. distance from the eye to the object

From these measurements you were able to get an idea of the size of the object. Can you state this relationship in a mathematical formula?

(Look back to Unit Two. There you may have tried to measure "work" by using a mathematical formula.)

2. In order to use the method in the investigation on page 379 to measure the size of an object, you must know the distance between you and the object. Thus, astronomers must know how far away a star is if they wish to measure its size.

Suppose scientists know the size of a certain star and want to know its distance from the earth. Could they use a similar method and a similar formula?

On your own, you may wish to visit the library to learn more about measuring distances in space. Guidebooks on astronomy will be of help.

## 3. Numbers of Stars

How many stars can you see on a clear night? Suppose you were to focus your eyes, without the aid of a telescope, on a part of the sky. What would you see? Perhaps you would see something like the part of the sky that is shown in the bottom picture. ■ Suppose, next, that you use a huge telescope to look at the same part of the sky. You might see what is in the top picture. ●

As we improve our techniques for studying the sky, we improve our understanding of it. Even so, man studied the sky long before he invented instruments such as the huge Hale telescope located at Mount Palomar. Soon man may use the moon or space stations as observatories. From such vantage points he will learn even more about the universe and what is in it.

How many stars can you see on a clear night? It would be an almost impossible task to count them all. Astronomers tell us that with the unaided eye we can see as many as 2,500 stars on a very clear night. If you used a telescope, you would be able to count many more. But, since you can see only half of the entire sky that surrounds the earth at one time, it is possible to see only about 5,000 stars, even with the aid of a telescope.

Ancient man built observatories many centuries ago. They did not have telescopes in them, but they were used to study the movements of objects in space. The remains of one at Stonehenge, England, consists of stone pillars placed in a circle. Through these, man could predict exactly where the sun and moon would rise at any time of the year. There is also evidence that this observatory was probably used to predict the eclipses of the moon.

The farther man looks into the universe, the larger it seems to be; the more stars and groups of stars he discovers. He does not yet know where, or even if, the universe ends. All he knows is that every time he develops an instrument for looking farther, he discovers that the universe is larger. Today, in addition to the giant 200-inch Hale telescope at Mount Palomar, huge radio telescopes are probing even deeper into space.

If you could make a star map of the sky section by section, however, you might be able to count all the stars. This is now being done for all the stars in our **galaxy** (gal′ək·sē), the Milky Way Galaxy. A galaxy is a large rotating mass, or system, of stars, having a common center. The Milky Way Galaxy is made up of all the stars

in the group of which our sun is a part. Astronomers say there may be as many as 100,000,000,000 (one hundred billion) stars in our galaxy. How do they arrive at that number? Is it fairly accurate? Is it just a guess? The investigation on the following pages will help you to understand one way of counting or estimating the number of stars in a galaxy.

381

# AN INVESTIGATION into a Way of Counting Very Large Numbers

**Needed:** 100 brown bean seeds; 100 white bean seeds; 100 corn seeds; a large box of toothpicks—red, green, plain (your teacher will be the only one who will know the actual number of toothpicks and the number of each color)

Be certain that the beans and corn are mixed thoroughly. Perhaps you might do this in a jar which you can shake again and again. Now how could you determine how many seeds of each kind are in the jar?

Try this: Scoop up some seeds. ■ Use your hand or a small cup. Each time you scoop some seeds, use the same scoop and scoop from different parts of the large jar. Count the number of white and brown beans and the number of kernels of corn in each scoopful.● Each scoop is a sample of the contents of the entire jar.

In two classes where this was done with the same jar of seeds, it took ten scoops to remove just half of the seeds from the jar. The results are shown on the opposite page. ▲

Would you conclude from this average that there are probably equal numbers of each kind of seed in the jar? Of course, you knew the answer in advance. How many seeds of each kind were in the jar? The jar was half full when you finished scooping. There must have been twice the number of those counted. You know this answer in advance, too. This is always good to know when you try out a new method of investigation.

382

| Scoop | Number of items | Kinds | | |
|---|---|---|---|---|
| | | Brown beans | White beans | Corn |
| 1 | 14 | 6 | 4 | 4 |
| 2 | 16 | 5 | 6 | 5 |
| 3 | 13 | 4 | 4 | 5 |
| 4 | 16 | 6 | 4 | 6 |
| 5 | 16 | 5 | 6 | 5 |
| 6 | 16 | 5 | 4 | 7 |
| 7 | 15 | 4 | 6 | 5 |
| 8 | 14 | 7 | 4 | 3 |
| 9 | 15 | 3 | 6 | 6 |
| 10 | 14 | 5 | 4 | 5 |
| | | 50 | 48 | 51 |

This new method of counting is known as **sampling.** Now try the same investigation with the toothpicks. This time the problem is a bit more difficult. You do not know how many toothpicks are in the bunch. Also you do not know how many of each color there are.

**Clue:** Scatter the toothpicks evenly over the top of a table where you can measure the entire area. Mark off several 1-square-foot areas.◆ Note the total area of the table. Then calculate the total number of toothpicks and determine the accuracy of your results.

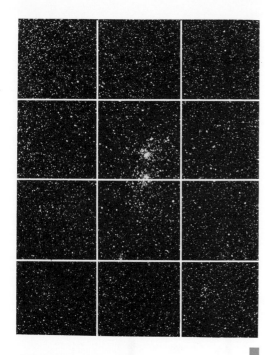

## Sampling the Stars

How can the results of the investigation be applied to counting the stars of the Milky Way Galaxy? Suppose we fix our telescope on different portions of our galaxy. The telescope is attached to a camera. The observer does not watch the sky to count the stars, he photographs them. Photographs are very accurate records and

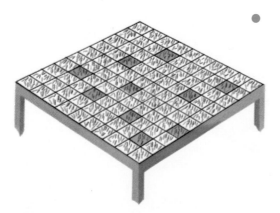

enable the observer to check carefully the parts of the sky he has photographed. Suppose he had photographed different parts of the sky—just as you (in your investigation) scooped out the beans (sampling). For example, the picture on the left shows a large section of the Milky Way Galaxy. ■ The lines show how twelve separate photographs could have been pieced together to make this picture.

Each photograph is like your scoop. It takes pictures of only certain parts of the sky. If you have samples of, for example, 100 parts of the galaxy, this is the *first* piece of information you need. What else do you need to know? You need to know the total area of the galaxy.

Recall this clue from the investigation on page 384. Scatter the toothpicks over a *known area*. It would make a great difference, would it not, whether you scattered the toothpicks over

    *a.* 100 square feet ● or
    *b.* 10 square feet.

In *a* above, if you took a sampling over several 1-square-foot areas and found that, on the average, there are ten toothpicks in each area, you might say that there are about 1,000 toothpicks on the table. In *b*, if your sampling again indicated an average of ten toothpicks per square foot, then there are about 100 toothpicks altogether. Notice the word *about*. Sampling gives you only a very good estimate of the total number. The word *about* shows that there is some error (however slight) in the count. In any event, you must know two things about the subject of the investigation.

1. You must know the size of the samples.
2. You must know the size or boundaries of the entire subject you are investigating.

Our galaxy, the Milky Way, has been measured. It has not, however, been measured in the units with which you are most familiar. The distances in space are far too great to be measured with the same systems we use to measure distances on earth. The measure, or ruler, for space is the **light-year.** The light-year is the *distance* that light travels in one year at a speed of 186,000 miles per second.

In one year light travels about 6,000,000,000,000 (6 trillion) miles. The unit, 1 light-year, therefore equals about 6 trillion miles. Our galaxy has been found, by careful probing with telescope and other ways of observing, to be shaped like a pancake thickened in the center. Across, it is about 100,000 light-years in diameter. ▲ Through the center, it is about 20,000 light-years. ◆ Slowly it whirls about in space. What does a sampling of its stars tell us about the number of stars in the galaxy?

There are about 100 to 200 billion stars in our galaxy. The nearest star is our sun. The next nearest, Alpha Centauri, a star about the size of our sun, is about 4 light-years away. If you

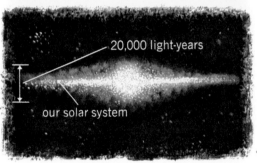

were to put a searchlight 27 miles away, you could, on a very dark night, see it as a pinpoint of light. This is about the way you see Alpha Centauri. We do not know if there is life elsewhere in space, but just suppose there was an observer on a planet in orbit around Alpha Centauri. Suppose he was using a telescope powerful enough to allow him to look at your school. Would he see it as it looks today? No. He would see it as it looked 4 years ago. Why?

BEFORE
YOU GO ON **A.** Study the statements below and choose the correct re- sponses. They will help you fix in mind the concepts of this section.

1. Our galaxy, the Milky Way Galaxy, has about
   a. 1,000,000 stars          b. 100 to 200 billion stars

2. In counting stars we can use a mathematical method known as
   a. sampling                 b. photography

3. The unit that is used to measure distances in space is the
   a. light-year               b. width of our galaxy

4. The diameter of our galaxy is about
   a. 100 light-years          b. 100,000 light-years

**B.** Write a paragraph or two on this topic: The Light-Year.

USING WHAT
YOU KNOW 1. A rancher who owns a large ranch is bothered by the gopher holes on his land; sometimes horses step into the holes and injure themselves. He wants to know how many gopher holes he has on his ranch because he wants to get rid of the gophers. He has a ranch of 10,000 acres.

a. What method do you recommend for finding out the number of gopher holes?

b. How would you do it?

2. Alpha Centauri is about 4 light-years away from the earth.

a. How long would it take you to get to Alpha Centauri in a spaceship traveling at a speed of 1 light-year a month? (By the way, no such spaceship exists.)

b. Suppose that there was a planet revolving around Alpha Centauri and that organisms living on it could use telescopes. One of them is viewing a football game being played on earth on January 1, 1968. In what year would the organism see the kickoff?

## 4. The History of a Star

Almost 900 years ago, in the year 1088, Chinese astronomers saw a "new" star born, or so they thought. Modern astronomers know something of the history of such "new" stars. They are really not new stars at all. How they become new stars, or, rather, how they appear to *renew* themselves and suddenly become much brighter, is an interesting story and an important one. ■ ● The story gives us a clue that indicates how the elements may have come to be.

### The Meaning of a Word

**Nova** means "new" in Latin, so the word "nova" was the name given to a so-called "new" star. These stars are really very old but have come to life again. How is this possible?

Certain stars, like our sun, slowly use up their atoms of hydrogen in the process of fusion. This process takes place in our sun and in many other stars as well. What can happen to a star which gets its energy from the fusion of hydrogen?

Recall that atoms of hydrogen fuse to form helium, and in so doing, some of the matter is changed into energy (page 371). Now, how long can this go on? It can go on as long as the star has enough hydrogen. If the change from hydrogen to helium continues, a time will come when no more hydrogen is left. Then what will happen? According to the best knowledge at present, this is what would happen.

Slowly, over millions upon millions of years, the hydrogen is used up. Why millions? A star is quite huge; for example, the sun has a diameter of 864,000 miles. Its volume is tremendous. 1,000,000 earth-sized globes could fit inside the sun.

As the hydrogen is used up, the helium increases. Where would you expect the helium to collect? First, a

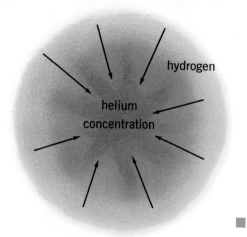

hydrogen

helium concentration

helium atom is almost four times heavier than a hydrogen atom. Because of its heavier weight, the helium slowly gathers toward the center of the star. The lighter hydrogen remains in the outer regions of the star, as shown. ■ As the atoms of helium gather toward the center, the weight of all the matter presses the atoms of helium gas closer and closer together. What happens as atoms or molecules

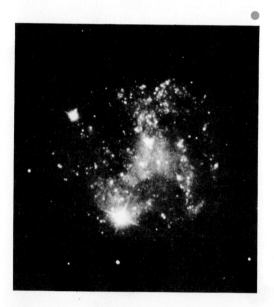

of a gas are pressed closer and closer? Try the investigation on the opposite page and see for yourself.

## A Star Explodes

As the hydrogen is used up, more and more helium is produced. The star becomes hotter and hotter as the pressure within it becomes greater and greater and greater. The kinetic energy of the atoms increases. The atoms of helium get even closer, bouncing against each other with greater and greater energy. The pressure builds up to such a point that the star explodes. It flares up in a brilliant, brilliant light and becomes a nova or a very huge nova, called a **supernova.** ●

## The Stars—As Factories

For a long time astronomers had been wondering how the elements were formed. There are 92 natural elements on earth; oxygen, nitrogen, iron, sulfur, and uranium are examples. Scientists have been looking for a theory (an explanation) as to how the elements were formed. One fact is certain: the elements do exist.

Experimentation provided a clue. As a result of many experiments and advanced technology, scientists have been able to make several new kinds of atoms by bombarding nuclei of certain ordinary atoms with atomic bullets. Two of these new atoms are plutonium and neptunium. There are nine others, among them curium, einsteinium, and others. Some of these

# AN INVESTIGATION into Compression of Gases

**Needed:** a bicycle pump; a deflated bicycle tire or a deflated basketball

Feel the bicycle pump and feel the tire. Now ask a friend to pump up the tire, and as he makes the downstroke, feel the pump below the piston. ■ Also feel the metal hose connection. What has happened? The pump below the piston has become hot. In other words, the kinetic energy of the molecules has increased.

What is your explanation of the increase in heat of the air (the gas) in that part of the pump?

The apparatus shown below the pump is called a J-tube. ● Suppose the mercury in the long part of the tube were increased in amount. The pressure on the air increases. What would you expect to happen to the temperature of the air in the J-tube as the pressure on it increases?

**Additional Investigation:** If a J-tube like the one shown and a small amount of mercury are available, fill the tube as shown in the diagram. ▲ What is the effect on the volume of the gas in the tip of the tube as the pressure increases? Use a ruler and measure very carefully. Which column of mercury rises more rapidly? the one on the left or on the right? How much more rapidly? Why?

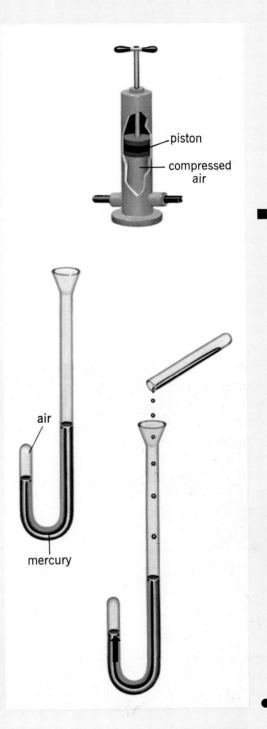

piston

compressed air

air

mercury

● ▲

new atoms were made in atomic piles, and others were made by using the cyclotron. By bombarding certain nuclei with atomic bullets, new and larger atoms can be created.

Imagine then that a supernova flares up, spraying its surroundings with atomic particles! Neutrons, protons, electrons, and alpha particles (helium nuclei) fly apart and then come together again. As they come together, new atoms form. Over a long period of time many different kinds of atoms are formed. Some of them are the ones with which we are most familiar on earth: nitrogen, carbon, potassium, iron, and others.

As a supernova begins to cool slightly, the different particles fuse with the different atoms. Heavier and heavier atoms are formed. The supernova becomes a factory of elements. This is a theory to explain what some scientists believe happens. How else could we explain the origin of elements? Do you have a better theory? Perhaps another will be developed in the next few years.

The elements formed in the supernova are the same as those that are found on earth and in other parts of the solar system. The atoms of elements find their way into space. Sooner or later they may become a part of a cloud of whirling particles like the Crab Nebula, shown below. ■ Astronomers believe that this great mass of whirling particles was once a supernova. Sooner or later these whirling particles may form a new

■

star; and perhaps around this star some planets may be formed. Perhaps this is the way our solar system was born.● Perhaps this is the way the elements which make up the earth came to be part of it.

As we have said, further investigation in the years to come will give more evidence and better explanations of the evidence. Our theories may change as new evidence is introduced.

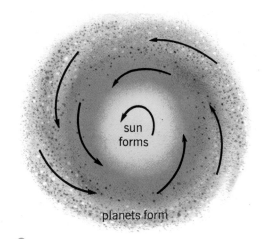

●

BEFORE
YOU GO ON **A.** Study the statements below and choose the correct responses. They will help you fix in mind the concepts of this section.

    **1.** A nova is an
      a. old star which     b. entirely new star
        becomes brighter

    **2.** A star has a supply of hydrogen which is never used up. This statement is
      a. true     b. false

    **3.** A star's supply of hydrogen usually lasts
      a. 10,000 years     b. millions upon millions
                         of years

    **4.** As atoms become compressed, their kinetic energy
      a. increases     b. decreases

    **5.** As kinetic energy increases, the temperature
      a. increases     b. decreases

    **B.** Write a paragraph or two on this topic: A Nova.

USING WHAT
YOU KNOW What theory is currently considered to be the best explanation for the origin of the elements?

1. What are the man-made elements? The names of some were given in the section you have read. As of now, how many are there altogether? In the library, a new reference book in chemistry should provide a complete list. They are sometimes listed as the transuranic (trans'yo͞o·ran'ik) elements. Why is it necessary to use a new reference book? Why would an older reference book not be satisfactory?

2. Robert Boyle discovered this law about the behavior of gases: If the temperature remains the same, the volume of a certain amount of gas varies *inversely* with the pressure. For example, if the pressure is doubled, the volume will be one-half. Can Boyle's Law be applied to the air in the J-tube (page 391)?

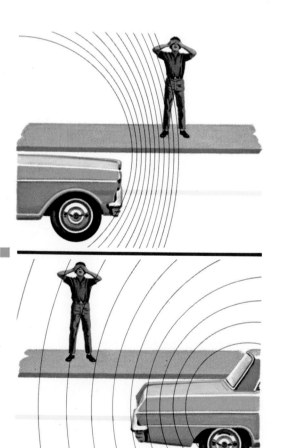

## 5. Motions of the Stars

You can find out something about the motions of the stars in an unusual way. You can get one clue by trying to find out whether an automobile is moving toward you or away from you, and you must determine whether it is moving toward or away from you *only from the sound of its horn.* Suppose you are standing on the sidewalk with your eyes closed while an automobile comes down the street with its horn blowing constantly.

Sound travels at a speed of 1,100 feet a second. As the car travels toward you, the sound waves will be crowded together. ■ When sound waves are crowded together, the sound of the horn is *pitched higher.* This is so because each second there are more sound waves coming toward you. As the automobile moves away from you, will the sound be pitched higher or lower?■ Why? Are the sound waves packed closer together or are they farther apart? The illustration will help you to decide.

What has this phenomenon to do with the motion of the stars?

## Clues from Light

The sound of the horn gives a clue as to whether an automobile moves toward us or away from us. In much the same way, objects in space that are giving off light give a clue as to how they are moving.

If a certain object were moving toward the earth, what would happen to its light waves?

## The Doppler Effect

Christian Doppler, a German scientist, wondered about certain phenomena in regard to sound. He finally described the phenomenon that is known as the **Doppler effect.**

The Doppler effect is: Sound that comes from an object traveling toward you increases in **pitch;** the sound is higher. As the object travels away from you, the pitch becomes lower. The reason is that sound waves traveling in front of a moving object are pushed closer together, thereby increasing the **frequency.** Frequency is the rate at which waves (sound or light) pass a fixed point and is measured in waves per second. For instance, the string for middle C on a piano vibrates with a frequency of 256 times per second. Frequency is the rate of vibration.

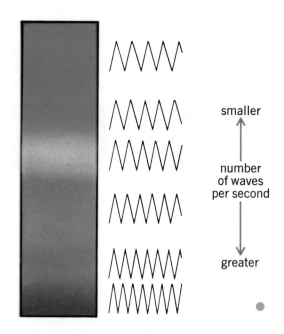

smaller

↑

number
of waves
per second

↓

greater

How can astronomers determine whether the light from an object is traveling toward the earth or away from the earth? The clue is in the Doppler effect, and the evidence is obtained by analyzing light with a spectroscope.

Just as sound waves that come from an object moving toward you have a higher frequency, so also do waves of light. The light waves coming from an object which is moving toward the earth would be of a higher frequency. That is, a greater number of waves would reach the earth each second. Each color in the spectrum has a different frequency.● The color having waves with the highest frequency (most crowded) is violet. Therefore, if a star were moving toward the earth, the line of its spectrum would be crowded toward the violet end. A star moving away from

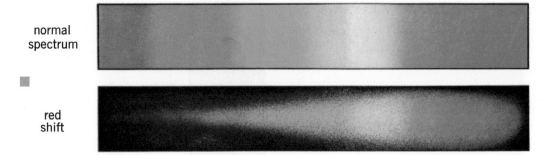

normal spectrum

red shift

the earth would have the lines of its spectrum crowded toward the red end. Red light waves have the lowest frequency (are the least crowded) of any in the visible spectrum. This is called the Doppler shift or sometimes the "red shift." ■

Scientists have used the Doppler effect to study the motion of other galaxies far away from our own. They have been surprised to find that each distant galaxy has shown a shift toward the *red* in its spectrum. Does this mean that all the other galaxies are moving away from us?

Many astronomers take this as evidence that the entire universe is ●

spreading apart or expanding, that all star systems are moving farther and farther away from each other.

## The Motions of the Stars

All stars are moving. The stars in our own galaxy are revolving around a center, like a giant wheel, as shown. ● Of course, our star, the sun, is moving, along with the other stars, around the center of the galaxy as well.

Sometimes the motion of a star can be discovered by photographs. Look at a picture of Barnard's Star (named for Edward Emerson Barnard) in our Milky Way Galaxy. ▲ Notice also the photograph of the same star taken twenty-two years later. ♦ The star has moved. It is moving even now.

Scientists can predict the motion of stars and other bodies in space, such as **comets.** For instance, it is almost certain that Halley's comet will appear again in 1985; its last appearance was in 1910. ★ Scientists can predict its orbit and know that it appears approximately every 75 years.

Why is it that you cannot see stars and other objects in space move as you watch them? The explanation is

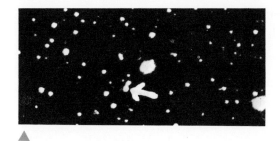

simple. Suppose you watch a friend walk by close in front of you. He walks quickly. If he were far away, for example, a mile, he would *seem* to move more slowly across your field of vision. Though some stars move at 50 or 60 miles a second, they *seem* to move hardly at all. The positions of the stars in the sky do not seem to have changed very much since man started to notice their movements. Barnard's Star, which moves across the sky with the greatest speed we know, has taken almost 180 years to move a distance that looks about the same as the diameter of the moon (as we see it).

All the stars move, even the North Star. It is rushing away from us at a speed of 15 miles every second. How much farther away will it be by the time you finish this sentence?

### The Meaning of It All

No one quite knows what all this means to us, except that the universe is vast, with a vastness the human mind cannot seem to understand. Yet the universe is not a place where things stand still. *In our universe all is motion. In our universe everything is changing.*

All is motion.

All is change.

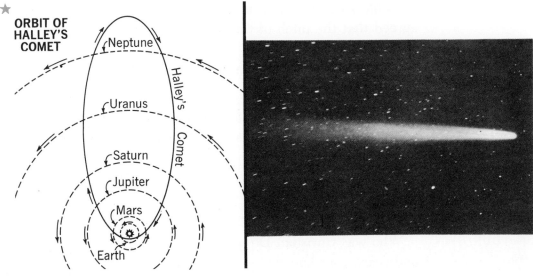

**ORBIT OF HALLEY'S COMET**

**A.** Study the statements below and choose the correct responses. They will help you fix in mind the concepts of this section.

**1.** An automobile traveling toward you, horn blowing, can be distinguished from one going away from you because the sound is pitched

    a. higher                         b. lower

**2.** A star moving away from the earth would have the lines of its spectrum shifted toward the

    a. red end                   b. violet end

**3.** The Doppler shift is sometimes called the

    a. red shift                  b. blue shift

**4.** There is evidence that the universe is

    a. expanding              b. getting smaller

**B.** Write a paragraph or two on this topic: The Uses of the Doppler Effect.

**1.** In trying to solve a mysterious bank robbery, a detective had to determine where a certain car was at the time of the robbery. Witnesses near the bank agreed that the car had been blowing its horn as it sped through the streets. They all agreed that the pitch of the horn dropped suddenly and got lower.

Was the car approaching the bank? Or moving away from it?

**2.** The light from a distant galaxy shifts toward the red end of the spectrum. Is it moving toward our solar system? Or away?

What is the reason for your answer?

Who was Christian Doppler? Report on his life and work, and share your knowledge with your class.

# 6. The Main Concept: The Changing Universe

On a dark, clear night. we look into the skies at the stars. We search out Polaris, the North Star—and there it is. ■ Ships and aircraft can be guided by the North Star. We look for other stars and there they are, just as they appear on sky charts. The moon seems always to be where it is supposed to be. All seems to stay the same; nothing seems to change.

We know differently. We know that our galaxy, the Milky Way, is whirling in the skies and that our star, the sun, is moving as well. We know our planet, earth, is moving. The evidence tells us also that all the galaxies of stars are moving away from us and away from each other. It seems clear that everything is moving; and change is taking place everywhere. Nothing in the universe remains the same as it was a moment ago.

Should this disturb us? Not at all. The movements of the stars are not helter-skelter. The fact that scientists can predict where the stars will be tells us that their movements are regular and uniform. Their movements are orderly. Isaac Newton discovered the law that tells us how an object continues in motion and remains in orbit. Also, Newton's *Law of Gravitation* explains how objects in space attract each other. There are many other laws which man, as a scientist, has stated as he tried to find out more about the universe. These laws enable us to

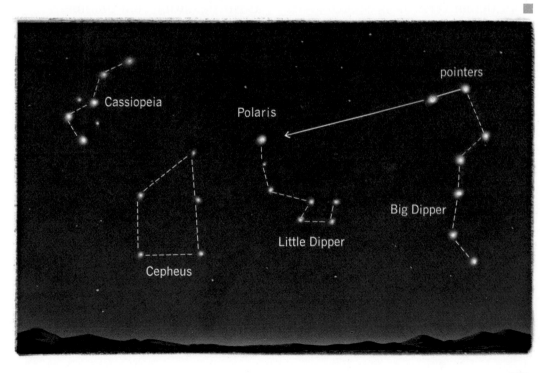

understand certain events, such as the revolution of the moon around the earth. Scientific laws also help us to predict events. Thus, Gregor Mendel's *Laws of Heredity* help to explain how plants and animals inherit certain traits and how man uses them.

Understanding Newton's Laws of Universal Gravitation made it possible for us to predict what happens to a spaceship as it approaches the moon.

A scientific theory can become a scientific law if, over many years, the theory is tested by observation and experiment. If the theory continues to explain new things (such as the behavior of a spaceship approaching Mars, Saturn, or objects in space), we call it a law. Newton's Law of Universal Gravitation has been tested for about 300 years.

In the universe all is change. Stars change. We know a star to be a nuclear furnace. It may be an active furnace, a dying one, or an exploding one.

If its nuclear fuel is hydrogen, the hydrogen is fusing into helium. It is the fusion of hydrogen into helium which gives certain stars their energy —light, heat, and other forms of radiant energy. As stars change more and more of their hydrogen into helium, helium atoms become packed near the center. Finally, this packing (which causes great pressure) can no longer continue. The star explodes and becomes a nova—a "new" star.

A nova is really an old star which suddenly becomes brighter as it explodes. Novas or supernovas (giant novas) create more changes in our universe. They seem to be factories of the elements—exploding newly formed elements out into clouds of particles. Perhaps these clouds are the beginnings of a new solar system.

Our sun and its planets *may* have started this way, as shown in the illustration.■ Notice how the swirling cloud of particles might have collected and changed shape to form our sun and planets. This is one way it could have happened. Much investigation must be done, however, before we will really know how our solar system started.

If you become a scientist some day, there is much for you to discover about the changing universe. If you do not become a scientist, you may still want to know what discoveries are made during your lifetime.

You must realize that you are living in a great age of investigation—investigation into the nature of the earth and of the universe.

A great deal is known but scientists realize that there is much more to be learned. After all, it has only been during the last 500 years that "modern science" had its birth. Scientists often consider that "modern science" began with Galileo, who lived from 1564 to 1642. It is only a short time that scientists have been exploring the secrets of the universe. More than half of all the scientists who ever lived are alive and at work today. It seems certain then that, in the future, much more will be discovered.

## ■ ONE CONCEPT OF THE WAY OUR SOLAR SYSTEM WAS FORMED

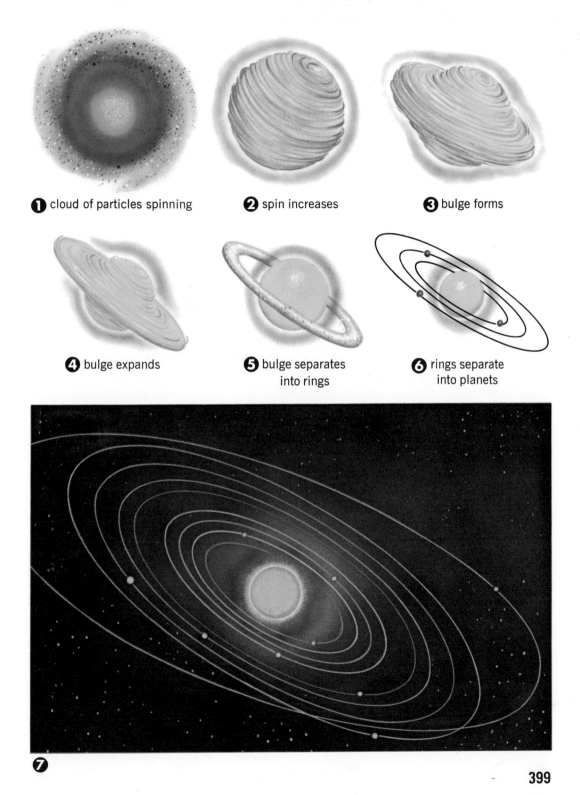

**1** cloud of particles spinning

**2** spin increases

**3** bulge forms

**4** bulge expands

**5** bulge separates into rings

**6** rings separate into planets

**7**

# Fixing the Main Concepts

Test your understanding of the important concepts in this unit by doing these problems.

**1.** An object is discovered in the sky. It gives off a bright yellow light. First measurements show that it has a diameter of about 800,000 miles. The object is probably a

    a. meteor          c. moon

    b. planet          d. star

**2.** The spectrum of an object in the sky shows that it is crowded toward the red end. The object is

    a. moving toward us      c. becoming a nova

    b. moving away from us    d. a dark star

**3.** Fusion of atomic nuclei and fission of atomic nuclei are two ways of getting energy from matter. We could say that on the sun

    a. matter is unchanged      c. matter gains weight

    b. matter is changed        d. energy is changed

        into energy                into matter

**4.** The Doppler effect could tell us all of these things except

    a. whether an object in the sky moves toward us

    b. whether an object in the sky moves away from us

    c. whether an automobile is moving toward us

    d. whether an object is undergoing fusion

**5.** Some scientists believe that the red shift in the spectrums of distant galaxies is evidence that the universe is

    a. expanding              b. revolving

**6.** By determining the exact colors of a star in the light spectrum, astronomers can determine its temperature. For this purpose they use a

    a. telescope             c. thermometer

    b. spectroscope

**7.** When four atoms of hydrogen fuse to form helium, 0.029 of a unit of matter is apparently missing. It has been converted into

a. water
c. energy
b. hydrogen
d. matter

**8.** A bathtub full of cool water has more heat in it than a hot nail because it

a. has a higher temperature
b. has more molecules
c. has fewer molecules
d. is water

QUICK TEST

**1.** A gas lighter than oxygen is

a. carbon dioxide
b. hydrogen

**2.** One of these equations is correct. Which one is it?

a. $2 H_2 + O_2 \rightarrow 2 H_2O$
b. $2 H_2 + O \rightarrow 2 H_2O$

**3.** When hydrogen atoms fuse, we have a

a. chemical reaction
b. nuclear reaction

**4.** We get energy from atoms whether they undergo fission or

a. fusion
b. diffusion

**5.** Which one of these stars would be most likely to have a spectrum with an even range from violet to red?

a. a yellow star
c. a red star
b. a blue-white star

**6.** The light-year is a measure of

a. light
c. distance
b. frequency

**7.** The factories of elements are thought to be the

a. stars
b. comets

**8.** Sound waves from an object moving toward you have a

a. higher pitch, or higher frequency
b. lower pitch, or lower frequency

**9.** The stars do not seem to be moving because they are

    a. really moving very slowly         b. so far away

**10.** The Doppler effect is based on observations of the shifting of both light and

    a. sound                   b. heat

**FOR YOUR READING**

**1.** *The Stars for Sam,* by W. Maxwell Reed, published by Harcourt, Brace & World, New York, 1960.

This book is a full account of the stars from the time the ancients first examined them to the work of the modern astronomer. The history of stars is discussed from their "birth" to their "death."

**2.** *The Stars: Steppingstones into Space,* by Irving Adler, published by John Day Co., New York, 1956.

This book will help satisfy those who are especially interested in the stars.

# A Concept of Change: A New View

People once thought that everything in the universe remained pretty much the same; that the earth remained in the same place; that the mountains were there forever and so were the seas. ■

Now we know that "things are not always what they seem." What seems to be happening is not always what really is happening. We cannot sense the motion of the earth; yet we know that the earth and eight other planets are rotating at the same time that they are revolving at a tremendous speed around the sun.

The moon revolves around the earth; the earth revolves around the sun. The sun is only one star among the many billions of stars in our galaxy and all the stars in our galaxy are moving. Furthermore, there are millions of galaxies in the universe, all moving away from our own galaxy at great speed.

The universe is so vast that we cannot as yet thoroughly understand it; but we have reached the understanding that all things in the universe are in motion, and that all things change. The changes may be so quiet or so slight as to go unnoticed, or they may be as violent and dramatic as an earthquake, a volcanic eruption, a tidal wave, a landslide, or a flood. They may occur daily, monthly, seasonally, or they may extend over billions of years. Some changes are observable, but some changes can only

be reconstructed from evidence recorded in the earth itself. Man is limited only by his short period of observation.

## Change in Matter and Energy

Even though our world is constantly changing, scientists know that it is not a world of disorder. As man learns and develops concepts about our world, he can predict many changes that may occur and, in some cases, control them.

For instance, scientists can predict where the moon will be at a certain time. Otherwise, they might never have been able to shoot Ranger VII

toward it or to photograph its surface, as shown in the illustration. ■ Because the movements of the earth and of the moon are precise enough to be predicted, it is even possible to think of landing men on the moon.

Man, as a scientist, does not limit his observation to only those things he can actually see. It is possible for him to explain things he cannot "see" with his eyes. He uses indirect evidence. The movement of distant galaxies, for instance, can be explained by means of the Doppler red shift.

Our understanding that matter can be changed to energy helps us to explain how the sun radiates light and

■

heat. The concept is restated here as: *Energy can be changed into other forms of energy. Matter can be changed into other forms of matter. Matter can be changed into energy. However, the total amount of matter and energy remains the same.*

Knowing this concept of matter and energy, it is possible to understand another great concept more easily. That concept is: *The universe is in constant change.*

As part of the universe, we too are changing. Birth, growth, maturity, old age, and death represent a life cycle of change. We change as we grow and learn. Our concepts of the world about us grow and change as we understand more science. This does not mean that what we have learned earlier is wrong. It merely means that we have learned more and, therefore, have a broader understanding. Man and, indeed, all living things are changing and have been changing ever since we began.

### Living Things Change

It is now known that the growth of all living things is affected by their chromosomes. Furthermore, by determining the code in the chromosomes scientists can predict the kind of offspring that will be born, and to some extent, how it will develop. It is the DNA molecule in the chromosome which carries the hereditary code of the organism. The DNA of the garden pea carries the code (in the form of genes) that causes the plant to reproduce garden peas and not geraniums

or whales. The DNA also determines traits of the garden peas, such as color and height. A DNA code determines the traits of cattle, and dogs, and oak trees, each having its own particular code, which makes it different from other organisms.

We can cross garden peas to get certain flower colors and not others. In other words, by controlling the pollination of garden peas, we can determine the genetic code to some extent. By radiation, we can perhaps alter and study the code. It has been possible to improve our food supply by selective breeding for desirable traits.

We have learned that the molecule DNA, or the genes, can change. In other words, when the DNA molecule changes, the code is changed. New traits appear. Over millions upon millions of years, genes mutate and produce changes in organisms.

Unless we provide the organisms with the best environment in which to grow, the traits will not develop to their fullest. The illustration shows how a poor environment can hamper the development of good traits. In order to understand what environment has to do with development, an important concept must be kept in mind. The concept is: *Living things exchange matter and energy with their environment.*

It is possible to predict changes in living things, once we know something about their heredity (their genes or DNA code) and also know something about their environment.

We have learned to understand how organisms develop as we have learned to understand and accept this concept: *All organisms are the product of their heredity and environment acting together.*

Over millions of years the kinds of animals and plants on the earth seem to have changed. Perhaps you have wondered why we do not see dinosaurs or the huge tree ferns that lived millions of years ago. ■ Scientists can understand this because they know that the universe and everything in it is in constant change. The organisms are in constant change as well. How have we come to understand this?

If an organism is to survive, it must be fitted to its environment. A fish, for example, is fitted to live in water, not on land. If, for instance, a pond dries out, the fishes die.

Over millions upon millions of years, the environment changed. The land environment became drier. The dry desert, shown in the picture, was once a moist, tropical forest inhabited by many kinds of dinosaurs. As the land became drier, those organisms that were able to adjust to a changing environment reproduced and survived. Those that were not, the dinosaurs perhaps, died out. This is one way that scientists explain why the same kind of organisms that lived millions of years ago are no longer found.

It is therefore not only the planets, comets, and stars which change. It is not only nonliving matter and energy which change. Living things change as well. Over millions of years, only the organisms on this earth that have been best fitted to the changing environment have survived.

As the scientist explores the universe, he looks for orderly explanations of the things he sees. Whenever he sees something new, he seeks to explain it. He tests his explanations by carefully controlled investigations—often in a scientific laboratory.

As the scientist tests the phenomena he seeks to understand and to explain, he comes to see that at least some things of the world of matter, energy, and living things can be explained and understood and predicted. As he understands the world about him, and can predict events, man can modify his environment. He can breed animals and cultivate plants to produce more food.

## Developing New Concepts

The more we investigate in the manner of the scientist, the more we learn about the concepts of matter, energy, and living things. Concepts like shown in the chart help us to understand the world in which we live. ●

Because we already understand the great concept *that the universe is in constant change,* we can also understand the concept that *organisms are in constant change.*

"Normal" processes over billions of years have changed the earth and its life to the present form. Rivers flow to the sea, cutting valleys and building deltas. They flow at different rates and carry different amounts of sediment. Rain falls, and rocks are weathered by wind, water, and changes in temperature. Waves break along the shore, washing it away in one place and building it up in another.

The earth moves through space; conditions in space change. Forces are at work on the earth; conditions on the earth change. Living things are dependent on their environment; the environment changes. As the environment changes, living things change.

Man, like all other organisms, is interdependent with his environment. Man, as an individual, changes; man, as an organism, changes; but man makes changes of his own—in his environment, in his concepts, and in his plans for the future.

As men change, problems change. As problems change, man is forever challenged to meet the new demands of each new day, for there is still a great deal to be learned.

●

### SUMMARY OF CONCEPTS

**1.** Energy can be changed into other forms of energy. Matter can be changed into other forms of matter. Matter can be changed into energy. However, the total amount of matter and energy remains the same.

**2.** The universe is in constant change.

**3.** Living things exchange matter and energy with their environment.

**4.** All organisms are the product of their heredity and environment acting together.

**5.** Organisms are in constant change.

# THE ART OF INVESTIGATION

Not everything can be learned from books or from other people. There may come a time when you find yourself in situations where the answers are not in the book, or where there is no one around to tell you what to do, or where the answer itself may not yet be known. Sooner or later you must find out some things for yourself by investigating in the same way that the scientist investigates.

The investigations in this section are for you to do *on your own*. You will be given some help but only enough to start you off. Some of the investigations are fairly easy, while others are more difficult. As you look through them, you should find one or two—perhaps more—that will interest you. Select one that does.

Just as you learn to run by running, to write by writing, to play the piano by practice, you can also learn to investigate by investigating. You learn to solve problems by solving them. While you should seek help where you can, it is important to learn how to find out things for yourself.

Let's take an investigation apart to see how it is made up. In other words, let's *analyze* an investigation to see what we need to be careful about as we work.

# 1. Analyzing an Investigation

We can use an investigation that is similar to one you may have already done in Unit Three.

### Background

Suppose you wanted to study bread mold under a microscope. To investigate bread mold, you would first have to grow it. You could grow some by taking a piece of white bread and exposing it to the air for a half hour. The spores of bread mold are in the air and they will fall on the bread.

Put a *few drops* of water on the bread, and place it in a closed jar. Keep the jar in a warm place. In a few days or a week you should find a growth of bread mold.■

*Suppose, however, that you want to find out whether bread mold grows better in the light or in the dark.*

### The Investigation

You could take two slices of bread and divide each into two equal parts. Place each part in the same kind of jar; then add ten drops of water to each piece of bread. Put two of the jars in the dark (in a closet) and two in the light.

From the evidence you might conclude that bread mold grows better in the light; but let's look into this a bit more closely. Was the temperature in the dark closet the same as it was in the light? Suppose it was not. Suppose that the temperature was higher in the light. The temperature could be higher in the light, could it not? After all, light energy can be changed to heat energy.

It is possible then that the greater growth in the *light* was *not caused by light itself* but was caused by the *higher temperature in the light.* In order, then, to do the investigation properly, it is necessary to control the temperature so that it is the same in both the *light* and in the *dark.*

What was wrong with the way you did the investigation? Scientists would say that the investigation was not well planned because not all of the variables were controlled. Temperature, light, and moisture are some of the variables in this investigation. One of the greatest mistakes made in doing an investigation is the failure to control all of the possible variables. Let's see what controlling the variables means and how important it is to control them.

## Avoiding Mistakes

Suppose you wanted to find out whether moisture was necessary for the growth of bread mold. You could first dry the bread (or whatever the mold is to grow on) until it is crisp.

You could put ten drops of the water that has been boiled to kill any mold spores into one of two clean jars. 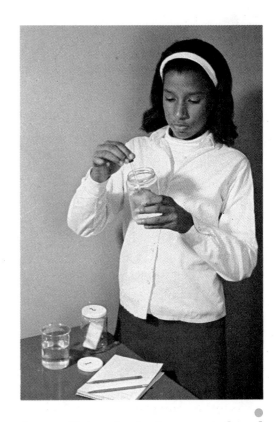 One clean jar should be kept dry. Keep both jars on a table, side by side. Every day, change their positions to make sure that one is not any nearer a source of warmth or light than the other. The variables, temperature and light, are therefore the same for both.

It would probably be necessary to repeat this at least five times (at the beginning) to be fairly sure that your results were no accident. After all, what happens once *could* be an accident. But if it happens the *same way* in all five trials, you could be fairly certain that it happens that way most of the time. No true scientist ever stops after only one trial. Sometimes he may repeat the same procedure for as many as 100, or even 1,000, times before drawing a conclusion. He may fail many times, but he continues to try until he succeeds.

By controlling the variables, light and temperature, you made certain that moisture was the only *variable* you were observing. It was the condition of moisture which *varied*, or was different, in each of the two jars. One jar *varied* from the other by having *moisture* in it. The difference between the conditions in the jars was reduced to *one* variable. If mold grew in the jar *without moisture* but did *not* grow in the jar *with moisture*, then you might say that bread mold did not need moisture for growth. If bread mold grew in the jar with moisture but not in the jar without moisture, then you might say bread mold did need moisture for growth.

You could come to this *tentative* conclusion, because other variables, such as light and temperature, had been controlled. The only variable which was being investigated was moisture. In doing any investigation, it is important to search out all the variables to be sure that one and only one variable is being studied at a time.

411

## Another Pitfall

There is more to doing an investigation than simply controlling all the variables. Look at the illustration and then read on to see why. ■ Both the boy and the girl tried to find out whether moisture is needed for the growth of mold. The boy and the girl did the same investigation and controlled the variables, temperature and light. The only difference in their procedure was that the girl used a larger number of samples.

From which investigation would it be more accurate to conclude that moisture is necessary for the growth of mold? Why?

Once you have decided what you want to investigate, you must consider *two* very important things:

a. You must be sure that you control all the variables.

b. You must plan to repeat your investigation enough times to be confident of your results.

Now before going further, we need to look into the meaning of several important *words* and *acts*.

## 2. A Word About Words— And a Word About Acts

Perhaps you have noticed that the word "investigation" has been used in this book to describe almost any activity in which you "saw" the results yourself. You may be surprised that the word experiment has been avoided.

An investigation includes many things, for instance:

a. *Reading.* ● A person who investigates any subject should find out what is already known about it. Otherwise the investigator may only waste time by repeating what has already been done. To repeat what has been done is sometimes necessary, however, as you will see later.

It is always important to know the concepts upon which an investigation is based. These can often be found by reading the work of investigators who went before you. For instance, it would be peculiar if you announced that you had discovered that bacteria cause disease. Bacteria have already been discovered; and much work has been done to demonstrate that certain bacteria cause disease in man. The work of Pasteur, Koch, Salk, and many others already has been done. It is important then to find out what has already been done or discovered.

Most scientists spend a great deal of their time reading about what other scientists have done. This is often called library research. Since scientists build on each other's work, the library is important; some would say it is as important as the laboratory.

b. *Consulting.* ▲ When a book does not have the information you need, it is always helpful to talk to someone who has done work in the field you are investigating. For instance, some of the investigations which you will deal with soon are concerned with light, heat, evaporation, and con-

densation, in the study of weather. If there were a weather station in your area, you could visit it and talk with a *meteorologist* (mē′tē·ə·rol′ə·jist) (weather expert). Of course, you should first make an appointment.

Perhaps you will need to use a light meter in your investigation. If you know a photographer, it would be wise to consult him on the use of the light meter.

Consult with those who have had experience, if you can. Make an appointment before you go to see them.

c. *Observing.* Most of the investigations you have done in science required that you *observe* what was happening. By observing you use any of your senses, aided in whatever way science and technology can help. ■ Your eyes, ears, nose, and senses of touch and taste are useful, but sometimes they are not good enough. For instance, you can tell whether a substance is hot or cold by feeling it, but you might also cause great injury to yourself by doing so. (Never touch a substance to determine whether it is hot or cold. It might be burning hot, or below freezing temperature, as is dry ice.) Using a thermometer (a piece of equipment, a result of science and technology) is a better way of *observing* whether a substance is hot or cold. It is also more accurate.

In most scientific investigations it is important to know not only whether a substance has a certain *property* (heat, in this case), but also how much of it. Only by making careful measurements can you be sure that the observations you will find in this section will give you an opportunity to learn to measure accurately, or, in other words, to observe accurately.

d. *Experimenting.* If you are unable to obtain accurate information by the methods already mentioned, you may need to find out for yourself by means of an experiment.● An experiment requires careful planning.

Later in this section, you will see that doing an experiment usually requires a good deal of preparation even before the experiment is started. You will see that *reading, consulting,* and *observing* are needed even before you can state the problem.

Probably the best way to learn how to do an experiment is to try to do one. You may wish to glance through those that are suggested (pages 418–22). Once you try to solve any one of these problems by *experiment,* you may discover many problems that can be solved only by experiment.

**Recording:** In any kind of experiment you do, it is not enough to trust your memory. You should always keep a record of your plans, your observations, and your experiments. Do this regularly and carefully in a notebook.

For example, it might be helpful to record the following things in an investigation of "weather."

---

1. **When you did it.**
   Date, Day (to check), and Time.
2. **Kind of day.**
   Weather conditions observed.
3. **Temperature.**
4. **What you did or observed.**
5. **How you did it.**
6. **Notes.** (Reminders)

---

**Planning.** Much time can be saved by careful planning. As well as having a good understanding of the problem, solving the problem is the real purpose of doing the experiment.

# 3. Investigations— On Your Own

Now you can proceed to a series of investigations in one field—**meteorology**—the study of atmospheric conditions, or weather. These investigations are intended to help you learn how to investigate, on your own. They are developed around one major concept: *Heat energy is the kinetic energy of moving molecules.* This concept is helpful in explaining the causes of different kinds of weather.

*Investigation 1.* **How accurate are the weather predictions for your area?**

The word *prediction* is an important one in science. Once a scientific concept is thoroughly understood and observations have been made to test it thoroughly, predictions can be made. The more thorough the understanding of the concept the more accurate the predictions.

There might be two parts to your investigation. First, you might record the predictions from radio, television, and newspapers, and then test them by observing what really happens. Second, you might make a prediction yourself based on reading the weather maps. In order to do this, you need to be able to understand the kind of weather map that is published in many newspapers.

One good way to do this is to select weather maps for five consecutive days. You will find a sample weather map on the following page.

Before you read the map be sure you know what each symbol on the map stands for. The important symbols are explained on the map. ■ (Where would you find out what the others mean? a dictionary? an encyclopedia? a science book?)

How accurate are the results?

Can you state them by giving the percentage of accuracy?

How accurate are your predictions in comparison with other predictions?

Were any of the predictions 100 percent accurate?

What do you think accounts for the results?

## Investigation 2. Can weather be predicted by observation of clouds?

Study the chart of clouds on the facing page. ● You can learn how to identify clouds better as you become an experienced observer. Soon you will see combinations of different clouds and different cloud types.

After you have learned to identify the clouds, try to predict the relationship between the different types of clouds and the weather. For instance, does a cumulonimbus cloud (thunderhead) always produce rain? Be sure to keep careful notes. ■

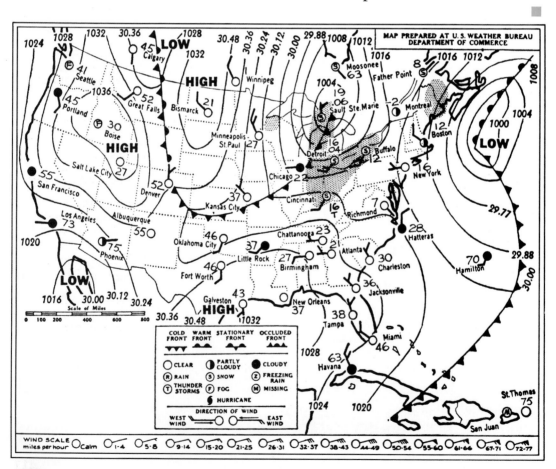

## TYPES OF CLOUDS

1. cirrus
   "mare's-tails"
   over 30,000 feet

2. cirrostratus
   (like a thin veil)
   causes a halo around
   moon

3. cirrocumulus
   (like rippled sand)
   over 20,000 feet

4. altostratus
   (like a thick veil)
   about 19,000 feet

5. altocumulus
   (like a herd of sheep)
   over 12,000 feet

6. cumulonimbus
   "thunderhead"
   lowest level about
   5,000 feet

7. fractus or "scud"
   (broken clouds)

8. cumulus
   dome shaped heaps
   4,000 feet and over

9. nimbostratus
   heavy rain clouds
   to about 3,000 feet

10. stratus
    light rain clouds
    1,800 feet

11. fog and haze
    near the ground
    "ceiling zero"

417

## 4. Selecting Your Own Problem for Investigation

Recall our basic concept: *Heat energy is the kinetic energy of moving molecules.* In other words, application of heat increases evaporation. On a hot day more water evaporates than on a cold day. This means that there is more water vapor to condense into clouds, perhaps. ■

***Problem 1.*** Have you ever wondered whether water evaporates faster from oceans than from fresh water? After all, oceans have salts (sodium chloride, potassium chloride, and others) dissolved in the water.

Is there a problem, or problems, for investigation here? What is the problem? How can you investigate it? (Be sure to control all the variables.)

***Problem 2.*** Have you noticed that oceans do not seem to freeze as often as do lakes or ponds? What is the reason for this? Is it because the oceans

are large in size, or is it because ocean water contains a great quantity of salt and other minerals?

Plan an investigation in which you control both of these variables. First design an experiment into the freezing of salt water as compared with the freezing of fresh water.

Suppose, for instance, that you were to take 1,000 milliliters (about one quart of water) of lake water, or tapwater, and were to add 40 grams of salt to it.

NOTE: 1,000 milliliters = 1 liter
1 liter = 1.1 quart
1 ounce = 28.5 grams

Would the salt water you have just mixed freeze? If it did, at what temperature would salt water freeze as compared with other types of water?

Suppose you added twice as much salt (80 grams) to a liter of water. At what temperature would it freeze then? Would it freeze sooner or not at all? You will need a good thermometer to find out.

Can you then design an experiment to test the effect that the size of a body of water has on its rate of freezing? What should your only variable be?

Now, on the basis of your investigation, try to predict whether the ice formed in the Arctic Ocean is salty or not. How could you set up an investigation to confirm your prediction?

***Problem 3.*** Try to set up an investigation to find the real cause of evaporation. Perhaps you could obtain two thermometers. Wrap the bulb of one thermometer in gauze that has been soaked in very warm water, and place it near the second thermometer which remains dry. ● Look at both thermometers about every 15 minutes for the next few hours. What is your hypothesis about the cause of evaporation? How would you test it?

*Problem 4.* Does the rate of evaporation remain the same at different temperatures?

Suppose you were to put 500 milliliters of tapwater, measured carefully, in a graduated cylinder and then set the graduated cylinder into a pan of water on a hot plate, as shown. ▲ This is a kind of double boiler. The thermometer tells you the temperature of the water in the graduated cylinder. You could heat the pan to a certain temperature and, by turning the heat on and off, keep it at that level.

Does water evaporate at about the same amount for every 10-degree rise of temperature? For instance, does 5 milliliters evaporate when the temperature rises from 40° C to 50° C, and 5 milliliters evaporate again from 50° C to 60° C?

NOTE: If the water in the pan shows signs of boiling, remove it from the heat to protect the cylinder.

Are the results different for salt water and fresh water? At what temperature does water begin to evaporate measurably?

Can you predict what will happen before you do the investigation?

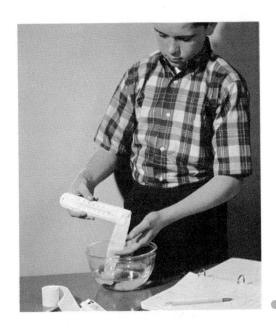

*Problem 5.* Water vapor in the atmosphere must *condense* (kən·dens′) (change to a liquid) before it can fall as rain. Meteorologists can determine the point at which water condenses; this is called the *dew point.*

Suppose you took a shiny can, taped a thermometer to the side, and filled it half way with water. Suppose you stirred and began to add ice cubes one by one to the water. At what temperature would you begin to see water condensing on the outside of the can? This would be the dew point.

Does the temperature of surrounding air have any effect on the dew point? What about the amount of moisture in the air? Would the dew point be the same on both wet and dry days?

Predict—if you can—the conditions under which the dew point would occur at a high temperature; and when it would occur at a lower temperature.

**Problem 6.** On page 58 you found ways to demonstrate that molecules move inside a flask or beaker of water. When water evaporates, the molecules must speed up enough to escape very rapidly out into the air.

Which color of light provides the most kinetic energy to the motion of molecules in a beaker of water? red? orange? yellow? green? blue? What effect do the different colors have on the rate of evaporation?

CLUE: Colored bulbs or colored cellophane or plastic will allow mainly that wavelength of light (color) to go through a glass.

**Problem 7.** What kind of insulation best retards the movement of molecules? Design an experiment to answer this question. Naturally you will use only those materials which are available to you. You may be able to obtain and to test some of the following: rock wool, aluminum foil, fiber glass, plastic foam, cotton, cork, wool.

**Problem 8.** What is the effect of pressure on temperature, evaporation, and condensation? Obtain a large bottle (1-gallon size), pour a little water into the bottom, and then pump air into the bottle until the stopper flies off. (Be careful to keep your face away from the stopper.) What causes the cloud to form? See if you can use this apparatus in designing an investigation into the effect of pressure on temperature, condensation, and evaporation of water.

**Problem 9.** Does ice evaporate even at cold temperatures? Can you design an experiment to answer this question?

**Problem 10.** Try to design an investigation into how the sun causes the winds. You might use an infra-red heat lamp or a large light bulb and smoke from a smoldering rope to show the motion of air currents. The figure on the opposite page may give you a clue. ■

As you investigated each problem, did you find yourself saying something like this: "If heat speeds up evaporation, *then* the greater the amount of heat I apply, the greater should be the rate of evaporation."

Or, suppose you asked yourself: "Does the movement of air increase the evaporation of water?" You might have answered: "*If* I increase the movement of air over a pan of water, *then* it should increase the movement of water molecules."

Notice the IF—THEN type of sentence. This kind of statement is one way in which you make a kind of prediction. *If* a first condition is true, *then* the other condition, which depends on the first, may also be true. This kind of statement is called a hypothesis, or working idea.

Before you design an investigation, or an observation, or an experiment, it is useful to state a hypothesis.

Here is a hypothesis about your work in science: *If* you investigate on your own whenever you can, *then* you will learn more about the ways of the scientist. How could you investigate the truth of that statement?

Of course, "on your own" does *not* mean completely without the help of others. Your parents and teachers may help you. So will books. You will en-

counter many problems that need investigation. Your work in school will also help you to learn the ways of the scientist. As you look about this world, you will find yourself asking why, or how, or when things happen. You will find, in short, enough problems to investigate. Look around you —and use the knowledge that is available from observation, in books, and from other people.

# KEY CONCEPT WORDS: A BEGINNING VOCABULARY FOR SCIENCE

To record what they have learned from their investigations, scientists use words that have the same meaning to every other scientist; that is, scientists try to use words accurately. You are building up a vocabulary of key concept words of science during this year. You will, of course, want to use them properly. The first time a word is used with a special meaning for scientific communication, it is in boldface type in your textbook. In this vocabulary of key concept words, a page reference is given in case you need more information or examples of the meaning than are given here. In other words, the definition given may need filling out. As you study science, the terms you use will take on a fuller meaning. A few terms you probably know from earlier work in science do not have a page reference; you should already know how to use these words in their correct meaning. The index gives other page references.

## PRONUNCIATION KEY

| SYMBOL | KEY WORDS | SYMBOL | KEY WORDS | SYMBOL | KEY WORDS |
|--------|-----------|--------|-----------|--------|-----------|
| a | add, map | o | odd, hot | u | up, done |
| ā | ace, rate | ō | open, so | y | yet, yearn |
| ä | palm, father | ô | order, jaw | zh | vision, pleasure |
| e | end, pet | oi | oil, boy | ə | an unstressed vowel |
| ē | even, tree | o͞o | pool, food | | as in the words above, |
| i | it, give | o͝o | took, full | | sicken, clarity, |
| ī | ice, write | th | thin, both | | melon, focus |

**action,** a force applied in one direction that is equal to the action of a force (reaction) in the opposite direction, 218

**adapted,** fitted by structure to carry on life activities within a given environment

**alloy** (al′oi), a combination of two or more elements, at least one of them a metal, which, when melted and cooled, has properties different from the original elements, 79

**alpha particle,** a certain type of positively charged particle given off by certain radioactive atoms; the nucleus of a helium atom, 287

**antenna** (an·ten′ə), a device for transmitting and receiving electromagnetic waves, 271

**antibiotic** (an′ti·bī·ot′ik), a substance, generally produced by a fungus plant, which, when introduced into the body, controls many bacterial infections, 121

**antibody** (an′ti·bod′ē), a substance made by body cells that acts against germs in the body, 126

**antiseptic** (an′ti·sep′tik), one kind of substance that stops growth of bacteria outside the body, 111

**armature** (är′mə·chŏŏr), a piece of metal or a coil of wire that moves through a magnetic field, thus causing a flow of electric current, 253

**associated**, related, as two stimuli given at the same time, 16

**atom**, a building block of elements; atoms combine to form molecules, 54

**atomic number**, a number assigned to identify an element; it is equal to the number of protons in the nucleus of the atom, and is an index of the properties of the atom, 296

**atomic pile**, a device in which atomic nuclei are made to undergo fission, 302

**atomic weight**, the sum of the protons and neutrons in an atom, 292

**automatic** (ô′tə·mat′ik) **act**, a type of behavior that does not require thought, 21

**bacilli** (bə·sil′ī), rod-shaped bacteria, 102

**bacteria** (bak·tir′ē·ə), **bacterium** (*singular*), the smallest single-celled plants without chlorophyll, 100

**behavior**, the ways in which a living thing responds to the environment, 4; also, the ways a substance reacts to a change of any kind, 76

**blend**, a trait in an organism for which the characteristics from the parent genes show neither dominance nor recessiveness, 342

**block and tackle**, a machine consisting of pulleys fixed in two frames with a rope or chain between them and a free end for applying a force, 166

**carburetor** (kär′bə·rā′tər), in a gasoline engine, a chamber in which gasoline vapor is mixed with air, 208

**caterpillar**, *see* **larva**

**cell**, the smallest living unit of structure and function in an organism

**cell membrane**, the outer boundary of a living animal cell; the boundary of a living plant cell, 104

**cellulose** (sel′yə·lōs), the substance that makes up the walls of plant cells, 88

**cell wall**, the outer nonliving boundary of a plant cell, consisting of cellulose, 104

**chain reaction**, a process in which neutrons from the fission of one atomic nucleus cause fission of other nuclei, 302

**chemical change**, any change in matter that results in a change in the chemical properties of its molecules, 210

**chemical reaction**, a change in a substance or substances, resulting in other substances with different properties; also, any recombination of atoms in a molecule, 368

**chlorophyll** (klôr′ə·fil), a green substance in green plant cells that is basic to photosynthesis, 104

**chromosome** (krō′mə·sōm), a structure, inside a cell nucleus, containing a substance that is basic to determining the hereditary characteristics of each organism, 328. *See also* **DNA molecule.**

**cilia** (sil′ē·ə), hairlike extensions of covering cells lining the tubes to the lungs, 111; also, hairlike structures on single-celled animals by which they move about

**circuit** (sûr′kit), a complete path through which electricity travels, 244

**classify**, to group objects and events by their likenesses, 146

**cocci** (kok′sī), bacteria that are spherical in shape, 102

**cocoon**, the silky covering made by a larva, from which an adult moth emerges, 85

**colony** (kol′ə·nē), a visible group of bacteria originating from division of a single bacterium, 101

**comet** (kom′it), a body in space that travels around the sun in a long narrow orbit; its head is apparently composed of many particles, and its so-called tail, of dust and other particles of matter that are most visible as it nears the sun, 394

**compound**, a substance consisting of two or more kinds of atoms chemically combined, 49

**compound machine**, a machine consisting of two or more kinds of simple machines, 177

**compressor** (kəm·pres′ər), a device in a jet engine that squeezes an amount of air into a smaller volume, 218 conditioning (kən·dish'ən·ing) a change in behavior resulting from substitution of one stimulus for another to achieve the same response, 18

conductor (kən·duk'tər), any substance through which an electric current can flow; also any substance through which heat can be transferred, 235

connecting nerve cell, a nerve cell (neuron) that transmits an impulse between one nerve cell and another, 14

control, that part of an experiment that includes all conditions (variables) except the condition (variable) being investigated, 11, 119

control rod, a device, in a reactor, which adjusts the rate of fission, 303

corrosion (kə·rō'zhən), the chemical combination of oxygen and a metal exposed to air and moisture, 80

covering cells, the outer cells of a many-celled organism or of organs inside the organism, 110

cross, see cross-pollinate

cross-pollinate (krôs'pol'ə·nāt), to transfer pollen from the stamen of one flower to the pistil of another, 337

culture, a colony of bacteria grown under controlled conditions, 100

current, or current electricity, a flow of electrons through a conductor, 235

cyclotron (sī'klə·tron), a machine that accelerates (increases the speed of) charged nuclear particles, controls their direction, and is used to study the structure of atoms, 298

cylinder (sil'in·dər), a hollow tube in which a piston moves, 208

diffusion (di·fyoo'zhən), the spreading of one substance through another, with or without passage through a membrane

digest (di·jest'), to break down a complex food substance into less complex substances so that the substance can pass through a cell membrane, 107

DNA molecule, a large protein molecule within a chromosome; it is basic in determining the hereditary characteristics of an organism, 334. See also chromosome, gene.

dominant (dom'ə·nənt), a trait that always appears in the offspring if it is carried by a gene, or genes, in the cells, 333

Doppler effect, change in pitch and frequency of a wave (sound or light) as an object moves nearer or farther from the observer, 393

effort, a force applied to a machine, 161

egg cell, a specialized cell in a plant or animal which when united with a sperm cell can develop into a new organism; the female cell in reproduction, 330

electric impulse, a single, usually sudden, flow of electricity, 261

electricity, a flow of electrons

electromagnet (i·lek'trō·mag'nit), a magnet made of a coil of wire wound around an iron core in which the magnetic field is produced by electric current flowing through the coil, 244

electromagnetic wave, a form of energy that travels through space as a wave at the uniform speed of light, 270; light is one kind of electromagnetic wave (speed is about 186,000 miles per second)

electron (i·lek'tron), tiny negatively charged particle revolving around the nucleus of an atom, 232

electron microscope, a microscope that uses a beam of electrons instead of light

element, a substance consisting of only one kind of atom, 49

embryo (em'brē·ō), the living organism in a seed (before germination), in an egg (before hatching), in a mammal (before birth), 330

energy, the ability to do work; the ability to set matter in motion

environment (in·vī'rən·mənt), all the surroundings of an organism, including all matter and all forms of life with which an organism is interdependent

enzyme (en'zīm), one of a group of substances made by cells; these substances help to break down or build up compounds in the body without generally being changed in the reaction of which they are a part, 107

evaporate (i·vap'ə·rāt), to change from a solid or a liquid to a gas

**experience,** knowledge and skills acquired from observation, investigation, and thought

**experiment,** an investigation carried out in a laboratory under carefully planned conditions in which known variables are carefully controlled, 118

**filtration** (fil·trā'shən), a method of purifying water by passing it through materials that hold back bacteria, other microorganisms, and undissolved substances, 132

**fission** (fish'ən), the splitting of the nucleus of an atom, 294; also, the division of a cell in reproduction

**fixed pulley,** a simple machine consisting of a single grooved wheel attached to a support. A rope passed around the wheel changes the direction of the force, 158

**fluid,** any substance that flows, as a gas or liquid, 214

**force,** a push or pull exerted on an object, 155

**frequency** (frē'kwən·sē), the rate at which wavelengths pass a fixed point in one second, 393

**friction,** a force, where two surfaces meet, that resists the motion of one surface across the other, 180

**fuel** (fyoo'əl), any substance that can burn and thus release energy, 206; also, a substance that can undergo fission or fusion and release energy

**fulcrum** (fool'krəm), the support around which a lever can turn, 156

**fungi** (fun'jī), **fungus** (fung'gəs) (*singular*), a group of plants without chlorophyll that obtain food from other living things, or from organic (that is, plant or animal) matter, 104

**fusion** (fyoo'zhən), the combining of atomic nuclei of one element, resulting in the nucleus of another, 316

**galaxy** (gal'ək·sē), a large group, or system, of stars which is rotating around a center, 381

**galvanometer** (gal'və·nom'ə·tər), an instrument for measuring a small amount of electric current, 239

**gears,** a simple machine consisting of toothed wheels which are meshed so that one wheel can turn another, 176

**gene** (jēn), a part within the DNA molecule that is basic to the development of a definable characteristic, 328

**germ,** any microorganism that can cause infection or disease

**goal-insight theory,** a theory that helps to explain learning of complex habits, 26

**graft,** to join the stem of one plant to the root or stem of a related plant in order to obtain more plants having a desired characteristic, 348

**gram,** the basic unit of weight in the metric system, 169

**gravitation** (grav'ə·tā'shən), a force that attracts all objects (masses) in the universe to one other; each mass tends to pull every other mass toward itself

**gravity** (grav'ə·tē), commonly refers to the attraction of a very large body on a small body, as the attraction of the earth or the moon for an object on its surface

**habit,** a learned automatic act, 21

**habitat** (hab'ə·tat), the environment to which an organism is adapted, 38

**heat** (or **heat energy**), the energy of moving molecules which, when transferred to or removed from an object, changes its temperature, 57

**heredity** (hə·red'ə·tē), the sum of all the traits inherited by an organism, 326

**humus** (hyoo'məs), decaying plant or animal matter making up a part of the soil, 102

**hybrid** (hī'brid), an organism that results from the mating of two organisms, each pure for a different given trait, 344

**hypothesis** (hī·poth'ə·sis), a possible explanation of an object or event which can form the basis for planning the design of an investigation, 119

**immune,** having conditions within the body unfavorable to disease-causing viruses, bacteria, or other microorganisms, 126; when these conditions exist, the body has **immunity**

**inborn act,** *see* **reflex act**

**inclined** (in·klīnd') **plane,** a machine consisting of a sloping surface placed at an angle with a flat surface, 154

**infection,** attack by disease-causing microorganisms, 108; such microorganisms are said to be **infectious,** 110

**insight,** in learning, an understanding of the means of achieving a goal, 26

**instinct,** a type of behavior consisting of a series of complex reflex acts, 6

**insulator** (in'sə·lā'tər), a substance through which heat does not travel readily, 62; also, one that stops the flow of electrons

**interdependent,** dependent upon one another and interacting with the environment, 39

**invertebrate** (in·vûr'tə·brit), an animal without a backbone, 146

**isotope** (ī'sə·tōp), an atom with the same atomic number as another atom but with a different atomic weight, 302

**kinetic** (ki·net'ik) **energy,** energy of matter in motion, 63

**larva** (lär'və), **larvae** (lär'vē) (*plural*), the young form of a moth that has hatched from the egg, 85

**learned act,** a type of behavior acquired after birth, 16

**lever** (lev'ər), a simple machine consisting of a bar with a support (fulcrum) around which it can be turned, 156

**lift,** an upward force produced by difference in air pressure on the upper and under surfaces of the wing of an airplane, 212

**light-year,** a unit of measurement in astronomy equal to the distance light travels in one year, 385

**lines of force,** the pattern of the magnetic field describing the amount and direction of forces around a magnet or a conductor of electricity, 243

**load,** the weight to be lifted by a machine, 161

**magnetic field,** area in which magnetic lines of force can be noted around a magnet or a wire carrying electric current, 243

**mass,** the amount of matter in an object, 322

**matter,** all substances on the earth or in space, or any part of them; anything that has weight and takes up space

**meteorite** (mē'tē·ə·rīt'), a bit of matter that has fallen to the earth from space

**metric system,** a system of measurement in which each unit is multiplied by 10 to obtain the next larger unit, or divided by 10 to obtain the next smaller unit, 169

**microorganism** (mī'krō·ôr'gən·iz'əm), an organism generally too small to be visible without a microscope, 100

**microphone** (mī'krə·fōn), a device that changes sound waves into electric impulses

**microscope** (mī'krə·skōp), an instrument that enlarges the image of an object, so that it becomes visible

**mineral** (min'ər·əl), a compound in the soil or dissolved in water in the soil that aids the growth of plants, 102

**mold,** a fungus that grows on plant or animal matter, 104

**molecule** (mol'ə·kyool), the smallest part of a substance that has the properties of the substance, 54, 197

**motor nerve cell,** a nerve cell (neuron) that carries a response to a muscle, 14

**movable pulley,** a pulley free to move; a system with a movable pulley multiplies the force applied to it, 167

**mucus** (myoo'kəs), a substance produced by cells lining the inside surface of the body and keeping them moist, 110

**mutant** (myoo'tənt), an organism different from its parents in one or more new traits that can be inherited, 347

**mutant gene,** a gene that has changed, resulting in a change in inheritance, 347

**mutation** (myoo·tā'shən), a new characteristic that can be inherited as a result of a change in the genes, 350

**nerve,** a bundle of nerve fibers, 12

**nerve cell,** 12; *see* **neuron**

**nerve ending,** the part of a nerve fiber where a nerve impulse begins or ends, 14

**nerve fiber,** the generally long threadlike part of a nerve cell, 9

**nerve impulse,** a "message" (perhaps electrical or chemical) that travels along a nerve fiber, 9

**nervous system,** the total of all the pathways along which nerve impulses may travel in an organism, 12

**neuron** (nŏor'on), a cell which can carry a nerve impulse, 15

**neutron** (nōō'tron), a particle in the nucleus of an atom, having no electrical charge, 288

**nova** (nō'və), a star that explodes and increases greatly in brightness, 387

**nuclear reaction** (nōō'klē·ər rē·ak'shən), a change in an atom or atoms as a result of fission or fusion; new atoms with different properties may be formed, 368

**nucleus** (nōō'klē·əs), the central part of an atom, 232; also, of a living cell

**nylon** (nī'lon), a man-made fiber having many of the properties of silk, 88

**orbit** (ôr'bit), the path of one body of matter around another, as a satellite around the earth or the earth around the sun

**ore,** a mineral or rock that is the source of a metal

**organ,** a group of tissues that carries on a specialized function in an organism

**organism,** any living thing that carries on life functions

**ovary** (ō'və·rē), in a flowering plant, the organ in which the seed is formed, 330

**oxide** (ok'sīd), a compound of oxygen and another element

**penicillin** (pen'ə·sil'in), an antibiotic produced by the mold *Penicillium,* 120

**physical change,** any change in matter that does not change its chemical composition, 210

**pistil** (pis'til), the part of a flower that contains the ovary at its base, 330

**piston,** a device fitting snugly inside a tube, moved by steam or gases, and connected to a machine to do work, 200

**pitch,** (*sound*) highness or lowness of a note on a scale; (*light*) placement in the spectrum according to frequency, 393

**plastic** (plas'tik), a man-made substance that can be molded, shaped, or cast, 82

**polio** (pō'lē·ō), a virus-caused disease that damages nerve cells, 124

**polled** (pōld), hornless, a result of a mutant gene in cattle, 355

**pollen** (pol'ən), powdery grain on the stamen of a flower; contains the sperm cell, 330

**pollinate** (pol'ə·nāt), to transfer pollen from stamen to pistil of a flower, 330

**potential** (pə·ten'chəl) **energy,** energy that is stored in an object by its position or chemical composition, 204

**pressure,** force exerted on the surface of an object from without or from within

**prism** (priz'əm), a device, such as a triangular piece of glass, that separates light into its different wavelengths, visible as a spectrum, 372

**property,** any characteristic that is generally true for a substance and for which the substance can be tested, as color, hardness, dullness

**proton** (prō'ton), in the nucleus of an atom, a particle having a positive charge, 288

**pulley,** a grooved wheel around which a rope may be placed, 158; *see also* **block and tackle, fixed pulley, movable pulley**

**pupa** (pyōō'pə), the stage between larva and adult in the life of a moth, 85

**pure,** in heredity, having a gene for a given trait from each parent, 332

**quarantine** (kwôr'ən·tēn), the keeping of a person having a serious contagious disease away from others who might contract it, 140

**radioactive** (rā'dē·ō·ak'tiv), describes an element whose nucleus gives off particles and radiations, 287

**radio transmitter,** a device that changes electric energy into electromagnetic waves and sends them through space

**rayon** (rā'on), a fiber made from cellulose, 87

**reaction** (rē·ak'shən), a force exerted in a direction opposite that of another force (action), 218; *see also* **chemical reaction**

**reactor** (rē·ak′tər), a device in which nuclear fission is controlled, 303

**receiver,** (*telephone*) a device for gathering electric impulses and changing them into sound waves, 261; (*radio and television*) a device for gathering electromagnetic waves from space

**recessive** (ri·ses′iv), a gene carried by the cells but whose effect does not appear as a trait in the organism, 333

**reflex act,** an act that is inborn, unlearned, automatic, 4

**reflex arc,** the nerve pathway followed by a nerve impulse from stimulus through connecting neurons in the spinal cord to response in a muscle or gland, 14

**reservoir** (rez′ər·vwôr), a lake, usually artificial, in which a city's water supply is collected and stored, 131

**response,** the reaction of an organism (or any part of it) to a change in the environment, 8

**reward,** something favorable obtained by an organism when it makes a useful or correct response to a stimulus, 16

**sampling,** a method of estimating the total amount by finding the average of small parts (samples) of the amount, 383

**screw,** a simple machine that multiplies effort. It consists of an inclined plane wound around a central post, 172

**secrete** (si·krēt′), to produce within a cell a substance that is used outside the cell, 110

**sensory nerve cell,** a nerve cell (neuron) that reacts to a stimulus and sends a nerve impulse to the spinal cord and brain, 14

**serum** (sir′əm), the liquid part of the blood that remains after clotting, 127

**simple machine,** a single device for multiplying force or for changing its direction, as a lever, a pulley, an inclined plane, or a wheel and axle, 154

**solution** (sə·lōō′shən), a mixture of two substances, one of which is dissolved in the other, 51

**sound wave,** a form of mechanical energy in which particles of matter move back and forth in a characteristic pattern, 262

**spark plug,** a device to ignite a fuel in an enclosed chamber in an engine, 208

**spectroscope** (spek′trə·skōp), a device used to analyze light from a glowing object to determine its composition, 372

**spectrum** (spek′trəm), a band showing the separation of light, or electromagnetic, waves into their wavelengths, 372

**sperm cell,** a specialized cell in a plant or animal that, when united with an egg cell, can develop into a new organism; the male cell in reproduction, 330

**spirilla** (spī·ril′lə), **spirillum** (spīril′əm) (*singular*), bacteria having a corkscrew or, rarely, a comma shape, 102

**spore,** a specialized cell of fungi and many nonflowering plants that can reproduce a new organism, 105

**S–R bond,** in behavior of organisms, the manner in which a stimulus is thought to be linked to a response, 18

**stamen** (stā′mən), the part of a flower that produces pollen, 330

**state** (of matter), any of the forms of matter; as, solid, liquid, gas

**static electricity,** an electrical charge (excess of electrons) on a substance, usually given it by friction, 234

**stimulus** (stim′yə·ləs), a condition in the environment that causes an organism to react, 8

**streptomycin** (strep′tō·mī′sin), an antibiotic produced by a mold, effective in treating tuberculosis, 121

**subatomic particle,** any particle of which an atom is composed, 315

**supernova** (sōō′pər·nō′və), an especially bright nova, 388

**technology** (tek·nol′ə·jē), the science of applying discovered concepts to the invention or improvement of materials or tools to do work, 55

**telescope** (tel′ə·skōp), an instrument that collects light from a distant object, focuses it as an image, and enlarges the image so that details can be seen

**temperature** (tem′pər·ə·chər), measurement of hotness or coldness; that is, the average kinetic energy of the molecules in a substance, measured in degrees

**tentacle** (ten'tə·kəl), in hydra and jelly-fish, an armlike structure that aids the organism in catching food, 8

**theory** (thē'ər·ē), a reasonable explanation that satisfies a set of observations, data, or investigations, 18

**threads,** ridges around a screw that form a winding inclined plane, 173

**tissue** (tish'oo), a group of similar cells that do one kind of work

**transmitter** (trans·mit'ər), a device for changing a form of energy into electric impulses and sending them along a wire, 261; or into electromagnetic waves and sending them out through space, 271

**turbine** (tûr'bin), a wheel which has blades that are moved by steam or other means and which is connected to another machine to do work, 201

**unlearned act;** *see* **reflex act**

**vaccinate** (vak'sin·āt), introduction of living or dead bacteria or viruses into the body to cause the body cells to produce antibodies, 126

**vaccine** (vak'sēn), a substance containing living or dead bacteria or viruses introduced into the blood to develop immunity to a disease, 127

**vertebra** (vûr'tə·brə), one of the small bones in the backbone through which the spinal cord passes, 146

**vertebrate** (vûr'tə·brit), an animal with a backbone, 146

**virus** (vī'rəs), a particle smaller than a bacterium (and not cell-like) that can reproduce itself inside a living cell and cause disease, 124

**volume** (vol'yoom), measurement of the space occupied by a substance, 61

**watershed,** all the area from which water flows into and is collected by a lake, a river, or a reservoir, 133

**wedge,** a simple machine, consisting of an inclined plane that can be forced into or between objects to spread them apart, 174

**weight,** a measure of the pull of gravitation on an object

**wheel and axle,** a simple machine consisting of a wheel attached to a rod passing through its center, to which a force may be applied, 158

**white blood cells,** special cells in the blood that can engulf and destroy bacteria in the body, 113

**work,** the result achieved when a force moves an object through a distance, 183

# INDEX

(Page numbers in **boldface** refer to illustrations.)

birds, 146
Black Death, 139
blast furnace, 76, 77, **77**
blending traits, **342**, 342–46, **344**
blinking, as inborn act, 4, 5, **5**
block and tackle, 166, 168, **168**, 170, **170**, 187, **187**, 189; use of, 169, **169**
blood cells, white, 113, **113**, 114, **114**, 126
Bohr, Niels, 287, 316
bomb, nuclear 312, 368, 369
boron, atomic nucleus of, 297
Boulder Dam, 246
bowline, how to tie, 25
Boyle's Law, 392
brain, 12, **12**, 39, 41, 53, 151
Braun, Wernher von, **55**
bread mold, 104, 105, **105**
breeding, *see* prize genes
bronze, 76, 80
brush, in electric motor, 253, 254, 255
bud of potato, 326, 327, **327**, 328, **328**
bull, Santa Gertrudis, 357, **357**
Burbank, Luther, 346

cadmium control rods, 303, 304, **304**, 305, 309
camera, 274, **274**
cancer, radioactive substances in treatment of, **312**, 312–13
candle, burning, 206, **206**, 207, **207**, 208
carbon, 75, 77, 78, 206, 208; atom of, 232, **232**, 289, **289**; atomic number of, 296, **296**
carbon dioxide, 75, 76, 77, 206, 210; formula for, 206, 208, 322; from burning fuel, 206; molecule of, 322; used by plants, 150
carburetor, 208
cast iron, 78
caterpillar, 85, **85**
cattle, hybrid, 344, 345, 350, **350**
cell(s): blood, white, 113, **113**, 114, **114**, 126; cilia of, 111, **111**; covering, 110; egg, in flowering plant, 330; nerve, *see* nerve cell; of potato bud, 328, **328**; secretion by, 110; sperm, in pollen grain, 330
cell membrane, 104, 107

cell wall, 104, 107
cellulose, 88, **88**, 89
Celsius scale, 67, **67**
Chain, Ernst, 121
chain reaction, 302, 303, **303**; control of, 303–04, **304**, 305, 310, 312
charcoal, 75
chemical change, 210
chemical energy, changed to heat energy, 60
chemical reaction, 368, **368**; in green plants, 150; matter neither gained nor lost in, 190, 322, 323
chemistry, 82, 87, 90, 92
chimpanzee, and learning process, 26–27, **27**, 28
chlorination of water, 132, **132**
chlorine, 132, 133, 136; atom of, 290, **290**, 320, **320**
chlorophyll, 104, 329
cholera, 131, 139
chromosomes, 328, 330, 333, 360; DNA code in, 333, 334, **334**, 359, 360, 405
cilia, 111, **111**
circuit, electric, *see* electric circuit
classifying animals and plants, 146, 148, **148**
cloud chamber, Wilson, 315, **315**
coal, 206, 279, 370
cobalt, radioactive, 313
cocci, 102, **102**, 113, **113**
cocoon, 85, **85**, 86
code messages, 257, 260, **260**, 261
coke, 77
colonies of bacteria, 100, 101, **101**, 117
color television, 275
comets, 394
compass, 268, 269
compound machine, 177–78
compounds, 49, 82, 321; obtaining metals from, 72, **72**
compressor, of jet engine, 218, 219
concepts: formulated by scientists, 53, 54, 55, 56, 64, 90, 93, 94, 148, 151; uses of, 57–65, **58**, **59**, **60**, **61**, **62**, **63**, **64**, **65**, 90
conditioning, 18, 22; theory of, 30
conductor of electricity, 235
connecting nerve cell, 14, 15

electron microscope, 124, 129

electrons, 232, 235, 288, 289, **289**, 290, **290**, 291 (table), 292, 322; flow of, in electricity, 236, 240, 243; in motion around atomic nucleus, 232, 316, **316**; negative charge of, 232, 288; transfer of, 232

elements, 49, 82, 291 (table), 321; and atomic number, 296, **296**; new, made by bombardment of atomic nuclei, 388, 390; number of, 321, **321**, 322, 388; origin of, 388, 390, 391, 398; in stars, and spectrum, 373, **373**

embryo of plant, 330

Enders, John, 127

energy: from burning fuel, 202, 206, **206**, 224–25; changed from one form to another, 189, **189**, 190, 209, 225, 236, 279–80, 405; changed to heat energy, 60; electric, *see* electric energy; kinetic, *see* kinetic energy; matter changed into, 322–23, 370, 372, 387; from nuclear reactions, 305, 308, 309; potential, *see* potential energy; and work, 189, **189**, 197, 238

engine: automobile, 208, **208**, 209, **209**; jet, 212, 218, **218**, 219; Hero's, 203, **203**; rocket, 220, **220**, 221, **221**

environment: adaptation to, 38, **38**, 39, **39**; changed by man, 39–41, **40**, **41**, 53, 91–94, 140, **140**, 151; control of, 139–41, **140**; dinosaurs fail to change with, 353; effect of, on living things, 326, **326**, 327, 328, 329; and heredity, 329, 359; interdependence with, 39, 148–51, **149**, **150**, 329

enzymes, 107

evaporation, of gasoline in carburetor, 208

experiment, as scientific tool, 118

explosion, 205–06, 208

Fahrenheit scale, 67, **67**

fibers, new, invention of, 86, 87, 88, 90, 93

filtration of water, 132, **132**, 135

fish, training of, 19, **19**; nest building by, 6

fission, nuclear, 294, **294**, 295, **295**, 296, 297, 298, **298**, 302, 304, 316, 369

fixed pulley, 158, 159, **159**, 166, **166**

Fleming, Alexander, 106, 117–21, **119**, **120**, 122, 141

Florey, Howard, 121

flowering plants, 148, 330, **330**, 332, 336, **336**, 337, **337**, 338, **338**, 339, **339**

fluids, pressure of moving, 212, 213, **213**, 214; *see also* force

food-gatherer, 70, 92, **92**

food-making by green plants, 150, **150**

food-producer, 70, 92, **92**

force, 155, 198, 212; direction changed by machine, 158, 159, **159**; of friction, 180, 181, **181**, 182; of moving molecules, 198, **198**, 200; multiplied by machine, 155, **155**, 156, **156**, 157, **157**, 173, **173**, 174, 175, **175**, 185, **185**, 186, 187, **187**; of steam, 200, **200**, 205, **205**

four o'clocks, heredity in, 342, 343, **343**, 344, 360

frequency: of light waves, 393, 394; of sound waves, 393

friction, 180, 182; investigation into, 181, **181**

fruit flies: bombarded with X rays, 352; DNA code in, 334, **334**; kinds of, 351, **351**; mutations in, 350, 352

fuel: energy from burning, 202, 206, **206**, 224–25; for rocket, 221

fulcrum, 156, **156**, 157, **157**, 161, **161**, 163; location of, 162, **162**

fungi, 104, 105, **105**

fusion, nuclear, 316, 368, **368**, 369, **369**, 387, 398

galaxy, defined, 381

Galileo, 398

galvanometer, 239, **239**, 241, **241**, 243

gases: compression of, 389, **389**; kinetic energy of, 198

gasoline, 93, 206, 208, 209, 210; model of molecule of, **208**

gear wheel, 176, **176**

Geiger counter, 300, **300**, 313

generator(s), 189, **189**, 202, 237, **237**, 238, 239, **239**, 240, **240**, 242, 243, 245, 246; at Hoover Dam, 244, 245

genes, 328, 329, 330, 332, 333, **333**, 336, 337, 360, 405; changed in fruit flies, 350, **350**, 352; and DNA code, *see* DNA code; dominant, 340, 342, 343, 344, 361, **361**; mutant, 347, 350, 352–53, 355, 356, 357, 361; prize, *see* prize genes; recessive, 340, 342, 343, 344, 361, **361**

genetic code, *see* DNA code

geneticist, 344

giant stars, *see* stars

gland(s): salivary, 14, 15; thyroid, 313

glucose, 150

goal-insight in learning, 26, 28, 30

Goddard, Robert, 216

gold, 80, 82, 92

government, role of, in health, 136

grafting, 348, **348**, 349, **349**

Grahame-White, Claude, 216, **216**

gram, 169

graphite, in nuclear reactor, 304, **304**

Gravitation, Newton's Law of Universal, 397, 398

green plants, 139, 150, **150**

guinea pigs, heredity in, 342, **342**

habitat, 38

habits, 21–22; forming, **23**, 23–26, **24**, **25**; practice in fixing, 33, **33**, 34; study, 32–37, **33**, **36**

halazone pills, 134

Hale telescope, 380, 381

Hall, Charles Martin, 48, 49, 52, 53, 55, 73

Halley's comet, 394

health, public, 131–37

heat, 57; changed into chemical energy, 60; changed into mechanical energy, 189, **189**; investigation into nature of, 59, **59**; kinetic theory of, 63, **63**; as motion of molecules, 61, 62, 198; from nuclear energy, 305, 308, 309, **308–09**; from sun, 279; and temperature, 374, 375, 376

helium, 212; atom of, 290, **290**, 368, 369, 388; atomic nucleus of, 297, **297**; atomic weight of, 369; fusion of hydrogen into, 368, 369, **369**, 370, 372, 387, 398; in sun, 369, 370, 372, 387

heredity, 326, 398; and environment, 359; and intelligence, 360; *see also* DNA code; Mendel, Gregor; traits

Hereford cattle, 355, 356

Hero's steam engine, 203, **203**, 218

Hoffman apparatus, 367, **367**

Hoover Dam, 244, **244**, 245

hornlessness (a mutant trait), 355, 356, **356**

humus, 102, **102**

hybrid, 344, **344**, 345, 350, **350**

hydra, 7–9, **8**, **9**

hydrogen, 208, 366, 367, 388; atomic nucleus of, 297; atomic weight of, 369; fusion of nuclei of, 368, **368**, 369, **369**, 370, 372, 387, 398; in sun, 369, 370, 372, 387; symbol for molecule of, 366; from electrolysis of water, 206, 321, 366, **367**, 368

hydrogen bomb, 368, 369

hypothesis, 119

immunity, 126, 127

inborn acts, 4, **6**, 6–7, **7**, 16, **16**; *see also* reflex acts

inclined plane, 154, **154**, 186; investigations into, 155, **155**, 173, **173**, 185, **185**; winding, 172, **172**, 173, **173**

infection, 108, 110, 113, **113**

influenza, 124

inheritance, *see* heredity

insects, cross-pollination by, 337

insight into achieving goal, 26, 28

instinct, 6

insulator, heat, 62, **62**

intelligence, inheritance of, **360**

interdependence, 39, 146–51, 149, **149**, **150**

invertebrates, 146, 148

investigation, art of, 409–21

iodine, radioactive, 313

iron, 74, 75, **75**, 76, 79, 80, 90, 93; atom of, 289, **289**; cast, 78; an element, 76, 82; furnaces for making, 76, **77**, 77–78, **78**; separated from ore, 75

iron lung, 125, **125**

iron ore, 71, 73, 75, 77, 78

iron oxide, 71, 77, 78, 79, 190, 321; *see also* corrosion

isotopes, 302

jack, force multiplied by, 156

jet plane: engine of, 212, 218, **218**, 219; speed of, 257

kerosene, 218, 219

kinetic energy, 63, **196**, 197, 198, 225, 374, 376; potential energy changed into, 208

kinetic theory of heat, 63

kitchen middens, 68, **68**

knee reflex, 12, 13, **13**, 14, **14**, 15–16

krypton, nucleus of, 296

larva, 85, **85**

Lavoisier, Antoine, 314

Lawrence, E. O., 298

lead, 73, 92

learning (learned acts), **16**, 16–18, **17**; automatic, 21; and environment changed by man, 39–41, **40**, **41**, 53, 91, 92, 94, 140, **140**, 151; goal-insight theory of, 26, 28, 30; investigations into problems of, 29, **29**, 30, 33, **33**; study habits formed in, 32–37, **33**, **36**; and theory of conditioning, 30; by trial and error, 74, 76, 80, 92

Leucippus, 286, 314

lever, 156, **156**, 161, **161**, 163, **163**; investigations into, 157, **157**, 162, **162**

lift of airplane, 212, 215

light waves: frequency of, 393, 394; speed of, 257, 323

lightning, 235, **235**

light-year, 385

lima bean plant, 329, **329**

lines of force, 243, **243**, 268, **269**

liquid oxygen, for rocket, 221

lithium: atom of, 288, **288**, 290, **290**; nucleus of, 297, **297**

load, and lever, 161, **161**, 162, **162**, 163

locomotive, steam, 201

longhorned cattle, 347, **347**

Lunar Orbital Rendezvous, 221, **222**

machines: compound, 177; and energy, 189–90; speed multiplied by, 158; simple, 154, 155

magnesium, 48

magnet, 239, 240, **240**, 241, **241**, 242, 243, **243**, 245; lines of force of, 243, 268

magnetic field, 243, **243**, 268, **269**, 270, **270**

malachite, 72, 74, 76

malaria, 140

mammals, 146

Manx cat, 355, **355**

Marconi, Guglielmo, **55**, 268

Mars: electromagnetic waves from, 276; orbit of, 378, **378**

mass, 322

mass-energy, and Einstein's formula, 323

matter: changed into energy, 322-23, 370, 372, 387, 405; changed from one form to another, 190, 405; composed of particles, 57, 60, 92, 151, 314–16, 322; force exerted by, 198

measurement, 141; of distance of stars, 376, 377, **377**

meat grinder, as compound machine, 178

medical research, 141

medicine dropper, **100**

Meister, Joseph, 99, 124, 127

memorizing, best place for, 35

Mendel, Gregor, 333, 342, 398

mercury, 73

Mesabi range, 78

metabolism, 144

metal(s): discovery of, 69, 70–71, 73; getting from compound, 72, **72**; methods of working, 80; separated from ores, 72, **72**, 73, 74, 75; *see also* aluminum; iron

metallurgy, 76, 80

meteorite, 74

meteorologist, 413

meteorology, 415

metric system, 169

microorganism(s), 100, 139; *see also* bacteria

microphone, 270, 271, **271**, 273

microscope, 100, 129, 139, 141; electron, 124, 129

milk, safe to drink, 131

Milky Way Galaxy, 381, 384, **384**, 385, **385**, 394, 397

minerals, in soil, 102

mining, 80

model(s): of atomic nucleus, 294, 302; of atoms, 287, **287**, 288, 289, **289**, 293, **293**; of electric bell, 250, **251**; of electric motor, 253, 254, 255, **255**; of molecules, 82, **82**, **88**, 208, **208**; of nuclear reactor, 306, **306**; of steam engine, 199, **199**, 200, **200**; of telegraph, 258, 259, **259**; of telephone, 263, **263**; of turbine, 201, **201**

moisture, a need of fungi, 104

molds, 104, 108, 117, 118, 120, 121, **121**, 148

molecules, 54, 82, 94, 197; of air, 197, 198; models of, 82, **82**, **88**, 208, **208**; motion of, 58, **58**, 60, 61, 62, 198, 199, **199**, 200, 225, 374; *see also* DNA molecule

Monkey (bull), 357, **357**

Montgolfier, Joseph and Jacques, 216, **216**

moon, landing capsule for, 221, 222, **222**; surface of, **404**

Morse, Samuel F. B., 261

Morse Code, 260, **260**, 268

moth, life history of, 85, **85**

motor, electric, *see* electric motor

motor nerve cell, 14, 15

Mount Palomar, 380, 381

movable pulley, 167, **167**, 168

mucus, 110, **110**, 111

Muller, Hermann, 350, 352

muscles, machines to multiply force of, 154, **154**

mutants (genes, mutations), 347, 350, **350**, 352–53, **352**, 355, 356, 357, **357**, 361

natural immunity, 126

negative charge, 232, 288

neptunium, 388

nerve cell(s), 12, **12**, **125**; connecting, 14, 15; motor, 14, 15; and polio virus, 125, **125**; sensory, 14, 15

nerve endings, 14

nerve fibers, 9, 14, **14**, 15

nerve impulse, 9, 14

nerve net, of hydra, 9, **9**

nervous system, 12, **12**

nest-building, 4, **4**, 6, **6**

neuron, *see* nerve cell

neutrons, 288, 289, **289**, 290, **290**, 291 (table), 292, 294, 316, 322; used for splitting nuclei of atoms, 295, **295**, 297, 302, 304, 310

Newton, Isaac, **54**, 218, 224, 228, 397, 398

nitrogen: atom of, 289, **289**; atomic number of, 296; and bacteria in soil, 108

Nobel prize, 121, 352

North Star, 395, 397, **397**

nova, 387, **387**, 388, 398

nuclear accelerator, 298, 299

nuclear aircraft carrier, 310, 311

nuclear bomb, 312, 368, 369

nuclear energy, 305, 308–11

nuclear fission, 294, **294**, 295, **295**, 296, 297, 298, **298**, 302, **303**, 304, 316, 369

nuclear fusion, 316, 368, 369, 387, 398

nuclear power plant, 308–09, **308–09**, 310, **310**

nuclear reaction, 302–06, **303**, 368, **368**; mass-energy remains same in, 322–23; *see also* nuclear fission, nuclear fusion

nuclear reactor, 303–06, **304**, **305**, 308, 310, 311, 312; building, 303–06; model of, 306, **306**; *see also* atomic pile

nuclear submarine, 310, 311, **311**

nucleus of atom, 232, 280, 288, **288**, 292, 316, **316**; radioactive, medical uses of, **312**, 312–13; splitting, **294**, 294–99, **295**, **297**, **298**; unstable, 299

nylon, 88, **89**, 93; molecule of, **88**

observation, in science, 141, 151

Oersted, Hans, 268

orange, seedless, 346, 347, 348

organism(s), 100; changes in, 361; as product of heredity and environment, 359

ovary, in flowering plant, 330

oxygen: in aluminum oxide, 49; atom of, 289, **289**; in carbon dioxide, 206, 208; in chemical reaction in green plant, 150; in iron oxide, 77, 78, 79; symbol for molecule of, 366; from water, 206, 208, 321, 366, **367**, 368

C 6
D 7
E 8
F 9
G 0
H 1
I 2
J 3
4